THE ETHER ZONE

U.S. Army Special Forces Detachment B-52, Project Delta

R. C. Morris

HELLGATE PRESS   ASHLAND, OREGON

THE ETHER ZONE

© 2009, 2014 by R.C. Morris
Published by Hellgate Press (an imprint of L&R Publishing, LLC)

Hellgate Press
P.O. Box 3531
Ashland, OR 97520
sales@hellgatepress.com

Editor & book design: Harley Patrick
Cover design: L. Redding
Cover photo courtesy of Jerry Estenson

Library of Congress Cataloging-in-Publication Data
Morris, R. C.
The ether zone : U.S. Army Special Forces Detachment B-52, Project Delta / R.C. Morris. -- 1st ed.
   p. cm.
Includes bibliographical references and index.
ISBN 978-1-55571-662-2 (alk. paper)
1. United States. Army. Special Forces Group, 5th. Airborne. Detachment B-52. 2. Vietnam War, 1961-1975--Regimental histories--United States. 3. Vietnam War, 1961-1975--Commando operations--United States. 4. Vietnam War, 1961-1975--Reconnaissance operations. I. Title.
DS558.4.M677 2009
959.704'38--dc22
                              2009016271

Printed and bound in the United States of America
Second edition 10 9 8 7 6 5 4 3 2

Advanced Praise for *The Ether Zone*:

The Ether Zone should be a must-read for those who are aspiring to enter our Special Forces, or other elite units where guts, innovation, and dedication are essential ingredients for success. Or, for that matter, anyone who would like a down-and-dirty vicarious experience in our Special Forces.

– David J. Baratto, Major General, U.S. Army Retired
Former Commander, John F. Kennedy Special Warfare Center and School

Project Delta arguably marked the greatest advance in U.S. Special Operations since Colonel Aaron Bank devised the A-team. Ray Morris lays it out chapter and verse, concept and combat…What a book!

– MAJ Jim Morris, USA (Ret)
Author, *War Story, Fighting Men* and *Above and Beyond*

Among Vietnam War recon units, Project Delta B-52 was the pioneer and class act that set the standard for everyone else. With The Ether Zone, there is at last a book worthy of that little known—and yet legendary—unit! The Ether Zone is truly excellent!

– Kenn Miller, author of *Six Silent Men II* and *Tiger the Lurp Dog*

Ray Morris, with skill, has assembled a remarkable true history of the then-secret actions of those few brave Nung, Montagnard, Vietnamese and American men who served in B-52 Delta.

– COL Alan Park, USA (Ret)
Commander, Project Delta – 1969

This is a story of unparalleled bravery of one of the most combat-effective units in the Vietnam War, the precursor of today's Delta Force. I was proud to be a part of that unit. An exciting read…places you in the middle of the action!

– John F. Flanagan, Brigadier General, USAF Retired
Author, *Vietnam Above the Treetops: A Forward Air Controller Reports*

"These men operate in the Ether Zone of military excellence."

General Robert Cushman
Commandant, United States Marine Corps

CONTENTS

FOREWORD

IN *THE ETHER ZONE*, RAY MORRIS CARRIES the reader behind the scenes of one of America's premier forces in the Vietnam War. Project Delta provided the eyes and ears for the commander of U.S. forces in Vietnam by operating in "no man's land," far from other U.S. forces in what would have been "behind enemy lines" in America's previous wars. The quietest of "The Quiet Professionals," these extraordinary men operated in the most desolate of places, near and in enemy sanctuaries, clandestinely seeking out the enemy and either delivering devastating air power or providing the intelligence needed to support the employment of larger American units in that region.

This small, but highly effective, group of men punched well above their weight! They were an incredibly brave and dedicated professional force who purged their own ranks of those who did not measure up; in some cases they were "characters," but characters that became legends among those fortunate enough to know them.

The personal stories captured by Ray Morris portray instances of incredible heroism, told in anecdotal fashion as the incident unfolded. This tightly-knit group operated clandestinely for five years; they suffered losses, but never missed a beat. To the man, they were single-minded in purpose and intent on being the best. They were proud but not cocky; they were quiet professionals in the finest sense. It is past time that America hears their story.

General Henry H. Shelton, U.S. Army Retired
14th Chairman, Joint Chiefs of Staff

The Quiet Professionals:
For all those brave men who have ever served on a
U.S. Army Special Forces A-Team,
and for comrades still missing in action.

In the Company of Heroes

THE CHILDREN WHO WOULD BECOME THE WARRIORS of Project Delta were born at a time of uncertainty; America was still engaged in World War II. As the nation struggled to revive a sluggish post-war economy, these young boys were developing stalwart character traits reflecting America's values, work ethic, courage and morals. The sons of sturdy American and immigrant stock, they were a diverse lot, representing the best of the best. Their geographical background was rich, an amalgamation of all walks of life. They hailed from cities, both large and small, obscure little towns, farmlands, flatlands, seacoasts, the Rocky Mountain region, low-country, cattle country, the hills of the Ozarks and from the swamps and bayous of Louisiana. At least four had emigrated from Europe, while one had been of French-Canadian descent. Three Project Delta members ultimately rose to the rank of general officer; one achieving acclaim as Chairman of the Joint Chiefs of Staff. Predominately, this collective body represented poor and middle class families, although a few would be from wealth. Most had enlisted while others were drafted—all would volunteer for Project Delta.

Ever since the middle ages and the Roman Army, armies have had elite volunteer units dedicated to the most difficult and dangerous missions. Despite America's relatively short history, historians have chronicled: Rogers' Rangers (Revolutionary War); Jeb Stuart's Cavalry (Civil War); the tough 101st and 82nd Airborne Divisions; Darby's Rangers; and the 1st Special Service Force—the renowned, combined American and Canadian World War II forerunner to today's Special Forces. The soldiers of these unique fighting units had one very important similarity—they all volunteered to fight with an elite unit. Modern soldiers serving in the U.S. Army's most elite combat unit, the United States Army Special Forces, each volunteer a minimum of three times; the majority are also Ranger and/or jungle warfare qualified. Barry Sadler's lyrics in the "Ballad of the Green Beret" state, "One hundred men they'll test today, but only three win the Green Beret." His words hit not far from the mark, but even after this strict selection process, it would still take at least three more years of intensive training to become fully qualified for specific mission deployment.

Among these elite Special Forces units, a relatively few men would become affiliated with even a more select group—they share the distinction of serving in one of the military's most selective, secretive organizations, Project Delta. Handpicked from the elite Special Forces ranks, they were identified as the best of the best from the highly trained United States Army Special Forces.

These noble warriors, caught up in an ignoble war no one wanted, returned home, not to ticker-tape parades as previous American war veterans had experienced, but rather to an ungrateful nation—jeered, derided and spat upon. After receiving little appreciation for their terrible sacrifices, all these men wanted was to quietly rebuild their lives and raise their families in tranquil obscurity. Peace looked good to them. Collectively, during a five-year span, they'd experienced more combat than any other unit in the Vietnam War, and had viewed enough killing and destruction to last a lifetime. Ultimately, some suffered emotionally and remain psychologically scarred; mentally they might wander the Central Highlands's misty hills, forever lost in that conflict—or hope to mend their minds in the relief of hard liquor. Most successfully put it behind them, yet none completely forgot what they once had—and lost.

As others wrote about their Vietnam experiences and Hollywood crafted movies depicting corrupt versions of that bloody conflict—the leading characters nearly always portrayed as potheads or psychopaths—the weary soldiers of Project Delta preferred to fade into the background to resume their disrupted personal lives.

Throughout the ensuing years, these men have remained close. An integral component within the exclusive Special Operations Association (SOA), they support worthy causes, share stories, resources and strength during annual reunions. While the wartime friendships and unique brotherhood has never diminished, their numbers have shrunk; the years have taken their toll. Many Project Delta members have succumbed to old war wounds, physical and mental, or other war-related illnesses, eventually coming to terms with the death they'd bravely defied so many times in the past.

These graying warriors rely upon their diminishing colleagues for strength, encouragement and purpose, silently grieving for those left behind while honoring those now quietly passing. Today their brotherhood remains as steadfast and strong as when they fought beside each other in Southeast Asia's rugged mountain jungles.

After the war, some former Special Forces soldiers did their best to educate the American public about several highly classified projects: the Studies and Observation Group (SOG), Omega and Sigma. John L. Plaster's *SOG: The Secret Wars of America's Commandos in Vietnam*; Jim Morris's *War Story: The Classic True Story of the First Generation of Green Berets in Vietnam*; and Robin Moore's, *The Green Berets*, are noteworthy. But strong perceptions persist, and the American public still has a hard time believing anything good might have come from this disputed conflict. Most have only heard details from distorted Hollywood script versions, in lieu of eyewitness accounts from those who lived through it.

Stunned by public rejection, Project Delta's members unanimously agreed they would deny interviews and withhold authorization for their story, preferring to remain in the shadows. Only a few citizens know of Project Delta; even fewer have any awareness of the vital contributions and immense sacrifices of this small band of men. Yet for this unique group, whose numbers never exceeded a total of 100 officers and enlisted men, uncommon valor was the order of the day. Delta members generally scorned medals and decorations. Still this small fighting force has collectively been honored with an astounding array: five Distinguished Service Crosses, thirty-seven Silver Stars, 102 Bronze

Stars, forty-eight Army Commendation Medals for valor, twenty-one Air Medals for valor and sixty-eight Purple Hearts for wounds received in combat. Several awards, including one for the Distinguished Service Cross, were flat-out refused by their recipients; the soldiers had insisted their efforts unworthy.

When the policy of being awarded three Purple Hearts could ensure a quick trip back home, scores of Project Delta members could have legitimately claimed the medal, but scoffed at such antics. Sixteen awards for valor are pending and may never be presented.[1] Numerous other decorations for valor (not acknowledged above) were also recommended and/or awarded. With member attrition, the loss of precious institutional memory and recorded documentation, those awards couldn't be included. Project Delta has also been recognized with an impressive number of Unit Awards, above and beyond those for personal valor.

Project Delta, Special Forces Operational Detachment B-52, was the most highly decorated unit of its size, and the second most highly decorated unit in the Vietnam War. (But the first, CIA's Special Forces Project MACV-SOG, larger in numbers, also sustained substantially more casualties than Delta). During the five years and three months of Project Delta's existence, between 1964 and 1970, despite a voracious number of combat operations, only nineteen U.S. personnel were killed while twelve remain missing. This statistic is astounding considering the magnitude of its combat operations, war wounds and personal bravery awards. Most Project Delta personnel received multiples of all three; it is a testament to their superb training and combat skills that such a relatively few men were lost.[2] Retired Army Colonel David Hackworth, in *About Face: Odyssey of an American Warrior*, referred to Project Delta as, "...pound for pound and weighed against its cost... the most effective fighting force in Vietnam."

Records are essentially unavailable for the brave Vietnamese Special Forces, Chinese Nung mercenaries, Montagnard Road Runners and

---

[1] Steve Sherman. *Project Delta, After Action Reports, Detachment B-52* (1964-1970).

[2] A list of awards is documented in the Annexes.

81st Airborne Ranger Battalion personnel—all vital to Project Delta. They fought bravely along side their American counterparts and will forever remain an integral slice of Project Delta history.

I am honored that the surviving Project Delta members have allowed me to write their story. However, this task was not easy. It was often difficult to get these former operatives to speak about their experiences. Their recollections were mostly about the brave deeds accomplished by others; the telling of others' feats while remarkably skipping over their personal participation as either nominal or insignificant. Only after my review of their awards and decorations, did my evidence indicate quite the contrary. Hence, this account of Project Delta and its brave men result from information I've gleaned from many sources, meshed and woven, much like a patchwork quilt. It's not as if there isn't an abundance of untold stories within this secretive entity, but the U.S. Army Special Forces have a motto: "Quiet Professionals." This trait is unique to their profession and they seldom speak of personal exploits or history, except during quiet conversations with those who have shared their experiences. Yet, if ever an opportunity arises to overhear one of them speak of some exemplary leadership or astonishing bravery, it's wise not to dispute them. It will be the truth. In Detachment B-52, Project Delta, there are no phonies or "wanna-bes."

The Special Ops community has long coveted its privacy. Many did not reflect too kindly upon fellow veteran Barry Sadler for his song "The Ballad of the Green Berets" and scorned Robin Moore's book, *The Green Berets,* and John Wayne's adaptive movie, based on it. In 1965, Robin Moore traveled to Vietnam and visited the 5th Special Forces Group. A Project Delta NCO bumped into him in Nha Trang at the "Playboy Club."

"I don't like your book," said the NCO.

"Have you read it?" Moore asked.

"No," was the curt reply. "I don't have to read it. I don't like it because of all the attention it's giving Special Forces, and for the trouble I know it'll cause us."

Many Special Forces soldiers believed this kind of publicity drew too much unwarranted attention to highly classified missions, inherently dangerous enough without adding notoriety that attracted others to volunteer, simply because they wanted to "cash-in" and become "heroes." This philosophy was not, and is not, held in high regard. Attention also tended to evoke jealousy within some conventional Army organizations that resented elite organizations; they often attempted to get their own guys in to share the glory. Schemes and manipulations of this type could cause serious disruption and made Special Ops work all the more difficult and dangerous. Needless to say, attention such as this was not appreciated by the Quiet Professionals.

Despite this notoriety, Project Delta's veterans seldom speak of their own exploits, generally shunning those who boast of real or imagined adventures while serving with the organization. While they may speak quietly among themselves while honoring those no longer with them, outsiders should consider themselves fortunate to be privy to these tales of bravery and sacrifice.

I'm convinced the recollections are but the tip of the iceberg. Names, dates and locations, while as factual as possible, may still be inaccurate due to lack of records, the passing of key personnel, or fading memories. Although I crosschecked material with Project Delta members or source documents prior to writing, mistakes do happen, and if so, they are purely unintentional. In a situation where information couldn't be verified, I simply listed the operation and the names of those wounded, killed, missing in action, or receiving awards for valor. If any inaccuracies or omissions are discovered, I humbly apologize to any I may have slighted or failed to mention. It is my sincere hope that my efforts may be judged as a way to honor those living, and in some small way document the enduring legacy of these Project Delta members, for them and their families.

Remarkably, none of the old warriors I interviewed would admit to being a hero, but to a man, they would stubbornly insist that the men they had fought beside certainly had been. Perhaps that's what makes a man a true hero—an unawareness of personal bravery, the chalking up of heroic actions to the notion that they were, in fact, just doing their jobs and taking care of each other.

In Stephen Ambrose' book, *Band of Brothers*, years after WWII had ended, Mike Ramsey was questioned by his grandson if he'd been a hero during the war. He pondered for a moment, then replied quietly, "No, but I served in the company of heroes." It's time for these Quiet Professionals to tell their tale. These are heroes America needs to hear about. Welcome home, Brothers.

> From this day to the ending of the world,
> But we in it shall be remembered—
> We few, we happy few, we band of brothers;
> For he today that sheds his blood with me
> Shall be my brother...
>
> *-William Shakespeare, Henry V*

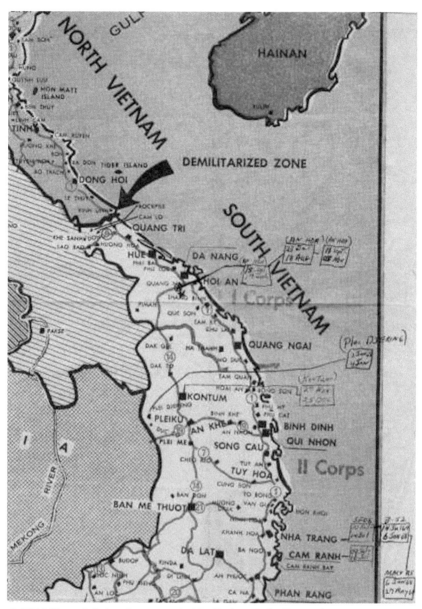

A 1966 "Stars & Stripes" map carried by Project Delta Recon Sergeant James Jarrett

ONE

1953 – 1964

Find the Ho Chi Minh Trail!

*"A nation reveals itself by the men it
produces and the men it honors."*

— *John F. Kennedy, President of the United States*

THE MUTUAL DEFENSE ASSISTANCE ACT OF 1949 allowed the United States to send a small military staff, equipment and related training technicians to Vietnam to act as advisors to the Army of the Republic of Vietnam (ARVN), primarily after the French left in 1953. As an unforeseen consequence, this then became a "foot in the door" for subsequent involvement in the eminent Vietnam War. Although these advisors formed into small military groups, they actually served as an extension of the U.S. diplomatic mission. By 1953, approximately 300 "advisors" were in country, many, highly trained Special Forces personnel stationed in Okinawa, Japan.

In essence, the War in Indochina really never ceased after the French surrendered to the Viet Minh at Dinh Bien Phu, and the country was divided along the 17th parallel, forming the two countries, North

Vietnam and South Vietnam. Almost immediately, the North began incursions into the new South, attempting to influence political decisions. For years, the South Vietnamese government knew that supplies had been reaching VC insurgents from North Vietnam, via the same trails through eastern Laos that'd been used to supply the Viet Minh on their southern battlefields during the French Indochina War.

Vietnam is shaped similar to an hourglass. The center (along the 17th parallel) is the smallest dimension, which allowed the French, and later the South Vietnamese Army, to effectively curtail the movement of supplies and personnel along that narrow point of entry. Aware of this strategy, Communist leaders decided to resurrect hundreds of miles of trails that side-tracked west into Laos. This allowed them to bypass the narrow, well-defended center along the Demilitarized Zone (DMZ), the North and South Vietnamese border, and veer into South Vietnam further south. What had been previously known as the Truong Son Route, the U.S. news media would begin to refer to as the Ho Chi Minh Trail.

The Ho Chi Minh Trail consists of hundreds of miles of small roads and trails, interdicting South Vietnam by way of Laos. This winding network of footpaths and small roads became a lifeline, essential to the North's incursion into its southern neighbor's territory. More than simply a supply route, it functioned for storage and as bases of operations for forces jumping off into the South. Estimates are that more than seventy percent of communist war materiel and personnel traveled down the Ho Chi Minh Trail.[3]

Since the Laotian military had little control over that rugged, isolated section of their country, Communist porters were soon moving men and supplies without fear of reprisal along these old supply routes. As one senior Laotian officer noted, "The trail runs through tropical, dense forest...The jungles along these trails are almost impenetrable primitive forests; the mountains are steep and rocky. During the French colonial regime, as well as after Laotian independence, this part of the

---

[3] *BDM Corporation: A Study of Strategic Lessons Learned in Vietnam, Volume 1, The Enemy.* McLean, VA, November 30, 1979, 5-14.

country was so remote, isolated and undeveloped that no effort was made to control it." [4]

Deeply disturbed by this activity, the authorities in Saigon approached its Laotian neighbors to allow forays across the border to suppress such activities. Early negotiations between the South Vietnamese and their Royal Lao Government counterparts allowed the Army of Vietnam (ARVN) to initiate intelligence-gathering operations from Lao Bao, along Route 9, across their western border, and into Laos. Because the Laotian authorities were having their own internal problems, the two governments mutually agreed that ARVN troops would disguise themselves in Laotian Army uniforms to hide the fact that they were Vietnamese. This agreement resulted in a semi-permanent ARVN outpost inside Laos. In 1960, the Royal Lao Government was overthrown by a relatively unknown paratrooper captain, Kong Le, who immediately declared Laos to be neutral. Soon, battles raged across Laos as Kong Le, backed by the Communist Pathet Lao, fought to retain power against a well-organized right-wing group of officers who battled just as determinedly to establish a counter-coup. This internal fighting allowed the NVA to strike up an alliance with the Pathet Lao and to cement them firmer into the border region of Laos. Within a few weeks, in December 1961, North Vietnamese Army elements overran the ARVN outpost in Laos, subsequently using that location to attack into South Vietnam's Kontum Province. Not since the end of the First Indochina War had northern troops used a base inside Laos to attack South Vietnam; reverberations were felt at top government echelons in Saigon and Washington, D.C.

Coups and political disorganization on both sides of the border prevailed for a few years as the Communists ran operations along the Ho Chi Minh Trail, while basing their troops with impunity inside Laos. It was during this period that U.S. Army Special Forces began to train commandos who would later become the nucleus of the South Vietnamese Army Special Forces (VNSF).

---

[4] Brigadier General Southchay Vongsavanh. "RLG [Royal Laotian Government] Military Operations and Activities in the Laotian Panhandle," *Indochina Monographs*. Washington, D.C., U.S. Army Center of Military History, 1981, 4.

General William C. Westmoreland, Commanding General of MACV and U.S. ground forces in South Vietnam, 1964 – 1968. (Photo courtesy of US Army)

In 1962, the Military Assistance Command Vietnam (MACV) was created as the Command and Control element for an ever-increasing volume of equipment, military advisors, technicians and staff to manage rapidly growing efforts to support the tottering Saigon Government. Although MACV's stated mission was to serve as an extension of the diplomatic mission, and as an allied headquarters, when the first major U.S. units arrived in Vietnam (1965), General William C. Westmoreland and his top military commanders became mired in a quandary. This wasn't like fighting in Europe and Korea. They hadn't been trained to fight in Vietnam's terrain, weren't equipped to fight a war like this, and Army doctrine needed a dramatic shift to accomplish its new mission. The difficult jungle terrain was much more than an obstacle, it offered a formidable place to hide for an enemy who preferred to fight with hit-and-run guerrilla tactics instead of slugging it out toe-to-toe, as the German war machine had done. Military leaders knew the well-trained and equipped U.S. soldiers could defeat this elusive enemy, but first they'd need an effective means to find him. In 1965, William Sullivan, Ambassador to Laos, pointed out, "…impenetrable tree canopy that high-speed, high-flying jets cannot see through…flying over slowly with a helicopter, a road was not discernable from above. It seems clear to me. . .that significant quantities of logistics can still be moving over routes which…our strike aircraft are unable to discern." [5]

---

[5] U.S. Department of State [DOS], telegram from Sullivan to DOS, 21 June 1965, *Foreign Relations of the United States [FRUS]*, 1964-1968, Volume 27, Laos. www.state.gov/www/about_state/history/vol_xxviii.

TWO

1964

Leaping Lena

THE ARVN COMMANDERS, ALONG WITH THEIR U.S. advisors, recognized the urgency for intelligence a full year earlier when initiating a classified operation, code-named "Leaping Lena," to conduct long range reconnaissance missions across the international border into neutral Laos and to locate enemy bases and foretell enemy troop movement.[6] U.S. Special Forces (USSF) had been operating in Southeast Asia under the Central Intelligence Agency's (CIA) auspicious control since the French had been kicked out in the 1950s, with, as yet, unpublicized achievements. Organized by the CIA, Leaping Lena initially consisted of several all-Vietnamese recon teams who were trained by U.S. Special Forces personnel on temporary duty (TDY), operating out of Okinawa. These were the predecessors of Project Delta or as the unit's old timers prefer to say, "Leaping Lena was the *operation*—Project Delta, the name of the *organization*.

---

[6] Steve Sherman. "History of Project Delta – Part 1," *Project Delta After Action Reports*, http://project-delta.net/delta_history.htm

As early as March 1964, U.S. Secretary of Defense Robert McNamara expressed his belief that reconnaissance teams were extremely beneficial and urged greater use.[7] In May 1964, Captain (CPT) William J. Richardson Jr., assisted by Sergeant Major (SGM) Paul Payne, handpicked volunteers from an Okinawa-based Special Forces company, flew them to Vietnam and began to train various indigenous ethnic groups; Chinese Nung, Montagnard tribesmen and Vietnamese army personnel for the sensitive Leaping Lena operation. Sergeants Paul Tracy, Bill Edge, Donald Valentine, Tony Duarte, Sergeant First Class (SFC) Henry M. Bailey and SFC Ronald T. Terry were among those on that first team, joined later in the year by NCOs Larry Dickinson, Norbert Weber, Harold "Catfish" Dreblow, Eddie Adams, Ronald Gaffney, James Malia and Sterling Smith. The Command's initial intention was for these USSF personnel to serve only as trainers and advisors, not to accompany the recon teams into the field. Initially, Leaping Lena recon teams were comprised of indigenous personnel (reflecting a cross-section of the local population) termed the Civilian Irregular Defense Group (CIDG) and a few of the new Vietnamese Special Forces (VNSF) the USSF had been training. In anticipation of their insertion into Laos, Leaping Lena teams had been trained by Green Berets, using proven long range recon patrolling techniques, such as the use of smoke jumping equipment for parachuting into dense foliage.

Vietnamese Army and Air Force elements provided aviation support for Leaping Lena in the form of Forward Air Controllers (FAC), troop carriers and on a limited basis, close air support. Before 1961, the Vietnamese had no system for directing or controlling air strikes. In December 1961, advisors from the 13th U.S. Air Force developed a plan for the first Tactical Air Control (TAC) system in Vietnam, to be located at Tan Son Nhut Airbase. The plan called for establishment of an Air Support Operations Center (ASOC), Air Liaison Officers (ALO) and Forward Air Controllers (FAC), manned by both USAF and VNAF personnel. The following year, an ASOC was created at Da Nang Air Base, which was assigned to I Corps combat operations, and subsequently ASOCs were also implemented in II and III Corps. Viet-

---

[7] Kenneth Conboy. *Shadow War: The CIA's Secret War In Laos*, New York: Paladin, 1995, 119.

namese pilots flew limited FAC support until the U.S. 19th Tactical Air Support Squadron (TASS), with its twenty-two O-1F aircraft assigned, arrived in July 1963.

During June and July 1964, five Leaping Lena teams, each composed of eight Vietnamese Special Forces NCOs, parachuted into the Laotian jungle along Route 9. Immediately, the operation ran into trouble; one man died from his injuries as he attempted to rappel 120 feet from the tall trees after his chute became entangled in its thick triple-layer canopy. Several more were also seriously injured in the tree landings, robbing the teams of critical skills they'd need to survive and send back intelligence. Without American leadership and expertise on the ground, the mission was doomed to fail, and despite being warned about going into villages, most teams ignored the orders. It didn't take long for the enemy to become aware of their presence and essentially wipe them out.

A broad consensus is that the first Leaping Lena operations were disasters. Of the forty Vietnamese team members initially dropped into Laos, most were either killed or immediately captured after their insertion. Only five survivors straggled back, weeks later. Of the data gathered, little was deemed to be useable intelligence, but it had still been more than MACV had collected prior to the operation. At the least, they knew the area across the border had been saturated with the enemy, many in NVA uniforms, clear proof that the North Vietnamese were sponsoring the South's insurgency. Roads and bridges were all guarded by a minimum of two personnel, and additional roads supported huge convoys that couldn't be detected, even from the air. Several battalion-sized units were reported just inside Laos, with evidence that one had already crossed into South Vietnam near Khe Sanh. Here, a Special Forces camp would be overrun in 1968, the site of one of the war's bloodiest battle between U.S. Marines and the NVA.

An immediate search for the missing Leaping Lena team survivors was initiated. MAJ Fred Patton and MSG Robert Mattox arrived as advance party for two SF teams deployed from 1st Special Forces Group Airborne (1st SFGA), A1/111 and B1/110, on a six month TDY assignment with orders to search for the missing Leaping Lena team members. Joined by teammates from Okinawa, their intensive search failed to turn up any more of the missing Vietnamese soldiers, except for the five initial stragglers. The others who had descended into the dark rugged jungle that fateful evening over Laos were never heard from or seen again.

After this first cross-border debacle, Leaping Lena shifted tactics and began to run Long Range Recon Patrols (LRRP), coined "Road Runners," using solely indigenous personnel. These teams were either brave Montagnard tribesmen from the Rhade and Raglai tribes, or Chinese Nung mercenaries employed and paid with CIA funds funneled through U.S. Special Forces personnel. They were trained to emulate North Vietnamese Army (NVA) soldiers or Viet Cong (VC), and then when inserted into hotly contested or suspected hostile territory, to run the trails, search for enemy units and gather intelligence. These teams would generally infiltrate wearing the South Vietnamese uniform, and then change into NVA or Viet Cong attire to blend in once on the ground. Since the majority of their time was actually spent within the enemy's encampments and defensive positions, they had to be extremely dedicated and have nerves of steel to accomplish their missions.

Using indigenous personnel as Road Runners dressed as enemy combatants often presented situations, that upon reflection, seem humorous to some of the Army's more conventional participants, such as in the following:

When 101st Airborne Division aviation elements were supporting Project Delta, a young, relatively inexperienced pilot, Bill Walker, confessed he'd nearly had to change his pants after a Road Runner team extraction. It had come soon after the loss of Gene Miller, a revered pilot and officer in the 101st Airborne Division, who along with his entire crew, perished while attempting a high overhead extraction of such a team by a hoist, the jungle penetrator. Walker had been assigned his first duty as Aircraft Commander (AC) and answered the siren, only to learn that a hoist had been put on his helicopter. He protested strenuously. He hadn't practiced a high overhead recovery since flight school, and the news substantially added to the stress of his first maneuver under combat conditions. To compensate, they'd given him the experienced and steady Keith Boyd as his right seat. The Command & Control (C&C) ship circled nearby, directing Walker's aircraft into a narrow opening in the jungle canopy, west of Khe Sanh, near a landmark called the "Rock Pile." He observed several orange panels in the tall elephant grass below, swallowed hard and nosed his vulnerable craft toward them.

"If there are six on the ground instead of five," the C&C ship told him, "kill 'em all."

Walker's stress index ratcheted up several more notches.

He dropped rapidly, hovering just beyond the treetops, amazed by the deafening sound of close combat over the noise of his rotary blades. He held the controls steady despite the gunfire streaking toward his exposed aircraft.

Through the chaos, he distinctly heard the ladder descending, mildly surprised that the crew hadn't used the jungle hoist after all. With ground fire pecking against his chopper's fragile skin, he heard the recon team scrambling up the ladder behind him. Finally assured everyone was aboard, Keith shouted, "We've got 'em all. Go! Go!"

Walker glanced back to ensure they were, in fact ready, and it was only then that he'd profess later, "I nearly shit my pants!" His chopper was packed with Asians in full NVA combat uniforms, pith helmets with red stars and NVA web-gear. Each carried the enemy's favorite weapon of choice, AK-47 Chi Com assault rifles. One camouflaged face stared back fiercely, then suddenly grinning, his gold teeth glistened. The grin seemed malicious and inherently evil, only adding to Walker's growing apprehension. He had a fleeting thought, "My God! We've picked up the bad guys!"Briefly flirting with panic, he considered ditching his aircraft into the nearby mountainside; he was not going to the Hanoi Hilton (the North Vietnamese's POW camp, near Hanoi). Keith quickly picked up on his friend's hyperventilation; he hastily explained their passengers were Chinese Nung mercenaries from an obscure Special Forces operation, Project Delta.

"Hey bud, don't have a heart attack," Keith said, grinning widely. "Delta inserts their Road Runner teams in ARVN uniforms, but as soon as they're on the ground, they change out of them and put on NVA uniforms. They do it so they can mix in with the enemy units and gather intelligence."

It quickly became obvious that tactic didn't always work as planned. That's why they were there, extracting them from a dangerous situation.

"Why doesn't somebody ever tell me this shit before it happens?"

Delta Road Runner in NVA attire.
(Photo courtesy of Gary Nichols)

Walker groaned in frustration. He listened as Eddie Hester and Felis Berto keyed their mikes so he and Keith could hear them laughing on the way back to Khe Sanh.[8]

The Road Runner's mission was dirty, dangerous work; the most hazardous assigned to any small force of only three to four men. The U.S. Special Forces soldiers of Project Delta highly respected the Road Runners, mourning each loss as one of their own. Inexplicitly, the NVA and VC frequently seemed to sense these teams as imposters, and would open fire on them without warning. No one ever determined just how the enemy knew the Road Runners didn't belong to one of their units, but the attrition rapidly proved much too high; tactics had to be changed quickly. The Road Runners continued to operate after Leaping Lena, with at least one major adjustment: Special Forces NCOs advised them from their initial deployment in 1964 until disbanding Project Delta, in 1970.

Operation Leaping Lena concluded with less than stellar performances by Vietnamese reconnaissance personnel, but future potential was clearly evident. Planners knew that for missions of this type to succeed, Americans would have to accompany indigenous soldiers on the ground. In late 1964, the decision was made to train combined recon teams, using both VNSF and U.S. Special Forces, and to develop the capability to quickly reinforce them while in the field.

Thirsty for intelligence, commanders realized that for operations to be effective, they would need not only U.S. Special Forces troops integrated, but more muscle as backup. In July 1964, the mission subtly

---

[8] *Lancers,* Volume 11, Issue 2, 9

shifted from being an operation, to becoming an organization, utilizing joint command of VNSF and USSF advisors from Okinawa, with command and control falling under MACV. This new composite detachment was designated B-52 (Project Delta), filled from within the Okinawa-based 1st SFGA with the most experienced, highly qualified personnel under that organization's command. A decision was made that only the best would be selected from U.S. Special Forces ranks to fill subsequent organizational vacancies. The muscle would come in the form of a reinforcement-reaction force, the 91st ARVN Airborne Ranger Battalion,[9] battle-hardened soldiers who had previously demonstrated they could take the fight to the enemy and hold their own if given the resources to do so. U.S. Special Forces advisors were immediately assigned to work with the Rangers, thus adding an enormous capability for calling in air and artillery support. Because of this substantially increased firepower with the addition of the Rangers, Delta forces would habitually kill more enemy soldiers than both Omega and Sigma, combined.[10, 11]

* * * * * *

The 91st Airborne Ranger Battalion and their American counterparts made significant contributions to Project Delta's overall mission throughout its tenure. In only one year, the 91st Rangers (referred throughout this book as the 81st Airborne Rangers, see footnote below) had spent on average 55% of their time in the field and accounted for 194 enemy soldiers killed in action. Project Delta personnel who had worked closely with them, praised their toughness and fighting ability.

The Vietnamese soldiers on Project Delta's new recon teams, much like the Americans, all volunteered and had been selected from among the ranks of Vietnamese Special Forces to receive further intensive

---

[9] The 91st designation for the Ranger battalion was later changed to the 81st, for unusual reasons. The Vietnamese rated everything from "Number 1" (very good), to "Number 10" (very bad). Adding the 9 and 1 (of the 91st), equals "10." To the superstitious Vietnamese and Montagnard tribesmen, the number 10 meant "very bad." Once their designation had changed to the 81st Ranger and they were issued the same M16 rifles as their U.S. counterparts, their combat performance dramatically improved.

[10] USSF Advisors to the 81st Airborne Ranger Battalion, Annex G11, 5th Special Forces Group Commander's Omega, Sigma and Project Delta Debriefing Report, June 66 – June 67

[11] *ibid.*

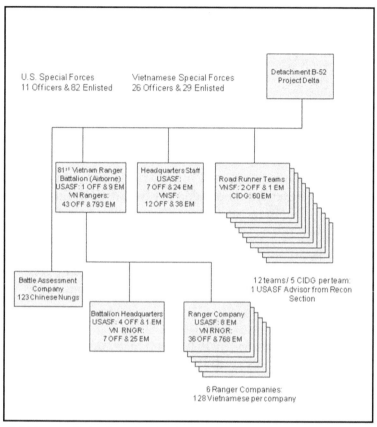

B-52 Project Delta Organizational Chart (courtesy of U.S. Army)

training, by and with U.S. Special Forces personnel. After the initial stage of specialized training, additional training in the form of "real world" exercises began in relatively secure jungle and mountainous areas where only small units of the enemy were known to be holed up, and then progressed into areas under total control of the Viet Cong or NVA. The training of each recon team often took six months, until all were satisfied about their capability to operate effectively—accomplished by running actual combat operations against the enemy.[12]

---

[12] See "USSF Personnel on Project Delta Recon Teams, 1964 to 1970," Annex E.

Vietnamese Recon Team members preparing for an operation, 1964.
(Photo courtesy of Len Boulas)

While the operational strength of Project Delta fluctuated, typically it was manned by eleven U.S. Special Forces officers and eighty-two enlisted men; twenty Vietnamese Special Forces officers and seventy-eight VN enlisted men; a 123-man Vietnamese Road Runner Company; and the 81st Vietnamese Airborne Ranger Battalion, consisting of forty-three officers, 763 enlisted men and a Battle Damage Assessment Company (BDA) of 107 heavily armed, Chinese Nung mercenaries, their salaries paid and controlled by the Delta Commander. The Project Delta organizational chart on the previous page depicts how this strength was assigned.

Although USAF Forward Air Control (FAC) section's strength fluctuated, it rarely exceeded ten personnel. The 281st Army Helicopter Company (AHC), (attached later), was an Army aviation unit of company strength.

* * * * * *

At the outset of Project Delta, USSF personnel lived, ate, trained and socialized with their respective VN team members. In doing so, rapport and close friendships fostered mutual respect, enabling U.S. personnel to exert greater influence on the Ranger companies and on recon teams in the field without usurping Vietnamese leadership authority. In this regard, U.S. personnel became well aware of the thin line they had to tread—particularly within the Ranger companies—to get maximum effort and capability without diminishing their leader's control, at the risk of rendering them ineffective. For recon teams on the ground, this line often blurred when USSF NCOs called the shots.

In the field, the USSF personnel always carried identical equipment and the same indigenous rations as the Vietnamese recon team members and their Ranger counterparts; they were not privy to any intelligence or special equipment unless like items were issued to the Vietnamese. In short, there were no shortcuts to the specialized training or resources, and no substitute for close personal relationships and rapport.

After Action Reports (AAR) repeatedly reinforced that with troops working and living so closely with indigenous military personnel, it was essential that only the most highly trained, experienced U.S. Special Forces soldiers be selected. Otherwise, trust and confidence—highly fragile commodities—could quickly deteriorate into contempt. This important concept is still used in Special Forces training.

Special Forces ranks are filled with highly skilled, brave and adventurous men; otherwise, they wouldn't have joined the military's most elite unit. But from even this illustrious group of overachievers, the mission of Project Delta still required the best. The meticulous search for replacements never diminished throughout the unit's existence. As H. Ross Perot once remarked about Special Forces soldiers, "Eagles don't flock. You have to find them one at a time."[13]

*   *   *   *   *   *

Unfortunately, some records of early operations have been lost to history. Often, due to poor record keeping practices or attrition within Project Delta's ranks, the names of some of the brave men who conducted those first operations are unavailable. Although personal knowledge of some of these earliest operations has diminished, by

---

[13] Tom Clancy & John Gresham. *Special Forces: A Guided Tour of U.S. Army Special Forces.* New York: Berkely Trade, 2001, 61.

meticulously researching and probing fading memories, the following account is provided:

The Commander (after Leaping Lena) had been MAJ Howard S. Mitchell, TDY for six months from the 1st Special Forces Group (Abn), when stationed on Okinawa. He'd taken command from CPT William J. Richardson while the project still had been known as Leaping Lena, and it was during his watch the "Project Delta" moniker was initially used. Mitchell's short command tour became a transitional timeframe as Project Delta struggled to develop a clear mission statement and establish its identity. Mitchell commanded for a period of six months, overseeing an important operation near the Nihn Hoa Peninsula in support of a deployed B Detachment from the 5th Special Forces Group (Abn), at Fort Bragg, NC.[14]

In December 1964, while still under Mitchell's command, Project Delta ran its first operation utilizing U.S. Special Forces personnel on recon teams, along with Vietnamese. Intelligence NCO, Sergeant First Class (SFC) Henry M. Bailey, in charge of the ground operation, was assisted by Sergeant (SGT) Ronald T. Terry and four Montagnard soldiers. The plan was to insert recon teams into an area on the peninsula extending east and south from Ninh Hoa, a small village complex north of the port city of Nha Trang. Three teams, consisting of five men each, were committed into separate operational areas. The concept for this mission was unique; it departed from usual dusk/night infiltration. Due to excessive rain and low-hanging cloud formations, it had been determined that poor night visibility would preclude a successful helicopter insertion. Instead, the teams were scheduled to go in at 0630 hours, with a hope that rain and the early morning mist would cover this most critical and dangerous phase of any covert operation: the insertion. Unfortunately, two teams were detected immediately upon landing. It is generally believed that because there were only a few suitable LZs in the designated area, the enemy had been keeping watch on them and were able to detect two of the teams as they landed. The third team, however, escaped detection and brought back valuable intelligence, as well as an enemy prisoner.

---

[14] See "Project Delta Commanders, Staff and Attached Personnel," Annex F.

Team One, although initially detected at the time of insertion, evaded capture and remained on mission while pursued doggedly by a determined enemy until extraction. During the process of extraction, they encountered a reinforced company of Viet Cong near the LZ, and its heavy fire drove the chopper off before it could land to pick them up. During the scrimmage, two team members became separated from the main group. However, both men, as well as the main body of the team, out-maneuvered the enemy's attempts to surround them, eventually escaping capture. The two missing men later rejoined the team at a designated rally point. A successful evacuation was finally concluded under sporadic enemy sniper fire, but only after the helicopter crew chief successfully engaged and killed a sniper with the ship's M60 machinegun.

Meanwhile, Team Two, led by SFC Henry M. Bailey, had descended down the mountain into the valley to an extraction point. As the chopper prepared to land for pickup, a VC ambush was sprung and the aircraft driven off under heavy fire. Bailey believed it had been the same group tracking them since their insertion. As the team took cover behind a rice paddy dike, three recon members, Bailey, SSG Ronald Terry and a VNSF soldier, were pinned down by heavy automatic fire while attempting to place orange panel markers on the LZ. After a short but fierce firefight, the remainder of the Vietnamese team members, presuming Bailey, Terry and their VN soldier were dead, withdrew to avoid being surrounded. A patrolling gunship had heard Bailey's radio exchanges and suddenly appeared, engaging the enemy. That timely intervention gave the beleaguered group the cover fire they needed to break contact, and allowed Bailey and Terry to crawl for the cover of nearby bamboo thickets while dragging their seriously wounded VNSF counterpart.

Due to extremely poor weather, darkness had fallen early, and although the enemy saturated the area with patrols searching for them, the pitch-black night and torrential rain gave them cover, temporarily allowing them to evade capture. However, the weather proved to be a double-edged sword; they quickly became disoriented, unsure as to their exact location. At daylight they found themselves in an even more precarious position than the previous night. They discovered that in the darkness, they had penetrated the outer defensive perimeter of the enemy's base camp. That day, they hid in a small thicket inside the enemy's defenses, scarcely daring to breathe, waiting for the cover of darkness to escape almost certain death. At one point, a VC search party stopped for a meal break within arm's reach of the three concealed men, remaining for nearly thirty minutes.

After what seemed like an eternity, darkness fell again, allowing them to crawl from the enemy encampment and make radio contact with a helicopter searching for them. Given directions to go to the area's only suitable LZ, it had been fifty meters on the far side of a village that sheltered two reinforced VC platoons. Just before dawn the two exhausted troopers, supporting the wounded VNSF recon man between them, simply stood and strode through the middle of the enemy encampment. They had counted on the darkness and rain to fool the VC into mistaking them for their own comrades. The gutsy ruse worked; they waved to a guard hunkered down, smoking a cigarette, and he nonchalantly gestured in return!

Upon reaching the far side of the village, they hid in a clump of bushes until nearly noon, when a slight break in the weather allowed the search helicopter to spot their orange panel. Totally surprised by the sudden appearance of a helicopter coming in to land, the enemy immediately opened fire from their nearby positions, but the young pilot never flinched, hovering just long enough for the three men to load, and then took off into the valley below—a remarkable extraction of the team under fire. Once airborne, Bailey called in an air strike, which, according to subsequent intelligence reports, destroyed nearly half of the enemy force and wounded many more.

Intelligence agents reported fifty-five enemy soldiers killed in the action, seventeen others wounded and twenty-four later captured. Twenty-two tons of rice and equipment had also been destroyed. Whatever was left of the VC Company had been forced to retreat into the hills. The small village of fifty-eight families, forced to provide rice and other support for the Viet Cong for nearly two years, emerged from VC domination. Friendly casualties consisted of only the wounded VNSF Recon man who Bailey and Terry successfully brought out with them. Higher command echelons all agreed that the first Project Delta operation had been an unqualified success; less than twenty men had been able to disrupt an entire VC network, nearly decimating a reinforced Viet Cong company. More importantly, the myth of the enemy's invulnerability was put to rest; Project Delta's teams had not only penetrated the enemy's camps, right under their noses, but wreaked havoc using the VC's tactics against them. The fact that the Vietnamese Army and Air Force could perform so well in combat also provided a psychological boost to the ARVN Command. Intelligence gathered indicated the venture had been a sharp jolt in the enemy's private bailiwick. Project Delta's first major operation against the enemy would set the tempo for others to follow.

* * * * * *

Project Delta's first recon endeavor had gone well, but unfortunately, the same could not be said for the Ranger's reaction force aspect of the operation. The ARVN Ranger Battalion saw little action, although through no fault of their own, for they were always packed and ready to move if called upon. In fact, each mission they'd been called to perform had been simultaneously aborted by their higher ARVN commanders, the major obstacle being the joint VN/US chain of command at I Corps level needing to commit the ARVN Rangers. This operation led to immediate changes in the way Rangers were to be used in the future. It also forced a decision that once an operation had been approved, and recon teams committed, the Rangers would become the prerogative of the VN/U.S. field commanders, to wit, the Project Delta Commander. Thereafter, once the Rangers came under the direct control of B-52, Project Delta, they performed effectively.

* * * * * *

For actions resulting in an important enemy defeat, SFC Bailey and SSG Terry were awarded this country's second highest award for bravery, the Distinguished Service Cross (DSC). SFC Terry later won the Silver Star and several other medals for valor. A year later, SFC Terry, while on a particularly bloody and costly operation in the An Loa Valley, did not return. He remains on Army rolls as Missing in Action (MIA).

* * * * * *

The growing demand for skilled recon personnel soon outstripped the combat experience and capabilities of the highly trained 1st Special Forces Group Airborne (SFGA). For months, detachments at Fort

Delta Recon Members 1964-65. *Standing, L to R*: Donald Hayakawa, Raymond Slattery, Bill Craig, Ken Hain, Jack Smythe, Lloyd Fisher, Larry Dickinson. *Bottom, L to R*: Norbert Weber, Paul Tracy (Photo courtesy of Jack Smythe)

Bragg, N.C. had been receiving orders for Vietnam deployment, for Special Forces' unique abilities that could support MACV's other rapidly expanding requirements. One alerted Fort Bragg detachment had been commanded by MAJ Art Strange, a tall soft-spoken amicable southerner. Although weighing in at about 250-260 lbs, his 6' 9" frame still made him appear tall and lanky. It was only when one looked closely at the size of his hands that his strength became obvious—his hands were the size of feet.

This team's Executive Officer (XO) was CPT Charles H. Thompson Jr.; the Operations Officer (S3), CPT Leonard "Greek" Boulas. Len Boulas, like many others, found his memories growing dim, but was glad to provide his perspective for the record, saying, "For those who may no longer be present to tell of their recollections, I want to help fill in some of the gaps of the history of this extraordinary military organization."

Boulas had been a handsome young captain commanding Headquarters Company, 6th Special Forces Group when he received orders for assignment to the 5th Special Forces Group. It was common knowledge that 5th Special Forces Group had been providing separate "A" and "B" Detachments, TDY to Vietnam, in support of MACV. But, for the

In 1965, before Project Delta built a compound of its own near the 5th SF Group Headquarters, this was "Tent City." Construction Supervisor was SFC Gerald V. Parmentier. (Photo courtesy of Len Boulas)

first time, it began preparing for deployment as a complete Group. According to Boulas's recollections, his new detachment had already been in pre-deployment training when he joined them, undergoing extensive physical training, team-building exercises and specialized training in weapons, demolition, medical, recon and patrolling. Having had one tour in Vietnam behind him as an ARVN Battalion Advisor, he was delighted to learn that MAJ Art Strange, a WW II and Korean War veteran, would be leading them. Captain Charles Thompson, SGM Charles McGuire and the other detachment NCOs were all experienced professionals. It appeared that his next tour would be with a group that really knew its business. McGuire, a barrel-chested, burley Irishman, stood six feet tall, weighed 225 pounds and had the bearing of a professional—every inch of him. An easy Irishman to stereotype, he loved to drink, would fight if you wanted to and belted out the most beautiful Irish tunes in a fine tenor voice. His rendition of Danny Boy at a 1st Special Forces Group formal affair on Okinawa brought tears to everyone's eyes.

Deployment orders for the original Detachment B-52 personnel (Project Delta Headquarters), 27 August 1964, list the following personnel: CPT Charles P. Thompson Jr., CPT Albert H. Deprospero, CPT Leonard A. Boulas, CPT Leslie R. Mason Jr., 1LT Channing M. Greene, SGM Charles T. McGuire, MSG Clyde J. Watkins, MSG Felix Z. Padilla, SFC Gerald V. Parmentier, SSG Daniel R. Redmond, SFC Lee B. Carter, SP5 Richard P. Loughlin, SSG Donald E. Valentine, SFC Marvin E. Dunbar, SSG Robert E. Harris, SGT Kelly D. Ellison, PFC Floyd L. House, SGT Leonard J. Karp, SGT Dennis P. Wash, SGT William D. Pool, SP4 Larry E. Melzer, and PFC Louis R. Hernandez. MAJ Art Strange had been listed on separate orders.

"The only information my detachment knew was that we were being assigned to a highly classified project which dealt with cross-border operations," Boulas relates. "That meant only one thing: we were going to be dropped inside North Vietnam to cause them stress. How little did we know?"

To become better prepared for this foggy, unspecified mission, Major (MAJ) Art Strange's team spent hours in the XVIII Airborne Corps G2 office, reviewing classified files, agent reports, engineer schematics of Hanoi's infrastructure and the bios of many who lived in Hanoi. More hours were spent memorizing staging areas and re-supply routes into the South through Laos. Although most was vintage information, at best, his research concluded, Boulas was convinced he knew more about the infrastructure of Hanoi than did those living there. Yet, as it turned out, other than for personal education, it was of little use for actual operations, a waste of his time. Unknown to him then, Leaping Lena's mission was continually changing, and the cross-border operations would soon be turned over to another newly created Special Forces organization, the CIA's highly classified Studies and Observation Group (SOG).

Boulas's team started deployment to Vietnam on 27 November 1964, with a closing date of 1 December. Their new base of operations, Nha Trang. By then Art Strange's team had been re-designated Detachment B-52, Project Delta. With Boulas's Greek nationality, he believed the Greek symbol, Delta, would bring good fortune. He recalls that upon reaching Nha Trang, the team met their new home with substantial alarm—and the alarm was warranted. The 1st SFGA team they displaced was located in a tent city, not far from the immaculate 5th Special Forces Group Headquarters. "Tent City" housed both U.S. and Vietnamese Delta personnel, along with all of their equipment. When it rained, as it did often, Tent City became a quagmire. Only the tents were above the waterline. If one inadvertently stepped from the wood-pallet sidewalk, they ended knee deep in water and muck.

Boulas, this his second tour, said, "The damn mud was everywhere, and on everything. I'd forgotten what the monsoon season is like in Southeast Asia."

The first few weeks in-country were spent transitioning the outgoing personnel who had been TDY from 1st SFGA, fighting a run of "god-awful weather," acclimating and becoming smart on what Project Delta was all about. Little time was lost settling in as more intensive training immediately kicked off. Detachment B-52 replaced the remnants of CPT Richardson's and Mitchell's Leaping Lena Detachment, and acting on hard learned lessons, Art Strange set his course to make tactical and organizational changes in his combat structure. It was during Strange's command that the first real changes began to take shape as Project Delta broke from its connection with the Leaping Lena image.

THREE

The Mind is the Greatest Weapon

FOLLOWING STRANGE'S INSTRUCTIONS TO "...get us ready to operate," Boulas and his operations NCOs adopted a vigorous training schedule to prepare recon teams for insertion and build a cohesive unit by implementing team and coordination exercises between the various VNAF resources, VN Airborne Rangers and U.S. Special Forces personnel. This included establishing an effective joint U.S./Vietnamese operations staff capability. Simultaneously, substantial logistical problems associated with supplying the activities of such a complex "joint" organization were being worked. These issues, tenacious since the project was classified and unique, were true of most Special Forces operations in Vietnam.

At the beginning, Project Delta's recon training was strict, unforgiving and grew more difficult as it continuously evolved. This would be true throughout the Project's existence. One commander, MAJ Chuck Allen, remarked that after a Delta Recon guy had an initial successful operation under his belt, he would become "one of the boys"; the more patrols, the more clannish. The most successful and best people were, according to Allen, "A real weird breed, usually loners—unless, of course, you were Recon."

The Recon guys would be the first to tell you they were, indeed, clannish. They didn't allow straphangers to go with them on recon operations because they had the Immediate Action Drills (IAD) and procedures memorized so well, they could almost perform them in their sleep. Teamwork came from working closely with each other, a simple facial expression, a wink of an eye in the jungle, or perhaps two blinks, meant for the team to do a specific thing. Outsiders, unfamiliar with this silent communication style would be completely lost, lose his life—or cause others to lose theirs. Besides, they didn't much trust those who weren't Recon—that general attitude persists within Delta's recon ranks.

* * * * * *

In Vietnam, Special Forces would also be given the task of setting up the first Recondo School in-country, that of training arriving American conventional divisions the art of long-range reconnaissance patrolling. Instructors came from within the ranks of the Project Delta Recon Section. Recondo training was hard, rugged, and designed to weed out those not cut out for this type of work. Initially, arriving Detachment B-52 personnel didn't go to Recondo School for training. Their mission was much more dangerous and unique; they trained their own. If someone managed to pass all the prerequisite interviews and personal muster by the Recon guys, and received an initial okay to continue, then those were the guys they trained with. The B-52 Headquarters Staff monitored the Recon training.

The "old" recon members, already trained and seasoned on the ground, were required to attend all aspects of the training with every new personnel assigned, no matter how many times they had been through it. When finished, all members of the team would know exactly the same thing, thereby keeping everyone up to date and "on the same sheet of music at all times." It also meant the new guy not only had the distinct advantage of that initial training, but benefited from the experiences of the others who'd already put the concepts to real world use in the field. It was hard and disciplined; the applications allowed no leeway or shortcuts. Get it right or be gone! Lesson plans were continually reviewed and updated, with lessons incorporated from previous combat-induced experiences followed to the slightest detail.

Normal operations consisted of small teams, (generally three Americans and three Vietnamese) inserted by helicopter at dusk into a known or suspected NVA or VC controlled area. Delta Recon men called this, "Going into the hole." Initially, the concept called for two Americans on each team, but with experience, the teams quickly adapted until three Americans went in, then at the last, some teams were strictly Americans. The rationale was that if there were at least three Americans, and one became seriously wounded, he had two buddies to carry him out. The rough jungle terrain made it nearly impossible for only one man to accomplish that feat, and since it was unheard of for a recon man to leave his wounded brother, the initial concept could have resulted in the death of both. In some instances it did anyway.

The most experienced man on the team, regardless of rank, was in charge of the mission. He was called the One Zero—the second most experienced, his assistant, the One One. The third was the least experienced, studying hard to become a One One, and eventually, perhaps the One Zero. Often, the third man was a new guy; the FNG (F_ _ _ing New Guy). Learning to operate in the jungle under conditions more intense than any he'd previously encountered, the FNG was always under close scrutiny by the other two, more experienced men. Upon returning to the Forward Observation Base (FOB), he'd be evaluated quickly and often, harshly. The final report would be either "he'll do" or "get him gone." If he demonstrated potential but lacked critical capabilities for a good Recon man, he might be recommended for another assignment within Project Delta, either with the Rangers or the Chinese Nung BDA Company. In any event, the team evaluation was the final call. Not even the Project Delta Commander would override it.

Delta's helicopter insertions were always accomplished in conditions of diminished visibility, without lights, a ground reception party, or an armed escort to secure the LZ. Just as it required a special breed to become Recon, a special breed of pilot was needed to volunteer to fly their missions. The helicopters usually flew in a trail formation, at treetop level, suddenly swooping low to unload their cargo onto a small, pre-designated LZ, while allowing those trailing to pass overhead. The pilot, hovering approximately six feet off the ground, would quickly disperse his team, then return to last place in the formation, falling in behind. This leapfrog maneuver was repeated until all teams had been inserted into the targeted area. With fading daylight, poor visibility and aircraft noise masking the sounds of landing, unless the enemy's position had been directly on the LZ, or very nearby, they wouldn't hear a helicopter land, nor realize a Recon team had been inserted. Despite precautions, on occasion, when a team exposed the enemy occupying their LZ, there was no alternative but to fight their way out.

Not withstanding an enemy encounter, insertion was still a dangerous undertaking. Night maneuvers in the dark called for nerve, skill and crew cooperation. Recon teams respected their early Vietnamese pilots and lavished them with praise. Under direct command and control of the Project Delta Commander, they pulled off some pretty wild and crazy flying. Some used their rotary blades like a weed-whacker to clear dense four-foot high elephant grass. One pilot positioned a strut on a tree trunk, six feet off the ground; another balanced one on a steep incline to pick up a wounded man. Often they flew rescue missions through mountain fog so dense they literally had to navigate using dirt trails while weaving drunkenly between trees. Many of the first Recon men were sorry to see the savvy King Bee pilots leave. In Colonel Charles Beckwith's book, *Delta Force*, he wrote, "They were some of the bravest men I'd ever met. They were handpicked, the cream of the Vietnamese Air Force, and they were the finest pilots in the country." In late 1965, American pilots and crews began to replace them. Soon Project Delta staff discerned that once trained in Delta's tactics, these new men's flying skills were just as formidable, often surpassing those of the King Bees.

The first Project Delta teams were purely reconnaissance; if discovered, they'd be immediately extracted from a dangerous situation. As the Delta Recon teams became more proficient with stealth and secrecy, at the discretion of the Recon team leader, if contact was made with enemy forces and safely broken, or the target size and disposition could be managed, they were permitted to use discretion toward exploitation and destruction. Hence, some teams evolved into hunter-killer teams. At the conclusion of Project Delta's existence, the mission of the Recon teams had substantially changed. They'd been granted various options for target exploitation: extracting to the FOB; providing intelligence; helping to formulate a plan of attack for the reaction force; remaining to observe the target until the Airborne Ranger companies arrived, then guiding them to the enemy's location; exploiting the target themselves; or, they could call in air strikes or artillery to eliminate the enemy.

Delta Recon men learned to blend into their surroundings, become one with the landscape. (Photo courtesy of Jerry Estenson)

Conceptually, Recon teams were committed for five days, the duration a team could operate effectively, transport enough rations and water without re-supply and account for the fatigue factor. Fatigue factor is the time span men can optimally operate in an enemy-controlled environment under the constant threat of danger, the inherent tension, the continual moving, reduced rations and lack of sleep, before losing the ability to remain alert and becoming careless.

Recon teams often crawled and scooted along on their bellies, spending days just inching forward. They learned to stay clear of ridgelines, roads, trails and streams—these were routes the enemy traveled. The Central Highlands, honeycombed by primitive native and animal trails, is where they lived and worked, preferring to slowly travel the steep slopes when navigating thick, rough brush. They often slept on slopes so steep, they had to straddle trees limbs to keep from sliding down, or in thick thorny patches, too difficult for others to get close without being heard. Underneath, their lightweight indigenous ponchos kept moisture from their chilled bodies.

Lying silently in the darkness, it was easy to hear the jungle vermin. Imagine legions of leeches crawling across a poncho, emitting tiny scratching sounds, slithering toward their next warm meal. The men's constant battle with leeches often provided fodder for serious, yet embarrassing experiences. One team member had to be evacuated when a leech attached itself to his penis, but when removed, the wound wouldn't stop bleeding. Engorged, the giant leeches of Southeast Asia are six to eight inches long, larger than a man's thumb. When attaching to a warm host, they inject an anti-coagulant that thins the blood, causing it to flow for hours after removal.

One radio conversation between a patrol member and the base camp medic went something like this:

"We pulled one of these giant mothers off his dick, and he's bleeding pretty badly," the patrol leader said. "What do we do?"

The medic, unable to disguise his mirth, didn't hesitate. "Put a tourniquet on it."

"Hey, no shit! This is no time to be screwing around! This is serious! He's been bleeding for more than an hour, and getting lightheaded!"

"Would you believe a pressure bandage, then?" said the medic, trying to maintain a serious tone.

The poor guy eventually got treated, but soldiers could be merciless, especially toward a buddy caught in an embarrassing situation, no matter what the circumstances.

It was common to awake and find two-dozen of those monsters sucking to their heart's content, their heads so deeply buried they couldn't be pulled off. The trick to removal was to either stick them with a lit cigarette, or apply a dose of insect repellant. It was easy to identify the men who'd spent time in the jungle, because of their quarter-size bite scars. These scars are permanent; some wounds never completely healed.

These earliest days were interesting times for the new Detachment B-52 Project Delta. During this period, they mastered the development and refinement of Long Range Reconnaissance Patrol (LRRP) operational tactics and techniques (a lost art in the United States Army) and constructed Camp Nguyen Van Tan, a permanent base camp at Nha Trang, replete with headquarters buildings, club and sleeping quarters.

They also field-tested a myriad of new weapons and field equipment—radio equipment, claymore mines, weapon silencers, various foreign weaponry, 9mm rocket ammunition, oriental freeze-dried rations, developed extraction devices, such as the McGuire Rig, and discovered the usefulness of the GPS-tactical breakthroughs, to name a few.

They also received dozens of items, obviously the result of someone's brainstorm, that were almost laughable in their presentation. One was a long plastic strip called a runway lighter, used for lighting up airfields and marking LZ/DZs at night. For years, SF soldiers had been using C-ration cans half-filled with a mixture of dirt and gasoline to do that. Who needed the extra weight? They continued to use C-ration cans. Another invention, lanolin-based insect and leech repellant, was, however, a huge success with all the troops. It'd stay on for days, and nothing but a river crossing would wash it away. But clearly the most ridiculous item delivered, as described by Special Forces Major (retired) Jim Morris, was an M-79 grenade-launcher round filled with luminous paint.

"What's that for?" Morris had inquired.

The guy said, "If you're ever attacked at night you can shoot the enemy with one of these, and then you can see them."

"And do what? Shoot him? I already shot him. When I shoot somebody I don't want him to glow in the dark. I want him to die."

Project Delta planners also fully developed a fledgling combined arms Unity of Command philosophy, trained Army aviation resources to support clandestine special operations, provided LRRP support and training to American troop units arriving in Vietnam, and ratcheted up training for their own LRRP program to levels never before met—nor achieved since.

* * * * * *

Project Delta had the full support of high-level commanders and staff; they came first on the supply system's priority-list. Major Strange knew that if his unit needed something and it was in the system, he'd get it immediately—if not, it was made available through commercial vendors—again, with a top priority. Watches, freeze-dried rations and camouflage uniforms were shipped direct from Okinawa. If an item wasn't available, someone invented it. Such as in the case of Asian LRRP rations.

Current Army field rations hadn't changed much since WWII, and it quickly became obvious they were not well-suited for the Vietnamese soldier's sensitive digestive tracts. However, there were other drawbacks to using C-rations in the jungle. Once opened, the VC could smell the aroma a long distance, and since this was a foreign odor, they'd be alerted to the presence of U.S. soldiers. Concealment of the cans also became a problem. The enemy learned to watch for the small, freshly dug holes for hidden C-ration cans. Command was aware they needed something new and soon, so new rations were developed on Okinawa, primarily for indigenous personnel.

"Ben," an agent at the CIA's Counterinsurgency Support Office (CISO) on Okinawa, received Delta's request for such rations, and put out requests for proposals to various companies with the capability to produce them. The best bid came back at three million dollars and about three years to produce them. That was way over budget, and the lead time far too long for Delta's needs. "Ben" called his girlfriend who was a dietician at the Camp Kue Hospital. They spent the afternoon in the main commissary on Okinawa, buying the items they would need, and a fifth of scotch. That evening they devised the rations, drank the scotch and spent a wild night together. It is appropriate to remain informed about how Project Delta's Asian LRRP rations came into being; a best case of "your tax dollars at work."

With the Japanese LRRP rations, the basic substance of the dehydrated meal was rice, one meal per package. Each meal consisted of a packet of brown rice, some type of meat (fish, beef jerky or shrimp) and vegetables (usually green beans). Very hot peppers were included, but only the bravest of souls ventured there. Before an operation, the U.S. soldiers would slice open a packet, mix the vegetables, meat, rice and peppers all together (supplementing with Tabasco sauce and dried onions, in some cases), add water, reseal and place in the large thigh pocket of their tiger-fatigues. As they moved through the jungle, their body heat and the humid jungle air "cooked" the meal—it was waiting to be eaten anytime the trooper was ready. If very hungry, one could eat it all, or apportion it over a longer period. Most men split it into more than one meal.

These Japanese combat meals were tasty and provided maximum energy for the amount of food consumed. The Recon teams found the new Japanese LRRP rations to be so savory that the supply officer had to quit issuing them while in garrison lest the teams devour them instead of the hot meals at the mess hall, then they'd run short for combat operations. The primary problem associated with the new rations was an almost uncontrollable urge to defecate within just a couple hours of consumption, and the copious amounts of human waste they produced. Recon teams knew full well that C-rations alone weren't the only way to emit long-distance odors in the pristine mountain air, and resisted the urge to defecate while on patrol. (Of course, there had been the distinct possibility the enemy might also catch them with their pants down at the precise moment of their maximum discomfort.)

Because patrols often continued up to five days, this was a serious problem. A story often retold as the "butt of many jokes," came to light when one of the guys told the team leader he had to "go" and "go right then," even if it meant he might die. So the team sent out tight security around the area while the suffering individual positioned himself aside a tall bush, placed his rifle within easy reach, pulled down his jungle fatigues and cut loose. According to an accompanying team member, the sounds were akin to incoming mortar fire and a simultaneous torrential rain. He remembered the crusty NCO team leader say, "My god! That boy could've shit right through a wire screen door!"

Enter an enterprising Special Forces medic, Larry Dickinson, who finally resolved Recon's problem by issuing everyone "no-shit" pills, which did the job nicely. No one knew exactly what they were and didn't care to ask, but few rarely left for an operation without swallowing some. Once the team returned to garrison, Dickinson simply gave them two big brown pills he affectionately called "Brown Bombers," designed to "correct" the situation. After ingesting those, the regularity issue was taken care of in about two days—no one dared stray too far from the nearest latrine.

If necessary, troopers could get by on only one of the Japanese meals per day, with the added benefit of substantially lighter combat loads. Conventional units—ground-pounders, legs or grunts, as they were often called—traveled with much heavier loads than did Special Forces, whom the conventional guys referred to as "Super-grunts." USSF learned that anything taken with marginal use took up space needed for more important objects: additional ammo, grenades, radio

This is a typically equipped recon team. *L to R*: SSG Parsons, SSG Brakeman, SFC Simpson, SFC Strick, SSG Sheppard, 1LT Sullivan. You can pick out the new guys because they have the hats with large brims. It only took one time out and then they took their hats to the Indian tailor to have two inches cut off. The wide brim restricted peripheral vision and when absolutely stationary, just moving one's eyes in a 360° circle, the brim interfered with upward vision. All the "old hands" knew this. (Photo courtesy of Maurice Brakeman)

batteries, food, water and extra first aid kits. Bill Roderick claims he carried 450 rounds of ammo, four hand grenades, and a 4x rifle scope to see farther than with the naked eye. He shunned the extra socks and change of dry clothing highly touted by conventional units, opting instead for the "necessities of life."

Extra medical kits were one such necessity. The standard Army-issue field dressing consisted of a single bandage with a gauze tail attached to each end. The inventor either had never witnessed an actual combat wound, or tried to save money. Most combat wounds are not at all like the clean little holes shown in the movies. High velocity rounds are so powerful they can often tear an arm or leg off. Then, there is another small consideration. When a bullet enters the human body, most of the time it exits. Therefore, two puncture wounds might need to be bandaged with that single field dressing. Morphine is not a standard issue item for most U.S. conventional soldiers, but no SF soldier in his right mind would have departed without at least two curettes in his makeshift first aid kit.

The typical Recon man dressed in tiger stripes (jungle camouflage fatigues). He carried a CAR 15 (shortened version of the M-16 automatic rifle) with an extra-large magazine (30 rounds). The CAR 15 was rigged to be carried suspended around their neck with parachute cord, about ammo-pouch height for easy access. The average time to put fire on a target, from acquisition to pulling the trigger, was less than a second. Most carried handguns as backup; either the standard Army issue .45 caliber automatic, or a personal weapon, normally a 9mm automatic or .357 Magnum. Nearly all Recon patrols found room for at least one of the issued silenced .22-caliber, high-powered automatic pistols.

Delta Recon didn't use the standard Army rucksack. Those issued to Delta were coated canvas, sterile (no U.S. Army markings), with three pockets, one in front and two on the sides. It contained an extra-large main pouch and had a flat narrow pocket sandwiched between it and the man's back, designed for carrying ground sheets. The ground sheet, a 3' x 6', thin, light-weight, green plastic sheet sufficed for sleeping. Most opted for two basic ammo belts, held in place by a web shoulder harness. Some also used a standard web belt with ammo pouches or filled canteen covers with loaded magazines. A few scrounged Browning Automatic Rifle (BAR) belts used in Korea. With six pouches, three on each side, they could carry an extraordinary amount of ammo. In addition, the BAR belts could hold two canteen

Weapons: M-16, "mini-pistol" modified from an M-79 Grenade Launcher (*left*); CAR-15. The mini-pistol, considered by the Recon guys to be "personal artillery," was shortened to 11" and carried in a shoulder holster. (Photo courtesy of Chester Howard)

pouches and a knife. Most Recon carried a knife, one either on their belt, or taped upside down on the harness. Field bandages lined the bottom of ammo pouches, which not only gave them extra bandages in case of casualties, but held the magazines notably higher so they could be easily grasped on the first attempt.

Signal mirrors, mini-smoke grenades, an orange panel and a couple of hand grenades typically went into a rucksack pocket. Additional grenades were taped to the web harness, carried in an empty canteen pouch or placed in a side pocket of the rucksack. A military issue compass was a necessity, as were wrist compasses, Army-issue olive drab plastic watches that didn't shine and topographical maps. Additional loaded magazines were typically placed in an ammo bandolier that held ten of them, giving each man between 380 and 560 rounds, plus four to six grenades. American team members typically carried a "mini-pistol," an M-79 grenade launcher, shortened to approximately eleven inches, tip-to-tip and fitted with a pistol grip; it had no sights and a shortened barrel. It was carried in a shoulder holster, pre-fabricated to attach directly to the web gear. Primarily used for close-in combat, with practice one became deadly accurate with this improvised weapon. Eighteen to twenty rounds filled with "double-ought" buck-shot or flechette rounds, a few high explosive rounds and some CS tear gas completed the armament for the mini-pistol. Some missions called for "silenced pistols," or rifles with scopes.

On the upper front shoulder strap of his web gear, every Recon man carried two morphine curettes and a pill-kit. The pill-kit was personally assembled by the Delta medics to fend off any possible pain or illness that might afflict them while in the hole. Some really didn't cure anything, but just gave the men the strength to continue. This arsenal included malaria medications, Darvon, amphetamines, allergy tablets, antibiotics, and "no-shit" pills. A snap-link and rope was attached to the shoulder-harness for tying a rappelling seat. While the rucksack might have to be dropped when running for your life, the web gear retained the necessary life-saving items essential to survive. When in the hole, it was never removed.

Additional canteens were placed in the side rucksack pockets. The front pocket held serum albumin (blood expander), more grenades and toe-poppers (a small mine one could quickly push into the ground). Smoke grenades were latched between pockets of the rucksack, and the team always found enough space for an extra battery for the PRC 25 radio. The team leader (One Zero), nearly always carried the PRC 25 radio, and the assistant team leader (One One) carried a "mini-ponder,"[15] which emitted a beacon signal the FAC could detect, if they ever became separated from the radio.

They always counted on a claymore mine or two, a pound of Composition-4 (C4) explosives, an additional bandolier of ammo, more ammo for the short M-79 and eight to ten small cans of C-ration meat or fruit. One can of meat or fruit, mixed with a small amount of rice, provided nourishment twice a day while in the hole. When they infiltrated, their pant pockets held a bag already mixed with water and indigenous rice. In the field, water was too precious to waste on food preparation.

All members wore canvas jungle-boots, a short-brim flop hat and an olive drab cravat around the forehead or neck as a sweat catcher. Unlike conventional U.S. units, Special Forces never issued steel helmets, flak-jackets, or toted gas masks, unless remaining stationary in an FOB for a long period. With grease-painted faces and hands, they carried a tube to replace the color as sweat and rain washed it off. Altogether, including fully loaded weapons, each man hoisted around sixty pounds. A six-man Delta Recon team could generate some awesome firepower. In Nha Trang, while on stand-down, the weapon, rucksack and all equipment was kept nearby, ready to travel at a moment's notice.

* * * * * *

Just ask any Army doctor, and he'll be the first to affirm that Special Forces medics are the best trained in the world, receiving substantially more than that given to the average combat medic. SF medics are the only ones who get to treat actual gunshot wounds during training, and if they lose one of these "patients" they simply fail to graduate. The Army's Physician's Assistant Program, prevalent in all Army hospitals,

---

[15] A small transponder, approximately 3" wide x 6" long x 1.5" thick, that fits into a fatigue shirt pocket and acts as a wireless communication, monitoring or control device that picks up and automatically responds to an incoming signal. The term is a contraction of the words "transmitter" and "responder. "

came into existence as a result of the Special Forces medic training. Project Delta was fortunate to have some of the finest medics in the world assigned in support of their mission: Roland Meder, John Burdish, Bill Erickson, James Dallas Chapman, Howard Wells, Ed Foshee, Dennis McVey, Mike Sterns and Larry Dickinson, to name only a few. If a Recon patrol had the good fortune to have one of these skilled SF medics along on an operation they were extremely lucky. Not only because one had been assigned, but because these medics are soldiers first and medics second; expected to lead, fight, parachute and successfully accomplish all the tasks other SF soldiers do. Regardless of their placement, the others were all cross-trained in life-saving techniques.

An intriguing example of how far the men would go to be medically trained was emphasized by one Delta member. When SFC Andy Shepard cut his leg to the bone with an ax while chopping metal bindings from a pallet of supplies, bleeding profusely, he hurried to the detachment medic, SGT Taylor.

"Doc, I need for you to put some stitches in this, and give me a tetanus shot."

"I'm not going to sew that up," Taylor told him rather bluntly. "And I'm not going to give you a shot, either. You're going to do it, because if I ever need your help while we're in the hole, you'll have to know how."

Under Taylor's close supervision, Shepard sewed up his own leg.

* * * * * *

Renowned for their language skills and cultural sensitivities as much as for their legendary military acumen, medics weren't the only ones highly trained. The extensive skill sets needed for Project Delta personnel went far beyond the typical requirements for a particular military occupational specialty (MOS.) For example, its weapons NCOs are trained to operate any light or heavy weapon found in the world arsenal, to include field-stripping them in the dark, then repairing them. SF demo men have the capability to demolish a five-story building using items typically found in most hardware and grocery stores. SF radio operators can send and receive Morse Code at an astonishing speed, as well as operate or repair any radio they might encounter.

Project Delta's Communication NCOs, or "Commo" men, were responsible for implementing communication innovations that changed the face of military field combat. It was said that, "These guys can rig communications from a strand of wire and a Coke bottle—and talk to the world." While the comment may seem farfetched to some, Delta's Commo men initiated several configuration modifications for the HC-162 radio set: a smaller, lighter, dry-cell battery; a power converter/transformer for ac or dc voltage; additional receptacles so the HC-162 could be attached to the new "burst" device; and changes to the type of antenna wire generally provided. Inventive SF Commo men had been improvising doublet antennas by using steel or deep-sea fishing line, which frequently shorted out due to lack of insulation. It's common to hear tales of reverting to wire coat hangers, a clothes line, barbed wire, or even the use of a vehicle as an antenna. Still, their fabricated innovations were superior to what was available through supply channels, and their recommendations a direct result of lessons learned during actual combat operations.[16] Skilled Commo men were always in high demand.

Most Project Delta commanders had a special radio operator accompany them when in the field. Early in his command, MAJ Charles Beckwith always took Don "Val" Valentine along. Valentine revolutionized the way Delta operatives communicated in the field. For example, on the ground, Recon men often had to make radio contact while operating within just a few yards of the enemy. Listening to the airborne radio relay was usually not a problem—it was the answering that always worried them. When close to the enemy, they couldn't always answer, so they'd just "break squelch" by pressing the "push-to-talk-button," to indicate they could hear but that it wasn't safe to reply. The first time it happened to Valentine, he told the Recon man to hit his push-to-talk button three times for "yes" and twice for "no." Then he posed direct questions answerable by a simple yes, no or "no response."

Initially, he thought of questions as the scenario unfolded, but by the next day he had managed to devise a list of direct questions a radio

---

[16] It is a commonly accepted fact that a Special Forces radioman can communicate great distances with the ANG-109 radio, using only a wire coat hanger, a clothes line, barbed wire, or a vehicle as an antenna.

operator could use in a similar situation, to remain informed even when given map coordinates. Valentine's procedure was integrated into unit Standard Operating Procedures (SOP), used frequently by Project Delta radio operators on radio relay flights. After Valentine rotated back to the United States, Beckwith's Commo man became Terry "Rolex" Morrone.

Delta veterans recall one operation, when a Recon team had been out of radio contact with the FOB for much too long, and the radio relay man had called repeatedly, yet failed to make contact. Finally, when the team leader answered, he spoke much too softly to be heard over the aircraft engine noise and it seemed his Vietnamese teammates were chattering loudly behind him. The irritated airborne radioman growled, "Speak up! I can't hear you through all your Vietnamese troops talking!"

Very slowly a faint voice came back. "T-h-e-y-a-r-e-n-o-t-m-y-t-r-o-o-p-s."

Yet another tale, quietly divulged by a Recon man, bears testimony to the harsh realities of war and the mental anguish that is obvious when speaking about the loss of comrades. One seasoned radio operator had served with Project Delta for a year and then transferred to MACV-SOG. During his very first operation into Laos, his entire small team, one fellow American and three Vietnamese, were surrounded and captured. The NVA lieutenant immediately executed the SOG Vietnamese soldiers. While two of his men restrained the young radio operator, the NVA lieutenant slit his stomach, his intestines spilling to the ground. His heinous act incomplete, the lieutenant sprayed highly combustible fluid over the intestines and the man's stomach cavity, and lit it with a flame-thrower. The NVA soldiers had bound his buddy's arms, making him watch. The enemy officer admonished the surviving U.S. member to return, the Americans to never again come to Laos, or this is what would happen to them. The young SF communication soldier who died that day was married, with two small children. Many Special Forces men prayed they'd be the one to run into that NVA lieutenant. Rest assured, if any had, it was never confirmed, nor made a matter of public record.

* * * * * *

In 1964, CPT Larry O'Neil worked in Air Mobility at the 5th Special Forces Group (Abn) Headquarters, as part of supply operations (S4). His job entailed sending tons of equipment and supplies all over Vietnam, to SF detachments and projects. Aware the new Leaping Lena and fledgling Project Delta operations were classified CIA missions, he wanted special handling for those items marked to go there. His concern was he didn't want to designate it in any way that would be obvious to VC agents, so he simply marked it with a small chalk triangle. The Greek symbol soon became Delta's trademark.

The McGuire Rig allowed hovering rotary-blade aircraft to extract Recon teams from the densely forested areas in the highlands. Vietnam, 1966.

Often surprised by the type of U.S.-issued or foreign equipment that might arrive on site, innovative adaptations frequently had to be made to make it operate effectively with other Project equipment. That entrepreneurial spirit shines through in the following incident:

A call had come in from the 5th SFG's Supply Officer (S-4) that they were in possession of some locked conex containers belonging to Project Delta. Because the S-4 staff had known Delta's mission was classified, the 5th SFG men weren't about to force the containers open. Instead, they demanded immediate removal from their holding area. Since keys couldn't be located, the Delta logistics troops cut the locks with bolt-cutters. The cargo, numerous types of silenced weapons, included long-barreled, .22-caliber automatic target pistols.[17] This bonanza proved extremely valuable as bartering material, and if rumors are to be believed, some have been carried home in personal luggage. It was a fact that the Project never suffered from a shortage of U.S. or foreign-made weapons.

---

[17] This unique weapon was often issued to Special Forces teams for classified CIA projects. The teams found them to be extremely accurate for "close-in work."

Besides the logistical cache ordered through the supply system, Project Delta often received items as forced issue. Items were sent for combat testing and required a rather lengthy report regarding their effectiveness. During this period, much activity was ongoing in research and development related to Project Delta, not only in the arena of tactics, but for unproven equipment. Some Project-tested equipment eventually became standard issue for the rest of the Army. For example, the Hughes HC 162 radio (eventually known as the PRC 72), the PRC 64 radio and the Claymore mine. Other innovations, such as "rocket ammunition" pistols and a vintage GPS using a converted C-47, all failed miserably.

During the development of Project Delta's operational tactics, combat planners had difficulty finding suitable Landing Zones (LZ) for their rotary-blade aircraft to land and extract Recon teams, especially in the densely forested areas of the Central Highlands, where triple-canopy vegetation was the rule. Even this problem was no match for the creative juices applied by Project Delta's inventive Non-commissioned Officer Corp. Sergeant Major Charles McGuire and other NCOs worked closely with VNAF helicopter crews to develop a sling harness that could be lowered to a team on the ground. They would be slipped into it and then hoisted above the treetops to safety. To complicate matters, they often had to complete this tricky maneuver under heavy enemy ground fire. The pilot had to first lift the loaded McGuire Rig straight up, clear the trees, apply full throttle and then whisk his live cargo away. As pilots were first learning new techniques on how best to hoist the loaded rigs, several team members sustained serious injuries. Frank Badolati was among them. He suffered broken ribs, a punctured lung and, after being dragged against a tree stump, had to be medically evacuated. Badolati had inadvertently locked his wrist into the slip-loop before the chopper had completely cleared the ground; this would later become a forbidden practice.

On that first experimental run, Jack Dawg Long had hooked up to the same chopper, but observing Badolati's predicament, quickly managed to get loose. One Project Delta spectator remarked, "Dawg was so scared he actually outran the damned chopper until he could loosen his wrist from the lock-down loop. I've never seen anyone out-run a helicopter before!"

It was quite a memorable day when Bob Hope and his USO troupe were in Nha Trang performing, while SGM McGuire and his NCOs were nearby, testing the rig at the Project Delta compound. Hope stopped his act in the middle of a joke, speechlessly eyeing the helicopter speeding past at 500 feet, three men precariously dangling 100 feet below it. The unexpected event broke up the show, as he and the audience gazed in wonderment. The famous McGuire Rig had been christened.

Perfecting the original McGuire Rig would be accomplished through practical application in the field, over several improvement iterations. Initially, the rig was constructed of a nylon mountain-climbing rope, with two loops sewn into the end, nearest the ground. One large loop and another much smaller were affixed to the rope by strong nylon thread. In 1966, a Delta Recon Supervisor, SFC Norm Doney, helped redesign the McGuire Rig with an adjustable wrist loop. The concept was simple. The man being extracted would sit in the large loop and slip the smaller adjustable loop around his wrist, thus locking himself in place so he couldn't fall out, even if hit by enemy gunfire. Being slowly lifted clear of obstacles, then rapidly flown away, the centrifugal force might still pull his arm out of its socket, but he wouldn't fall out—and he'd still be alive! The other end of the rope was anchored securely to a sturdy 4"x 4" yoke, and then snap-linked into a set of rings in the floor of the extraction helicopter.

The pilot first had to hover above the treetops while up to three recon team members hooked themselves into the rig, then he had to slowly lift the chopper until the man (or men) were clear of any trees before he'd fly off with his load dangling high above the ground as enemy fire peppered the air. Once the helicopter found a safer location, it could land and take the men aboard. It probably beat dying—but not by much. The simple fact was, for those who truly believed they were ready to meet their maker, they might've opted to remain behind and fight to the death rather than climb into that evil contraption and be whisked away through thorns and tree branches, swinging suspended over 100 feet beneath a pilot who's only thoughts at the moment were getting the hell out of that area as quickly as possible. All of it, while an adversary tried their level best to shoot them from the saddle. It was that scary. While each extraction helicopter was equipped with more than one McGuire Rig, most men hoped they'd never need them. SFC

Norm Doney and others redesigned the rig and made modifications to it to improve its effectiveness and safety. The McGuire Rig was eventually replaced by the "Stabo Rig."

* * * * * *

If Project Delta team members lived a Spartan existence while in the field, after only one short year, its garrison facilities were, by Vietnam standards, luxurious. Initially, when replacement teams began to arrive during autumn 1964, they were given the most undesirable location available, under the worst conditions imaginable. It was commonplace to wade in muck up to the knees, sleep in leaky tents, take cold showers and eat C-rations—when they were available. Yet, by the time Project Delta deactivated and left Nha Trang in 1970, their facilities, especially Delta's club, called the Delta Hilton, were among the plushest digs in Vietnam. Using primarily "scrounged" and "borrowed" materiel, they built a modern camp and an enviable club that possessed a coveted Delta-symbol padded bar, rock garden, fountains, paintings and tasteful furnishings. The menu was one of the most palatable in theater: steak, baked potato, fresh salad and—always—cold beer.

However, Delta's first attempt at establishing a unit club had not been quite as successful. The "Bamboo Club" had been simply a bamboo lean-to with wooden benches, a BBQ grill converted from a fifty-five-gallon metal drum and several garbage cans to cool the beer. As materials could be located and scrounged, the Navy Sea-Bees had been bribed with beer and booze to help build the new club, and a respectable facility eventually emerged. Erecting these clubs was eventful; as if Project Delta needed more adventure!

The original Delta Club had operated only forty days before the Inspector General (IG) shut it down at the request of the 5th Special Forces Group Commander—there were persistent rumors of rowdy behavior, raucous misconduct and, heaven forbid, fights! Of course, those were just rumors—except maybe for the fights. What began as a hangout to unwind between missions, with just a few bottles of booze, a scarred wooden table, a cooler of beer and a few rusty old metal chairs, actually made a profit; in fact, it took business away from the 5th Special Forces Group's legitimate clubs. No one ever thought it would

Inside the Delta Club, 1965. (Photo courtesy of Len Boulas)

become a "real" club, because they knew a "real" club brought unwanted regulations, required a board of governors, published rules, etc. Early B-52 operatives blamed their "club" troubles on one of their own. Fancying himself as a news reporter, he'd "ratted out" his Delta brothers, causing them to lose their club. Suffice it to say, that individual didn't last long. The word was, he left the Army and eventually found work at a liberal West Coast magazine. Like a shunned Biblical sinner, within Delta circles his name hasn't been mentioned since—and it won't be mentioned here.

The good news was, in the relatively short time the Bamboo Club existed, its profits paid the civilian labor force and made enough for material and labor to build a better club. Plans were drawn up and it was constructed within Project Delta's secure compound, using generated funds. A private club, it didn't cost taxpayers one red cent, and unlike most other Army military clubs, turned a profit. It was common knowledge during that era, that many club managers had skimmed non-appropriated funds (e.g., club profits), then rotated back to the States while leaving their facilities deeply in debt. It's a fact that one of the Army's top command sergeant majors stole millions from Southeast

Asia NCO club funds and deposited them in a Swiss bank account using the name "Fishhead." Dishonorably discharged, he was incarcerated at the Fort Leavenworth Federal Prison in Kansas.

After being burnt by one they trusted, this new Delta Club was classified secret; reporters were never again allowed inside. They had learned much from their first experience, and once the club was built, it operated strictly by the book by having elected club officers, keeping immaculate books, paying distributors on time and establishing by-laws. The Delta Club generally set the standard for others.

DELTA CLUB RULES

1. Uniform Regulation: Something on your feet and something on your ass—shower shoes and jockstraps suffice.
2. Guests: Any female is to be allowed entrance whether accompanied or not, but no female shall be allowed to exit without permission of a club member. Only Delta personnel may bring guests into the compound or club.
3. Associate Members are allowed from any branch of service.
4. No reporters or non-Special Forces Officers are allowed inside the club.

The Delta Club became famous within Special Forces circles and with some of the other units Delta worked with. It was the place to go for fun, good drinks and great food at reasonable prices. Everyone was welcome, with the exception of non-Special Forces officers and reporters. Few who visited could deny it was a class act.

* * * * * *

Due to the clandestine nature of Special Forces operations, units traditionally have fallen outside the perimeters of normal Army supply channels. They've always had to scrounge materials and supplies, which led to a tongue-in-cheek rumor that a Special Forces required skill was "scrounging." Adept soldiers on SF teams excel at "acquiring" items the unit needs to operate in relative comfort, anywhere in the world. The majority of the stuff for the Delta Club renovations was "borrowed" from the logistical center at Cam Ranh Bay, or from sister units that had "much more than they needed." While conventional leaders might prefer to refer to it as pilfering or thievery, some SF NCOs contend it's been essential to their existence in a combat theater of operations. Two unnamed NCOs assigned to B-52, who excelled in these skills, would make twice monthly trips to the logistics center. With a can of white paint they would stencil a Special Forces number onto the bumper of a new truck or jeep, get in, drive past the gate guard and head home. But not without a detour first to the supply depot, where they'd load up with air conditioners, cement, tin roofing, food, beer or other essentials. Their authorization was a simple rationale; since goods were readily available to other U.S. units, and Project Delta was part of the U.S. Army, they figured it was just meant for their use, too.

This philosophy had not been limited solely to the scrounging of supplies; it extended to food and drinks. Without mess sergeants, field cooks and mess halls, like other U.S. Army units, SF teams received extra pay to purchase food outside the Army's supply channels. The funds were never enough to cover the cost of rations, particularly after conventional forces began to arrive and drove up prices. Again, by taking the initiative and using their natural entrepreneurial talents, SF supplemented rations through trading highly coveted captured weapons, crossbows, Viet Cong flags, etc. Detachment B-52 also had issued each Recon member a .25 caliber pistol as an emergency hideout gun. The Recon guys referred to these little gems as "cathouse pistols." As highly classified as Project Delta was, the serial numbers of these weapons were never recorded, and any information about their issue was purged from the Army's supply records. The reason: if that weapon had ever been captured in some god-forsaken place that it shouldn't have been in the first place, it couldn't be traced to U.S. involvement. Occasionally, after an operation, someone would turn in his little pistol and be issued another. The returned weapon, usually listed as "lost during combat operations," ended up in trade to the Air Force supply guys for steaks or choice cuts of meat.

Running short on pistols and captured weapons, they'd trade almost anything else of value, figuring "a fighting man's gotta eat!" Even when SF felt they had nothing of value to trade, they could create it. One story about this creativity lingers: a clever SF camp hired a Vietnamese tailor to mass produce "genuine" VC and NVA flags, replete with bullet holes and dried chicken blood. Crumpled, they'd be dragged through the dirt, and often had burn-holes singed into them for good measure. These had been traded in Da Nang to the Air Force and Marines, who simply loved them. Like they said, "A man's gotta eat."

* * * * * *

Hollywood, TV scripts and many books have often described Special Forces soldiers and their operations, mostly concentrating on their high training standards and combat skills. While it's true that SF soldiers are intelligent, take initiative and have superb leadership abilities, little has been written about their keen sense of humor. Special Forces humor should be considered inspirational, creative and awe-inspiring—it is deserving of military history recognition! The black humor was a great wartime stress reliever; wild, edgy and a bit crazy, it often crossed the line between good taste and outright cruelty.

Men who see a lot of combat are naturally close, and perhaps Delta Recon was closer than most. They would sometimes go to great extremes to play harmless pranks on each other, or show affection and trust, most of which seemed lurid or uncouth by other's standards. While such things were considered normal behavior by most Project Delta guys, to others they might seem unnatural, shocking or even perverted. In part, it was an act of defiance—daring someone to criticize their actions, while delighting in shocking them. It was great sport to make bystanders sick enough to vomit by consuming some loathsome object—bugs, frogs, leeches, etc.–or by biting the head off a snake. Did every Delta member commit these harmless yet gross acts? Absolutely not; such behavior was restricted to a few brave and gallant individuals. But it was always accepted.

Practical jokes were considered a sacred mission. Cooperation and assistance was expected—and almost always provided. Pranks could be targeted at officers and enlisted men, and simply being the Commander was no protection. No one ever felt completely safe. If a fellow SF soldier could pull off a really good prank, it was a sign the recipient was well-liked; after all, pulling off a really good prank takes a lot of time and effort. Secrecy was a must, especially when payback was involved.

Jim Jarrett confirms this story about an operation in 1967 with Gary Stedman:

They'd been on recon, west of An Hoa for several days, when discovered by the enemy and forced to run for their lives. After a day and a half of playing the ambush/counter-ambush game with the Viet Cong, by mid-afternoon they managed to position themselves on a small knoll, listening for the enemy's movement. A FAC appeared overhead briefly, confirming they'd been essentially surrounded. The circling FAC pilot called in airpower, while the small recon team prepared for a serious fight.

The sunshine and small trees appeared surreal; they could've just as easily been in a Colorado state park, but they knew if they let down their guard for an instant, they could be dead before that beautiful sun set. The six desperate men established their final defensive position, lying head-to-foot, thighs touching. With magazines stacked and hand grenade pins straightened—they waited. The enemy began to fire 60mm mortar rounds, but luckily, nearly all failed to explode. Whether these duds had been caused from the VC's inexperience or unfamiliarity with American mortars was never clear. The team counted their blessings—and continued to wait.

Everyone has an irrational fear. For some it's snakes; for others, it's rats, spiders or bats. Some become claustrophobic in close spaces. A few Recon men were annoyed by those ugly, slimy, clinging creatures that would suck blood until bloated, then fall off only to be replaced by more. Leeches were a part of life for the Recon men, an inconvenience, a minor nuisance. But Gary Stedman hated them.

As the team lay still in the damp grass, listening to subtle sounds of enemy movement all around them, praying for the whooping of chopper blades overhead, Stedman rolled onto his side suddenly and whispered frantically to Jarrett.

"Get it off! Oh shit, get it off me!"

Startled, Jarrett shifted his eyes. He stared directly at his friend's bare derrière, no more than a foot from his face. Affixed to Stedman's hairy bottom was a large, black elephant leech. Stedman, one of the most steadfast, courageous Recon men in Project Delta history, was about to lose it—over a leech.

"My thoughts of our impending doom were instantly forgotten in the excitement caused by that damned leech," Jarrett recalls. "I calmly took out my Army-issue mosquito repellant, squeezed a single drop of the fluid on it and fried the little bastard."

The dead critter dropped free, but Stedman wasn't yet satisfied. He immediately inspected his backside for others, muttering sentences that tended to start with "mother" and "son of a...." From Jarrett's vantage point, it was a very unwelcome sight to see Stedman's hairy private parts swinging in the jungle breeze. Army-issue repellant is largely alcohol-based, and most men understand alcohol and scrotums don't fare well together. Jarrett must have considered the consequences of his impending actions, under the circumstances. Yet, a chance like this might only come along once in...what...a lifetime? There they were, Stedman's crown jewels, hanging in the still air like ripe fruit, and Jarrett with this tube of repellant in his hand. It was a no-brainer.

"Besides," Jarrett said. "Things really didn't look all that bright for us, anyway, so I just thought, 'why not?'"

Jarrett leveled a stream of Army-issue insect repellant straight at SSG Gary Stedman's pride and joy. Stedman shot straight into the air, howling and scrambling, his partially discarded pants around his knees, desperately struggling to get his canteen out of its pouch to put out the fire. "After that," Jarrett says with a small smile, "if the subject ever came up, Gary would give me a look of pure dejection, wounded betrayal. Like...'How could you have done that to me?'"

Jarrett said he laughed so hard, tears ran down his face as his friend tenderly inspected the mistreated area for signs of permanent damage, completely oblivious to the creeping enemy around them. Even in the face of doom they were enjoying a friend's predicament. "It was, without doubt, the funniest incident I ever witnessed during my entire tour in Vietnam," Jarrett contends. Their Vietnam team members also found it hilarious.

There are stories around Delta that Jay Graves had done something similar to the legendary Moose Monroe one day in the FOB after an operation. Whether Jarrett got his idea from Graves, or the other way around is unclear. Maybe great minds just think alike. But the fact remains, even friends weren't safe from a good prank if these guys got a wild idea into their heads.

Other pranks are also etched into Project Delta's history. Before the Delta Club was built, soldiers made do with a large concrete pad and only picnic tables for partying. On one, hot Sunday afternoon, Delta members erected a silk parachute as protection from the sun, stoked up the barbeque grill and iced beer in garbage cans to celebrate "stand-down," the pause after one operation ends and the next begins. Nearly all the NCOs were present and a few officers, primarily lieutenants and captains who had paid their dues and been accepted by the group. Because the B-52 compound was adjacent to the 5th Special Forces Group Headquarters, NCOs and lower ranking officers from the Group's staff had been invited. When most of the senior staff officers hadn't shown, an energetic participant accepted the task of sending an invitation to the Officer's Club, inviting them to join in the celebration. Still, not one of the Group staff officers arrived. Becoming irritated after the second invitation had been rendered, and a respectable amount of time had elapsed and still no one came, an adventurous Recon NCO took it upon himself to motivate the Group staff to action.

A CS grenade is often called "tear gas." In reality, it is much more. Ask anyone who has ever breathed it, and I'm certain you will believe the stamped "CS" means "concentrated shit." It not only makes one tear-up and gasp for breath, it incapacitates and makes them physically ill for a substantial amount of time. That enterprising Recon NCO dropped CS into the air-conditioning vent of the Officer's Club that bright Sunday afternoon. Complete pandemonium ensued, resulting in a hasty exodus of the "O" Club. Gasping, heaving, cursing and sometimes laughing majors, lieutenant colonels and one full colonel, the Commander of 5th Special Forces Group, spilled onto the lawn. Helplessly prone, suffering and trying to recuperate from their "CS" ordeal, they lobbed verbal threats toward the raucous party under full swing at the nearby concrete pad that was Project Delta's improvised club.

The 5th Group Commander ordered a full investigation. He admonished MAJ Charles "Bruiser" Allen, the Delta CO, to discover the culprit so he could be brought to justice. Whether he put forth any real effort, Allen was unsuccessful—no one talked, so apparently the threats did no good. Eventually, tempers cooled and the tempo returned to normal.

For years, this secret was kept confidential, only to be revealed to Allen just before his death in 2003. It was at the 50th Special Forces

Reunion; the last time Bruiser would attend a gathering of the Delta men. He'd lost a leg to diabetes and had been suffering, but he wanted to attend a last reunion and see his old Recon guys. Jay Graves brought him a drink and sat beside him; they silently stared at each other. Jay said, "Bruiser, you remember the CS grenade in the "O" Club?"

"I sure as hell do and if I ever find out…"

"It was me, Bruiser."

"You…asshole."

They laughed until tears ran down their cheeks. Graves still didn't disclose that it had been Joe Singh who'd handed him the grenade, cocked his eyebrow and said, "You know what to do with this, right?"

Sometimes, pranks were perpetuated solely as an act of revenge, the target generally a non-Special Forces type, an enlisted goof-off or a greatly disliked officer. Good grace was never allowed. When an SF guy screwed up, his buddies delighted in pestering the hell out of him for days. This punishment was often harder to bear than what the Commander had in store. The only sympathy one might expect was, "Just hang in there until the next guy f _ _ _s up." It usually didn't take very long, and then the next foul-up would become the prime source of entertainment until another poor guy dropped the ball.

* * * * *

There is an old military mantra that states, "A unit will always reflect the personality of its leader." If a commander is a hard-charging, no-holds-bared type, his unit will be the same. On the other hand, if he's laidback, timid or egotistical, that will also be reflected in their training or combat operations. Project Delta commanders had a hard job and were key components in the development of the organization, especially early on. One aspect making the commander's job so difficult was Project Delta's high visibility. Suddenly, a major or lieutenant colonel, or even senior NCOs were dealing one-on-one with major generals and receiving personal communication from the President of the United States. Under those conditions, egos tend to inflate. It is to their credit that most commanders were able to push that aside and put the welfare of their men first and foremost. In one or two cases that did not happen, and as a result, the unit's overall mission suffered—but only for short periods. Fortunately, those incidents were very rare, and due to the quick turn-over of commanders and the stability of senior NCOs, Delta rebounded quickly. As an added benefit, many of the NCOs were not bashful about telling their commanders when they were screwing up. As one old SOG Recon guy, Major Harry E. Jones, Sr. once told some inflated ego, "Yes, there is a God—and no, it's not you."

The majority of Project Delta's commanders believed field soldiers had braved so much while deployed, that in garrison, other than normal training, nobody asked them to give more. They were to relax, train when told to do so, yet be ready to travel at a moment's notice. Most lived like it was their last day on earth—and for some it ultimately was. Revered as gladiators, they partied hard, ate high quality food and enjoyed the best entertainment and morale of any unit in Vietnam. That arrangement seemed only fair. On any day, these men could be in their air-conditioned bar, sipping a drink, listening to country or soft rock on the antiquated jukebox, watching Andre St. Laurent gyrate to the "pre-insertion boogie," or listening to Jim Tolbert as he strummed a slow, sad country ballad. The next day they might be hugging the moldy jungle floor, trying to will themselves invisible, watching while a dozen NVA soldiers only a few feet away searched the brush, their demise clearly in mind. Most Delta commanders figured it really wasn't too much to ask for their men while they were in garrison. Not for these men.

FOUR

"Watch Out for Guys in Black Pajamas"

THE DIFFERENCES BETWEEN NORTH VIETNAMESE ARMY (NVA) units and the Viet Cong (VC) were substantial. During the early years of the war, VC units often carried older, outdated weapons of Indo-China War vintage, and had been successful in organizing only small unit tactics such as ambushes, raids and sniper attacks. In late 1965, that changed dramatically as they began to be supplied with newer, more deadly AK-47 Chi Com assault rifles, machineguns, mortars, and received professional military training and leadership from their NVA counterparts. The NVA, an entirely different adversary than the VC, had been well-trained in both small- and large-unit tactics, and was well equipped. While the NVA wore dusty-brown-khaki uniforms, web gear and green pith helmets with red stars, the VC fashion was black pajamas, straw hats or headbands. Yet, there was little reason to see any clothing before determining the foe, for it was often their abilities that foretold the type of unit encountered. Most likely, the VC would ambush a small patrol, then pull back and snipe for hours, while the NVA would try to over-run a position, or encircle it. It soon became clear that the NVA units were formidable foes, their fighting ability superior to the Viet Cong, a lesson the Recon teams learned quickly.

When any enemy contact was made, communication with the outside world became a matter of life and death. Often they had only minutes to call for fire support and evacuation. Communication was accomplished by using the HC-162 radio to check in once a day, or as the situation required, and by pre-planned over-flights by Air Force C-47 and FAC aircraft. A spectacular configuration of the C-47 was dubbed "Puff the Magic Dragon."

"Puff" consisted of either six 7.62mm or 20mm mini-guns that could fire 2,500 high explosive rounds per minute into a narrow killing zone, each approximately one foot apart, as though the barrage came from a single weapon. For example, a target the size of a football field could be blanketed in less than a minute, killing anything in its path, while demolishing masonry into pebble-sized rubble. Since every sixth round was a tracer, the mini didn't seem to have a single muzzle flash. It appeared the plane had been attached to the ground by a wiggly line of flame, thus, Puff the Magic Dragon. After dark, the show was spectacular; day or night, it was devastating.

Another deadly weapon was the B-52 Bomber. The high-attitude B-52 crews would cruise at 50,000 feet, arriving about daybreak at an eight-digit coordinate provided earlier by either recon or conventional units. With exacting precision they'd dump their pulverizing cargo and return to Guam just in time for cocktails. When these bombs hit, each carved a crater sufficient to envelope an average-sized house—and they dropped dozens on the target. The powerful explosion caused, sent an arc of light nearly blinding to those within a thousand meters. These strikes became known to the troops as "Arc Lights."

* * * * * *

Delta Recon teams employed utmost stealth and secrecy, often operating within the inner most perimeters of the enemy's defensive positions. Detection would've meant almost certain death; many teams had been chased for days after being inadvertently sighted. Tactics were needed to ensure deception, to fool the enemy. It was standard practice for helicopter pilots to use the "leap-frog" maneuver and go in at dusk, so if the teams were spotted and chased, it would soon be dark, easier to lose their pursuers. But if no enemy was in pursuit, the teams would distance themselves from the LZ to wait until dawn before moving.

During Project Delta's advanced in-country training, all teams, American and Vietnamese, had the potential to infiltrate either through a helicopter insertion via landings, rope ladders, rappelling; or by parachutes, including deliberate night tree jumps.

Early planners continually tested new methods, such as parachute free falls from high altitude, use of smoke screens, or they would often remain after the main combat unit on routine operations had moved out. Some methods caused unintended consequences, as in this reported incident:

It was a Sunday. Personnel had been discussing parachute insertion dispersion patterns (there was a distinct possibility that some beer had been consumed). They all agreed a big problem of a parachute insertion was that troops became so dispersed that it was difficult to locate everyone. This always caused the unit to remain too long, with the possibility of detection.

The guys seemed to agree upon the notion that if they could be dropped from a helicopter or C-130 aircraft at minimum altitude, it would drastically limit their dispersion pattern and could benefit large Ranger unit operations. Len Boulas was designated to check with 5th Group's Parachute Maintenance Officer concerning their plan. After they had the Warrant Officer estimate a parachute's safe opening distance, tacking on an additional hundred feet for good measure, they decided upon 400 feet for the drop altitude (1250 feet is the typical altitude for conventional airborne units in a static-line training jump). Their next step was to convince a Vietnamese helicopter pilot to run the test.

Captain Boulas, Captain Leslie P. Mason and four volunteers assembled a team to try it. The jumpers held back until the pilot had made two passes over 5th Group Headquarters, then aimed for the rice paddy beyond. On the third pass, they all bailed out. Boulas barely had time to check if his main chute had deployed before his feet hit. The entire team landed fast, within a fifty-meter circle.

As they congratulated themselves, the Delta Commander and some 5th SF Group Headquarters staff drove up. Apparently, the 5th Group Commander, Major Art Strange, and some of the staff had been playing poker when the low-flying chopper rattled their flimsy headquarters, scattering men and cards. They quickly exited, just in time to see Boulas and his cronies bail out at 400 feet. "To say the least," Boulas related, "we got a real serious ass-chewing." The crusty old warrant officer from Parachute Maintenance needed to come to their rescue, to convince the Commander that their experiment, while unusual, was really not that dangerous for "experienced jumpers." He reinforced that the 101st Airborne Division had used the same tactic during the WWII D-Day invasion in Normandy— he failed to mention how many had been injured.

Had this been an isolated instance of Project Delta risk-takers simply pushing the envelope, it might've fallen by the wayside, overcome by other events. In reality, this was but one of many shenanigans that Project Delta personnel pulled to keep Major Strange in trouble with his boss. Early on, the troops had been described as among history's "finest combat soldiers"—albeit a "commander's nightmare" in garrison. Major Charles Beckwith had remarked about these soldiers, "These are the finest, goddamned combat troops in the world. Now if I could just get away with keeping them in a cage until time to send them back out, my job would be a hell of a lot easier."

Another incident involved Delta medic Larry Dickinson, Harold "Catfish" Dreblow and their friend, Don Hayakawa. After a lengthy recon operation in the Central Highlands, the trio lingered in a Nha Trang restaurant late one evening, catching up on good food and some Ba-Me-Ba Beer (Beer 33). Since Beer 33 was viewed mostly as formaldehyde, it didn't take much to change human behavior, and the trio grew drunker by the minute. Upon leaving, the three inebriated warriors discovered none had any money.

"Don't worry," Dickinson slurred. "I've got a plan."

Dickinson always had a plan and most didn't work very well. Leaving the others behind at the table, he went outside, pulled his pistol and fired three times into the air, then stuck his head back in the door, shouting, "VC! VC!"

Catfish leaped to his feet. "Everybody out! Everybody out! We're under attack!" He bolted for the door.

Don Hayakawa, an American Recon NCO of Japanese-American decent, would've liked to have gone, but the simple truth was that he was just too drunk to move. So like all good Recon men, he also had a plan; he calmly continued to sip his beer until the MPs arrived. In his tiger-striped fatigues, without insignia or rank, he blended in perfectly with the other Asians in the bar. After the MPs had questioned him about the two Americans who'd skipped out without paying, they'd attempted to get Don to pay. His response, "Me don't know nuttin. Me just interpreter. Ask GI, dey say dey pay."[18]

He got away with it.

Ex-radioman Don Valentine remembers this about Hayakawa: "Don was quite smart. When ready to retire from 10th Special Forces Group, he persuaded the company SGM into allowing him to attend school while still on active duty, to acquire a civilian trade. The deal made, he was covered administratively by the SGM while training as a 'cable-splicer' for the local telephone company. He'd agreed to work for them without pay, without any expectation of a job upon his completion. Turn down a deal like that? They agreed, he graduated with flying colors, and of course, they hired him on the spot. As a Special Forces Communications specialist, why wouldn't he graduate with flying colors?" Valentine figured this ploy had been at least as good as Hayakawa's interpreter scam in Nha Trang.

* * * * * *

Before Delta completed their highly coveted club at Nha Trang, they either had to party at the nearby 5th Special Forces' Playboy Club, under constant observation by the Group staff, or anywhere they could, which generally meant an unused area, beyond a ditch where concrete picnic tables were protected from the elements by a parachute canopy. No one seemed to notice its shortcomings. They held a party there after a particularly difficult Bien Hoa operation in which they had lost some men. While no one seems to recall the food, they do remember their libations—two gallons of 180 proof medical alcohol, blended with Hawaiian Fruit Punch and fresh fruit. Larry Dickinson had prepared the food and punch, and it was generally accepted that when Larry prepared anything, it was better not to inquire too deeply about his ingredients.

---

[18] Donald Valentine's website; http//www.don-valentine.com

Two Air Force buddies, with whom they usually traded pistols and captured crossbows, joined them for beer and steaks. The Delta group frequently invited others in a position to help in re-supply endeavors, particularly from the Air Force, since they had easy access to the daily planes from the Philippines and the United States. As vaguely as anyone remembers, their names were Simpson and Tufin. The inebriated Delta guys decided to "adopt" these two new Air Force buddies, and began coaching them on "jump training," making parachute landing falls (PLF) from the concrete tables. After finishing off the punch, they retired to the Playboy Club, continuing to perform the PLFs from the barstools and bar, to the chagrin of the 5th Group staff. Whether the culprit or not, SFC Ayers gets the credit for the idea to include them in an actual parachute jump, an initiation of sorts for their new buddies. In retrospect, the participants admit, "What were we thinking?"

When the club closed at midnight, the remaining partygoers retired to the Bamboo Bar in downtown Nha Trang, where they continued the "training" until nearly daybreak. Then at dawn, they escorted their Air Force comrades back to camp to awaken Cowboy, the only Vietnamese helicopter pilot halfway crazy enough to fly for their parachute drop.

Valentine, appointed as Drop Zone Safety Officer (DZSO), was too drunk to drive and had to be driven to the DZ, a small rice paddy adjacent to the main gate of 5th Group Headquarters. Valentine still doesn't remember how he ever notified the jumpers it was safe to jump (he felt they must have had a radio on the ground), but they did jump.

A Delta guy exited first followed by an "Air Force dude," alternating with another Delta man, then an AF man, then the last one, a Delta guy. Their explanation for this jump order was that the first Delta man would demonstrate how to exit the aircraft, while those following would ensure both AF guys jumped. Valentine was too drunk to remain upright and observe, so he reclined, watching the jumpers as they exited the aircraft. Others recall him tightly clutching his .45-caliber pistol, believing he had to secure the DZ in the event the VC attacked during the jump. His companions felt he made an excellent choice of weapon, because its effective range generally matched how far he could see.

All four jumpers exited the chopper, their chutes opening successfully. One jumper flailed his arms and legs all the way to the ground; he hit so hard that dust billowed from the hard-packed clay. Valentine, alarmed that he'd probably broken every bone in his body, rushed over to him. Luckily, he was the nearest jumper because Valentine could barely stagger toward his moaning, motionless body. It was SGT Simpson, one of the Air Force NCO daredevils, covered with dust, his eyes tightly clinched.

"Just what the hell were you doing?" Valentine screamed.

Simpson peeked up at him, squeezing out a small tear. "Val, I did just like you taught me," he mumbled. "I jumped and counted to four—pretty fast—but then I suddenly thought, what in the hell am I doing here, and I tried to climb back inside that damned helicopter."

The poor guy was as sober as a judge and nearly as white as a sheet by then, so Val lay off chewing his ass too severely. SGT Simpson quietly collected his dignity, brushed off some dirt and departed, never again to attend another Delta party. Air Force SGT Tufin, on the other hand, enjoyed his experience. He attended every Delta gathering thereafter; he'd been converted. Most figured old Tufin was a little touched in the head anyway and would fit right in, so they took a liking to him and he became one of their Air Force boys. They even pinned jump wings on his chest that fateful morning on the DZ.

The Air Force often reciprocated, inviting Delta guys to attend some of their parties. More lavish than Delta's, they seemed to be not nearly as fun, so the Delta gang often decided to ratchet them up. It was during a "bring your own booze" dinner party at an Air Force sergeant's pad that things really got lively. The sergeant lived off base in Nha Trang with a pretty Vietnamese girl. Valentine and his companion stopped at the Class Six Store for booze, and against sound advice, Larry chose Irish whiskey.

"Larry," Valentine reminded him with his best fatherly advice, "The damn Scots and Irish have been fighting among themselves for centuries, and I think it's because they drink their own whiskey."

Larry laughed, and bought the whiskey anyway.

Since their host's girlfriend was very pretty, the more Larry drank of that damned Irish whiskey, the more desirable she became. Despite

Valentine's discouragement, Larry remarked within earshot of their host that he had to have her.

Their host became incensed. "I think you'd better leave, now!"

It was an unlikely match; the host towered over 6' tall and weighed in at 200 pounds, while Larry stood all of 5'8" and 150 pounds soaking wet. Valentine had seen Larry become involved in incidents of this kind before, and knew no good was going to come from it.

"Larry, you best leave this man alone. You're drunk and out of order. You're also out of your weight class. Let's go home."

"Hell, no," Larry replied, wobbly climbing to his feet. "I'm gonna whip his ass, then I'm gonna take his girlfriend home with me. Haven't ya noticed? She's hot for me."

"Larry, you're making an ass of yourself, and believe me, this is a huge mistake. Let's just drop it and go home."

Larry stubbornly ignored this sound advice and proceeded to assume his best karate stance (under the circumstances). The large host incredulously absorbed the scene—he couldn't believe it.

"Are you ready, big boy?" Larry asked drunkenly.

"Yep."

Larry attacked first with lightening speed; no one expected it. His fist caught the big guy in the chest, knocked him off his feet and onto his butt. Yet, all he'd accomplished was to piss off his host even more. No sooner had his butt hit the floor than the big guy sprang back, knocked him down then sat on his chest, all the while savagely pounding at his face.

After a few good licks Valentine tapped their host on the shoulder. When he paused, he leaned forward and said, "Hold off for a second there, Bro. Let me see if he's come to his senses yet. Larry, I told you not to drink that damn Irish whiskey. Have you had enough for one night?"

"Yes, Val. I believe I have," Larry answered politely.

While Larry staggered to his feet and brushed off his clothing, Valentine shook hands, thanked their host and his girlfriend for their kindness, then guiding his battered friend by the arm, marched him out. He left the remainder of Larry's Irish whiskey with their host. "If I were you," Val said, "I'd pour the rest of that shit out."

Larry was in such bad shape that Val decided he'd first take him to the MASH unit for the doctors to patch up before going home. Val recalls that when the medical personnel worked on him, Larry, a trained SF medic, gave them his diagnosis and sage advice on exactly how to treat him, none of it appreciated by the medical staff. Larry eventually transferred to the Special Forces camp at A Shau, a Vietnam hotspot. Although the camp was overrun in 1966, Larry survived and returned to live in New Jersey.

FIVE

Teamwork and "Jointness"

B-52 PROJECT DELTA MAINTAINED MINIMAL LOSSES throughout the war as long as they operated by their own rules; Recon members decided who would be on Recon teams. Nominations could only be made by recommendation of a current Recon member, one who could flatly state, "I personally know him and would trust him with my life." They stipulated that teams would only be comprised of the most experienced Special Forces NCOs. Officers might be allowed, in exceptional circumstances. Since most NCOs had spent years in Special Forces units, and were well-trained in all Special Ops-type missions, they were apprehensive about younger, inexperienced officers placed in charge, without the high level of skills needed to pull off the day-to-day missions. Some officers served with distinction on Recon teams. Among these: 1LT Guy H. Holland, CPT Billy J. Turner, 2LT Jerry D. Estenson, 2LT Tommy L. Richardson, 1LT Douglas E. Coulter, 1LT John M. Sullivan, 2LT Michael K. Carney and CPT Henry H. "Hugh" Shelton.

Jerry Estenson's autobiography places the decision to use young officers into perspective.[19] He contends that when the "powers-to-be"

---

[19] Jerry D. Estenson. Autobiography, http://www.projectdelta.net/bios/estenson.htm.

Captain Hugh Shelton, who later would become a four-star general and Chairman of the Joint Chiefs of Staff. (Photo courtesy of Maurice Brakeman)

first suggested the idea that Project Delta Recon teams would benefit from leadership provided by Special Forces lieutenants, even some young officers viewed the decision as flawed. Still, the theory would be field-tested to determine if it would hold up under combat conditions.

Estenson researched who had been responsible for the decision to use officers, tracing it to General Jack Singlaub who had been receiving pressure from the conventional Army hierarchy to make it happen. This meddling by conventional-mindset officers continued to chafe the Special Ops community and made their job much more difficult.

Any officer volunteering for Project Delta Recon had to first attend Recondo School. Many quickly fell out and were eliminated, either unwilling or unable to meet the harsh training demands. Upon graduating, they would report to Project Delta Headquarters in Nha Trang, only to face additional intense rugged training. Those demonstrating abilities were mentored by level-headed NCOs in charge, like Joe Markham, tough but fair. His leadership molded many of the young lieutenants earmarked for Delta Recon teams.

Jerry Estenson's first time in the hole came in 1966. He was in the northern An Loa Valley with a young sergeant named Brewer and an old Delta hand, Jay Graves. That's where he would learn certain principles that have remained with him to this day.

The An Loa Valley constricts to less than 250 meters in some areas. The team, out for three days, was tired. Reaching a river, they set up defensive positions in tall elephant grass and contemplated their best route across. In the grass behind him, Estenson heard what he described as a water buffalo thrashing. Checking, he discovered Jay Graves, pasty-

A Delta Recon team ready to go. *L to R*: SSG Pappy Gleason, SSG Andy Shepard, SFC Joe Markham, SSG Brewer, SFC John Seal, Jr., 1LT Jerry Estenson, SGT Jay Graves. (Photo taken just prior to the An Lo Valley operation; courtesy of Jerry Estenson)

faced and convulsing. Suspecting he'd been bitten by a snake, he scanned his arms and found small puncture wounds, apparently the imprint of a poisonous viper. Only through the quick action of SGT Brewer, who applied a tourniquet, was Graves able to make it until extracted. Graves was one of four Delta men documented as snake-bite victims.

On that first operation, Estenson claims he learned the value of teamwork and "jointness." He described this incident: The Recon team carried both the PRC-25 FM radio and the AN-GRE 109 radio, a Morse Code-sending device, as their primary and backup means of communication. Beyond FM radio range, the short-wave system sent Morse Code messages that would be picked up by Air Force units, then relayed to the right Army folks.

Team Lesson One: Unless the Commo folks kept the equipment in top shape, no communication could have taken place.

Al Groth, the Air Force FAC assigned to Delta, circled above Estenson until the C&C ship arrived.

Jointness Lesson One: The Air Force will be there to help when motivated by a skilled FAC or one of their own.

A small sandbar was located in the center of a two feet deep river. Estenson's job was to place an orange panel marker on it to bring in the extraction chopper. Estenson recounted how he felt that day. He'd been clearly concerned about leaving the relative safety of the river bank to venture out onto that sandbar, but it was the only spot a chopper could set down. Waiting for the whooping of the helicopter blades to tell him they were in-bound, he felt his nerve slipping. From the signs he'd observed during the past three days, they were in the middle of "Indian Country." He admitted he'd rather have done anything other than walk onto that barren sandbar, to be a sitting duck for the enemy snipers. His thoughts flashed back to his training at Recondo School and his old mentor, SFC Joe Markham.

"What would Joe do?" he thought, then silently answered himself. He'd say, "You're in charge, L.T. Now, get your sorry ass out there and do your job." As he heard the ship approaching, he stood and ran to the sandbar. It has been said, "Courage is being the only one who knows you're afraid."

Once the choppers arrived, a robust conversation ensued

First Lieutenant Jerry Estenson, 1967.
(Photo courtesy of Jerry Estenson)

between Estenson and the C&C ship, resulting in a decision to pull the team out. The Command's staff man insisted they should extract the ailing Graves, and then leave the team to continue their mission. What had been Estenson's stance on this matter?

"You're f_ _ _ing crazy! We're used up, the place is crawling with bad guys, and if they didn't know we were here before your chopper hovered over us for fifteen minutes, they sure as hell do now. We're coming out!"

Leadership Lesson One: Regardless of rank, the Team Leader on the ground makes the final call and is accountable for the decision.

As noted previously, the extraction site was only a narrow valley with its small river; the sandbar was the LZ. The 281st Army Helicopter Company (AHC) pilot who had inserted them, returned to retrieve them from a very tight spot.

Jointness Lesson Two: Although Project Delta was all about placing recon teams on the ground, their mission couldn't have been accomplished without the superb flying skills of the 281st pilots and their crews who risked their lives to insert and extract these teams.

According to Estenson, that mission was accomplished repeatedly and well, ". . . even when some of us Recon guys behaved like arrogant unappreciative pricks."

Estenson recalls his seven months in Delta taught him life-long lessons. He observed the professional NCO behavior, those who had to train some numb-nutted lieutenant to do a job they were far better at, and remembers an incident that left him with enduring memories of these men. During an extraction, after his team had climbed the rope ladder and he'd been the last man, the chopper "red lined"—lost power—in immediate danger of crashing. Estenson had only reached halfway up when the pilot pulled pitch and lifted off, dragging him through the trees as it struggled to gain altitude. The airspeed, rotor-blade wash, his equipment, and just having to hang on for dear life, wore him down. As he was about to lose his grip and plummet to the valley below, some welcome hands gripped his web-harness and pulled him aboard. Those hands were Doc Simpson's, one of the most outspoken NCO's about officers on Recon teams. "For him to believe as he did," said Esterson, "then to risk his life to save mine, well, we had some remarkable NCOs in Project Delta!"

Estenson, now a professor at California State University, Sacramento, wrote, "I learned to appreciate the permanent bond between men who do hard things together in hard places. The experience is my privilege of being able to share a life-long pride among this group of men who placed duty, love for their brothers and professionalism far beyond self. The price for these lessons might have been great, but my rewards are extraordinary."

Another effective Recon officer was an athletic lieutenant from Virginia, Doug Coulter. Coulter was traveling in Madagascar when the Selective Service tracked him down with a draft notice. Estenson emphasized that Coulter's intellect and deductive abilities, when combined with his innate leadership traits, appealed to even the most hardened and opinionated NCOs; they all wanted him to be with them on dangerous missions.

In *Special Forces: A Guided Tour of U.S. Army Special Forces*, co-authored by Tom Clancy and John Gresham, Clancy interviewed General Henry "Hugh" Shelton, Chairman of the Joint Chiefs. He shared this about Coulter:

"But to go back to the original question about special or unique individuals. One I remember particularly was Doug Coulter, a Harvard graduate who came to Vietnam when that was not a very popular war, and said, 'I'm going to do my duty. My number came up and I'm going.' He did, and was a very professional guy, one of the best officers I saw during my two years over there. Today he teaches Harvard business case studies in China. Before that, he also taught in Russia. He's as professional as they come, and went out on some missions and did some things that would make the hair on the back of your neck stand up; all out of range of U.S. forces and artillery. He was truly good."

Specialist 6 Estelle Kerley, a tall youth from the hills of Tennessee, had been assigned to run recon with Estenson. About the same height, they made a good team and became close friends. Whenever possible, Recon teams were paired with other members similar in stature, in the event one became wounded and had to be carried. Estenson gave Kerley high marks for his quiet, solid approach to running field operations; he never lost his cool. Kerley and Estenson remained together throughout the An Lo and A Shau Valley operations. After returning to the States and marrying the love of his life, Kerley was killed in an industrial accident. The pain of his friend's untimely death still troubles Estenson.

* * * * * *

Recon personnel always stipulated duties would be strictly on a volunteer basis—anyone could choose to leave at any time. The most experienced Recon man was in charge of the operation, regardless of rank. They had an implicit agreement with the Project Delta Commander, MAJ Art Strange: "If you don't trust us, don't use us; but if you use us, trust us. If we request extraction don't question it, just come and get us. No discussion, no questions. We can discuss it later."

These were the rules, and they proved to be good ones. It wasn't as if they didn't exactly trust officers, although many were younger and less experienced than the seasoned NCOs. Most learned quickly and did their jobs well. After a short shakeout, several were released for employment elsewhere. For the most part, the primary concern of NCOs was more about the officer chain of command, beyond Special Forces channels. They knew it could take just one conventional-thinker or less adaptable officer to get them killed.

In the summer of 1965, B-52 began to operate near the Cambodia border, to the north of their Forward Operations Base (FOB) at Bien Hoa Air Base. It was their first operation after the CIA acquiesced and relinquished control of Project Delta to MACV. The men were apprehensive about falling under a non-Special Operations commander with not a clue as to how Special Ops troops were supposed to be used. The apprehensions proved to be well-founded. The area, War Zone D, had the largest concentration of NVA and VC in South Vietnam; this was a dangerous place for Americans.

SGT Morley had been among those on the first team inserted, and was shot through the thigh immediately after the team hit the ground. They'd inserted into a large enemy encampment and had to run for their lives from the very start. Morley and his Vietnamese medic quickly became separated from the rest of the team, but finally managed to break enemy contact and made it to the riverbank. Evading the enemy, they survived three days by using a large log to float down the river during darkness, and then hid in the brush during daylight. The remainder of Morley's team, split up at first contact, had managed to evade the enemy until the next day, despite the Viet Cong and NVA saturation searching for them. As soon as they could break enemy contact, the team leader radioed the FOB that Morley and their Vietnamese medic were

Recon men running to board an extraction chopper. (Photo courtesy of the family of Roy Sprouse)

missing and that others had been seriously wounded. He reported the NVA had been waiting for them on the LZ. With half his team missing, and the mission compromised, he requested immediate extraction. But, when MAJ Strange told the MACV G3 Operations Officer that he was in the process of extracting a team, the G3 colonel said, "Major, you tell that team to continue its mission. This is only the first day of that operation, and they're scheduled for six."

Major Strange told the colonel he was extracting his troops ASAP, and that's what he did!

During the next two days, the Delta Commander had choppers in the air from his 145th Air Lift Platoon, searching for the two missing team members, with no luck. On the third day, SGM McGuire, MSG Shaw and SFC Valentine were on one of two search choppers scouring the area when Shaw spotted Morley's orange panel near a river that flowed toward Bien Hoa. As soon as the chopper began to circle, it started taking automatic weapons fire from the trees. Other U.S. aircraft in the area were still searching, but out of sight. McGuire told Valentine to inform the FOB of what they'd found.

"We've located our missing MIAs," Valentine reported. "We're taking heavy automatic weapons fire, but we're going in to get them out."

To avoid the enemy's fire, the pilot "dead-sticked" the chopper, spiraling it toward to the ground. When only a few scant feet before impact, he pulled up and leveled off. It was a risky maneuver, but he figured he had no other option. Captain Thompson, on a chopper minutes away, broke in on the radio.

"Wait for us to support you."

"No," Valentine declined. He never much liked Thompson, considering him pushy, a bully and disrespectful to NCOs. He knew those guys on the ground personally and wasn't going to let him risk their lives. "We're going in to get our troops out, now!" Valentine told Thompson. He proceeded to not answer when Thompson called him back. While some Delta officers and NCOs agreed with Valentine's opinion of Thompson, others thought him to be a fine combat leader, smart, low-key, a great sense of humor. Strong personalities and strict leaders often clashed, even between officers and NCOs.

As the chopper spiraled down, the rounds pummeled its thin metal fuselage. The staccato of the left door M60 machinegun ceased as the Vietnamese door gunner was slammed backward, hit in the shoulder. Others fired as fast as possible from the chopper's side doors, trying to keep the enemy's head low until the pilot could get the fragile craft level. Valentine's carbine jammed; it would only work single-shot, but since Shaw and McGuire had been armed with new, shorter CAR-15 rifles, they worked over the area on full automatic.

The helicopter was peppered with hits, as if "leprechauns were banging on it with ball-peen hammers," Valentine said later. Bullets cut the hydraulic lines and flammable fluid began to spurt onto the floor, making it slick and dangerous for those standing near the door's edge. The pilot leveled off about four feet above the elephant grass, and they could see the two Recon guys slowly making their way toward the hovering chopper. SGT Morley hobbled through the tall grass, using his M-16 as a crutch, leaning on the medic for support.

To those in the chopper, they were moving too slow. McGuire yelled above the racket, "We're taking too many hits! We're gonna go down if they don't haul ass!"

Valentine jumped from the door of the chopper to help the wounded Morley, before realizing they were hovering four feet above five-foot elephant grass, which made it a nine-foot leap to the ground; he hit hard. Luckily he hadn't broken anything. Limping toward the struggling Morley and the medic, he grabbed Morley's useless weapon and flung it away. Wrapping the wounded man's arm over his shoulder, he helped Morley to the chopper and inside. The enemy fire remained relentless, but the pilot held his chopper as steady as if it were a training exercise.

"They're on!"

The pilot pushed the stick forward and the battered helicopter lifted away as sluggishly as an overloaded dump truck. By then, it was so full of holes that the pilot couldn't get more than thirty feet of altitude out of it, so he lifted off as far as possible and then flew practically along the water, down the river to Bien Hoa. The 145th pilot performed some pretty gutsy maneuvers, and had it not been for his courage, Delta men would've surely been lost.

Behind them, the other chopper and the gunships arrived and their mini-guns could be heard blasting away at the enemy's positions. Shortly, Air Force fast-movers the FAC called in arrived—then the party really began.

Sergeant Morley ultimately recovered from his wounds. He went on to become an instructor at Fort Bragg's Special Forces Medic's Course.[20]

* * * * * *

Many seemed to lose track of Major Strange; he simply vanished from the scene. Boulas remarked, "One day he was there, and the next, gone." Boulas seems convinced it might have been one of the antics he'd been subjected to, perhaps related to the secret club the Delta NCOs ran at the beach in Nha Trang. But "insiders" know the reason. It was that incident at Bien Hoa when he'd stuck up for his troops who asked to be extracted that caused his demise. He had bucked the MACV G3, offering to let him "kiss his ass" when told to leave Morley's team in for another three days. It had simply gone against the agreement he had made with his NCOs; and Art Strange was an honorable man.

* * * * *

While in garrison, problems magnified after conventional troops arrived. New commanders attempted to impose stateside rules on Special Forces troops who'd already been in combat for years. SF had been in countries throughout Southeast Asia since the mid-1950s, killing and being killed; on the other hand, conventional units only began to arrive in late 1964. When Project Delta personnel returned

---

[20] Donald Valentine's website; http//www.don-valentine.com.

after a dangerous and stressful operation in enemy controlled territory, or had survived a savage battle with the Rangers and Nungs, they just wanted to wind down, drink some beer, play a little poker and have a fight or two among friends. Then just as quickly, it was always back to training; followed by another mission. So maybe they did pull off a few crazy antics, but usually the Commander looked the other way. He knew if he fired them he'd never find any others crazy enough to do their job, or be half as good at it. He also understood that after a few days of wild socializing, they'd be ready to go back out again—and do it damned well. Then, someone tried to change the routine.

A military police unit assigned to Nha Trang began to detain Delta personnel for speeding, and issued them speeding tickets. The explanation—they didn't want anyone to get killed. SFC Don Valentine was among the first recipients. Infuriated, he marched that ticket straight to SGM William Fuller. Fuller, 6'6" and well over 260 pounds held a black belt in Karate. But beyond being large, he became ugly when angry—and he'd become very angry. Fuller stormed into the Provost Marshall's Office waving the offending ticket, cussing a blue streak. He reminded the PM Duty Officer that his men got killed nearly every day, and had been doing so longer than any of his fuzz-faced MPs had been drinking Army coffee…and not by any freaking jeep accident! He tore up the speeding ticket, threw it on the Desk Sergeant's desk and stormed out; finishing his tirade by yelling, "Shove it, where the sun doesn't shine!" No further tickets were issued to Special Forces personnel.

* * * * * *

The men in Project Delta were like a close family, and like most families, they had their share of disagreements. Often issues might lead to fisticuffs, but outsiders were better off not to interfere in the disputes. If anyone outside of the "family" attempted to intrude, they usually ended up being blamed for the entire mess, and had to take on the whole bunch. Troops cheerfully recall one such disagreement between SGM McGuire and Major Strange. It had been smoldering, and something finally brought it to a head during a party in the mess hall of a nearby aviation company.

"Come outside and we'll duke it out, Major," McGuire said, puffing out his barrel chest as he challenged his commander. McGuire, known

With few exceptions, air transport support for early Leaping Lena insertions (June-July 1964) was provided by VNAF pilots, the King Bees, utilizing H-34 helicopters [21]

to put away a substantial amount of booze when off duty, was never one to walk away from a fight. The Major, a light drinker at best, politely refused the challenge and ordered his SGM to sleep it off. Although the dejected SGM McGuire left, in his mind it was just too big a deal to simply ignore. Within minutes he returned, shouting again for Strange to come outside. Strange realized this issue wouldn't go away unless addressed, head-on. As Strange was huge, with tremendous strength, Delta folks often wonder exactly what McGuire was thinking when he challenged him. It was clear the Major didn't want to fight his top NCO, but at McGuire's insistence he relented and they moved outside to settle their differences.

They no sooner squared off than McGuire attacked—that was the end of it. Art Strange had been a wrestler in college. He mashed McGuire's face into the sand and pinned him with a painful arm lock. When a guard from the helicopter unit, on his rounds, saw the two men struggling in the dirt, he became excited.

"Okay, knock it off you two," he shouted, rushing up. "Get up right now!"

---

[21] Detachment B-52, 5th Special Forces Group (Airborne), 1st Special Forces, Operation 1-66, After Action Report "Mallet," dtd: 25 Jan 1966, para 1.b. (2)

Delta troops never wore rank on their collars and although they knew each other's rank, outsiders didn't. In Project Delta, particularly Recon, rank mattered much less than in other units; experience and ability counted most. On occasion, higher-ranking NCOs and officers might have participated in operations led by someone of lesser rank. The two exceptions for wearing rank were reserved for SGM McGuire and Major Strange, each having metal rank insignias pinned to their collars. While securing McGuire in a torturous arm hold, Strange glanced up, exposing his rank to the young guard for the first time.

"Go on about your business sonny, or I'll kick your ass, too," he said calmly. When the guard saw the rank of the two combatants, his jaw dropped and he beat a hasty retreat. To McGuire, Strange said, "Do you want me to break off your damned arm, Sergeant Major?"

"No, Sir."

"Then how about a drink?"

"Okay."

He let the SGM up, and it ended.

In yet another incident, upon returning to Fort Bragg as a Group Command Sergeant Major, McGuire called two of his NCOs into his office after they returned late for duty. Closing the door, the sounds of physical conflict could be heard inside for several minutes. The two NCOs emerged, battered and bruised, then asked the clerk to call an ambulance for the Sergeant Major. As Don Valentine related, "At times, you had to admire McGuire's warrior spirit if not his judgment."

Today, Charles McGuire resides in North Carolina not far from the retirement home where Art Strange once lived. In a role reversal, McGuire gave up drinking, fighting and Irish ballads for the church choir, and serves as a part-time minister, while Strange, the mild mannered teetotaler, purchased a cocktail lounge. Arthur Strange passed away at Cape Fear Valley Medical Facility in Fayetteville, NC, 31 October 2005. He served five distinguished tours in Vietnam and at the time of his death, had retired as a high school teacher. He'd also been a successful businessman, with his popular Silver Fox Lounge and Ken-Art Realty Company.

* * * * * *

In January 1965, a feverish Captain Boulas was diagnosed with pneumonia, malaria and myocarditis (inflammation of the heart). Evacuated to the 8th Army Field Hospital, he remained for forty days; a Vietnamese-French priest gave him his last rites at a low point in his progress. He swears he had an out-of-body experience, floating above his bed, watching as the doctors and nurses struggled to save his life. His friendship with one of the nurses, Julie Klebaum Thornton, a farm girl from Washington State, has endured through the years. Boulas says she was a no-nonsense professional who didn't suffer fools lightly, always providing a helping hand or a word of encouragement, and represented the best in the Army Nurses Corp. If anything, Boulas's hospital stay had some positive aspects, for Delta troops always maintained a close relationship with the medical staff who cared for them when they were sick or wounded. B-52 reciprocated by providing security, making the medical team's tour a little less stressful and perhaps even a little more enjoyable.

Upon returning to the States, Leonard Boulas was hospitalized for hepatitis at Walter Reed Army Medical Center, costing him an assignment as a CIA training officer. He eventually retired as a lieutenant colonel. Today, he teaches at a community college and consults on emergency management issues.

* * * * * *

A majority of the earliest arrivals served more than one tour, remaining through the changes of several Delta Project commanders; MAJ Art Strange, Charlie Beckwith, John Warren and others. Some extended beyond, long after most soldiers departed to "The World."

After Leaping Lena's demise, VNAF pilots continued on as Delta's primary source of air transport for the next year and a half. The VNAF pilot talent ranged from extremely good to barely acceptable. It wasn't that they lacked flying skills or the sensitivity to their unique missions, for once trained with Delta they were as good as any other pilot. Their problem was turnover—after crews had been highly trained for Delta-type missions, they'd suddenly be transferred, and a raw new crew would take their place. In essence, Delta had become a training unit for the Vietnamese helicopter pilots. Vietnamese H-34 Helicopters (the

Recon team boarding a "Slick," 1966. (Photo courtesy of James Jarrett)

King Bees) were transferred to the CIA for use in SOG. Many of the valiant VNAF pilots who supported Project Delta were eventually killed while with SOG.

The VNAF rotation, in combination with insufficient U.S.-operated rotary-blade aircraft, nagged and frustrated Delta commanders throughout 1964 and 1965. Inexperienced pilots often inserted recon teams into the wrong landing zones. After one operation on 30 July 1965 at Binh Dinh, MAJ Strange, the Project Delta Commander, commented in the official After Action Report (AAR), "This Project cannot operate effectively without a group of efficient, determined and motivated helicopter pilots."[22]

Neither the Commander nor Recon teams had cause to worry about one pilot, Lieutenant Khoi, a long-time Section Chief of the King Bees. He'd been with Delta its initial two years, then transferred along with other King Bees when they left to support SOG missions across the border in Laos. Many of Project Delta's old hands wouldn't have recognized him by his name, Khoi. He was known simply as "Cowboy."

As Len Boulas tells it, "How do you go about describing someone who is the cream of the crop in their technical skills—fearless, nerves of

---

[22] *Project Delta After Action Report*, Opn 15-65 (Binh Dinh), 30 July 1965.

Choppers with recon teams, going into the "hole." (Photo courtesy of Steve Adams)

steel, yet with a sense of humor, one who enjoyed life to its fullest?" He said two things about the flamboyant Lieutenant Khoi were immediately noticeable; first, he was only a lieutenant who supervised several captains in his helicopter section, and secondly, he'd been given the nickname Cowboy by the Americans. This term was not only because of his Western-style hat or his pearl-handled pistol, but to recognize that he was the cream-of-the-crop, the best the Vietnamese Air Force had to offer. When he dropped off a recon team, he always knew exactly where they were, and when they needed to be extracted he always came back for them, regardless of the situation or weather.

Boulas said, "If he'd been an American aviator, he'd be wearing a chest full of DFCs (Distinguished Flying Cross, awarded to pilots and crews for extreme valor.) There are an awful lot of Recon folks who owe him their lives—some who've never even met him. Cowboy set the standard the Recon personnel expected from all aviation support personnel. They expected that when they called to come get them, the aviators would come, no questions asked, no matter how bad the situation. That's what Cowboy always did."

One day Boulas encountered another SOG pilot using the name Cowboy, wearing the same type hat and brandishing the same pistol as Lieutenant Khoi. Boulas asked him if he knew Khoi. The new pilot informed him Cowboy Khoi had been killed flying a particularly dangerous mission across the border for SOG. When Boulas inquired about his nickname, the pilot grinned and said, "Comes with the territory. You get it when you're recognized as being the best." It had become Cowboy's legacy.

* * * * * *

Although the 145th Airlift Platoon supported Project Delta intermittently as early as 1965, their first appearance in direct support began to be documented in After Action Reports following an operation near Binh Hoa, 2 January 1966, when they flew out of the Di An FOB. A sketchy history details the 145th Airlift Platoon (UH-1B) as "Slicks," meaning the helicopters had been stripped of nonessential equipment to increase air speed, range, maneuverability and troop capacity. Slicks specialized in the dangerous, often vulnerable feats of insertion and extraction of teams in enemy controlled territory.

On 6 January 1965, the 145th Airlift Platoon initially moved to Nha Trang to support Headquarters, Field Forces. That same year, on Christmas, they were reassigned to the 10th Combat Aviation Battalion, and began training with Project Delta Recon teams. A month later, 25 January 1966, the 145th platoon merged with the 6th Aviation Platoon (UH-1B gunships), forming 2nd Platoon, 171st Aviation Company (AC), thereby combining the 145th troop transport capability with the 6th Aviation's combat punch that Delta needed.

Whereas the 171st Company had been providing helicopter support for the entire 5th Special Forces Group headquartered in Nha Trang, the primary purpose of 2nd Platoon, 171st Company, became direct helicopter support for Project Delta's recon operations. Remaining under operational control (OPCON) of the 5th SF Group Commander, conflicts often occurred; they were frequently skimmed off to support other Special Forces requirements throughout Vietnam. It would not be until 1966 that Delta received its own direct support organic helicopter unit—the 281st Army Helicopter Company. Its heroic insertions, air support cover and death defying extractions became legendary as Delta's operations evolved over the next four years.

By July 1966, the 281st Army Helicopter Company had assimilated all aviation assets of the 171st and was attached to Project Delta for direct support, thus combining airlift capability and firepower under the OPCON of Commander, Project Delta. The 281st AHC remained as Delta's primary helicopter support unit until early 1970, near to the time of Delta's deactivation.

The 145th Platoon was unique even after absorbed by the 171st, and later by the 281st AHC. They were the first clandestine helicopter unit in the traditions of Special Ops; sterile uniforms—no rank or unit patches—and under the direct control of a non-aviation commander, the Commander of Project Delta. While this presented autonomy to operate secretly without interference by the aviation chain of command, it also aligned them beyond conventional re-supply channels. Unlike Special Forces units who were designed to operate in this manner, it proved to be a great hardship for aviation pilots and crews. This remained a bone of contention until 1965, when Delta Commander MAJ Charles Beckwith arrived and assumed full command responsibility for them.

The 145th Airlift Platoon (later 2nd Platoon, 171st Aviation Company and 281st ACH) was an outstanding organization with the most talented pilots. Their unselfish acts and bravery beyond duty requirements unquestionably resulted in the safe return of many Delta personnel who might have easily perished.

*　*　*　*　*　*

Fixed-wing aircraft were also becoming much more accessible to the unit's operations. Following President Johnson's decision to introduce U.S. aircraft and pilots into the Vietnam conflict, with the arrival of the 19th TASS (Tactical Air Support Squadron), three additional TASS's rapidly followed. By 1965, 120 O-1F aircraft were being flown by USAF pilots. On 8 May 1965, the 21st TASS activated, and became operational December 1965. Shortly thereafter, the 21st TASS assigned a FAC, a radio operator and one 01-F aircraft in direct support of Project Delta. The U.S. Air Force touted its association with Project Delta as "one of the most innovative aspects of the entire Project."

Once enemy units had been identified by Delta's small recon teams, FAC pilots were called in. They directed deadly air strikes onto the exacting coordinates provided by the recon teams, and assisted in locating their precise position on the ground. The FAC mission also helped teams in trouble, extracting from hot areas by providing radio relay and air cover. According to a 1969 Air Force study, this new joint tactic was "One of the most significant and more productive applications of airpower in Vietnam, and represented a high payoff for a small investment of resources."[23]

Leaping Lena and, subsequently, Project Delta operations, gave birth to Long Range Recon Patrol (LRRP) techniques used by conventional U.S. Army and Marine Corps. Special Forces and CIA projects, SOG, Omega and Sigma, would similarly be organized using the skills and lessons gleaned from the early Leaping Lena and Project Delta endeavors; many conventional divisional LRRP units were trained by Special Forces personnel who had become experienced running recon patrols in Project Delta.

Although divisional LRRP personnel were capable leaders upon graduation, their level of training still fell short of that for Delta Recon personnel, primarily due to Delta's constant and repetitious training exercises using advanced infantry, special and unconventional warfare tactics. Their skills were finely honed to a higher level. All were skilled shooters and airborne operations qualified, map, compass and land navigation experts, trained in advanced tracking methods, silent movement techniques and hand and arm signals. They executed infiltration and extraction techniques; developed a mastery of as many types of weapons as time permitted; conducted practice ambushes, raids, defensive positions, recon and observation techniques; and mission support sites (MSS) and LZ/DZ sterilization procedures. In essence, Project Delta set the standard for all Special Operations projects to follow. Many of their techniques are still taught in Special Forces training exercises and are being used in Afghanistan and Iraq.

---

[23] U.S. Air Force. "USAF Support of Special Forces in South East Asia," HQ PACAF, Directorate, Tactical Evaluation,

SIX

"We're Thinking About You. Hold Out As Long As You Can. God Bless You All."

- Lyndon Johnson

IN JANUARY 1965, PROJECT DELTA CONDUCTED a series of operations around the small village of Vung Tau. On 15 January, two Delta Recon teams were inserted north of Vung Tau where two VC battalions had been reported. Over two days, these initial teams were involved in a series of running gunfights with enemy forces, killing several and returning with valuable intelligence. One American received minor wounds. Ultimately, seven, five-man recon teams would infiltrate during the operation.

Sergeant First Class Eddie Adams had been assigned to a Ranger reaction force called to action as a result of one of the recon team's intelligence reports. On 21 January 1965, Adams led a company of Airborne Rangers into a defensive built-up village reported by the recon team. Under heavy automatic weapons fire, Adams formed his force into an assault line, entered the village and initially forced out the enemy, although one house had been so heavily defended that it completely bogged down the attack. The Rangers, pinned down by the hail of fire, held up and returned fire; it was plain they weren't going anywhere. Adams knew he had to get them moving before the enemy regrouped and counterattacked.

He ordered a small huddled group of Rangers to follow him, stood upright in the face of direct enemy fire and charged the fortified house, firing as he ran. Without hesitation, the Rangers followed. The VC platoon guarding the house was so surprised by this audacious affront that it fled in panic, abandoning its weapons, grenades and documented intelligence information. Adams's Bronze Star citation reads, "...continuously exposed himself to enemy small arms and automatic weapons fire to rout the Viet Cong from their positions, wounding many NVA and capturing one enemy POW."

* * * * * *

On 19 February 1965 in Nha Trang, Ranger advisors were briefed about an unidentified ship sunk near Vung Ro Bay. They were tasked to deploy two Ranger companies; 2nd Ranger Company would assault a nearby beach and travel overland to secure the wreck-site until the ship's cargo could be determined. 1st Ranger Company would traverse the small mountains then meet to reinforce them on the beach. The Rangers weren't trained on how to conduct a seaborne assault, but were ordered to conduct one against heavily fortified positions and a determined enemy. Despite the Delta Commander's heated protests that they were sorely unqualified, it didn't seem to affect the higher Joint Command decision. In the end, Project Delta did what they always did. They simply saluted and said, "Yes, Sir," carrying out their orders in the most professional manner possible.

The Delta staff was well aware land travel would be extremely difficult due to the harsh terrain with its immense boulders, dense vegetation and vine-choking mountains more than 300 meters in height. They expected to travel 250 meters (the length of two football fields) per hour. Ninety Rangers and four USSF advisors of the 2nd Ranger Company would load helicopters to bring them within several kilometers southwest of the wrecked ship's location, where they would board the small landing craft that would carry them to the beach assault location.

Meanwhile, the 1st Ranger Company had air-landed on the far side of the rugged mountain range and began their long, difficult trek toward the sea.

Due to late arrival in the target area and 1st Ranger Company's slow progress through the mountains, a decision was made to postpone the 2nd Ranger Company beach assault until the following morning. In the evening, the Americans reviewed their difficult mission, fine-tuning final plans. It was apparent only two acceptable sites were suitable for beach landings. The Americans preferred to hit the beach nearest the target area to facilitate surprise and limit heavy casualties, while the Vietnamese (VN) Flagship Commander and Vietnamese Ranger Company Commander felt enemy fire would be too heavy closer to the objective. Over objections of the three U.S. Ranger advisors, the beach farther from their objective was selected for the landing.

The following morning, two support ships and a small landing craft began to move toward the objective. All could fire weapons; 40mm cannons, 20mm guns and one five-inch gun on the escort craft. As the LSM approached the beach, it became apparent the enemy was well dug-in. They prepared for their assault. Heavy automatic fire, which intensified as more small arms and automatic weapons joined in, caught them in a carefully planned, deadly crossfire from heavily camouflaged positions. As the ships continued toward their objective, the LSM took considerable pounding from the devastating small arms fire, several Rangers fell wounded. When one of the Vietnamese Navy 20mm gunners was hit in the head and mortally wounded, other gunners ceased firing and sought shelter.

It was then that SSG Malia rushed to the wounded man, fully exposing himself to enemy fire, and pulled the wounded gunner to a safer position. His actions seemed to galvanize the other gunners, who returned to their firing positions. The action had little affect on the enemy; the supporting ships soon gave up their attack and withdrew, forcing the LSM landing craft to also retreat. Enraged that the Vietnamese Navy would leave them high and dry without supporting fire, the Americans raised hell with all who would listen until they finally relented, launched another attack and encountered the same vicious crossfire. Only this time, the LSM continued forward until it hit the beach. Staff Sergeant Malia was with the lead platoon when the ramp began to open; he fired his rifle over the top of the lowering ramp. Three Rangers fell severely wounded; another was shot and killed instantly. Malia glared at the frightened Vietnamese sailor tasked with lowering the ramp, as if daring him to try to interrupt its decent. He didn't back off, and the outer gates of the LSM were swinging wide by the time the beach was just a few meters away. As the ramp leveled so the Rangers could deploy, the officers and many troops shifted further toward the rear of the LSM seeking safety from the fusillade of small arms fire, until only a thin line of personnel extended along each side of the landing craft. Without officer support to motivate them, the troops had simply frozen.

Malia, positioned with his platoon leader several men behind the lead man, saw what was happening and seized the initiative. Leaping to the front of the ramp, he began firing rapidly, and without looking back, led a charge onto the beach. His bravery galvanized the entire company into action; they hit the beach and quickly established fire superiority over the entrenched Viet Cong. The ferociousness of this assault caught the enemy by surprise. They immediately gave up their positions, retreating into the dense jungle. The Rangers had conducted a successful beach assault, despite their lack of training on this type maneuver. Within thirty minutes the beach was secure—SSG Malia spread the Rangers into a horseshoe-shaped defensive position against the base of the mountain, then they attended to the wounded.

Although the enemy had been forced to withdraw, he was not yet beaten and continued to pour heavy fire into the Ranger's precarious defense. Contrary to his orders from the VN Special Forces Command, the Vietnamese Ranger Company Commander opted to attack toward Vung Ro Mountain on the right, the path of least resistance. Malia and other U.S. advisors moved within full sight of the enemy, knelt beside the frightened Vietnamese officer, trying to persuade him to drive toward their assigned objective. After a heated discussion and obvious threats, he acquiesced and the column moved out. Once the base of the Vung Ro Mountains was positioned on their left, and with the ocean to their right, they had no alternative except to retreat or continue toward their objective—the damaged ship.

After traveling only a short distance, the column again came under heavy attack, this time by 60mm mortars; the first two rounds hitting directly in the middle of the column, wounding four more Rangers. Then a round exploded twenty feet from SSG Malia, lifting him off the ground. Miraculously, other than a bloody nose, he was not injured, but the VN Ranger Company Commander had disappeared. Malia again left his cover under heavy mortar fire to seek the officer, finding him hiding in rocks nearby. Infuriated, Malia strongly suggested they move out of the mortar bombardment before they all became casualties, as 60mm rounds continued to rain on their position. The VN commander hunkered down, steadfastly refusing to move from the relative safety of the boulders. Several mortar rounds landed within fifteen to forty meters from SSG Malia's exposed position, yet he remained, calmly speaking to the commander until he could get him to agree to move—but not until the VN Navy ships began to place naval gunfire on the enemy.

As the column again moved out, SSG Malia positioned himself toward the front of the column to better control their rate of march. Mortar rounds continued landing among the Rangers as they struggled through the difficult terrain, their casualties quickly mounting. The column suddenly stopped and SSG Malia cautiously moved forward to find out why.

He learned the point element had discovered a large enemy cache: two houses that were being used as a VC command post, several small boats and rafts, Chinese anti-aircraft sights for a .50-caliber machinegun and numerous belts of .50-caliber armor-piercing and tracer ammo. As the destruction element team (DET) prepared to destroy the items, SSG Malia, anxious to get to the objective, led them out again. Movement became much more difficult as the jungle closed in. Soon, the point element again encountered enemy resistance. Fighting became "up close and personal," as the Rangers closed with the enemy in the dense jungle and combat quickly broke down into hand-to-hand struggles between small groups and individuals. This was the kind of warfare the Rangers liked best, where they could finally confront a faceless enemy and put their extensive close combat training to work. They suffered no additional casualties, but killed four and wounded many more, forcing the enemy to withdraw just as suddenly as they had appeared. Malia, in the middle of the confrontation, killed one in close combat before breaking contact. After directing the collection of combat intelligence information, he once more struck out toward the objective.

They'd been moving steadily nearly an hour through almost impassible terrain, mostly under enemy sniper fire, when the lead element paused, passing back information of a heavily fortified machinegun emplacement blocking their way. With the mountains on their left and the ocean to their right, there was no way around; the Rangers would have to assault the position to advance. Malia backtracked for his VN Company Commander and found him behind yet another large boulder refusing to budge. Disgusted by the officer's reluctance to lead, SSG Malia detached himself from his platoon and took over the point element. For the third time in an hour, he usurped the commander's control and inspired the rank and file to follow him in battle.

Once the machinegun position was destroyed, SSG Malia stayed on point for more than three more hours, constantly exhorting his men to move faster. The Rangers, now essentially commanded by SSG Malia, had by late afternoon moved onto the fringes of the second beach— their final objective. Observing a fresh set of footprints in the soft sand, he followed the tracks into the bushes and discovered an enormous cache of weapons, medicine and munitions. To let the ineffectual company commander save face in front of his men, SSG Malia started back to tell him of the discovery, and let him determine how it would be recovered, but the VC had left behind an element to guard the supplies and they suddenly opened fire, forcing Malia and his Rangers to retreat to the safety of some rocks.

Malia finally exhausted efforts on finding the commander and instead, located 1LT Bay, his platoon leader. Bay had proven himself repeatedly and Malia trusted him to do his job. Together, they led a charge across the open beach in the face of enemy fire. Men, who had retreated only minutes before, left their positions and vigorously charged the beach while spraying a lethal rain of small arms fire on the enemy's position; the results were so devastating the VC broke ranks and dispersed in full retreat, leaving the position for the Rangers. The U.S. Special Forces advisor's After Action Report stated the bravery of the Rangers was unquestionable, including many of the NCOs and junior grade officers, but leadership at the company command level had been almost non-existent. This situation would slowly change over time as weak company commanders were weeded out and replaced by more competent officers, like the formidable 1LT Bay.

Throughout the remainder of the day, U.S. advisors Malia, Florio, Spinaio and Graham continued to exhort men to move the captured ammunition, rifles, medicines and explosives to the beach for loading and removal. The cache proved to be the largest discovered during the Vietnam War, nearly 100 tons of explosives, recoilless-rifle ammunition, grenades, more than 20,000 rounds of .50-caliber ammo and large quantities of high quality, critical medical items, including Japanese blood plasma, Bulgarian penicillin, streptomycin and other North Vietnamese, Chinese and Soviet produced medicines. Thousands of rounds of Soviet ammo were recovered, along with 2,000 Mauser 98s, quantities of Chinese "Burp" guns and Russian light machineguns. The cache was reported by the media, on TV and viewed throughout the world. It was also analyzed by technical Asian intelligence personnel and scrutinized by the United Nations International Criminal Court (ICC). General Nguyen Khanh, ARVN Army Chief of Staff, personally visited the cache site.

The valorous acts by SSG James J. Malia, Jr. were cited in both U.S. and ARVN After Action Reports (AAR), and in his award citation, which documented that he deliberately exposed himself to enemy crossfire while aboard the landing craft to assist a wounded soldier, personally led the beach assault and refused protection when advising the ineffective commander during a constant mortar barrage. He also led the point element for their forward movement, galvanized an entire Ranger company into action, disregarded his own personal safety as he led the beach assault, killed numerous enemy soldiers (one in hand-to-hand combat) and led an effective attack across an open beach. His actions contributed substantially to locating and securing some of the greatest historic material finds of the war. His U.S. and Vietnamese comrades stated that throughout the day of 19 February, he repeatedly disregarded his own personal safety in more than eight separate incidents. Malia's acts notably inspired the Vietnamese Rangers and greatly aided accomplishment of a very difficult mission. For his acts of bravery, SSG Malia was awarded the Silver Star for valor.

The Delta staff anticipated that the 1st Ranger Company, traveling overland, would run into enemy resistance and fail to arrive to participate in the cache recovery, yet they succeeded in destroying a substantial number of the enemy on route while tying up troops that might have been used to reinforce the cache site. SFC Sterling Smith won the ARCOM/v for his heroic actions on their march to the sea. It was during this operation that Specialist (SP5) Ronald Gaffney was listed as KIA.

Project Delta continued launching recon operations, sharpening its skills as intelligence demands steadily increased. On 12 July 1965, MSG Henry Gallant and SFC Fred Taylor conducted an operation near Pleiku in Kontum Province; both are still carried on Army rolls as missing in action.

* * * * * *

Love him or hate him, Major Charles Beckwith was a hard-charging officer who pushed himself and others hard—hence his nickname, "Charging Charlie." Under his command, the Delta compound transformed itself from an ugly, muddy quagmire where people walked on wooden pallets, to an enviable complex. He built desirable living quarters, established a motor pool and filled it with jeeps and trucks "found" on other installations until the 5th Group Commander expressed, "Your motor pool is large enough, Charlie. Cease and desist."

During his introduction speech, he told the Delta troops, "There are only two kinds of soldiers; dip-shits and piss-cutters. I only want piss-cutters in this outfit. If you don't like that, get the hell out. If you stick with me, I'll send you home with a chest-full of medals or I'll send your mother a foot locker full of them."

Most Delta men didn't much like that kind of talk; Charging Charlie took a lot of getting used to. He pulled a tour of duty with the British SAS where he almost lost his life, but in the process adopted many of their ways, and much of their language, modifying both as he went along. When he wanted to, he could charm the pants off anyone and had a knack for playing the role of the "good old country boy hick" who didn't know too much, especially with those senior to him. From Boulas' observations, "He was much more intelligent and had a better handle on things than most men he dealt with. Many times I heard him say that there were two kinds of folks—those who should be in the Army, and those who should not be. He felt it was his mission to get rid of those who should not be in the Army."

One day he asked Boulas to review an Officer Evaluation Report (OER) he'd been preparing to send to one officer's official file in the

Department of the Army. He had given the officer all zeros out of a possible score of ten, and in the narrative had entered a single sentence, "This officer is a dipshit."

Boulas read it a couple times and commented, "Sir, you can't be serious about sending this in!"

"Sure I am. The folks in DA will know exactly what I mean."

Apparently, the officer was one Beckwith felt shouldn't be in the Army. For those he thought should be in the Army, he gave them a full ten points and entered the one-sentence comment: "This officer is a piss-cutter."

While Len Boulas remembered being impressed by Charging Charlie and his leadership style, many others weren't.

Beckwith has been described as a soldier who deeply loved his country and would do anything to defend and protect it and its citizens. Some respected Special Ops NCOs who worked with him, such as Command Sergeant Major (Ret.) Eric L. Haney, portrayed him as a highly moral man who held that all human life is precious. Others find that notion hard to believe, having been sent into situations by him where there was a good chance they might not come back. His record confirms he never asked anyone to do that which he was either incapable of, or unwilling to do himself, attesting to his 1966 life-threatening wounds during Operation Masher in the An Loa Valley. According to Haney, now a Fox News analyst, "Charging Charlie... always acted on what he thought was in the best interests of the nation, the Army, and the unit...and damn the consequences to his career." [24]

Boulas said, "He brought with him a sense of soldiering and professionalism which many in the Project had begun to drift away from...the first thing he did was to order everyone out at 'O-dark-thirty,' in full combat gear for a forced road march."

There was a lot of grumbling and a few close to becoming burned out, either left or were fired. But Beckwith's energy revitalized the rest and gave Project Delta a new focus. He instituted increased recon team insertions and subsequently won the commitment of the 81st Airborne

---

[24] Jerry D. Estenson, DPA, Professor College of Business Administration, California State University, Sacramento. *Leading Professionals in High-Risk Environments: Perceptions of Critical leadership Attributes Provided by Three Generations of Military Special Operations Personnel*, 66.

Rangers to Delta. Under his command, contact with the enemy became more and more frequent; more often than not, with "Charging Charlie" right in the middle of it.

Soon after Beckwith took command of B-52, Communication NCOs Bill Pool and Ronald "Robbie" Robertson were selected to be radio men with the Airborne Rangers, to reinforce the Special Forces at Plei Mei under siege by a suspected NVA regiment. The 1st Cavalry Division was supposed to provide air transportation, but backed out at the last minute, causing them to wait for Delta's pilots to fly north from Nha Trang. They had to follow roads, flying just above the trees, because the fog was too dense to navigate otherwise. But they made it. Arriving at the launch pad, Pool caught up with Cowboy, one of Delta's Vietnamese pilots, exiting a running Huey. They exchanged greetings and Pool said, "I thought the Cav was providing chopper support on this boondoggle, Cowboy."

The slender pilot shook his head. "They say, 'too foggy.' No fly when too foggy." He pushed his western hat back, grinning widely, "Pussies."

Pool had to agree. If he had to go up in this pea soup, he'd rather have one of his own pilots than some stranger.

Getting into the Area of Operation (AO) was a dangerous proposition; the weather didn't improve as the day wore on, and hugging the treetops was a good way to get shot down. Eventually landing a short distance from the besieged camp, they were ambushed and pinned down immediately. But they had expected it and didn't take any initial casualties, despite being unable to advance. Hunkered down in partially open terrain with only a few scattered trees to the front and right, and rice paddies on their left, Pool and Robertson took cover in a deeply rutted dirt road ditch, straining to determine the direction of the firing. Pool raised his head slightly to find someone to fire at, but with his visibility limited, he leaped up and moved toward the crest of a small hill to their right front. He never made it. Shot high in the upper shoulder, the bullet lodged against his shoulder blade.

The M-16 rifle has three settings: Safe, Fire and Automatic. "Fire" is semi-automatic—pulling the trigger each time to fire a round. "Automatic" allows a shooter to hold the trigger down until the magazine is empty, or to simply waste ammunition. A sharp-witted SF man dubbed these settings, "Slow, Fast and Awful Fast." Pool had his setting on

"Awful Fast," so when the shot drove him backwards he instinctively gripped the closest thing handy, in this case his trigger, holding tightly as he fell backwards, spraying the area. One of his wayward rounds hit Robertson in the big toe, barely nipping the tip, but tearing the toe off his boot. Robertson dropped his rifle, leaped up in the middle of the firefight, grabbed his distressed foot and hopped around on the other— cursing at Pool for all he was worth. Despite his own injury, Pool felt badly about it, but since he didn't know how Robertson might retaliate, he dropped into a shallow rut and quickly yelled apologies until Robertson had quieted down a bit. Before Robertson could become a target—of the enemy this time—he sought cover and closely inspected his foot, which appeared allright; he ignored a small group of Rangers huddled nearby, laughing and pointing at him. They apparently had gotten quite a kick out of the whole event.

Robertson, grateful he hadn't lost any toes, realized the Rangers were already in the attack and doing pretty well against their ambushers. Then he saw one of their best officers, who had motivated their forward movement, struck in the forehead by a .50-caliber round. This infuriated the Rangers. They attacked in a frenzy; screaming, firing and running straight at the machinegun nest. They found the dead VC gunner inside—handcuffed to his machinegun. While politicians back home might be playing political games with the war, the Viet Cong, known respectfully as either the VC, Victor Charlie or Mister Charles, were playing for keeps. They wanted to win.

* * * * * *

When Charging Charlie Beckwith went on an operation, he nearly always ordered either Terry "Rolex" Morrone or Don Valentine to be his radio operator. When Valentine's tour was up, Beckwith sent for him.

"Sergeant Valentine, you're a good man. Why don't you extend your tour and stay with me?"

"No, Sir," Valentine told him. "You're going to get this outfit wiped out, and I don't want to be here when it happens." Beckwith laughed as Valentine headed out the door for Fort Bragg, NC.

It was October 1965 when Beckwith volunteered to insert Project Delta B-52 teams a mile outside the surrounded Special Forces camp at Plei Me. Their infiltration was to help stiffen the resistance against enemy buildup around the encampment. Pleiku Province had become the most hotly disputed area in the war-torn country. The Special Forces camp near the small town of Plei Me had been battered day and night by several NVA regiments. By circling the encampment with Chinese 12.7mm anti-aircraft guns, they'd already shot down two Air Force fighter-bombers and a Huey helicopter. Before Beckwith's deployment of his Delta force, the camp was defended by 400 Montagnard tribesmen and their families, a twelve-man U.S. Special Forces A-Team and a Vietnamese Special Forces A-Team.

Fifteen American Special Forces and two Ranger companies of approximately 100 men took off from Camp Holloway, heading south to relieve the encircled camp. The LZ Beckwith had earlier chosen on an over-flight, was prepped by two air strikes by bombers and gun ships. On 21 October 1965, at 0900, the small force of Rangers and American Special Forces of Project Delta landed by helicopter about a mile from the besieged camp and began moving overland to enjoin the fight. A young officer and Ranger company advisor, CPT Thomas Pusser, was among the Americans deployed with them. Beckwith personally led the air-assault.

Successful in maneuvering around NVA positions, but concerned that they might be mistaken for the enemy in the darkness, Beckwith decided to enter the camp the following morning. Under cover of darkness just before dawn, they stealthily approached the camp and broke for the main gate, taking the enemy by surprise. Still, a Ranger lieutenant and an American news photographer were killed, and several others wounded. Almost immediately after arriving inside the camp, Beckwith received orders to send his unit outside the wire to locate and destroy the enemy's anti-aircraft and artillery firing positions.

"Major, I want you to get outside the camp . . . clear the enemy out of there," COL Bill McKean told him.

"Sir, that's not a good idea," Beckwith replied.

"I don't care, Major," was McKean's reply. "I'm ordering you."

Beckwith knew his officers well and, with serious misgivings about the operation, sent his best officer, CPT Thomas Pusser, along with the stronger of the two Ranger elements. Pusser had expressed a desire to command the weaker company—he'd been worried about it and had wanted to "keep it moving." On his second Vietnam tour, Pusser once

Plei Me Special Forces Camp, 1965. *L to R*: CPT Tom Pusser (KIA); LT Julie Klebaum, 8th Army Field Hospital, Dong Ba; "Thin" (the monkey); CPT Leonard "Greek" Boulas

was questioned by a friend as to why he wanted to go back. Pusser had replied, "It was hard before, and this time will be harder. But, I might as well do it as anybody else. I have no wife or children, and those are wonderful people over there. At first they don't trust you, but once you've won their trust, they'll give their lives for you."

Beckwith comments in his book, *Delta Force*, "In the afternoon, we mounted up both Ranger companies. Captain Thomas Pusser, a West Pointer I thought a lot of, was the adviser to the Vietnamese Rangers."

Beckwith's strategy was to first clear the northern slope; most of the firing was coming from there. The NVA waited patiently until both companies reached points outside the encampment and then popped up from well-dug holes, hitting the Ranger elements with the full force of automatic fire and mortars. Fourteen were killed, including Thomas Pusser, who was gunned down while leading an assault against an enemy machinegun nest. Pusser had been directing the action, encouraging his Vietnamese Rangers to maintain fire discipline. The enemy had his troops pinned down; they were in danger of total annihilation when he led his charge. Many others had been wounded, so Beckwith pulled his battered force back inside the camp and hunkered down for a long difficult siege.

During his radio messages, Beckwith estimated the camp was under attack by "2,000 to 3,000 enemy troops…two to three NVA regiments." News of the fierce prolonged attacks came to the attention of President Lyndon Johnson, and on 23 October, he sent a message to the defenders: "We're thinking about you. Hold out as long as you can. God bless you all."

On 24 October, with the siege in full swing and Beckwith laboring to strengthen the camp's fortifications, the American element of the task force decided to run a dangerous operation to recover Pusser's body from where it had fallen outside the defensive wire. The senior Vietnamese Ranger Commander, Major Tut, had been adamant that he and his troops would be the ones to recover the body of his young American friend. Tut was insistent. "No. We will go. The Vietnamese soldiers will recover Captain Pusser. He was our advisor and died on the field of battle with honor and courage, fighting for us and with us. He is ours. We will do it."

This time they were ready for the enemy's resistance, and braving intense fire, were successful in their endeavor without further loss of life. The following day, the weather cleared enough for the Air Force to send in fighter bombers—these broke the enemy's back. On 25 October 1965, the siege of Plei Me came to an end. Captain Tom Pusser, soft-spoken southern gentleman, exemplary West Point cadet and pride of Chesterfield, SC, proved to be a dedicated leader and heroic Army officer. Along with others who lost their lives during that operation, he remains on the Project Delta rolls as KIA, forever etched into the memories of his brothers. A Delta warrior, he epitomized those who unselfishly died for a cause they believed in, even if that cause had not been supported by others in the United States. For his heroism, Captain Thomas Pusser was awarded the Silver Star. Buried in the Pusser family plot in the Chesterfield Cemetery, the words on his stone are powerful in their simplicity: "Rest in Peace, Tom. Well Done."

Staff Sergeant Jimmie L. McBynum was another among those killed conducting operations against hostile forces on the Plei Me operation, which continued intermittently into early 1966 with even more losses. Beckwith, was so severely wounded he was sent back to the U.S. for treatment. Seven other Silver Stars were awarded from those tenacious battles: MAJ Charles Beckwith, MAJ Charles H. Thompson, CPT A. J. "Bo" Baker, SFC Marion C. Hollaway, SFC Robert J Wren, SSG Larry R. Dickinson, SGT Terrence SSG "Rolex" Morrone and SGT Ronald L. Robertson.

Beckwith lost so many men during that siege and subsequent operations in the surrounding hills that Project Delta had to temporarily suspend business for several months before suitable replacements could be found. Fortunately, the ranks of Special Forces are filled with men such as these; those who can be counted on to give their best in a dire situation.

* * * * * *

In 1965, the epic battle in the hills of Pleiku and throughout the Ia Drang Valley involved LTC Hal Moore's famed battalion. This battle was recorded by war correspondent Joe Galloway, who co-authored a best-selling book about these events; it became the basis for the screenplay and movie "We Were Soldiers Once...and Young."

The battle for Plei Me had been as costly for the much smaller Special Forces team and Project Delta units as the Ia Drang would prove to be for LTC Moore's 1st Cav Battalion. The reason was clear. Subsequent intelligence reports reported both LTC Moore's Battalion and the Special Forces troops at Plei Me faceD the same crack NVA units. Joe Galloway, who would write of Moore's brave exploits, also documented the earlier conflict at the Plei Me camp. Hearing about the Special Forces camp under siege, he talked his way into the area despite his awareness that another news photographer had been killed attempting to infiltrate with Beckwith and his small Delta group.

Galloway had barely missed out on finagling himself into that action, but he knew a lot of people and was respected by the combat community. So, he went looking for favors. Stomping in frustration, Galloway caught the eye of CPT Ray Burns, 119th Aviation Company.

"Why so pissed, Joe?"

Galloway played poker and had been known to drink Jim Beam with the 119th guys, so he knew most of them pretty well.

Major Charlie Beckwith (*left*), Commander of B-52 Project Delta, and war correspondent Joe Galloway, during the siege of Plei Me Camp, October 1965. (Photo courtesy of Joe Galloway)

"I've been trying to get to Plei Me, a Special Forces camp near the border that's been catching hell. Looks like it'll all be over before I can get there."

Burns had him wait while he checked the clipboard at Flight Ops. He returned, only to tell Galloway what he already knew—the airspace around Plei Me was closed to traffic. Then Burns grinned. "I'd kinda like to see the place myself, so if you want to ride along...."

Galloway was on his way.

At Plei Me, to avoid machinegun fire from the enemy positions ringing the camp, Burns literally dropped his chopper as if he'd run out of gas. Galloway bailed out as it touched down, simultaneously with the arrival of some camp defenders placing their wounded aboard. Through the Plexiglas cockpit window, Ray Burns grinned, flipping him the bird as he shot away. A young sergeant ran toward him, cupped his hands around his mouth and shouted over the racket of Burn's departing chopper, "I don't know who you are, Sir, but Beckwith wants to see you. Now!"

"Who's Beckwith?"

The sergeant grinned, motioning with his thumb over his shoulder. "He's the big guy over there, jumping up and down on his hat."

No novice, Galloway had been around, so he wasn't too concerned that he'd be reporting to the legendary Charging Charlie Beckwith. He decided he'd be respectful…just in case.

"Who the hell are you?" Beckwith growled as approached.

"A reporter, Sir."

No one could beat Beckwith's disgusted look, and the big guy definitely was disgusted. "I need just about everything in this goddamned world: I need reinforcements, I need medical supplies and evacuation helicopters, I need ammunition, I need food, I would dearly love a bottle of Jim Beam whiskey and some good cigars. And what has the Army in its infinite wisdom sent me? A reporter. A goddamned reporter! Well, I'll tell you what, son. I have no vacancies for a reporter, but I do have one for a machinegunner. And I've got some more really bad news for you. You're it!

"Uh…me?"

"Follow me." Beckwith headed off without looking back.

He led Galloway to a sandbagged corner of the trench-line and gave him a short lesson in the care, loading and firing of the M-1919A6, .30-caliber, air-cooled light-machinegun. All Galloway really knew was that it was dark, ugly and menacing. Beckwith explained how to un-jam it, just in case, and how to arm it with new belts of ammo stacked nearby. His directions, simple and direct: "You can shoot the little brown men outside the wire; they are the enemy. You may not shoot the little brown men inside the wire; they are mine."

Galloway spent the next three days hunkered in the muddy trench beside his dark, ugly, menacing weapon, with the enemy unrelenting in their efforts to kill the camp's defenders. On 23 October 1965, the Air Force found a break in the ceiling, dropped supplies inside the camp, and followed up with massive bombing runs. Later in the day, a South Vietnamese armored column arrived. The NVA had endured enough and left, leaving behind the never-to-be-forgotten smell of human flesh rotting and baking in the hot tropical sun. The following morning, the sky blanketed with U.S. Army helicopters, the 1st Air Cav arrived to sweep the surrounding hills of any remaining enemy. Eager to join the hunt, Galloway went to tell Beckwith goodbye.

"You done a good job," Beckwith told him simply. "Where's your weapon?"

"I'm a reporter," Galloway answered. "I don't carry a weapon. I'm what they call a non-combatant."

Beckwith smirked, and then spotted one of his NCOs. "Sergeant, bring me an M-16 and some loaded magazines."

He handed the weapon and several magazines to Galloway. "In these mountains there ain't no such thing as a non-combatant, Son. Take the rifle."

Galloway took the rifle and slung it over his shoulder, hurrying to catch up with Hal Moore's battalion of the 1st Cav Division. It was now their time to make military history.[25]

* * * * * *

Joseph L. Galloway resides in Arlington, Virginia and works in Washington, D.C.; he frequently travels for speaking engagements. Soon to retire, he has a retreat planned near Copano Bay on the Texas coast. "I have a lifetime deficit to catch up on," Joe says, "…fishing and bird hunting." Joe Galloway is the only civilian decorated by the military for bravery in the Vietnam War. The United States Army awarded him the Bronze Star Medal for valor. Joe managed to come closer to the fighting than any other reporter, and he reported the truth. He'll forever remain a part of the Army family.

---

[25] Joseph L. Galloway. *A Combat Reporter Remembers the Siege at Plei Me,* http://www.projectdelta.net/plei_mei.htm

SEVEN

Stay Out of the An Loa Valley

ON 29 DECEMBER 1965, B-52 PROJECT DELTA was alerted to support the 1st U.S. Infantry Division near Bien Hoa on Operation Crimp. Aware the area was hotly contested, Delta began celebrating New Years Eve as if they had just been given a few days off. On 30 Dec 1965, Detachment B-52 departed Nha Trang with three recon teams, each composed of three Americans and two Nungs. Upon arrival at the 1st Infantry Division FOB, the division staff generally decided their capabilities would be better served if they supported the much larger Operation Mallet. It had been programmed into five separate phases; its ultimate objective the clearing of Highway 15 of VC and NVA, from Bein Hoa to Vung Tau. Due to the operation's extended time span and the extensive area covered, even more recon teams would be utilized, if available. On 4 January 1966, three additional Delta teams arrived at Di An.

Delta had its standard mission: First, to conduct detailed reconnaissance and report intelligence information within their Tactical Area of Recon

(TAOR). Secondly, place surveillance on identified or suspected enemy units, activities and installations, with the objective of acquiring targets for air, artillery and troop exploitation. POWs would be a plus.

The initial six recon teams quickly grew to nine, as the division's graduating Recon School class supplemented Delta for the rapidly expanding mission. Supporting the nine teams would be the 145th Aviation Platoon (Project Delta), 2 USAF FAC aircraft (Project Delta), and one company-size reaction force (2nd Brigade, 1st U.S. Infantry Division). Delta's Ranger Battalion was not available for use as the reaction force due to other commitments. The Division's reaction force would only be used if a Delta recon team became compromised and had to be extracted by force, under fire. At the onset, Delta staff had serious misgivings about not being able to use their own Rangers— their skepticism proved to be well founded. It was only after the mission was underway that they learned the 1st Infantry Division had no plans to exploit targets discovered by the teams. Beckwith was livid, and expressed his frustration with the 1st Division staff. What was the purpose of locating enemy targets if they couldn't be exploited by a reaction force? It placed his men in jeopardy, and for no good reason. Regrettably, this Division staff's conventional mindset led to disaster. Lucrative targets were discovered and reported, but nothing was done; this shortcoming led to one of Delta's bloodiest operations.

Recon Team-1, SFC Marcus L. Hudson (Team Leader), SFC Robert K. Price, SFC Robert P. Whitis and two Nungs, infiltrated at dusk. They reported several well-armed enemy, and after completing their assigned mission, were extracted without hostile contact. Recon Team-2, SFC David W. Disharoon (Team Leader), Billy McKeith, Norman Dupuis and two Nungs, also infiltrated without enemy contact, but reported extensive enemy activity as they covertly moved toward their objective. On several occasions they held up to allow small enemy units to pass; the sound of barking dogs led the patrol to conclude the enemy was using canines in their search.

Two days into the operation, Disharoon's team, Recon Team-2, came across a stationary VC unit dug into a densely wooded hillside. They called for napalm and a 750-pound bomb air strike, which nearly annihilated the enemy platoon. As the air strike echoes faded, Recon Team-2 withdrew to a secure location to set up a cold camp for the night. Throughout the evening, they observed torch flares and detected voices, assuming the VC trackers were searching for them. They moved out at first light, silently, cautiously. Always primed for immediate action, for several hours they saw no one. Then about noon, on a small trail in dense vegetation, they encountered six VC preparing lunch. This chance meeting forced them to open fire, killing five, seriously wounding one. Considering his team compromised, SFC Disharoon decided to withdraw to the extraction point and call for pickup. By radio, he contacted the FOB, requesting an immediate airlift, directing his point man to proceed toward the extraction point.

An even larger surprise was in store for them—an estimated fifty soldiers had surrounded the LZ, waiting to ambush any extraction aircraft. Realizing helicopters were on the way, the team knew they had to engage the enemy and secure the LZ before the choppers arrived. Normally, it would be pretty gutsy for any six-man recon element to fire-up a company of seasoned NVA soldiers, but they had no choice. Disharoon placed his small team on line, waiting silently until the choppers came into view before opening fire. His team members recall how surprised the enemy was, initially disorganized by the devastating automatic fire raining on them. But as seasoned NVA regulars, they recovered quickly. In a matter of minutes, Recon Team-2 was in a life and death struggle. Nearby, extraction choppers circled while gunships pounded the LZ, then skirted low and hovered to pick them up during a lull in the fighting. The experienced WO3 pilot was a familiar sight, for he had pulled them from dangerous situations before; he held the chopper steady as the team scampered aboard under a renewed hail of enemy gunfire. Sergeant First Class Disharoon saw to it that his team boarded first, and he was last to leave. The accompanying gunships again swooped in, their mini-guns and machineguns rattling, forcing the enemy to fall back to seek cover in the jungle. Disorganized firing continued to pepper the chopper until they were well away. Once safely airborne and beyond range, Disharoon called in a tactical air strike on the LZ. Navy planes arrived within minutes, killing or wounding many of the enemy with napalm canisters. Remarkably, Recon Team-2 suffered no friendly casualties during these encounters. Disharoon was awarded the Silver Star for valor for his personal acts of bravery.

Five of the six teams deployed during this operation made enemy contact, describing it as "light to moderate." Reporting numerous enemy sightings, they returned with important intelligence on VC and NVA units. After Action Reports indicate that recon teams had been in just as much danger of being fired upon by friendly troops and divisional air support as from the enemy, since the Division repeatedly violated established No Fire Lines (NFL). Frequently, 1st U.S. Division gunships would fly over the teams, forcing them to hide for fear of coming under friendly fire. Still, the Delta Commander figured theywere lucky to get everyone out safely. Their luck was about to change.

Other Recon team members in the An Loa Valley operation:

Recon Team-3: SSG Brooke Bell (Team Leader), 1LT Guy H. Holland II, SSG Charles McDonald, one Nung.

Recon Team-4: SFC Marlin C. Cook (Team Leader), SSG Agostina Chiarello, SFC Donald E. Shautz, one Nung.

Recon Team-5: SSG George A. Hoagland III (Team Leader), SSG Charles F. Hiner, SSG Donald L. Dotson, one Nung.

Recon Team-6: SSG Frank N. Badolati (Team Leader), SSG Roland T. Terry, SGT Charles A. McDonald, two Nungs.

Recon Team-7: SFC Lucius T. Untalan (Team Leader), SSG Charles H. Gray Jr., CPT John P. Sanders (1st Inf Div), SGT Richard H. Finlan (1st Inf Div) and William B. Allen (1st Inf Div).

Recon Team-8: MSG Loyd R. Fisher (Team Leader), 1LT Howard S. Stanfield (1st Inf Div), SSG Walter K. Korber (1st Inf Div) and SGT Clarence E. Pitts (1st Inf Div).

Recon Team-9: SFC Walt Shumate (Team Leader), SFC Marlin Cook, 2LT Fredrick H. Evans (1st Inf Div), SP4 Donald C. Wombough (1s Inf Div) and SSG Willis W. Conley (1st Inf Div).

* * * * * *

In July 1965, as MAJ Art Strange handed off command of Project Delta to Beckwith, one of his parting comments had been, "Stay out of An Lao Valley, Charlie." It was only two months following the Plei Me siege when the admonition returned to haunt Beckwith. Delta had been tasked to support the 1st Air Cav Division in the largest search and destroy operation yet conceived; it would be an extension of the conflict at Plei Me.

Near Bong San, the An Loa Valley hosts some of the most unforgiving combat terrain found in Southeast Asia. Framed by steep mountainous slopes and dense vegetation, intelligence reports testified to dug-in anti-aircraft gun emplacements cleverly concealed along the ridgelines. The valleys were a ground commander's worst nightmare. The cultivated, flooded rice fields, four-foot tall elephant grass and triple-canopy vegetation with high ground on each side, were ideal for ambushes and enemy fortifications. Delta recon teams were fully aware of intelligence indicating the presence of several NVA regiments, supported by hundreds of VC insurgents. They recently had received confirmation of sophisticated warning systems and the enemy's extensive use of tracking dogs. For a six-man recon element, this was not good news.

Delta was given operational areas at the northern end of An Loa Valley, a hotly contested enemy stronghold. Their mission was to provide surveillance of the main supply routes to determine if the VC and NVA units were using them to reinforce or withdraw units engaged with Marine forces. The Marines had been pushing south while the 1st Cav units and Vietnamese Airborne Ranger Brigade pushed north in a pincher movement.

From the start, the operation was plagued with problems. Beckwith had decided against employing his teams with their Vietnamese or Nung team members, the usual practice, because of the 1st Cav Division staff's ardent mistrust of all indigenous personnel. Ground intelligence was unusually scarce, with helicopter and tactical air support limited due to the heavy concentration of anti-aircraft weapons. The weather had also been poor, deteriorating by the hour and to top things off, they were in the enemy's backyard. In the spring of 1948, the French were the last friendly forces to set foot into An Loa Valley; they suffered heavy casualties and withdrew, defeated. Despite these omens, Beckwith asked for volunteers—he had no shortage of men willing to go.

Three teams of six U.S personnel, supported by elements of the 145th Aviation Platoon (Project Delta), readied for insertion into this "valley of death." With so much against it, the mission quickly disintegrated.

Team One, (Eskimo), SFC Al Keating (Team Leader), SFC Whitis, SSG Bell, SSG Norman C. Dupuis and SFC Chiarello, infiltrated at dusk, spending the first night 300 meters from the LZ. Before daybreak, they continued northeast to their objective, arriving at 0900 hours. The treacherous terrain was rough, vertical and wet—the team's uniforms were soaked before moving a hundred feet. Climbing a tree to observe the valley to the east, a weary SFC Keating figured it would be a long five days. From this elevated position, he detected no movement, but that didn't mean much. Dense fog began to blanket the valley and within minutes movement became extremely dangerous. Keating decided to risk it, traveling farther to the north where he thought the team might be in closer proximity to the trails leading in; where they could hear traffic along the trails. Edging silently forward, his weapon always at the ready, Keating and his point man, SSG Dupuis, simultaneously caught sight of three armed VC a few meters ahead.

As the man in front raised his weapon to fire, both Keating and Dupuis fired, killing him instantly. When another grabbed his fallen comrade's rifle and rapidly fired off two rounds, Dupuis lofted a hand grenade in his direction—the firing ceased. Keating motioned for his team to stay down and threw another grenade; this time another VC fell from the bushes. Uncertain as to what they might be up against, Keating motioned for Chiarello and Whitis to flank the right as he and the others cautiously inched forward, their rifles combat ready. It was apparent that the man on the trail was dead, but then they discovered two bloody paths leading into the jungle. That would account for all three VC, but they wouldn't know if the two might live long enough to report the patrol's presence. This did not bode well for Recon Team-5.

Keating decided to keep moving north with his original plan, trying to evade if a larger VC unit picked up their trail. As he prepared to signal his team forward again, he was held up by a soft whistle.

"Hey Al…hold up. I've been hit."

It was Dupius. His head oozed blood; his dazed eyes stared back at Keating as he examined him. Dupuis had been struck by grenade shrapnel above his left ear.

"You okay to go on?" Keating asked.

"To tell the truth, Al, I'm dizzier than hell. I don't know if I can take the point any longer, but I'm not going back."

Keating hated to take him off point, but under the circumstances he had little choice. He moved Dupuis to a spot farther back, and told Bell to take over as point man. Bell was a solid trooper, and Keating knew he'd do a good job. They moved out quickly for about 500 meters, anxious to vacate the area where they had caused so much havoc. Safely away, the small patrol stopped, intently listening for any pursuit. Hearing nothing to alarm them, they attempted to make radio contact, but the bad weather and atmospheric conditions interfered. Heading north along the ridgeline, the patrol began to observe heavily trafficked trails, making each step forward more dangerous. Because the trails generally traversed northeast to southwest, Keating decided to take his patrol west to avoid the more heavily traveled routes. The last thing he needed was to come head-to-head with a large enemy unit, unable to contact the FOB for help. He tried to make radio contact again, but failed. Six men in enemy territory and, as usual, on their own.

Higher in this new location, the team detected cultivated rice fields through the shifting fog patterns. They spotted numerous huts in the valley, but observed no inhabitants—this seemed odd. Keating paused long enough to attempt another radio contact with the FOB, and this time reached the Air Relay in their approximate area. The pilot tried to pinpoint their position for nearly two hours, but the weather was still so poor he finally had to give up. He informed Keating he had to leave to refuel but would return in about an hour to try again. Within the hour the pilot returned, and the weather had cleared sufficiently for him to see the team's deployed orange panel. He directed Recon Team-1 to an LZ 300 meters away. One-by-one, they left the blackness of the jungle floor, climbed the rope ladder to safety and were extracted just before dark.

EIGHT

"Hang On, Recon... We're Coming to Get You."

RECON TEAM-2 WOULDN'T BE AS LUCKY as Keating's team. The team consisted of SFC Frank R. Webber Jr. (Team Leader), SFC Marlin C. Cook, SFC Jesse L. Hancock, SSG Charles F. Hiner, SSG George A. Hoagland and SSG Donald L. Dotson. Infiltrating at dusk on 27 January 1966, they spent their first day trying to avoid woodchoppers and minor foot traffic; no enemy contact was made that day. The next day out, they came across a vacant old hut adjacent to a hard-packed trail. Webber decided to avoid the trail, instead heading into the relative safety of the trees. Continuing to move parallel to the ridge, a small stream came into view, and he decided he'd let his weary troops pause for lunch. The lunch break was more valuable for psychological recovery than to abate hunger pangs, but still proved to be a smart move. After the brief pause, the team seemed more alert, more relaxed.

Movement became increasingly stressful, as the woodcutters' chopping sounds and voices periodically drifted to them. They knew not only the farmers needed firewood; the VC needed vast amounts for their cooking fires to feed large numbers of men. Frequently, they'd spotted men in black shorts or pajamas, the accepted attire of both the local farmers and VC soldiers. It didn't matter. Anyone in this area was considered to be sympathetic to the enemy. Sensing a group of woodcutters might have spotted them despite their attempts at concealment, they withdrew deeper into the dense vegetation, distancing themselves from the main trail. Movement was rough; they often crawled through the thick underbrush where they'd be less likely to come upon on an enemy force. Without warning they broke through into a "buffalo wallow," an area devoid of triple canopy, with only a few ten-foot-tall scrub trees. Webber felt he needed to get the team across fast. They moved through the middle swiftly, trying to return to the jungle cover as quickly as possible.

Instinctively, he felt their luck begin to sour. As soon as they cleared the open area and had reached a grove of banana trees, a dog began to bark—they were near a village. His point man froze in place, rifle at the ready. He looked toward Webber, his expression an unspoken question. Webber urgently pointed north, his fingers making a rapid walking motion. The point man quickly led them away from the barking dog. Leaving the open area, they were startled by banging on a metal basin less than 200 hundred yards away. They sensed it was a prearranged signal; the beat had a definite pattern, begininning, pausing and beginning again in the same tempo. Webber grew anxious about their evolving situation. The banging continued until they moved beyond hearing distance.

Cautiously, the team remained alert for potential contact as they crossed heavily used trails. They continued to hear voices, but not enough to know whether others were looking for them or just conducting daily business. It was easy to get spooked in these situations and no one wanted to cry wolf, leaving before their mission was completed. Besides, just the act of calling for extraction might place them in even more danger. They hadn't found anyplace suitable for a chopper to set down, so they would have to be hoisted out by rope ladder or McGuire Rig—either would be dicey, particularly if enemy units were nearby.

Webber paused, held up he team. Gathering everyone close, they discussed the situation in whispers and decided to hole up for the night and let the activity die down. They felt certain they had been compromised; if not by the woodcutters, then by those banging on the pot. The point led them into a thick grove of thorn bushes that would be their home for the evening. Inside, before settling in, they discussed strategy. Webber thought they should traverse the main north-south route, heading south toward a small village—he'd pointed to it on the map. After conferring, they all agreed that upon reaching the village, the team would split; three remaining to observe, the remainder continuing south to a better vantage point where they could see most of the valley and gather more intelligence. The team liked this idea, for if they ran into trouble they would be closer to the valley floor and more open areas for the extraction choppers.

They slept little, ready to move again at first light. The weather had deteriorated; a drenching rain greeted their day, along with some heavy fog that provided zero visibility. Making matters worse, they soon encountered very difficult terrain, heavy undergrowth and large slippery rocks. Having started the day without food, at around 1000 hours they finally stopped to eat. The team anxiously eyed their surroundings, hardly tasting the indigenous LRRP rations, careful to maintain tactical silence. Only upon getting under way again, did they realized they had stopped a mere thirty feet from a main trail. The vegetation was so compact that they were completely unaware of the trail. Cautiously crossing the trail, they turned south toward the village where they agreed to eventually split up. They had only advanced a few minutes before they hit unusually rough terrain, and a severe drop-off; Webber had no choice but to turn west.

They traveled on for thirty minutes, when, without warning, they broke into a fifty-by-twenty-yard clearing, devoid of any underbrush, but littered with large rocks, three to four feet in diameter. The precarious terrain and poor weather made concentrated listening nearly impossible. Webber halted the patrol for a five-minute break and to check activity. The order of march had been SSG Hiner, on point, then Hancock, Webber, Cook, Dotson and Hoagland. In this sequence they entered the open area, settling into a hasty defensive position. Immediately, the jungle vibrated with automatic weapons fire from only a few yards away.

Webber heard a yell, "Sonofabitch!" followed by a loud groan.

The undergrowth was too thick for them to see their adversary, but it was only moments before they'd taken a deadly toll on the small patrol.

Hiner had estimated the enemy to be platoon-sized, twenty to thirty men. When the firing first broke out, Hoagland, Hancock, Cook and Webber were hit almost instantly. Hoagland, the most seriously wounded, lay motionless after the initial burst. Webber watched as he crumpled onto his back, but was left with an impression that he was still alive. Hancock died instantly. Cook took a round in his back and fell forward; he called out that he couldn't move his legs. Though badly wounded, he remained lucid enough to pour deadly fire into the enemy's position.

Webber's left arm had been shattered below the elbow; it was useless, so he continued to fire using only one hand. Hiner and Dotson were the only two unscathed by the initial burst. While under intense fire, Hiner scurried to the top of a small rise to better blanket the area. Cook, paralyzed, called out for Hiner to return, to retrieve the radio from his rucksack. As Hiner started back, Webber, despite his critical wounds, covered him, suppressing enemy fire long enough for him to reach Cook's position. He dropped beside Cook, who, although mortally wounded, continued to steadily fire his M-16. Retrieving the radio from Cook's backpack, Hiner crawled to Webber's position behind a large rock to attempt radio contact.

Hiner worked the radio while Webber, dragging his useless arm, crawled forward, past Cook, to a point where his fire would be more effective on the enemy's position. Hiner got the radio to work, answered almost immediately by a C-47 aircraft in the area. After Webber assumed his new position near Cook, Hiner called on Dotson to occupy his previous position on the small hill. Dotson grinned, gave him thumbs up, but had only advanced ten feet before hit in the chest; he fell, killed instantly.

The C-47 aircraft Hiner had contacted relayed their information to a FAC, piloted by USAF Captain Kenneth L. Kerr, call sign "Robin One." Kerr called Hiner immediately, requesting the team's location; Hiner provided his coordinates and a quick summary of their situation. Robin One replied that he had two Huey gunships en-route to their location.

"Hang on," Kerr told him. "Just a little while longer."

Clouds frequently obscured the mountains of the Central Highlands making low-altitude flying treacherous, attempted only in dire circumstances by the most experienced pilots. The visibility had become so poor that Robin One had to lead in the gunships. Hiner threw a yellow smoke canister but they couldn't see it—then a red one. He heard the FAC pass low through the swirling clouds.

"I see it," Robin One finally reported. "Where do you want it?"

"Just put your stuff fifty meters around this clearing," Hiner replied. "There aren't any good guys further out than that."

During this time, the VC firing continued, heavy to sporadic. After the gunships made one pass, the firing briefly paused, only to commence again—this time, heavily from every direction. The team was effectively surrounded. Hiner surmised the VC knew the recon team would be trying to get out, so they'd be intent on inflicting as much damage as possible, or in capturing them before a rescue could be made. Growing desperate, he demanded the FAC have the gunships make a pass through the middle of the team's position. After initial resistance they agreed, and although he and Webber remained down, Hiner had been hit in the head by shrapnel from their fire and was barely conscious. Weak and lightheaded, his ears ringing, he heard the FAC advising him the gunships were out of ordnance and they'd be leaving, but others were on the way.

"Hang on," Robin One urged.

"You keep saying that."

"Can you make it to an LZ?" Robin One inquired.

"Negative. We're all either dead or wounded so badly we can't move. See if you can get some napalm next to this position. Maybe it'll burn an LZ," Hiner said. He felt himself growing weaker.

The FAC garbled something about B-57s being in the pass, or something entirely unrelated, but Hiner, dizzy from shock and blood loss, couldn't comprehend what he was saying.

"The ceiling isn't high enough for the fast-movers to come in this low," he recalled the FAC saying, as he drifted in and out of consciousness. He realized it pertained to them being afraid they might collide in mid-air.

"Can you find a reaction force that will come in to get us? We can't move," Hiner mumbled. He felt instant panic as he wondered where his rifle was, and then realized it was still in his hands. He shook his head, trying to clear it.

Heavy small arms fire erupted at the southeast corner of the clearing. Hiner informed the FAC that he thought they might be overrun at any moment. There were still no gunships in the area. The FAC, despite having no ordnance on board, decided to buzz the area to fool the VC into believing air cover was still overhead, forcing their heads down until the gunships arrived. It was clearly a gutsy maneuver for a small, unarmed, fixed-wing aircraft, yet on more than one occasion the FACs had put their lives on the line to get recon teams out of trouble. They knew these guys; they considered it all in a day's work.

Webber, huddled near Cook, suddenly shouted, "Grenade!"

He fired off a quick burst at a man wearing a red star on his baseball cap; hammering him backward. Although the grenade was of the old "potato masher" type and didn't have the bursting radius of the U.S. variety, Webber still decided to retreat from the edge of the clearing. As he passed Cook, he picked him up with his one good arm and carried him to the rock where Hiner waited beside the radio. Cook was alive but unable to speak, his eyes glazed from pain and shock.

Webber injected him with a shot of morphine and watched as relief washed over his features. Then he gave one to himself. Webber was weak from shock and blood loss, yet kept watch as Hiner wrapped a field dressing around his shattered arm. Pale and ready to pass out, Webber was fading quickly. Hiner hoped he'd remain conscious; there were only the two of them left in case the enemy charged their position. Hiner looked up at the roar overhead—the gunships were back.

"Give me some smoke," one of the pilots radioed.

"I'm out of smoke grenades," Hiner replied. "Wait."

Under intense fire, he staggered to the position where Hancock had fallen, retrieved a smoke canister from his dead comrade's backpack, then returned, pulled the pin and flipped it behind him.

"Hit everything within fifty meters of the smoke…360 degrees, all around."

Simultaneously, gunships came from four directions. The one approaching from the east misjudged his path and strafed the team's position, right down the middle. Hiner and Webber huddled together behind the rock, saving them. Hiner recollected that he didn't know if Cook had been killed during that run, or if he'd died earlier, but when they checked, he'd stopped breathing. They were both certain their time had come—they were out of options and lacked strength to fight much longer. All they could hope for was that, those nasty gunships would kill the enemy.

Through a deepening haze, Hiner heard the FAC speak, advising someone that the whole team was either wounded or dead, but needed help ASAP. As his mind became sluggish he couldn't tell if the conversation had actually happened—he didn't care. In a panic, he couldn't find his rifle trigger and then relaxed as he located it. He vaguely wondered how many rounds might be in his magazine; he didn't have the strength to check.

"Stay with me, Recon. The reaction force is on the way," the FAC said, his voice cutting through Hiner's fog.

Hiner may have mumbled something in reply—he couldn't remember. All of them had been in tough spots before, but with Webber so weak from blood loss that he could barely remain upright, and his own disorientation from his head wound, they'd given up hope of getting out of it this time. Hiner suddenly realized how silent it had become. All firing had ceased and the two men's eyes locked. Each silently wondered if the VC might be crawling toward their position. While they could only pray the VC had had enough of the gunships and pulled back, they really didn't believe it. Using grit and determination, Hiner used his rifle to pull himself up. His legs wobbling, he quickly scanned the edge of the clearing for enemy activity, then impervious to any surrounding danger, moved among the bodies of his fallen brothers, checking each for signs of life, collecting any ammunition they hadn't had the chance to fire. Webber was awake and lucid when he returned to the relative safety of the large rock, but just barely. He and Hiner prepared themselves for the end. They laid out all their ammunition and grenades, checked their loads and settled in to wait for the enemy assault, convinced it was inevitable. It could come again at any moment, but they were as ready as possible. The two men agreed they wouldn't be leaving alive, but when the VC came back, hell would be waiting for them.

Hiner radioed the FAC with what he figured would be his final report. He listened as the FAC resumed his urgent call for any reaction force that could hear him. Hiner drifted off briefly, then came back, dizzy and nauseous. He heard the FAC saying, "Come in Recon. Answer me! Hold on. The reaction force is on the way."

"Better hurry. Tell them to drop a rope ladder on top of us," Hiner said groggily. "We won't be going anywhere."

Photo taken by SFC Webber before insertion into An Loa Valley. *L to R*: SSG Donald Dotson (KIA), SFC Jesse Hoagland (KIA), SFC Marlin Cook (KIA), SFC Jesse Hancock (KIA), SSG Charles Hiner (WIA). (Photo courtesy of Jim Spooner)

Instantly, the FAC came back on. He related that 1LT Guy Holland and his Rangers were on the ground, within 300 meters of their location. He told Hiner to throw smoke and then fire three shots in the air so Holland could locate his position. Hiner feebly threw the smoke while Webber fired three times; it was all the strength they had left. A 1st Air Cav gunship nosed its way into the clearing and hovered above them, standing guard while guiding the Delta reaction force in. Hiner looked up once, saw the chopper pilot grin and give him thumbs up. It was the only moment Hiner felt he and Webber might actually get out alive. He recalled the helicopter pilot also pointed in the direction of the reaction force and within ten minutes, 1LT Holland's Rangers broke through the trees. Jesse Hancock, Donald Dotson, Marlin Cook and George Hoagland all died that day in the jungle clearing. Charles Hiner and Frank Webber eventually recovered from their wounds.

Webber, initially transported to a hospital ship then returned to the States, said, "Staff Sergeant Hiner continuously exposed himself to enemy automatic fire to recover that radio, and then, although wounded in the head, he directed air strikes around and on our position throughout the conflict. I feel that without Hiner's heroic actions, none of us would've come back." Hiner sufficiently recovered to run more recons, and for his actions in An Loa Valley he received the Bronze Star for valor. Many believed his award inadequate.

NINE

"Greater Love Has No Man Than This, That He Lay Down His Life for His Friends."

- John 15:13

RECON TEAM-3 (ROAD RUNNER) WAS ALREADY on the ground while Hiner's and Webber's patrol was being decimated. They had infiltrated at dusk on 27 January, with SFC Marcus L. Huston leading the patrol. With him were MSG Wiley W. Gray, SFC Cecil J. Hodgson, SSG Billy A. McKeith, SSG Ronald T. Terry and SSG Frank Badolati. The weather was poor and deteriorating as the chopper dropped them off and then disappeared into the evening's fading light. Once on the ground, Huston led out rapidly. He kept the team moving for 200 meters before deciding the terrain was too rough, and the darkness made it impossible to travel further. They set up a cold camp in the rain, made radio contact with the FOB and waited anxiously for daylight. At daybreak, the patrol proceeded northeast until it hit a trail adjacent to a small stream. Moving higher up the ridge, from this new vantage point they observed fresh dirt piles beside the trees. Huston posted Hodgson twenty meters further down and the others off to one side so they wouldn't be surprised from the rear. Respecting Frank Badolati's experience and jungle-tested knowledge, Huston took him along to gather intelligence and to search for recently prepared bunkers. They discovered the hill saturated with firing positions—it was clear the dirt was fresh.

Huston and Badolati had just returned to rejoin the team, when Hodgson suddenly opened fire from his position below them. Huston immediately pulled him back as he and Badolati covered Hodgson's withdrawal with automatic fire. Although unsure of the effectiveness of their own fire, they discovered Hodgson had killed the first two VC in the file, wounding at least another. After detecting voices and hasty movements behind them, Huston instructed his team to move out rapidly, cross the stream and quickly get up the other hill while he covered their rear. If they were being chased, Huston couldn't tell, so he rejoined the team within a few minutes. Realizing their situation was desperate, he sought a defensible location where he could use the radio. Exposed, his mission already compromised, Huston decided to ask for immediate extraction.

Continuing slowly and cautiously, they noticed the hill was saturated with individual fighting positions and machinegun posts. Woven baskets, food and hanging clothing all indicated the area was still occupied; they realized they were in the midst of a large, unidentified NVA unit. Whispering urgently, Huston told the others not to pick up anything for fear it might be booby-trapped. Their senses tingled as they made their way through the danger zone. Huston knew they were in grave trouble, but he was determined to get his team out as quickly as possible.

Terry, bringing up the rear, moved forward and whispered, "There's a large bunch of 'em coming up on us fast. I saw maybe thirty or forty moving up the trail behind us."

Huston's fears were justified, and they'd have to move fast to evade their pursuers. The team traveled briskly for a couple of hours, hoping to locate a good spot to stop, make radio contact and request extraction. All but giving up on finding a defensible position, Huston finally called for a break on the side of a heavily wooded hill to attempt radio contact. They paused less than five minutes when a hail of gunfire rained down on them, from not more than fifty meters above. Badolati was instantly hit in the left upper arm with a force that nearly severed it. The impact knocked him past Huston, but he was able to maintain his foothold and continued downhill, through the trees. Simultaneously, just as Badolati was struck, a round knocked Hodgson's rifle from his hands with such force that he landed on his back. Stunned, he blankly stared up at Huston.

"You hit?" Huston asked, calmly firing uphill.

"No."

"Well? Move out then!"

Huston, McKeith and Gray ferociously returned fire, forcing the enemy to seek cover. He motioned the team to move farther down the hill, remaining behind to cover their withdrawal. Then he and Billy McKeith leapfrogged, covering each other until they could break contact. Hodgson, his rifle blown from his hands, was armed with only a 9mm pistol; Huston told him to assist Badolati, who, with his severed arm dangling precariously, was in severe pain. Badolati asked for morphine, and in the coming hours he received four more doses. Although it failed to completely diminish his pain, he never complained.

Huston planned to move north, then west beyond their operational area, then again to the south to re-enter near their emergency rendezvous point. They managed to continue 200 hundred meters without further enemy contact—then hit a rock wall approximately three-feet high and eighteen-inches thick. It would provide a good barrier to attend to Badolati's arm, as well as a stronger defensive position if still being chased, and he felt certain they were. In any event, he hoped the wall's concealment would allow the team to hurt their pursuers badly enough that they'd break off, permitting more time to reach a suitable extraction LZ. Just as they settled into their new location, a hail of fire came from the woods behind; everyone immediately returned fire. This firing continued for several minutes, both sides pouring fusillades into the other's position. Deafening grenade concussions shook the ground. Through all the smoke and confusion, Huston suddenly realized three members of his team were missing; Wiley Gray, Ron Terry and Cecil Hodgson. Only he, McKeith and Badolati remained behind the wall of stone. Huston sprayed the area with a long burst of automatic fire, helped

Into the An Loa Valley. *L to R*: MSG Wiley Gray (WIA), SFC Cecil Hodgson (KIA), SSG Billy McKeith, SSG Frank Badolati (MIA), SSG Ronald Terry (MIA). (Photo courtesy of Jim Spooner)

Badolati up and began to move up the ridgeline while McKeith covered for him. He and McKeith took turns assisting Badolati, who was weak and deteriorating quickly. Just like a bloodhound on a hot trail, their pursuers weren't about to give up; they stayed close, sporadically peppering them with fire. Huston handed off a CS grenade to McKeith, who tossed it behind into the direct path of their pursuers. The blast slowed the pursuit for a few valuable minutes.

Listening intently for the sounds of aircraft, but hearing only the persistent buzz of flies, Wiley Gray contemplated his situation in a patch of elephant grass. In the confusion, he and the others had become separated from Huston at the rock wall, and he had no idea where they were. Being the senior man in his small group, he felt a heavy responsibility to ensure they all made it out alive. Since their split from Huston, Badolati and McKeith, he'd become disoriented, the brush and trees making it difficult to determine their exact location. As soon as he felt safe to stand and shoot a couple azimuths with his compass, he'd be able to use his map to intersect some prominent terrain features. Once he knew where they were, he could find their predestined rendezvous point.

By late afternoon, although they'd been able to evade the enemy, it was apparent the Viet Cong and NVA units were concentrated; he wondered how long his small group could hold out against these odds. Only he and Terry were armed with M-16 rifles because Hodgson's had been lost when Badolati was wounded. Hodgson had only his 9mm pistol, and they were all critically low on ammunition. The outcome didn't look promising, but they'd been in these situations before. Gray knew if they kept their heads, and reached an opening where a helicopter or FAC could be flagged down with their florescent orange panels or a flare, they could make it out alive. Unfortunately, the NVA also knew they'd be looking for a clear LZ and had been covering the one they selected.

Master Sergeant Wiley W. Gray was a lanky but athletic 6'2". Moviestar handsome with a devastating smile, he could've stepped out of a Special Forces recruitment poster. But with his two friends, thousands of miles from home, he'd been precariously evading a determined foe trying their level best to kill him. Actually, this was right where he wanted to be—well, perhaps not precisely at this moment, but with his Delta buddies, doing what they all did. He'd had several chances to leave, but couldn't quite bring himself to do it. Not yet. So, here he was, in a predicament. He glanced at Ron Terry seemingly dozing in the grass beside him.

Gray suppressed a grin, thinking here we are, deep in enemy territory, with thousands of Ho Chi Minh's boys scouring the bushes dead-set on killing us, without any communication, very little ammo and only a slight chance of getting out alive...and these two guys are catching forty winks. What a bunch! No, he couldn't be anywhere else.

At the stone wall after being overwhelmed by the second VC attack, Wiley Gray and Ron Terry returned fire, depleting most of their magazines. They noticed Hodgson, rapidly firing his pistol, moving west up the hill away from the wall. In the confusion, both he and Terry thought he'd been tailing the rest of the team, so they followed. Only after fifteen minutes of brisk movement, when they stopped to catch their breath, did they discover the team had split. Gray didn't blame Hodgson. He'd probably have done the same if armed only with a pistol.

Later, Hodgson would remark, "Hell, the bad guys have guns that are accurate for more than five-hundred yards. Mine shoots about fifty—give me another rifle and I'll hang around."

Within minutes of leaving the rock barrier, intense firing could be heard 500 meters north; they presumed the others were being extracted under fire. At least they hoped so. Badolati needed a doctor quickly if he was to survive. Concluding they were completely on their own and without radio communications, they continued westerly before reaching a trail junction. A recently dug firing position situated above, commanded a good field of fire in both directions. They took a vote, unanimously agreeing to wait there in the event more of their team had scattered and would join them. They waited several hours; Gray knew they had to move soon.

Suddenly, Gray caught movement down the trail. He slipped the safety off his M-16 as two VC appeared, passing them by a mere five yards. One wore a lightweight "Delta" style poncho. Gray figured it belonged to one of his team, wondering if they'd taken it from a body, or found a discarded rucksack dumped while running. Suppressing a surge of anger, he watched them pass without alerting Terry and Hodgson. He hoped they had outrun their pursuers, but seeing these two convinced him otherwise. Motionless, he pondered alternatives.

The evening before, at about 1900 hours, they decided to head south, toward their designated emergency pickup point. They advanced until it became too dark to see. Through the night they picked up the sounds of troop movements and barking dogs—trackers. Sensing their route to the south was blocked, at first light they struck out westerly toward an alternate pickup point, traveling at a brisk pace for two hours. A hundred yards beyond a trail, they encountered a thick patch of five-foot tall elephant grass. The grass would give them ground cover, yet permit visibility from the air, should an aircraft fly overhead. They remained in the grass, hoping someone would be looking for them.

From their position, lying within an arm's reach of each other, Gray could observe the trail running north and south. Suddenly startled from his speculation by a small sound behind, he couldn't turn for fear of detection. Within a few moments a small enemy force moved right on past them, and except for the sounds of birds, total silence. In late afternoon, Gray again was alerted by a slight sound from his right rear. Slowly turning his head, he observed three VC, dressed in black, lying prone. Four others in khaki stood only a few feet away. By their demeanor, he discerned they weren't going anywhere soon, and as close as they were, it would only be a matter of time before the team was detected. He tapped SGT Terry on his left leg. Instantly alert, Terry opened his eyes then tapped Hodgson. Gray silently indicated they were all to fire together. He rose to his knee, simultaneously firing his M-16 on full automatic. Four were hammered down immediately, but the two remaining stood their ground and returned fire.

"I'm hit!"

It was Terry. He held his right side, the blood oozing between his fingers. His body shook viciously as he took more rounds, then he lay silent. Fighting back rage, he checked Terry and confirmed he was dead. Glancing around hurriedly, Gray couldn't see Hodgson, thinking he could have fired and then quickly moved. Gray knew that he too must move; the VC knew his location and more would come. He scurried about twenty yards deeper into the elephant grass and dropped, facing the rear, waiting in ambush for the VC who were sure to follow. Pistol shots rang out across the trail, then loud gasps, followed by three more rounds from an M-16 rifle—and silence. The pistol shots sounded like a 9mm, which could have been Hodgson's. The M-16 shots might have come from the one the VC recovered from Terry's body. Resigned, Gray acknowledged that Terry and Hodgson were probably both dead, and that he was on his own. At the least, he hoped Huston and McKeith had gotten Badolati out.

* * * * * *

Huston, McKeith and the mortally wounded Badolati, continued south toward their emergency pickup point. Encountering another stream bed, they used it to cover their trail, hoping to throw off the tracker dogs. Once, they observed a helicopter farther up the valley, and watched helplessly as thirty to forty enemy troops moved from their cover to fire on it. Because these men were all well-armed with AK-47 automatic weapons, equipped with web gear and wearing tan caps with yellow stars, Huston knew they were NVA. That fact didn't bode well for getting out alive. Within minutes of the helicopter taking fire, Badolati suddenly stopped and dropped to one knee.

"I'm done. Can't go...any further, guys," he gasped, obviously depleted and in great pain. "Leave me here...get the hell out."

"No way," Huston replied grimly, scanning the trail behind them. "We're all getting out."

"Please...."

"No."

Huston and McKeith selected a position with a good field of fire, three feet up the steep creek bank on a bend in the stream. It was fairly well concealed, offering good cover with shrubs and small boulders. Positioning themselves on either side of their wounded friend, they laid out extra magazines and all their grenades, planning to take a few tormentors with them. It was the only thing they could do. Badolati couldn't go on, and they wouldn't leave him. They were out of options. There was a slight chance if they could kill sufficient numbers of them, the others just might pull back and leave them alone. It was their only plan and hope.

After nearly three hours, around 1600 hours, Badolati was still breathing but appeared near death. All they could do was to check on him every few minutes and pray for a miracle. Unfortunately, that miracle never came. When Huston knelt to check him around 1730 hours, it was clear Frank Badolati had succumbed to his injuries. Saddened by the lost of their friend, yet relieved his suffering had ended, the two friends hid his body near a prominent terrain feature so it could be found later. With heavy hearts, they moved out once more toward the south. Stopping only after it became too dark to travel, they each took turns sleeping and watching. At first light they resumed their trek, traversing the difficult terrain continuously from 0600 until 1500 before pausing on an elephant grass-covered hill. They hoped to be spotted from the air. No sooner than they dropped to rest, the distant drone of an aircraft shook them from their foggy exhaustion. After five passes to the south the FAC pilot inexplicably headed toward their location; he'd spotted their orange panel. They prayed he was calling for a helicopter evacuation.

Within minutes, firing broke out 500 meters down the hill. Believing the enemy had found them again, and they were under yet another attack, Huston and McKeith contemplated running, but then, as if they could read each other's minds, they silently agreed this was where they would make their stand. If they ran, the choppers would never be able to find them in the dense vegetation. The sound of others returning enemy fire became apparent; their shouting drifted up to them. Huston figured it just might be the other three men from his patrol.

He and McKeith discussed going to the aid of the besieged men, but Huston decided to first bring the chopper in, and then to try to locate and rescue their teammates. None stood a chance of making it out without the helicopter. Upon hearing it approach from the south, Huston popped red smoke. The chopper came in low, hovered and picked them up without a shot fired. Safely inside, he told the pilot and door gunners to do a fly-by to see if they could spot anyone else from the location where they'd last heard firing. The chopper began to receive fire from concealed enemy gunners, but the door gunners returned it with a devastating volley, quickly silencing them. After several fly-bys, it became apparent none of the others could be spotted from the air. Huston reported the firefight to the Tactical Operations Center along with his assessment that it might have been the rest of his team. He urged a reaction force to locate

The dense, triple-layer canopy affected team infiltration and extraction

them, but Delta's Ranger Battalion was extended beyond its capacity—this time it would be up to the 1st Cav Division.

* * * * * *

Back at the FOB, efforts were underway to get the 1st Cav to agree to reinforce the teams and get them out. Their argument seemed simple. Delta supported the Division; it was reasonable that they would help. Besides, the arrangement had been mutually agreed upon from the very first. The Cav Operations Officer refused; the weather too bad, the enemy too strong and their location unknown.

As the weather cleared, Beckwith mobilized all remaining SF resources in the base camp. While smaller than what was needed for such a rescue attempt, it was everything available under his control. Beckwith would personally lead the reaction force to rescue the teams. His rationale was that if he went in, his deputy, CPT "Bo" Baker, could use his presence to leverage the 1st Cav Command to make the rescue. His landing force immediately came under intense fire while still on the LZ, so in addition to having Beckwith's teams in grave danger, his reaction force was pinned down by a far superior enemy force. The operation deteriorated so quickly that Beckwith urged his pilot to land so he could join in. Eager to be in the fray, Beckwith was wounded by a .51 caliber round as he jumped from the hovering craft, shot in the stomach. The round passed through him, wounding his door gunner. Terry "Rolex" Morrone had been assigned as Beckwith's radio man, and was with him when he got hit. He put his Commander back onto the chopper for evacuation, noting he looked near death. The helicopter had taken so many hits there was speculation about how it ever made it back to the FOB. Beckwith nearly died several times while being treated, but survived, though his injuries were so serious that he had to be medically evacuated to the States.

Beckwith's ploy to get the Cav to react also failed. Exhausting all options, Baker asked the Delta staff manning the FOB for volunteers to reinforce Beckwith's element. Of the twenty-one men available—all volunteered. In their urgency to run for the choppers, grab rifles and extra ammunition, the Americans noticed several Nungs had joined in.

One Delta NCO recalled, "I remember the young, Nung private seated beside me on the chopper as we went into that hot LZ. He didn't have a clue. He just saw us all running toward the choppers in a state of emergency, armed to the teeth, and he reacted the same as most did, joining their American friends for whatever lie ahead." Project Delta members always had high praise for the Nungs—they were fine soldiers.

Under fire, the small reaction force inserted in a nearby rice paddy. They managed to make it to the base of the hill, reaching one element who had managed to fend off attacks since landing with Beckwith's force. Despite heavy fire, they carried the wounded back for extraction. One of the rescuers later said, "By the time we got back, Luke Thompson, the team medic at Bong Son, was helping Morrone place Charlie Beckwith on a chopper. He'd taken a round through his abdomen, side to side. I didn't think he'd make it, but was very glad to hear differently. He'd been standing in the doorway at low altitude, waiting to jump when they hit him. We should've never been there.

The weather was too bad for air support, we didn't have the reaction support from the Cav and we couldn't get the teams out once they were hit. But you know Beckwith—he's crazy. What the hell was he doing, going in that way? And, I couldn't believe the goddamned 1st Cav wouldn't even go in to help us. I mean shit—we were working for them in the first place. Supposedly all the support requirements had been worked out in advance, but when it came right down to nitty-gritty show time, they didn't have what it took!"

In retrospect, this was pent-up frustration speaking, for the 1st Cav had provided flawless support to Delta many times, and although the 1st Cav ground elements were among the finest combat troops in Vietnam, this operation had been orchestrated by conventionally trained staff officers with little experience with Special Operations troops, or how they should be used. From that point on, when the chips were down, Delta decided they could only depend upon Delta.

* * * * * *

Resigned he would probably never make it beyond his patch of elephant grass, Gray decided he'd at least make it costly for his enemies. Hope briefly drifted toward him on the whooping blades of a helicopter overhead, and the welcome sound of automatic fire as its M-60s opened up on the NVA's position. The enemy popped a few rounds, but it seemed their hearts weren't in it and they soon ceased firing to withdraw into the jungle seeking better concealment. Gray later learned it was the helicopter rescuing Huston and McKeith, but he wasn't in a position to pop smoke or display his orange panel—the close proximity of the NVA precluded him from trying to gain the pilot's attention. His heart sank as the chopper's lonely drone faded into the dark evening sky. Lying motionless, scarcely daring to breathe, Gray listened to the sounds of the enemy as they chopped litter poles to carry off their dead and wounded. Despite his situation, he fought back a smile. That door gunner must have really kicked their ass.

Gray decided to remain where he was, hoping they would leave once finished with their chore. He also prayed the chopper had spotted him and would soon return. Alas, it did not, and alas, the VC weren't yet through with their search. Five NVA soldiers appeared only a few feet from his position, their approach secretive and deliberate. He cut loose, depleting a magazine, and watched as they crumpled into a bloody heap. He dived and rolled thirty feet, paused, breathlessly waiting to either return fire or expecting an outright assault.

By late afternoon the steamy jungle temperature and blazing sun were intense. He fought back a desire to drink some of his precious water, and waited; soaked tiger fatigues stuck to his skin and a river of sweat stung his eyes. Several stressful minutes passed before a slight movement jolted him once more. His crushed grass path was leading them straight to him. As he watched two khaki-clad NVA soldiers move along his earlier route, his heart beat so loudly he was amazed they couldn't hear him. He let them advance to within six feet of his position, then cut them down with a burst from his M-16. A larger group of VC farther up the hill immediately opened fire, their rounds clipping at the grass overhead. Well aware it was much too dangerous to remain, Gray rolled again, tumbled a short distance and then set another ambush. He was desperately thirsty, but didn't dare drink what little water he had; he never knew when he'd find more. Less than ten minutes had elapsed when two more khaki-clad soldiers came into view, following his flattened path. As before, he let them get within six feet before he killed them.

He wanted to scream at them to stop coming—what the hell could they be thinking, walking into his fire? Gray continued to slide farther down. He figured he'd bought some time and paused to fluff up the grass to hide his trail. He continued more slowly, inching through the tall grass and down the dangerous slope, careful not to leave a path for them to follow this time.

Fifteen minutes elapsed when he again heard voices; harsh Vietnamese military orders and the sound of a crew-served weapon being positioned. Two words repeatedly floated toward him; "American" and "officer". Having come to the edge of the jungle at the base of the knoll, he lay silently while the NVA searched the tall grass and barked some radio orders. Concealed and quiet, Gray remained another two hours, hoping against hope that another team member might join him. When finally dark, he began to crawl toward an area he'd earlier picked out on his map as a possible extraction destination.

This time, luck was with him. Exhausted and dehydrated, he reached the pickup point at dusk, just as a FAC flew overhead. Gray popped a

Left to Right: Recon NCO, MSG Wiley Gray; MSG Leonard Booth; Ranger NCOIC, Delta S-4 Charles Moore; Ranger Advisor for 81st Ranger Battalion, Tony Jantovski; FAC, John Flanagan. Gray and Flanagan were preparing to launch in support of Project Delta operations at Tay Ninh, May 1966. (Photo courtesy of Charles Moore)

white flare and waited. Thirty minutes passed before he heard aircraft; this time he shot two white and two red flares at four armed helicopters. Determined to be seen, he also tossed a yellow smoke canister into the clearing for good measure. One of the choppers suddenly swooped in, landed and picked him up—he was the only one to make it back alive. Intelligence reports indicated more than 1,000 NVA soldiers, in four-man groups, had been searching for him.

* * * * * *

The remains of Cecil Hodgson and Ron Terry were never recovered; the Army carries them as MIA. On 16 April 2001, Wiley Gray, age 70, passed away from a heart attack. Returning from the fateful operation, Gray unceremoniously refused a nomination for the Distinguished Service Cross, remarking, "I wasn't able to save anyone but myself. I don't deserve a medal for that."[26] On a beautiful May morning, six draft horses hauled the caisson and Wiley Gray's casket on his final patrol. As was appropriate, he was laid to rest at Arlington National Cemetery beside this nation's other heroes. With profound sadness, yet pride from his family, friends and veteran Delta buddies attending— Wiley Gray's passing makes the world seem a lesser place.

* * * * * *

After Badolati was hit, he told Huston he'd never make it out alive. Even before the team split up, Badolati urged Huston to go on without him. He'd argued that he and McKeith would stand a much better chance if they didn't wait around for him to die. Throughout the ordeal, he pleaded with Huston to leave him behind. He knew he was dying and didn't want to do so with the knowledge that he had taken the others with him. Badolati sensed that if he stopped, the others wouldn't leave him; yet, he knew they couldn't afford to stay with him and remain alive. Miraculously, Frank Badolati remained on his feet, more dead than alive, longer than any man with a severed arm could be expected to.

As they waited by the stream, Huston leaned close to Badolati's lips as Badolati whispered his final words, "Save yourselves."

"These guys operate in the Ether Zone," General Robert Cushman told Delta Commander Chuck Allen. Badolati had surely been in the Ether Zone that day—he didn't want his brothers to die because of him. Huston said of Badolati, "…by his determination to keep going in order to spare us, Sergeant Badolati saved my team from complete annihilation." Staff Sergeant Frank Badolati's body was never recovered.

It was February 1966 when the 1st Cav Division ran the ill-fated operation near Bong Son in the An Lao Valley, and Major Art Strange's prophecy to Charlie Beckwith came to pass. Regardless of the outcome, uncommon valor was the order of the day, and Project Delta took the field. Five Silver stars were won during that operation: SFC Marlin C. Cook (KIA), SFC Jesse L. Hancock (KIA), SFC Cecil J. Hodgson

---

[26] Roger L. Albertson, U.S. Army Special Forces."The Last Survivor: A Memorial Day Tribute." http://www.projectdelta.net/gray_story.htm

(MIA), SSG Donald L. Dotson (KIA) and SSG George A. Hoagland (KIA). Staff Sergeant Charles F. Hiner was awarded the Bronze Star for his extreme bravery under enemy fire. Master Sergeant Wiley Gray's nomination for the Distinguished Service Cross was refused—by him. Ronald Terry and Cecil Hodgson remain on the Army's rolls as MIA.

And so it has been written: "Greater love has no man than this, that he lay down his life for his friends."

SSG Frank Badolati, Project Delta Headquarters, 1965. (Photo courtesy of Ray Davidson)

TEN

Why We Fight

"Every man in Delta Recon deserves the Bronze Star with
'V' device each time he steps off a helicopter for a mission."

- General William C. Westmoreland

IN JANUARY 1966, NORM DONEY WAS in Panama helping to establish the
relatively new 8th Special Forces Group when orders came for South
Vietnam. Married, his young wife pregnant with their first child, he
figured he'd spent enough time away from his family and viewed his new
orders with trepidation. All Doney knew was that he was being assigned
to the 5th Special Forces Group (Airborne) in Nha Trang, and would
receive specific assignment orders upon his arrival. He'd only been
informed that due to losses relating to some obscure secret project in the
An Loa Valley, Project Delta was seeking experienced men to fill critical
slots. Doney enjoyed a solid reputation, and since he had previously
deployed on White Star, a classified project in Laos during 1961, he was
just what they were looking for. Learning that Ron Terry, his demo

sergeant during White Star, was among the men missing, Doney immediately volunteered for Project Delta.

During the early years, Special Forces circles were small, and nearly all the NCOs who'd been around for a while knew everyone else; a man's reputation followed him. Project Delta, with some of the most experienced and capable NCOs, was no exception. Arriving in Nha Trang, Doney discovered he knew most of those assigned. He reported to B-52 in April while Wiley Gray was in charge of Recon, and was immediately assigned to a recon team. Lieutenant Colonel John Warren was the commanding officer. Doney acknowledged that Warren was "a pretty good commander." Typically a commander would turn-over every six months, but the NCOs, especially in Recon, were Project Delta's backbone. Many NCOs stayed on, or returned for several tours to ensure the continuity and experience of the Project. Master Sergeant Jim Shoulders was among those, and the first to welcome Doney to Recon.

Doney vividly recalled his first recon operation with B-52, Project Delta. B-52 had just deployed six recon teams, one company of the 81st Rangers, the 2nd Platoon of 171st Aviation Company, and one USAF FAC in support of the 1st Infantry Division operating near Tay Ninh. Sergeant First Class Charlie Telfair was his One Zero, and four VNSF recon personnel went along. Doney's team, Recon Team-1, was to conduct reconnaissance and surveillance within their assigned area, determine the location and movement of enemy units on the eastern flank of the 1st U.S. Infantry Division and conduct air strikes and direct artillery fire against targets of opportunity.

Team-1, along with two other teams placed in adjacent areas, went in without incident at last light on 7 May 1966. As the helicopter lifted away, leaving them on the LZ, Telfair started his point man into the jungle. Doney felt a strong feeling of being alone. They moved rapidly and silently to distance themselves from the commotion caused during their drop off. Traveling until too dark to navigate further, Telfair signaled the point man to stop, and in a dense thicket they set up a tight perimeter defense to wait out the night. Doney recalled being awakened around midnight by loud rumbling—it sounded like a freight train headed through their campsite—and being lifted a foot off the ground. It was only after he cleared the fog of sleep from his head that he realized what had made the commotion. Someone had forgotten to tell them about a scheduled B-52 bomb strike nearby with 2,000-pound bombs. That "friendly" incident scared him as much as any subsequent enemy encounter.

Back at the FOB, it was being reported that Team-2, dropped into an adjacent area, had encountered heavy enemy concentration; they were on the run and had requested immediate extraction. Three additional recon teams were slated to infiltrate the following morning, but had to abort due to poor weather. They'd be unable to deploy until the evening of 8 May. On the ground, Team-5 had successfully penetrated the enemy's outer defenses and reported VC work details preparing fighting positions. They also observed numerous well-equipped NVA troops milling about. Inching forward slowly and cautiously, they tried to traverse the forces' flanks to determine how far the defenses stretched, but after encountering enemy forces from several directions, knew they had been detected and were being systematically surrounded. Eventually, the mission deteriorated into a running gun battle to simply stay alive, and a wild helicopter extraction under intense automatic fire.

Compromised, Team-3 had also been extracted under heavy fire after they directed forty-four air strike sorties, killing an estimated 150 NVA soldiers. It was now obvious the area was saturated with NVA and VC units, and further recon team movement would be extremely dangerous.

Through radio traffic, Doney's team picked up enough information to understand that large enemy concentrations were moving through their area; they knew they had to be extremely careful. Using stealth and secrecy, the team moved cautiously throughout the next day across mostly flat but dense vegetation. They determined the enemy was not using any main roads or trails, but always had a security force of at least two-to-five men, well in front of the main body. The point man held them up as they came to a small clearing; they observed two bicycles leaning against a hut while men's voices came from inside. They could've taken it out, but it wasn't their mission. Instead they pulled back, skirted the clearing and then dropped onto a rocky creek bed. They followed the creek for a mile, finally coming to a bridge that had been partially destroyed by previous air strikes. Doney climbed a small tree and spotted two NVA soldiers coming toward him.

He motioned for the team to remain silent, and waited, scarcely breathing. "One of them looked right at me," Doney recalls. "I think he saw me…but didn't see me…if that makes any sense. Think what it's like when you look at something but it doesn't register, because you don't expect it to be there. Anyway, they walked right past us."

As Doney began to descend, he froze. A larger contingent of uniformed men appeared, camouflaged with shrub limbs and brush, headed directly toward him. Doney whispered down to Telfair, "Get on the horn and call for an air strike. There's a squad coming down the trail."

Telfair moved away from the trail, contacted headquarters and had begun delivering his report when Doney urgently whispered, "Make that a platoon."

Telfair began to broadcast again, but then was interrupted again. "No, wait. It's a company."

Amazed by the sheer size of this adversary, Doney watched as an officer directed troops to either the right or left side of the trail, apparently for a break. He surmised he'd been wrong. It was at least a battalion of NVA soldiers, and he suspected even more, because he could hear movement and voices in the thick vegetation. He was concerned they would hear his heart pounding. Telfair whispered urgently into the radio handset, calling for an air strike, as Doney scurried down the tree.

It was an anxiety-filled hour before the FAC finally appeared. When the pilot saw the massive numbers, it didn't take long for the jets to arrive—within minutes a jet sonic boom startled them into action. Then others came in lower, their 500-pound bomb blasts and napalm shattered the jungle quiet. Doney and Telfair both grinned—this was the sound of freedom and they loved it. As soon as the air strike began in earnest and they could tell the ordnance was falling accurately, Telfair called for extraction. The only clearing suitable for a LZ was close to the enemy battalion being blasted by air strikes, but they had little choice. It would have to do. Covertly, they successfully traversed around the air strike, reaching their destination without incident—they waited breathlessly, expecting to be attacked at any moment.

Time dragged as the team huddled near the edge of the LZ, precariously close to at least a regiment of swarming NVA soldiers. When Doney finally saw the chopper coming in, his team leaped up and ran onto clearing, anxious to be in position, so as to limit their exposure in the opening. The chopper's skids were still six feet from the ground when the enemy realized what was happening and opened up. The pilot took a hit in the foot, while the door gunner took one through his hand. The team watched helplessly as the chopper pulled up and flew off, leaving them stranded on the LZ. There was no time to make plans; if they were to survive, they'd have to get away fast! The helicopter's aborted attempt had given away their position; the enemy would be upon them within minutes. Quickly, they faded into the jungle, miraculously evading enemy detection. They soon found a spot to hole up until dark, when they would try to slip away.

It was nearly dark when Telfair was given another pickup point, but they had to reach it before dark or look forward to being holed up another night. Their concern was that the suitable LZ they'd been given was only a short distance from the enemy-occupied village that had been previously pounded to rubble by air strikes.

"We've got no choice," Telfair shrugged. "We either make it to that LZ or we're stuck here. Move out."

Reaching it involved using all their skill and stealth. At times, the team scooted along on their bellies between machinegun bunkers—one enemy patrol passed within five meters as they lay beside a narrow trail. Skirting through the enemy's positions and the heavy patrols between them and their potential designation, the team finally made it at dusk to the edge of the LZ. They knew they weren't yet out of the woods, for when the chopper arrived, the enemy patrols opened up again. This time, the pilot held firm until all were aboard and extracted them under heavy fire. Although bullet holes dotted the chopper's fuselage, remarkably neither the team nor helicopter crew sustained casualties. Norm Doney, relieved to survive his first Delta recon experience, and no longer the FNG, asked Telfair if they were always that tenuous. Telfair never hesitated, replying, "Always."

Project Delta spent much time in the Tay Ninh area of operations before being pulled back to Nha Trang. They'd lost a FAC, a number of Rangers and other Recon colleagues while there. When General William Westmoreland visited the FOB to receive a briefing, he commented to MAJ Allen, "Every man in Recon deserves the Bronze Star with 'V' device each time he steps from the helicopter for a mission."

One month later, Doney accompanied SFC Charlie Harper and four VNSF recon men into Tay Ninh to support the 25th Infantry Division.

MSG Norman Doney (*left*) accepts the Bronze Star with "V" device from MAJ Charles "Bruiser" Allen, CO, Project Delta, Nha Trang, 9 Feb 1968. (Photo courtesy of Norman Doney)

Plans were quickly drawn for B-52 to deploy a combined U.S./VN Delta Headquarters for the FOB; six recon teams, the 81st Airborne Ranger Battalion, previously designated as the 91st Airborne Rangers, one USAF FAC and a platoon of the 281st AHC (Project Delta).

"We went in just before dark," Doney reminisced. "That's the way I liked doing it because if we ran into trouble on the LZ, they'd have only an hour or so of daylight before it got too dark for them to chase us. We wanted to go as far as we could before darkness set in, so we followed the river, then a small tributary leading west toward where we'd seen smoke rising above the trees as we flew in. We knew around dusk would be when they lit their cooking fires. We figured to hone-in on that and call in an air strike as they were having dinner. We had to be careful in the dark though, or we might just stumble into their camp."

As Team-1 moved silently along the small river, they could hear bamboo reeds clicking in a rhythmic cadence from the opposite bank. The team dropped to the ground, crawling until they could observe across the river. A formation of NVA soldiers appeared to be conducting

Physical Training (PT), exercising in cadence to the clicking bamboo. Doney quickly got on the radio and reached the circling FAC, who was waiting for their call. Within minutes, the malevolent roar of jets filled the sky while bomb concussions shook the jungle. Doney noticed some smoke near his location and on his side of the river. He asked for an air strike on that position, and two jets came in low, splashing their napalm death over the targeted area. That strike was devastating, and as the NVA soldiers broke and ran for their lives, they headed straight toward them and their concealed location.

"To this day I don't know why they didn't see us," Doney mused. "I could've tripped some with my rifle if I'd wanted to. A few nearly stepped on me as they ran, trying to escape that terrible napalm rain. I figured we'd be history if we didn't get out quickly."

In the impending darkness, Doney and his team crawled away from the enemy's encampment, evading small groups of scattered NVA soldiers. After he figured they were far enough to safely do so, he called for extraction, "Get us the hell out of here." A helicopter had been circling, waiting for their call, and within a few minutes they acted. As the pilot brought it down on their orange panel, the jungle erupted with a barrage of automatic fire. The chopper pilot, oblivious to the metallic sounds thumping against the thin skin of his helicopter, focused on landing the craft without shattering a propeller blade against a tree. Finally, he managed to get low enough to pick them up; they'd been crouching nearby, returning the enemy's fire. Despite the heavy fire, the pilot continued to hover, holding it steady until Doney and his entire team were safely aboard, then pulled pitch and shot away.

"Joe Alderman was riding shotgun on the chopper that day," Doney said. "I remember that he grinned as he gave me his hand and pulled me inside. I was never so happy to see anyone in my entire life."

That day, they counted thirty-two bullet holes in the helicopter. Once more rescued from certain death, any one of them could have sent it crashing to a fiery end. Doney doesn't recall the name of the young pilot, but offered that he was just one of many who had put his life on the line for the recon teams.

"Two operations and two near misses—it's going to be one hell of a year," Doney reflected on the ride back.

His team hardly had time to eat a hot meal before they were heading back again—into the same area. Command needed to assess the previous bombing run damage and to engage the enemy further if they persisted in hanging around. No one knew the territory as well as Team-1; they'd been there—they'd go back. This would be an extremely dangerous situation and they knew it. The air strike had dispersed the enemy, permeating the dense jungle with small groups. In every aspect, this mission would be far worse. Before, they had some idea of the enemy's proximity, now they had no such information. The dispersed NVA units might be anywhere, and this time those guys would be mad as hell. This time they'd be anticipated, and if captured, they could expect little mercy.

Team-1 jumped off the chopper skids as it hovered four-feet above a small thick bamboo clearing, fading into the vegetation before the pilot could take off again. Once airborne, the pilot and his crew remarked that the team had already disappeared into the jungle as if ghosts; they couldn't even be detected from the air. Using only hand signals and facial expressions to communicate, Recon-1 traveled slowly and silently toward the river, expecting to come under fire from a hidden enemy at any moment. Suddenly, the point man signaled and the entire team dropped as though a single entity. He indicated he had the river in view. Crawling closer, they watched in amazement as rafts loaded with dead and wounded carried scores of earlier casualties down river.

"Just seeing all those dead and wounded...that we'd been responsible for, quietly floating down the river...washed over me with mixed feelings. I just couldn't put any more air strikes on them that day," he said quietly. "I had to let them go...let them retrieve their dead."

Doney, recalling that event from forty years earlier, filled with emotion, his voice fading as he softly said, "Hitting them again, that way...that wouldn't have been a very nice thing to do."

Doney served a year with Delta before returning to the States. He shared his feelings; they were similar to what others who had served felt. Landing in San Francisco, he was shocked by the venomous hatred the anti-war groups displayed toward their country's returning military. They seemed to believe that the returning soldiers were to blame for the country's failed policies. Simply wearing a uniform in public was sure to invite a confrontation, particularly when traveling through an airport or train station. Many Delta soldiers chose not to wear uniforms when traveling. After a year or more of operating in a stressful combat environment, they weren't quite sure what their reaction might be if accosted by some pimply-faced college kids who had never been out of the United States.

The obnoxious protesters and a general disrespect for the military weren't the only changes that required getting used to. There had been a cultural shift during their absence—the hippies, flower children, free-love fests and men with long hair traipsing about in tie-dyed trousers. Many soldiers hadn't been exposed to any of this and were agog at the spectacle. On his first trip to Saigon, prior to his departure for the States, Gary Nichols was riding in a rickshaw with SFC Donald (D.J.) Taylor, trying to adjust to the swarming masses after a stressful year in the jungle, when he noticed some skin-tight jeans and long black hair ahead of them.

"DJ, look at that babe! Now, that's a nice ass," he remarked.

With an embarrassed half-grin, DJ responded, "That's not a babe, Gary. That's a guy. All the guys wear their hair long now."

Nichols stared in disbelief as they passed the subject of his admiration, and sure enough, it was a guy. Sullen and pensive, he stared from his side of the rickshaw as they rode in silence, and then quietly said, "It was still a nice ass."

Whether it had been the difficulty of trying to come to terms with civilian attitudes, or that they just longed to be with the brothers they'd left in harm's way, many soldiers who came home following a Project Delta tour returned within only a few months—victims of a war that tugged at their memories. Doney was no exception. He'd spent barely three months with his family before returning in early 1967 for a second year-long tour. The mantra was the same as that repeated by an old recon man as he sipped a drink with a buddy in the Delta Club at Nha Trang, "When I'm here, all I can think about is being home…and when I'm home, all I think about is being back here." This feeling continued to haunt many Vietnam vets, years after the war ended.

Lieutenant Colonel John Hayes was the Delta CO during Doney's second tour; MAJ Chuck Allen, the Deputy Commander/Operations Officer. Allen immediately sought Haye's permission to use Doney as his Operations NCO, and he was approved. The most experienced recon man was always the Recon Section Leader, and Doc Simpson long had held that position. But following his departure in a few months, Doney would take over.

Although his heart remained with the guys out on recon, his new job gave him the opportunity to make some improvements. Within the week, Delta set up the FOB at Phu Bai, and then he asked Gary Nichols to visit the 1st Air Cav with some good whiskey to trade for some of the Cav's new aluminum rung, steel-cable ladders. Once that mission had been accomplished, James Lee Coalson and Paul Spillane figured a way to attach them to a Huey Slick. The innovation was a success; everyone agreed it undoubtedly saved many lives. Doney also saw an opportunity to convert the old hand-loop of the current McGuire Rig into a "slip-loop"; it slid over a man's wrist, then his weight kept him from falling out even when wounded. In March 1969, Doney served a third tour in Vietnam, conducting recon operations with MACV SOG. During this time he collected and compiled "Tips of the Trade" about recon operations. Joe Alderman updated them just before Delta's closing in 1970; many of them are still in use. In 1989, he returned to Vietnam again, but this time to Hanoi, to locate American POWs and MIAs.

* * * * * *

Today, Norm Doney resides in Oregon, and although his hearing and once sharp eyes are failing, he remains actively involved in the POW/MIA quandary, critical that the country he and others valiantly fought for fails to honor its missing Vietnam Vets and unresolved POW/MIA issues.

ELEVEN

A Different Breed

AS AN ORGANIZATION, PROJECT DELTA WAS a marvel in its efficiency and operational methods; perfected, smooth, it remains the model for many Special Forces classified projects. When a mission was tasked, the advance party's first troops established the FOB; its Tactical Operations Center (TOC), Intelligence (S2), Operations (S3), Supply (S4) and Communications Center. Teams didn't deploy with the FOB, remaining instead at Nha Trang until called for by number, and then only two teams at a time reported for their mission briefings. By the evening, the teams pre-planned their mission, re-packed rucksacks, checked weapons and munitions (all kept in their rooms), tested radio equipment and packed extra batteries. The following morning those alerted would load onto a Vietnamese C-47 cargo plane for the flight to the FOB. The USSF and VNSF team leaders would receive detailed briefings at the TOC, be given final mission instructions and link-up with their over-flight pilot. Within the hour, the over-flight recon would take off with the team leaders and primary/alternate routes chosen, along with primary/alternate LZs.

Once the recon leader returned, the team refined their plan, rehearsed immediate action drills and tactical movement, briefed-back the Commander and his staff, and then waited for last light—and infiltration. After insertion, the operation continued until the mission was completed, or until the team was compromised by enemy contact. From experience, they learned they had to extract the team as soon as possible once the enemy discovered them, as their adversaries would quickly attempt to surround, annihilate or capture them. After extraction, the team would be taken directly to the TOC for debriefing by the Commander or Operations Officer. Once debriefed, they would load onto the Vietnamese C-47 for the flight back to Nha Trang. From start to finish the process was smoothly orchestrated; there wasn't a moment wasted.

According to Charlie Beckwith, "My Delta guys are the most professional combat soldiers I've ever seen. Now, if I could get away with locking them up in a cage when they're not in the field, commanding them would be a piece of cake."

Beckwith's remarks were well-founded. Delta personnel, particularly those in Recon, tended to raise a little hell during "stand down." If something didn't happen, it was probably more because someone hadn't yet thought of it, than lack of restraint. Most Project Delta commanders understood the wildness was just a safety valve for built-up combat stress, and precisely what made them so daring in the field; therefore, they overlooked most of the shenanigans and tried to protect them against the conventional hierarchy's ire.

Andre "Saint" St Laurent, a young, capable, well-liked French-Canadian, had seen the feisty men in their green berets a few years earlier and hadn't rested until he'd been accepted and made it through their training. However, once in Vietnam, his life seemed a bit too tame on a regular Special Forces A-Team, so when he began to hear rumors about Project Delta—whatever it was—he wanted to be part of it. The evening before he was to report for his assignment with Project Delta, he went to a Nha Trang off-limits hotspot and "kicked up." An MP squad raided the place, and later he was accused of dismantling most of them. Hauled in and written up for drunk and disorderly conduct in an off-limits establishment, he reported to Charging Charlie the following morning, hang-dogged, bruised and hung-over.

Properly humbled, he said, "I guess you won't want me in the Project now, right, Sir?"

Beckwith grinned. "You're exactly what we're looking for. Those MPs said you kicked their asses pretty good."

The unspoken policy was "Raise hell if you want, but be prepared to pay when the time comes." Most believe it was either Doc Simpson or Wiley Gray who started to make the teams conduct a forced road march around "Stink Village" with rocks in their rucksacks to dry them out and get them into shape for their next mission. Stink Village was a small settlement just beyond Nha Trang's city limits. Its major enterprise was *nuoc mam*, a savory sauce produced by rendering liquid from decaying fish. In the hot sun, the potent smell traveled a great distance—hence Stink Village. To any man suffering an affliction of too much booze and late night hell-raising, the stench would make the most ardent partier heave his guts before completing the road march. Still, no one really felt the marches to be a serious deterrent to their fun, and the partying never noticeably let up during a Delta stand-down.

* * * * * *

The first two FAC pilots attached to Project Delta were Air Force Captains Kenneth Kerr and Jim Ahmann, both TDY from the 19th TASS. In June 1966, 1LT Carlton Skinner replaced Ahmann. Another early FAC pilot assigned to Project Delta was USAF Captain John F. Flanagan. Flanagan, author of *Vietnam Above the Treetops,* recalled, "When the secret CIA/Special Forces projects of Omega and Sigma were formed, Skinner left to fly for one of them, leaving only one FAC pilot to support Delta. For several months that was just me because we didn't like to use TDY FAC personnel for Delta's operations; the learning curve was just too steep."[27] Flanagan, who replaced Kerr in April 1966, retired as an Air Force brigadier general.

In November 1966, CPT Charlie Swope arrived just before Delta was slated to kick off a large operation near the Special Forces base camp of Khe Sanh. Swope was shot down and killed one month later

---

[27] Brigadier General John Flanagan, USAF Retired. *Vietnam Above the Tree Tops: A Forward Air Controller Reports.* NYC: Praeger Publishing, 1992,.

while supporting the operation; Recon men Bott and Stark also lost their lives. Sergeant Irby Dyer, B-52 medic, was also killed along with the entire recovery chopper crew when the helicopter was shot down while trying to rescue Bott's surrounded recon team. Sergeant First Class Arthur Glidden, along as an observer in CPT Swope's 0-1F aircraft when it went down, is listed as KIA. This had been only Swope's fifth mission. Sergeant First Class Tom Carpenter led a small force to retrieve the bodies of Swope and Glidden.

All FAC pilots had to have at least six months tenure in-country to volunteer for Delta, and then had to pass muster by the Recon Section after their initial "wet-run" operation. One FAC pilot was fired because the recon guys said, "He's nuts. He's going to get himself—or some of us—killed." Their phraseology might have been a bit more colorful, but that is the gist of their comments. After Swope and Glidden died in the crash of Swope's plane, Al Groth replaced Swope as Delta's second FAC, and would later be awarded the Distinguished Flying Cross for bravery.

But a new change in policy was in the works for the FACs supporting Delta. The Air Force hierarchy decided that Delta operations were far too dangerous for only one pilot to fly, and to do so was tantamount to attempting suicide. Thereafter, two FACs were to be in the air whenever Delta was supported. In July 1966, USAF Captain Ralf Miller was assigned as Delta's second FAC. He served a full year with distinction and, on several occasions, with extraordinary bravery.

Delta had the highest in-country priority for fighter support of any combat unit, since most missions were classified as "immediate in nature" As a result, Delta's close-air support remained some of the best. One primary reason was that the FACs could call for and approve air strikes on their own, without interference from the chain of command. As Flanagan put it, "What Delta wanted, Delta got." This policy undoubtedly saved many U.S. and Vietnamese lives. It remains a long-standing Special Forces operational concept.

Delta's Air Force attachments were quality men who risked their lives whenever Recon or Ranger operations were underway. Beyond FAC pilots, the Air Force also provided a Tactical Air Control Party (TACP) consisting of two officers, one or two enlisted radio operators (ROMADS) and a communications jeep with FM, VHF, UHF and a powerful HF/SSB (single side band radio). Airman Rudy Bishop, AF

ROMAD, was assigned to Project Delta for most of its existence. Unlike some aviation support elements Delta periodically used, the FACs and their support personnel lived with and were integrated into Project Delta, deploying to the FOB each time Delta elements went to the field. The desperate calls over their radios for help weren't just nameless voices; these were men the FAC pilots and ROMADS knew intimately. Delta's FAC pilots braved enemy gunfire on countless occasions to get them safely out of harm's way; a young ROMADS Airman would be sitting in the back seat every time.

In mid-1966, Airman Alfred Montez was assigned to the Tactical Air Control Party at Project Delta Headquarters in Nha Trang. Upon his arrival, he was given two sets of jungle fatigues, a handgun, and canvas jungle boots. Familiar only with Air Force personnel, he was shocked by the Special Ops guys. At the airstrip, a mean-looking, muscle-bound sergeant picked him up in a battered jeep and told him to report to the gentleman in charge of supply for the rest of his equipment. The stocky sergeant described the unit supply sergeant as a happy, very gentle E-7. Arriving for his new issue of clothing, Montez said he was met by a blond, shirtless, loud, vulgar sergeant who "made my asshole pucker up." According to Montez, the big guy spoke to him harshly, as if he already disliked him intensely, though they'd never met. The big blond guy contemptuously tossed him a rucksack, three sets of tiger fatigues, a knife, machete, web belt and harness, two canteens with covers, field bandages, four ammo pouches, poncho and liner, field sweater and two floppy hats. Blondie's snarled advice had been, "Take good care of it. I'll expect it all back in the same condition when you leave—that is, if you don't get killed."

When Montez reached his room, he discovered his new roommate had dumped all his stuff onto the floor—all except for his rifle.

"Who the f_ _ _ are you going to kill with that?" Herb growled at him.

It seemed everywhere Montez went someone wanted to bust his balls. Finally, he ran into an honest-to-god Air Force man, 1LT John Flanagan. Even Flanagan's demeanor seemed abrasive. He wondered if the Army might rub off on him, too.

Later, Montez met with his new supervisor, Air Force Captain Groth, and he told Montez why he'd been assigned. FAC missions were always over enemy territory and there were no backups—and few airstrips; a dirt road and the plank-sized metal strips called PSP, would be the best they would find in "Indian country." Montez would go along each time a FAC was airborne, to operate air-to-ground communication to the Recon guys. Groth handed him a long list of supplies necessary to keep their two aircraft operational, and he told him to memorize their SOPs. That was his introduction. Montez would spend the next two years in Project Delta and leave a changed man.

After he'd been out on a few operations, what hit him the hardest was learning that someone with whom he'd had a beer, shared a family story or joked, was lost and wouldn't return. Everything, gone in the blink of an eye. After each mission the Delta group seemed to shrink, with fewer returning than had started out. They shared some good times, but those seemed shallow measured against thoughts of who had been killed or wounded. At first Montez worried little about dying—until A Shau. He'd flown in a few birds that had taken small-arms fire, but it was in the A Shau Valley where he got his first look at a Chicom 12.7 anti-aircraft round coming straight toward him. Like quarter-sized footballs tossed toward his fragile craft, some seemed close enough to catch. It wasn't until one of the pilots told him what they were, and about their destructive powers, that he felt scared—then terrified. Once he understood how much damage they could inflict, he realized what would happen if one ever hit him. He'd seen choppers, and even a few fast-movers that had taken on 12.7 rounds, and there had been nothing left. From a thousand feet away, he once watched a chopper vaporize in an orange-black smoke cloud. Each of those scenes became personal; made him feel vulnerable. Knowing the men who died in those choppers left him disheartened, numbed beyond pain; when praying, he made promises to a god he no longer fully believed in.

Montez claims that living among these men and flying for Project Delta was the highlight of his life. He said he has never met braver or more gallant Americans, including the TACP personnel. They were responsible for keeping the birds safe and in the air, and often the 125-hour flying deadline had to be stretched to 150-hours due to mission requirements and not enough aircraft to cover all the operations. The pilots trusted him and he did his best; they all knew the rules had to be broken, but that he did so with the best of intentions. Once the 81st Rangers had been inserted, the non-stop action required them to frequently fly eight to twelve hours daily; most missions involved close-air support. He learned to recognize the voices of the men on the ground. With the sounds of battle in the background, some remained cool, while others yelled, cursed, and threatened the FACs if they didn't place the ordnance exactly where requested.

Montez says, "Our pilots were the best in the world—the Special Forces guys had no equal. I am deeply humbled and proud to have known such soldiers. Never before or after my time with Delta have I known such men."

He went on to say that personally working with those legends was unimaginable, yet gratifying. After coming home, when he would speak to civilians of their fearless deeds, his remarks were often met with a you're-full-of-shit look, so he eventually stopped talking about them altogether. He says he learned much from the men he served with in Delta—not only about war—but about dedication, character, loyalty, devotion to duty and *America*.

"These are qualities I've tried to teach my children," Montez said. "Today, I just feel great when I think about the little things; like the only words Doc Simpson ever spoke to me. Early in the a.m., after I'd walked into a room full of Recon men shooting holes in the ceiling with a mini-flare gun, he came in and said, 'Montez, get the f_ _ k out

Project Delta's "state-of-the-art" Forward Air Control (FAC) aircraft and communication jeep. (Photo courtesy Steve Adams)

John Young (*right*) and USAF Airman Al Montez (*left*) fueling up at
Nha Trang, Vietnam, 1966. (Photo courtesy of Steve Adams)

of here! Everyone else go to bed!' Well, that was Doc—he didn't talk
to you if you weren't Recon—I guess you just had to have been there."

* * * * * *

In August 1966, Delta sent twelve U.S./VN Recon Teams, one
USAF FAC and elements of the 81st Airborne Ranger Battalion
(minus), north to support the 196th Infantry Brigade in War Zone C,
near Song Be. The teams were comprised of thirty American and thirty
Vietnamese Special Forces personnel, three USSF and three VNSF per
team; however, many names have been lost to history. Some names of
those documented: SFC Norm Doney, SGT Joe Alderman, MSG
James Shoulders, SGT Eugene Moreau and SGT Vincent O'Connor.
Lieutenant Colonel William C. Norman was the assigned Delta Commanding Officer. Another twelve USSF Delta advisors accompanied
the 81st Airborne Rangers reaction force.

On August 11, Recon Teams 11 and 12 inserted at last light. The
following day, Teams 6, 8 and 10 also were dropped into their assigned
TAOR. By that evening, it was evident the local VC and NVA troops
had absolute control of the operational area. The teams called for continuous air strike sorties; countless enemies were reported KIA and

supply and equipment stockpiles destroyed. The 81st Rangers were inserted, and despite heavy opposition, conducted a successful search and destroy operation. Another two recon teams were inserted on 15 August and the remaining teams inserted the following night.

Across the board, radio contacts confirmed the teams were making heavy enemy contact. Team-1 had been hit by at least a company-sized element, one of their VN members had become separated, another wounded by grenade fragments, a third hit in the ankle. Requesting extraction, they had to be lifted out by McGuire Rig as there were no suitable LZs in their area. Team-9 reported they sighted two enemy platoons, but since they'd been too close to back off, they requested gunship support, air strikes and immediate extraction. As their extraction chopper went in, it took on heavy automatic weapons fire and crashed. Fortunately, the crew and pilot were able to evacuate the downed chopper and join the team on the ground; a U.S. Recon member was reported as seriously wounded.

Teams continued to be extracted and reinserted throughout the next week, all reporting heavy enemy losses due to the air strikes and prompt reaction by the 81st Rangers. At one point, the Commo-Relay pilot couldn't establish radio contact with Team-2. Lieutenant Colonel Norman, the out-going Delta CO nearing the end of his tour, went along with Delta's new Commander, MAJ Robert E. Luttrell. As they circled, they observed the flashing of a signal mirror, then an orange panel and smoke. The FAC flew over and reported two men lying in the elephant grass; one face-down, the other, face-up. The CO immediately ordered an evacuation chopper to rescue the team.

Special Forces medic, SGT Timothy O'Connor, accompanied the medivac chopper into the LZ. Upon landing, O'Connor jumped out and ran through a hail of bullets to the wounded men. Sergeant Johnny Varner was seriously wounded in the chest and leg, and SGT Eugene Moreau lay nearby; Moreau didn't appear to be breathing. Still under heavy fire, O'Connor carried Varner to the chopper. Another VN team member reported missing had found his way to the helicopter and jumped inside through the opposite door. Sergeant O'Connor, convinced Moreau was dead, still tried repeatedly to retrieve him, but intense enemy fire drove him back. Finally, he was forced to give up during his last attempt after being wounded in the leg.

Recon Team-2, Aug 1966, Tay Ninh (Operation 10-66 Phase III). *L to R*: VN Tm SGT (captured),VN team Leader, VN Radio Op (KIA), VN Pointman, Senior Advisor SGT Eugene Moreau (KIA), Ass't Advisor SGT Johnny Varner (WIA). (Photo courtesy of Norman A. Doney)

Lifting off as enemy fire poured across the LZ, they spotted another VN team member waving frantically to them, and the pilot hovered long enough to hoist him out by McGuire Rig. During all this activity, the hovering helicopter remained under intense fire from concealed enemy positions. The 4th Ranger Company, 81st Airborne Rangers were alerted and deployed to recover Moreau and look for other scattered team members. American advisors, 1LT Hamilton, SSG Munoz and SGT Haggard, accompanied them when they recovered Moreau's and Corporal Mo's (VN) bodies. Although the team had suffered one USSF soldier KIA and one WIA, one Vietnamese recon soldier KIA, another MIA and presumed captured by the North Vietnamese, Delta- initiated air strikes inflicted heavy damage on the VC and their infrastructure.

* * * * * *

Continuing well into September, twenty-eight recon operations were conducted, with intense enemy contacts, hair-raising escapes, continuous air strikes and scores of dead and wounded enemy accounted for. From a village hut, one team recovered two typewriters, a stack of intelligence documents and, much to the delight of higher command, a healthy VC prisoner. With the lack of suitable LZs, sixteen teams had to be extracted by McGuire Rig or rope ladders, many under direct enemy fire; ten extraction choppers received hits. It soon became obvious the recon teams were in the bivouac area of several battalion-sized units, with their carefully prepared defensive positions concealed so well that the teams often came within ten meters before being aware of them.

The morning of 14 August, 1LT Deaton, SFC Winder, SSG Musselwhite, SSG Raines and ninety-four soldiers from the 2nd Ranger Company, entered the village of Phuc Hanh. All the huts had been heavily booby-trapped, and fighting bunkers had been constructed beneath their structures. An aged Montagnard couple informed them that the NVA, normally 150 strong, had quickly left as the Rangers approached. Many others came and went on a regular basis. Armed with this information, the Rangers knew an NVA regular army regiment was operating in and around Phuc Hanh. Searching the village, they came across numerous tunnels and supply bins, along with a human arm, two dead VC soldiers and Soviet-made weapons—but no VC or NVA soldiers. Bloodied by air strikes and artillery barrages, it seemed clear the enemy didn't want to engage the aggressive 81st Airborne Rangers, and had hastily fled.

As the Rangers followed the path of their fleeing enemy, they began to receive heavy automatic weapons fire from an estimated platoon-sized element left behind to slow their advance. The firefight lasted thirty-five minutes, diminishing only after the Rangers called in close-air support. While two Rangers were killed and eight wounded in the exchange, their scouts observed that many enemy soldiers were being carried off, leaving only three dead behind. From the old woman's information, they were certain the enemy must have had advanced intelligence concerning the Ranger's operation; it was possible they had a spy in their ranks.

* * * * * *

Major Robert E. Luttrell took command of Project Delta from LTC John Warren, and teams continued to conduct operations in support of the 196th Infantry Brigade at Song Be, War Zone C. During the operation, MSG James R. Shoulders was seriously wounded and was evacuated; Eugene Moreau was killed. Lieutenant Colonel William C. Norman, SFC Norm Doney, Sergeants Joe C. Alderman, Vincent D. O'Connor and Eugene R. Moreau were all awarded Silver Stars for valor in combat.

TWELVE

Brotherhood

BILL RODERICK WAS ON HIS SECOND TOUR with a job he really enjoyed—radar technician testing new GPS ground radar systems. He'd been assigned to Dak Pek previously, so when they requested the radar system for a nearby hilltop, he was selected to set it up. While completing the project, a radio message instructed him to report to Pleiku with "bag and baggage." After he met with Henry Gold and Alvin Young, they informed him he'd been "volunteered" for Operation Blackjack 21, Special Forces' newest classified project, the Mobile Guerrilla Force. When Blackjack 21 ended in late September, Roderick was "volunteered" again—for Project Delta. This time they requested him by name.

Initially, he'd been paired with SFC Willie Stark, who soon left for Khe Sanh; he was killed in December 1966. Roderick's next roommate was SFC Allen H. Archer; Archer was killed three months later. After that, no one wanted to be his roommate. He roomed alone until rotating to the States a year later. Archer was a heavy smoker and was nursing a bad cough when he left Nha Trang on his last recon mission. Many felt he shouldn't have gone, but the managers either didn't know about his cough, or he BS'ed them into believing he was fit.

By all accounts Delta's most experienced recon man, Doc Simpson, had been assigned as One Zero for the mission; SFC Archer and SSG Parsons were the other two Americans. All day they'd been navigating through difficult terrain and were exhausted by the time Doc Simpson called a halt, unaware that they had paused just beyond the perimeter of a large NVA encampment. Cigarette smoke can be detected a great distance in the fresh jungle air and many Recon One Zeros didn't allow cigarettes on a mission, so it's uncertain why Archer knelt behind a tree to light up. Doc Simpson recalled that Archer never had a chance to lower his hands; he just keeled over, dead from a single round through the left eye.

All hell broke loose. The team executed Immediate Action Drill (IAD), firing off a full magazine as they backed into the jungle. Simpson carried the radio and immediately called for artillery and TAC air support. Although temporarily separated after the initial burst, the team was successfully extracted without further injury. After the target was bombarded throughout the night and well into the next day, Doc Simpson personally led the Nung force back to recover Archer's body.

Maurice Brakeman recalled that back at the Delta Club that night, many drinks were tossed down in Archer's memory. The air was permeated with a deep sadness as Archer had recently married a British woman just before his current tour. As Archer's roommate, it was Roderick's task to pack up his personal affects. It hadn't been all that long since he'd packed up Willie Stark's belongings. It was one of the toughest tasks he ever had to do—it was going to be a very long year.

Roderick had been inserted with recon teams north of Khe Sanh earlier, in the same area where several of their guys had been killed. Before going in he was briefed that it was a hot spot for enemy activity. But after his first trip, he believed the remark substantially understated the facts.

On a three-day mission with Team-3, they noticed some peculiar vehicle tracks and followed them. During the team's debriefing, Team-3 reported tracked vehicles operating in A Shau Valley—namely, enemy tanks. Nobody believed them.

He laughed, "They looked at us like we were nuts."[28]

---

[28] In 1966, the 1st Mobile Guerrilla Force LRRP Platoon operated in A Shau Valley for more than a month. The Platoon leader and Platoon sergeant, SFC Henry "Hank" Luthy, reported tanks, which was viewed with skepticism. The NVA eventually overran the Special Forces camp at Lang Vei using tanks. Hank Luthy went on to become the Special Operations Command Sergeant Major.

"I've mostly forgotten about many of our combat operations," Roderick recalled. "Or perhaps I've simply blanked them out. But what I do remember most was the strong camaraderie and bond between all us guys. They always stepped forward, regardless of the consequences, to save another."

His tone changed and his eyes grew misty, continuing, "There were disputes—of course. We gambled a little, and didn't always think some of the others were particularly honest, but even if you weren't part of that and you saw it, the best thing was to keep your mouth shut, or else you'd have us all to whip. We developed this special relationship—particularly within Recon— we were closer than brothers."

Roderick is a strong man, one not easily affected by sentiment, yet in his life the impact of those close relationships remains powerful and enduring.

* * * * * *

Intelligence reports all indicated the area around the Special Forces camp at Khe Sanh (eventually occupied by the 1st Marine Division) was heavily populated with VC and NVA regulars; precisely in the midst of the main supply route, the Ho Chi Minh Trail. Recon teams discovered an extensive storage area just south of the DMZ near the Laotian border. They called in air strikes and observed numerous secondary explosions as ammunition and fuel supplies went up in smoke. The NVA High Command couldn't let the U.S. military forces remain for long to disrupt those supplies, and poured troops into the area to dislodge them. Within only a few months, the Marines at Khe Sanh would be attacked by five crack NVA divisions, and the bloodiest battle of the war would ensue. The enemy would suffer more than 100,000 casualties before retreating into Laos.

It was on a recon mission into that same area, near the small village of Bong San, that Roderick's team had been cut off and nearly overrun. Recon Team-3 consisted of three Americans, Roderick, Gary Budd and SFC James W. Smyth, and three veteran Montagnards. Loaded aboard a "Slick" supplied by their reliable 281st AHC, they first made an attempt to infiltrate on their primary LZ, but were driven off by a barrage of enemy gunfire. Reviewing alternative courses of action, they spotted a clearing, another potential LZ, high on the side of a mountain. Wind currents were strong and space was scarce, but the 281st pilot finally got them close enough to be inserted. Exiting from a height of about six feet, they quickly melted into the jungle then headed due west. Advancing only one hundred yards, they came across a platoon-sized VC force. The VC were startled, the team alert and ready – the point man firing off half a magazine as they broke contact. Backing off, they evaded until dark, trying to avoid further enemy contact. The next morning, backtracking and traveling east, again, they encountered another substantial force. It quickly became obvious they were in the midst of a large enemy encampment.

As a strategy, both the NVA and VC were known to establish two defensive lines; an outer-perimeter and inner-perimeter. By making contact in both directions, the team concluded they had landed between the two. That left little choice but to return to their original LZ and request extraction. As it became evident they wouldn't make it before nightfall, they searched for a concealed spot to hold up until daylight. With their backs against a thirty-foot drop-off, they set up a night defensive position in a bamboo grove—and waited. In the blackness of night, they detected torches as the VC combed the mountainside searching for them. The buzz of a generator indicated either a regimental- or division-sized headquarters element was nearby. The team got very little sleep that night. Just before dawn, an enemy patrol stumbled upon their position in the thicket, a fierce firefight broke out and one of their Montagnard soldiers was killed instantly. The fight persisted for more than an hour with heavy firing on both sides, but repeatedly the recon teams' deadly accurate fire held them off. The team leader was well aware they were in serious trouble; they couldn't hold out for long with their backs against a steep ravine. It seemed as if they had few options; they were low on ammo and hadn't made contact with the FOB to request reinforcement or extraction.

Roderick's team pulled together in a tight circle to whisper about their alternatives, aware they had to move soon or be annihilated. It appeared the only escape route was over the cliff into the bamboo grove; they hadn't a clue as to what might be waiting—rocks, punji pits, booby-traps, the enemy—all possibilities. Once a decision was made, without hesitation, Smyth went first. Budd paused, then winked at Roderick and led the two remaining Montagnards over the edge. Roderick, covering their rear, positioned himself to jump when a grenade went off behind him, helping him complete the act. He landed hard, thankful he wasn't dead or didn't have any broken bones; but his body ached for days afterward. He sustained a wound to his left wrist when the grenade exploded, but it wasn't serious enough for him to be evacuated to the States. As a souvenir, he still wears that dark bit of blue shrapnel in his wrist.

Bruised but safe, they wanted to put as much distance between them and the enemy as possible. After thirty minutes of sprinting with sixty-pound rucksacks, exhausted and dehydrated, they finally paused to call for a helicopter and extraction. Since there was no suitable nearby LZs, they were told to expect extraction by rope ladder. As the chopper approached and hovered at forty feet, Roderick remained behind to cover the others as they laboriously climbed. He was the last one up, and just as he started his ascent, he caught sight of several VC closing in at the edge of the LZ. One-handed, he pointed his M16 and fired off three rounds; it was all that remained of the 450 rounds of ammo he started with.

When asked if he received a Purple Heart for the shrapnel in his left wrist, he laughed softly and held up his arm. "For this little thing? Hell, I was back in the field in a week."

Within a few months, Roderick was out with Smyth and Budd when he was wounded again, under circumstances he now laughs about. After being chased across a rice paddy by a hostile force, he lost his balance and sprawled forward as though pushed from behind. Leaping up quickly, he was off again when he detected a warm oozing wetness in the seat of his pants. Keeping up his pace, he wiped his hand across his buttocks and held it up to observe the red dampness. Heaving a sigh of relief, he was immensely grateful he'd only been wounded. What if it hadn't been blood? How could he ever explain in the Delta Club that he'd shit his pants? A wound in the butt, no matter how embarrassing, was bad enough—but it was a much easier thing to explain than loss of bodily control. He caught some ribbing anyway, but not nearly as bad as if he'd messed his pants.

Roderick sustained yet another wound before he left Project Delta, this time through his right elbow. His aging body still carries lead from those wounds, and although he has no Purple Hearts to show for them, it doesn't bother him. It never even occurred to him to ask for one.

"We all got wounds and injuries," Roderick said. "We'd simply drink a beer and ignore them for the most part, unless it was a really serious wound that required evacuation. We usually just put on a field dressing or band-aid and were told to quit belly-aching.

"In other words," Roderick's eyes twinkled, "in Delta you didn't get a John Kerry Purple Heart. You just expected a body leak for a while and were told 'Suffer through it, buddy—have another drink.'"

Roderick remembers the terrain as being extremely difficult. Mostly it was dense, compact, triple-canopy jungle and steep mountains. When the fog hung heavy and low, it was easy to stumble into the enemy without warning. He had only the highest praise for the gutsy chopper pilots who flew under those conditions.

He recalled that after an operation, no one ever bragged about their enemy kills, nor discussed the mission. What went down in the field was private among those who shared it. He admitted many of the guys were heroes. While praise was always bestowed on others, humility and a lack of self-aggrandizement were accepted traits; never did he imply he'd done anything particularly brave, noteworthy or heroic.

"There were no braggarts in Delta. All we wanted when we got back was to have a few beers and enjoy each other's company before time to go out again. We were more than buddies, like…brothers."

His voice soft, he said, "No, closer than brothers. That's what I remember the most about being with Delta—the camaraderie—we never spoke of it. The brotherhood endures to this day."

Roderick recalled that among his most difficult tasks was having to pack and ship a fallen comrade's affects home, as with Archer and Stark; those memories still bother him. With a voice still deep and strong, it is easy to tell how he could have been a member of this famed group.

In his sixties, William C. "Bill" Roderick's hair is touched with gray, and his movements are more measured and careful, but he remains tall and lean; his physique is much as it was in 1966 when he was a young Project Delta warrior.

* * * * * *

Maurice Brakeman had been on another mission the day Roderick was wounded and rotated back to the States. While it was Roderick's last mission, it was Brakeman's first."Brake" was then the FNG, tacked onto a team led by SFC Smyth. Sergeant First Class Strick and three Vietnamese Special Forces personnel were the others. They all inserted onto a ridgeline at last light and had moved a mere fifty yards into the black jungle before darkness forced them to halt for the night. A trail intersected the small LZ, leading the team to set up an RON position beyond it. Strick and Smyth, with the radio, moved a few meters to one side, while Brakeman, with the three VN, remained on the other. It was raining, the ground was soft and soggy, the air musty, and, as usual, leeches were everywhere.

As the evening breeze shifted, it wafted the most horrific, putrid smell he'd ever encountered. Even to a FNG, it was undeniably the stench of rotting corpses—human or animal. It didn't matter. They were all stuck there for the night. Using a wet handkerchief or a headband to cover their noses, two of the Vietnamese became nauseated, only adding to their misery. The stench was so powerful it permeated their clothing and skin. Whatever was rotting, it was very close.

Then they heard it. Someone—or something—was moving along the trail. Footsteps could be heard trudging down the trail between the two groups. It sounded large, and like a lot of...whatever it was. The VN personnel were scared stiff, but to Brakeman the sounds were a quandary. Unlike the squishing of sandals or boots treading on the damp jungle floor—these were more like sucking noises. Besides, they heard no whispered commands, no rattle of equipment and no lights. It would be impossible to move in that black jungle with so little noise, and with no illumination. The VC often moved at night, but they used torches. The sounds continued throughout the night and the small recon team froze in place, unable to move for fear of detection by this unknown entity.

The long-awaited dawn arrived and the mystery was finally revealed. The trail between them had been churned up—by pigs. As the team moved along the ridgeline toward their objective, the reason for all the traffic became apparent. Fifty meters to the left of the trail, a shallow grave and the remains of enemy corpses lay in the mud. The stench, while overpowering, never seemed to bother the pigs one bit. They grunted as they rutted in the mud, occasionally squealing with delight as they turned up a fresh corpse. Brakeman observed bones sticking up through the freshly churned mud—a hand here, a foot there—the scene would stay with him a lifetime.

* * * * * *

Sergeant First Class Gary Nichols spent four years with Delta, carrying the heavy PRC-25 radio on every mission. He smiled as he said, "It really wasn't all that heavy and because of it, I was never alone. It seemed everyone wanted to stay with me, no matter what happened."

The PRC-25 was a recon team's lifeline. Without the radio a mission might be more of a one way trip than they frequently were anyway. Nichols credits his survival to the Delta men and their camaraderie.[29] "We were closer than brothers and after all these years, still are. Their attitude in a wartime atmosphere set them apart from others I've ever served with. Never did any selfishness, fear or personal concern interfere with risking their life to assist a teammate."

By Nichols's recollections, Project Delta had it all; just traveling to work and living through each day was exciting—it might cost you your life—yet the sheer excitement was unmatched. He remarked that the anticipation was a "hoot," but once on the ground, the adrenalin rush was remarkable. Nothing could compare to the sensation of stalking others while being stalked, and of being on missions so secret it was difficult to convince those who had sent you of what you had seen. Tongue-in-cheek, Nichols offered, "I believe our mission documents should've carried the highest security classification, 'Burn Before Reading.'"

He retold what happened in 1969 when Roy Sprouse and Burhl Cunningham were running recon missions near the Rock Pile. They reported 125 loaded NVA trucks heading south across the DMZ. The Marines met this intelligence with skepticism and disbelief.

In recalling his first recon mission, Nichols remembers he left the Delta "Hilton" late, with SFC Richard "Buddha Belly" Delany, Roland Marque and Earl Sommeroff in tow. (Later, Sommeroff would be killed near the Laotian border.) During the first day out they confronted

---

[29] Gary Nichols. "Personal Reflections." Detachment B-52 (Project Delta), 1966-1970. http://www.projectdelta.net/nichols_story.htm

a Bengal tiger and two Viet Cong—by far, the tiger was the more intimidating. Later, Marque and Sommeroff detected a hidden trail, followed it and glimpsed an NVA unit eating lunch. A short distance away, an NVA radioman squatted on a rucksack with his rice pouch. Marque took a notion to capture him. He spent a lot of time crawling close enough, grabbed him by the scruff of his neck and picked him up, his radio and rucksack too, and ran like hell, while the entire NVA unit chased after them.

In the confusion, Marque became separated; for two days he was alone, despite his HT-1 radio and prisoner of war to keep him company. It was on this operation the HT-1 began to be referred to as "the little black box nobody listened to." Although he claimed to have called continuously, he never once made radio contact; however, he did manage to bring back his prisoner.

About Marque, Nichols said, "After that, he'd been pretty hard to live with."

During Nichols's next operation, Dennis Hapman and Edgar Morales, retreads from the 101st Airborne Division, joined him. The team was making good time before stopping for a break in a thick bamboo grove at the base of a steep hill. Suddenly, the distinct sound of a crowing rooster floated toward them from higher up. Nichols recommended retreating into the valley; the dense bamboo was making movement impossible, and they'd certainly be detected if they continued. The VN Warrant Officer disagreed, arguing they should continue forward and up the hill. Their VNSF point man sided with Nichols, claiming the orders stupid and steadfastly refusing to budge. The discussion became quite heated as they lobbed loud obscenities. The angry WO had just pushed the point man aside and taken a few steps when all hell broke loose. He was instantly hit in the head and chest; the point man was hit in the head. Blood, guts and bamboo splinters flew.

The small patrol returned fire as Nichols quickly checked on the downed WO and NCO. While the Warrant Officer was clearly dead, their point man was still alive, but critical—although much of his head had been blown off, he still breathed. The others, splattered with blood and bits of flesh, mainly sustained small cuts when nicked by the flying splinters. They all looked appalling, but miraculously none of the others had been hit in the hail of bullets. Nichols quickly gained control of the

SFC Walter "Doc" Simpson (*left*) and SFC Gary Nichols (*center*) preparing to infiltrate. (Photo courtesy of Gary Nichols)

team, moved them back into the jungle and toward a previously selected rally point, while calling for extraction. Standing by, the 1st Ranger Company was immediately dispatched to assist them, and to retrieve the dead officer.

* * * * *

During Nichols's four years, he counted numerous close calls, but none quite like the day his recon patrol arrived at an LZ for extraction after a fruitless three days out. Tired and dirty, he could almost taste the cold beer and steak awaiting him in Nha Trang. Unfortunately, they'd both have to wait. While his team hadn't made enemy contact, it was apparent some others had by the ruckus in the hills. In the distance, they knew a ferocious firefight was ongoing. They were informed all assets were being diverted to assist the Rangers, in heavy contact with a much larger enemy force. The LZ they'd chosen was in a large overgrown rice paddy. They set up security, hunkered down and waited. As usual, Nichols stayed close to his radio for news about their chopper, with an eye on his assigned perimeter. Suddenly he glanced up, straight into the muzzle of an SKS rifle held by a Viet Cong soldier. Time stood still—as did Nichols's heart.

Staff Sergeant Ken Eden turned and instinctively cut loose with his M-16, blasting the VC. Apparently, he'd fled the firefight with the Rangers and just happened to stumble upon them. Carrying two rifles, he strode across the open rice field and into the recon team's position without detection. Concerning Ken Eden's actions, Nichols remarked, "There will never be enough words to thank him."

Nichols had worked recon for ten months straight when he was offered one of two positions: either the Recon Supervisor job held by the departing Doc Simpson, or Joe Singh's job as Road Runner Supervisor. He decided to take Singh up on his offer. The Road Runners were mercenary Montagnards from all ethnic tribes who performed some of the most hazardous missions assigned to a four-man unit. Dressed in enemy uniforms and armed with enemy equipment, they moved at will on well-traveled trails and supply arteries deep inside enemy controlled territory, gathering intelligence on enemy units and caches, as possible targets. If discovered, they had only a slim chance of getting away with their lives, yet they returned time and again for this mission—their casualty and attrition rate was enormously high. Nichols held the Road Runner Supervisory position for sixteen months, and then returned to Recon for the duration of his time with Project Delta.

Nichols greatest honor was MAJ Charles Allen's recommendation for a direct combat commission. Allen also made the offer to Chuck Odorizzi and Bill Walsh. While Odorizzi and Walsh accepted, Nichols, already on the E-8 Master Sergeant's list, declined. Upon his retirement, he held the Army's highest enlisted grade, Command Sergeant Major.

* * * * * *

In January 1966, MAJ Charles Beckwith, seriously wounded during Operation Masher, returned to the United States. (He would later be called upon to form the famous Delta Force, and lead the Iranian hostage rescue attempt.) Following Beckwith's departure, MAJ John V. Keefe commanded Project Delta for a brief two months, then, in March 1966, LTC John S. Warren assumed command, remaining four months, followed by LTC John Hayes.

THIRTEEN

Team Viper:
"We're Hit, Bad!"

IT RAINED HARD THE DAY OF 29 November 1966, the sky gray and overcast. Six camouflaged men lugging rucksacks and automatic weapons made their way along the flight line toward a waiting Slick. There was no small talk or banter as they moved toward the idling chopper—their blackened faces calm and reflective. Each man exuded an air of confidence, innate capability. They'd done this before. This was Team Viper, Norm Doney's old recon team. With a ping of regret, Doney watched them load; he should be going—he was scheduled, but then at the last moment he had been reassigned as NCOIC of Recon Operations, albeit against his will. The shift was actually a promotion of sorts, well-earned, too; yet in his mind, he was still Recon—he wanted to stay. Perhaps it would be for the best. The interlude would give him time to change things he'd been fretting about—like eliminating those despised rope ladders that were either always breaking or causing his men to fall.

Team Viper consisted of SGT Russell Bott, SFC Willie Stark and four tough Vietnamese Special Forces personnel. They loaded onto the waiting chopper, oblivious to either Doney's concerns or the pummeling rain. Doney had no way of knowing the small group would be dropped onto a flat, room-sized plot in the mountainous jungle on the wrong side of the Laotian border or that only half would return.

With an ominous foreboding, Doney watched them load and lift-off. It wasn't just the damned weather that irked him. Russell Bott had been Doney's Demolitions Sergeant in Panama, and he liked the young man. But Russ was an experienced Recon man and good in the jungle—he'd do all right. Doney sighed, silently wished them well and turned toward the FOB Operations Center. Still, he couldn't shake the bad feeling.

* * * * * *

Bott sat nearest the door so he'd be the first one out, halfway convinced the pilot would abort due to the shitty weather. Although junior in rank to SFC Stark, Bott was still the most experienced and therefore, the One Zero in charge. As they flew west, the pilot suddenly increased altitude and his passengers' stomachs churned—the cloud cover was too low to fly between the mountains. There'd been many a rough flight when the men would whisper a familiar prayer, "If I'm gonna die . . . please God, don't let it be pilot error!" Bott noticed Willie staring at him and as he rolled his eyes, his buddy grinned back. If these expressions meant anything between them, they weren't the least bit funny to the VNSF troops. They sat motionless, their eyes wide, staring straight ahead. Below the small craft, white clouds were fluffy, soft and clean.

Bott and Stark both understood the importance of their mission. Higher command needed some vital information they were certain could be found along the international border, and they put pressure on the Delta Commander to get some boots on the ground quickly. In retrospect, some of the sage old Delta hands said the pilot should have aborted the operation—simply turned back, taken his ass-chewing like a man and drank some beer until the weather improved.

The team experienced a sudden gut-wrenching lurch as the pilot rapidly decreased altitude; he'd spotted a small hole in the thick cloud ceiling. The white void closed around them, then without warning, they popped though it, tree limbs poking through the low-hanging mist like boney fingers, reaching out for an elusive prey. The clouds, only moments earlier serene and white, suddenly became dark and menacing. Bott and Stark realized they were flying almost on the deck; their Vietnamese comrades appeared terror-stricken. Treetops flashed beneath them, barely a few feet below. They held on tightly, eyes searching the jungle floor as the pilot weaved a path between the mountains and the trees, seeking a reference point to pinpoint their location. Then the young pilot, who'd always been dead-nuts on with his navigation skills in the past, made a critical error. He mistook a rain-bloated stream for the river checkpoint he'd been searching for.

The chopper had barely settled when the team unloaded. They scampered into the wet, dank jungle, and instantly disappeared. The pilot shot his craft upward, glad to have blue sky above him once more. It wasn't until he returned to base well after dark that he cross-checked his reference points. Only then did he realize he missed the LZ entirely and had inserted Team Viper somewhere inside Laos.

Devastated, he argued to return immediately to search for them, but with the wind howling and the rain gusting in horizontal sheets across the runway, getting airborne would be impossible. Any attempt to rescue Team Viper would have to wait until the weather improved.

* * * * * *

Project Delta Commander LTC John Hayes was in a foul mood. One of his teams was lost in Laos. When the MACV Commander found out, there'd be hell to pay. The media would undoubtedly blow up this simple mistake, inadvertently made during a high-risk insertion into an international incident. He could almost envision the headlines: "U.S. Aircraft Lands Combat Troops Inside Neutral Laos." After spending thirty minutes behind closed doors—pacing, stomping about and cursing the weather, helicopter pilots, reporters and politicians of all ilks—Hayes was unusually subdued when he summoned his staff.

"We have to get those guys out of there and I want ideas on how to accomplish it. No one sleeps until we get it done," he ordered.

The next day, a Thursday, the weather had changed somewhat—it was worse. A radio-relay plane flying out of Da Nang had arrived on station, flew over the area where Bott and Stark's team had been dropped off, and reported back that the entire region was socked-in. They couldn't see a thing—only clouds. No one would be going up anytime soon.

But there had been some good news; Team Viper had made contact with the relay plane and they now knew they were in the wrong area. The requested a FAC ASAP to help establish their exact location as they attempted to move toward the border. Reporting a brief firefight with NVA regulars, they successfully broke contact and were moving east, trying to get back into Vietnam.

By midday, although the winds had subsided, the ceiling and visibility remained at less than 200 feet. Unannounced and undeterred, CPT John Flanagan and SGT Tommy Tucker strode to Flanagan's small fixed-wing plane, climbed aboard and, to everyone's amazement, took off into the thick pea soup. They would try to find Team Viper before the enemy did.

Flanagan performed some remarkable flying that day, finally contacting the team and pinpointing their location. They were still inside Laos but close to the Demilitarized Zone—and in the middle of a reported North Vietnamese Regimental headquarters. Returning to base, Flanagan pointed out that Team Viper was nearly 4,000 meters from where everyone originally thought. Flanagan also reported sighting numerous NVA units closing in on their position. If the team wasn't rescued soon, it would be too late. That night, the winds picked up again and the weather deteriorated even more, keeping all aircraft anchored to the runway. Hayes fumed and paced, and the staff stayed out of his way.

Friday morning dawned with more of the same; thirty-knot winds, overcast skies and dismal rain. The rain, although sporadic, was slammed horizontally by strong wind gusts. Staring at the dark sky, Delta personnel milled about helplessly, pacing and cursing the muck. The men's thoughts were not only on Team Viper, but with yet another recon team still out in the storm; one led by SSG St. Laurent. They hadn't been able to make radio contact with him either, and had no clue as to his location. St. Laurent was typical of Delta's NCO caliber; savvy and jungle smart. If anyone could survive in those conditions, he could. Listening to the radio traffic on Bott and Stark, St. Laurent felt badly, probably worse than he should have. He was the guy who had backed Bott's bid to become a recon member when no one wanted to take a chance on a demo sergeant.

The FOB staff and the other teams silently milled around the main tent, straining to hear any word about the lost team. The silence was unbearable. Again, John Flanagan had enough. He simply walked over to his small plane, climbed in and took off through a brutal side-wind. Within thirty minutes, he made contact with St. Laurent's team.

"…just hunker down and stay where you are. We've got a team in trouble on 'the other side,' and we're trying to locate them. Try not to stir up a hornet's nest, because no one can come for a while. Copy?"

"Copy," St. Laurent replied. "We'll be right here. Out."

Flanagan turned his small craft toward Laos.

Another transmission came through from the radio relay plane to the FOB; the room exploded in cheers upon learning that Flanagan had made contact. Then elation quickly shifted to gloom after hearing the news that Viper had taken casualties. Flanagan was returning to refuel, but relayed the battered team had to get out ASAP or they were finished. The Rangers, American advisors and several SF medics were all standing by, ready to go at a moment's notice—but the weather still wasn't cooperating.

Hayes finally decided "to hell with it" and made the decision to go. The men hustled to ready a Slick as the pickup aircraft, another as backup, a Hayes Command & Control (C&C) chopper and two gun ships. Without a word, SGT Irby Dyer hoisted his medical bag and double-timed it toward one of the helicopters. He'd man the machinegun and, as a medic, attend to the wounded once they were extracted. Only a few minutes out, the C&C ship made contact with Team Viper. Bott asked if the rescue helicopters had been launched; Stark was so badly wounded he couldn't be moved. The transmission interrupted briefly, then Bott came back on—they were under heavy attack and others were wounded.

Those remaining at the FOB anxiously huddled, listening to the C&C ship's choppy, one-sided radio conversation with Bott, trying desperately to fill in the blanks left by the loud static interruptions. Their area was still socked in, and they heard the C&C helicopter tell Bott they were having difficulty locating him. Viper reported they could periodically hear a chopper, but through the thick low clouds

Aug 1966, Tay Ninh (Operation 10-66 Phase III). *Front, L to R*: SGT Johnny Varner (WIA), SGT Eugene Moreau (KIA), SFC Norman Doney, SSG Andre St. Laurent. *Rear, L to R*: SSG Rolfe Raines, SGT Vincent O'Connor. (Photo courtesy of Norman A. Doney)

they couldn't tell where. A transmission relay to Khe San asked if John Flanagan would come again to help try to pinpoint the team—Flanagan never hesitated. Delta Recon NCO Tom Tucker climbed into the rear seat of Flanagan's small fixed-wing plane, and together they took off in a vicious cross-wind with fifty-knot gusts. How they made it, no one could explain. By the time Flanagan arrived, the helicopters had only twenty minutes of fuel remaining. Flanagan made contact with Viper and immediately recognized Bott's voice above the background chatter of automatic weapons fire and exploding grenades. It was evident a vicious firefight was underway.

"We're surrounded," Bott informed him, his voice more calm than it should've been. "Willie's been hit pretty bad...I can't move him... and I won't leave him. We're split from our indigenous guys, and we're alone. What can you do for me?"

"Keep the key to your handset depressed, and I'll try to guide in on your signal."

Guided only by the signal, Flanagan finally flew over Viper's position, rewarded by Bott's prearranged codeword.

"Payoff. Payoff."

"Throw smoke," Flanagan told him, "so I can guide the rescue ship in."

Purple smoke wafted up, indicating that Bott's location was in a thicket of elephant grass at the crest of a small knoll. Flanagan flew low, and when he drew no ground fire, cleared the recovery helicopter to go in. Just as the pilot managed to maneuver his chopper to less than ten feet from Bott's position, the hillside erupted in automatic fire. Tracers streaked as the elephant grass parted, and NVA soldiers popped from camouflaged "spider holes" that had been concealing weapon emplacements. The vicious fire concentrated on the hovering helicopter—it was literally shot to pieces.

"I'm hit!"

Flanagan flinched at the chopper pilot's startled cry.

"We're all hit! Going down…going down!"

The chopper pilot grunted as he took another hit. He watched helplessly as the wounded pilot struggled with the ship's controls, hopelessly trying to keep it airborne. The chopper strained and shuddered violently as it drifted sluggishly to the left about two-hundred feet, then plunged, struck the ground and dissolved into a fireball. It continued to roll with its cargo of two pilots, two door gunners and Delta Recon medic, SSG Irby Dyer. Flanagan fired a rocket at the enemy's location, marking it so the gunships could bring them under fire and protect the downed helicopter crew. But with the craft's condition, Flanagan knew they were all dead. It had been a trap. It was the helicopter they were waiting for, and Viper was the bait. Now, the rescue crew was down too, probably dead. Remaining in contact, he overheard one pilot say the lead gunship had its fire-control system shot out leaving it useless as a gun platform. They would have to return to base.

Bott came back on the radio just long enough to report he had used up all of his and Stark's ammunition; he was now armed only with the silenced .22 pistol he always carried and two remaining magazines. The radio sputtered loud static and what may have been gunfire, then the transmission faded as it had before.

Back in Khe Sanh at the FOB, they listened to the helicopter pilot's final words, then the words came that would give them all chills—the ones they all were silently dreading and praying wouldn't come. The Delta Commander in the C&C ship directed Viper to escape and evade back toward base camp—the helicopters were out of fuel and had to return to Khe Sanh. Viper was alone. Every Recon man fears this the most—being abandoned to fend for themselves. It was gut-wrenching news. Someone whispered hoarsely, "We've got to help them."

Long after the other aircraft departed, Flanagan's small, single engine plane circled over Bott's position, reluctant to leave, yet helpless to do anything for the battered team. As a witness to this experience, it would haunt him his entire life; he documented it in his book, *Vietnam Above the Treetops.*

Bott's last transmission continued to echo in his mind. "FAC, please help us, we're hit bad and can't hold out."

These last words were spoken by a very brave man who simply wouldn't leave his wounded friend as ordered. In a fatalistic attempt to forestall the inevitable, Flanagan then expended his last rocket at the enemy emplacements. He flew a wide circle over Viper's position again and saw no sign of them, only the mashed down grass where they had lain. He circled again above the downed chopper; there were no signs of life, only a small trail of smoke drifting from the twisted wreckage.

LLDB (VNSF) MG Doan van Quang (*left*) presents Vietnamese Jump Wings to Project Delta's two FAC pilots, USAF 1LTs Flannagan (*3rd from right*) and Simpson (*2nd from right*). SFC Donald Roberts (*right*) looks on. (Photo courtesy of Norman A. Doney)

No movement. No signs of life. Only the silent jungle. Team Viper was gone. His heart heavy, John Flanagan turned his plane eastward toward Khe Sanh; he landed in the raging crosswind again, but it hardly mattered now.

* * * * * *

Lieutenant Colonel John G. Hayes assumed command of Project Delta in September 1966 as they continued support of the 196th Inf Bde. He weathered the political storm caused by Delta's insertion into Laos, and went on to serve another three months as Delta's Commander. Sergeant First Class Arthur Glidden was KIA with CPT Swope while assisting a team in trouble during a FAC over-flight. In December 1966, Delta was deployed to support the 3rd Marine Division near Khe Sanh, in Quang Tri Province. This was the operation where Recon men SGT Russell P. Bott, SFC Willie E. Stark and Ranger Advisor SGT Irby Dyer of the 81st were all lost. Bott was posthumously awarded the Distinguished Service Cross; Stark, the Silver Star.

Russell Bott and Willie Stark both remain on Army rolls as missing in action (MIA), presumptive finding of death (PFD), yet some evidence persists that this might not be the case. It was clear from Bott's radio communication that Willie Stark had been badly injured and that Bott had refused to leave his wounded comrade. Earlier, he'd told the two surviving Vietnamese to leave and evade back toward Khe Sanh. These two Vietnamese were picked up several days later, exhausted but unharmed. During debriefings, they reported after they'd left the two Americans at Bott's insistence, they remained nearby, but no other shots were fired that day. They related how they hid in the tall grass, and overheard an NVA officer say, "Ah, here you are. We've been looking for you."

Reports from intelligence agents on the ground state the following day Bott had been seen alive, his hands bound, walking northward on trails leading into Laos. Three years later, an agent reported Bott and Stark were in Laos in a POW compound. Unresolved POW issues remain a grave bone of contention for Project Delta survivors, Special Operations Association members, prior service vets and dependents. No one really knows how many American POWs, or their remains, are still in Southeast Asia.

B-52 CO LTC John Hayes (*far right*) with unidentified Marine chopper pilots working with Project Delta at Khe Sanh during Operation 13-66. (Photo courtesy of Norman A. Doney)

* * * * * *

In March 1967, Delta Recon teams were again inserted in the An Lao Valley to support the 1st Cav Division. Sergeant First Class William C. Roderick was again wounded and evacuated. This time he received a Purple Heart. Sergeant First Class Allen H. Archer, KIA, was posthumously awarded the Silver Star; Walter L. (Doc) Simpson received the Bronze Star for valor.

FOURTEEN

Heart and Soul

PROJECT DELTA MAY WELL HAVE BEEN THE GREATEST collection of talent and combat skill ever assembled in a small group. A closed society, there was little debate that those belonging to this exclusive club were an unmistakable alliance, analogous to the blending of King Arthur's knights with Robin Hood's merry band of thieves. They could easily down voracious volumes of booze and beer, and occasionally fought among themselves with as much zeal as against their enemies, yet rallying to each others' aid if ever threatened. Names such as Chuck Allen, Norm Doney, Charlie Beckwith, Wiley Gray, Joe Alderman, Moose Monroe and others, became legendary, yet none dominated; all were leaders who stepped forward when situations warranted it, then stepped aside when time to do so. Among these was "Doc" Simpson.

Master Sergeant Walter "Doc" Simpson was an MOS 18D, Special Forces school-trained medic. Simpson, a hard-nosed ex-Marine, was a no-nonsense guy who incessantly kept his conversational tone serious. Gary Nichols described him this way, "…tall and lanky, straight brown hair, his face weather-beaten; he seemed hard pressed to smile."

Most folks noticed it; "Doc" Simpson never smiled. Some say he laughed on the inside; but if true, it never reached his lips or eyes. Some worried about his stoic expression, whispering that he was just a little too mechanical. But, you never heard that from those who had been with him on patrol. It didn't matter if he never smiled or showed warmth; Doc Simpson knew Special Forces operations better than anyone, and especially how to conduct recon. Serving nearly three years with Delta's most experienced and capable, when he spoke, everyone, regardless of rank, listened. Recon was what Doc did, and you'd better think twice before going with him if you weren't as deadly serious as he was about his profession.

To a man, Simpson was highly respected, if not necessarily liked. He was given the responsibility-laden job of Recon Supervisor and although only a sergeant first class, his word was never disputed nor overridden—by officer or enlisted. He became the confidant of commanders, advisor to staff officers and mentor to the NCOs and young officers. All followed his recommendations without question. The consensus was unanimous: no better man could be in charge of the Recon Section—or your life.

After the An Loa Valley operation, when numbers in the Recon Section fell to only four teams, due to casualties and attrition, Doc Simpson took his turn in the hole as a team member. Delta had less than a half-dozen "fieldable" recon teams during this time, yet higher command requirements for viable intelligence dramatically increased. Frequently, exhausted teams would be picked up from one area, only to be briefed on a new mission while still on the helicopter, provided fresh rations, water and ammo, and then reinserted.

Bobby Pruett served three tours in Vietnam. Among his awards for service and valor are the Silver Star and three Bronze Stars. It was during his second tour that he met Doc Simpson, whom he credits with saving his life many times over. Pruett, having served with Project Delta's BDA Company (Nungs), the 81st Airborne Ranger Battalion and as a Recon Team Leader, said, "Between Doc Simpson's wisdom and Joe Alderman's 'tricks of the trade,' well, I definitely owe them my life." Pruett served with both Project Delta and SOG, retiring as a command sergeant major.

From October 1967 to October 1968, Al Greenup served as a recon team leader under SFC Simpson's tutelage. Shortly after assignment, Greenup and two other FNGs were summoned to meet with Doc Simpson; Simpson held the men's longevity in his hands. If he didn't want to keep them, they were gone. No one would override his decision. The FNGs had just completed two of their first "wet" operations during their "probationary" status. Greenup recalled the meeting did not go especially well for them. Never one to mince words, Doc went straight for the jugular about how pathetically they'd screwed up on their recent "piss-poor" recon mission and proclaimed he'd given them both an "unsatisfactory" performance report. He chastised them for everything: bad eye-sight, poor self-discipline and being as noisy as a "herd of water buffalo" in the brush. Downtrodden after being severely critiqued by the Master, they left the meeting with heavy hearts; Greenup more determined than ever to demonstrate he had what it took to become Recon with Project Delta. However, he noticed the other NCO had been sent to collect his belongings. Without fanfare, he quietly departed; his departure hardly caused a ripple.

Years later, Greenup contemplated that incident and what occurred that day, and finally it all became clear. When first assigned, he'd been reminded it was strictly a volunteer outfit; he could quit at any time without repercussion. Then he learned that everyone, not just the FNGs, were being continually evaluated, even the veterans, and they might be involuntarily removed if diminished skills or attitude warranted. While some realized up-front they weren't cut out for this kind of work, others never would figure it out, or were determined to stay and get it right. Delta's missions called for tough decisions to be made by tough men—and Doc Simpson was a tough man. His decisions affected not only these men, but the lives of his other recon men; put a marginal man in the field, and he might well get the whole team wiped out. When the other FNG was let go, Greenup was impressed by how Doc Simpson went about it—quietly, without excessive embarrassment to the individual. In the process, he demonstrated removal was never an indictment of one's courage, values or personal standards. While Delta's mission simply wasn't for everyone, it was important to complete an involuntary release without personal humiliation.

One of the rare photos of SFC Walter "Doc" Simpson. 1966. (Photo courtesy of Bill "Pappy" Gleason)

Greenup said, "Doc Simpson was a tough man who made tough calls, but he did it intelligently, and always left a man with his dignity."[30]

If the term "Mister Recon" could ever be applied to any one man in Project Delta, it would undoubtedly be Walter "Doc" Simpson. By all accounts, he was a man's man, a strict task master, mentor, warrior and patriot. He was the kind of soldier that one did not simply like or dislike—but all respected. Many Delta Recon men will say they owe their lives to this man called "Doc," either directly, as a result of his actions, or indirectly, through his mentorship and strict training. Doc Simpson retired in 1978 then piloted a Missouri Riverboat. He eventually moved back to his home in Tennessee, where in 1981, while mowing his mother-in-law's lawn, he suffered a heart attack and died. Doc will always be remembered by his Delta Recon brothers as a master of the craft.

* * * * * *

As an NCO, Greenup was a recon operator for a year. Upon completing several years with Special Forces, the majority of them in Special Ops, he left the service and returned to college. After graduating, he joined the Air Force and became a pilot, flying Special Operations aircraft. He retired with the rank of Air Force Colonel. His intelligence and determination attests to the high caliber of Delta's NCOs.

---

[30] Jerry D. Estenson, PDA, Professor, College of BA, California State U., Sacramento. "Perceptions of Critical Leadership Attributes Provided by Three Generations of Military Special Operations Personnel," 49.

FIFTEEN

A Shau: Valley of Death

AFTER LEAPING LENA'S 1964 DEBACLE OF USING only Vietnamese-cadre on recon teams, Project Delta combat operations started out small, both in terms of personnel involved and in duration. Activity quickly expanded as Delta's capabilities and combat expertise evolved, and with higher command's increasing demands for more intelligence. By 1967, Delta was launching full-blown combat operations requiring as many as thirty-six C-130 troop transport aircraft to move the unit for an operation, relying on the 81st Airborne Ranger Battalion as its quick reaction/reinforcement force. However, rotary-wing aircraft support was still difficult to obtain; teams frequently stared at the ominous black sky, waiting anxiously for the drone of a rescue chopper to whisk them to safety, or simply back to Nha Trang for rest and medical treatment.

Recon was Project Delta's sole purpose, but without helicopters, it couldn't have survived. These odd contraptions performed an important role in Project Delta operations; they were essential for insertions, extractions, command and control, close-fire support and medical evacuations. Early on, this support had been provided by VNAF elements using CH-34 helicopters, L-19 fixed-wing observation aircraft and C-47 troop carriers for parachute operations and re-supply drops.

Hughes "Slick" helicopter with recon team. The bundles beneath the doors are rolled 30-foot rope ladders. While the rope facilitated retrieving the men, the exterior lines were aircraft cable; the rungs ribbed, aluminum-alloy pipe. (Photo courtesy of Maurice Brakeman)

After 1966, air support was primarily furnished by U.S. assets, but since there was never enough to go around no matter whom provided it, augmentation was always provided by the Marines, VNAF or other U.S. divisions.

Delta veterans are prolific in their recollections about helicopter support, both good and bad. Almost to a man, they have fond memories of the unit that had served them the longest and best—the 281st AHC pilots and crews. The men knew if they called on the 281st for extraction, the crews would recover them or die trying. This sense of confidence about the 281st wasn't felt for all other helicopter units that supported Project Delta.

Sergeant Major (Ret.) Donald Taylor recalls the day Edgar Morales was stuck on the ground near Quan Loi. Sergeant First Class Jerry Nelson had been flying recovery with a chopper crew from a different helicopter support platoon. The tall vegetation at the extraction site made landing the aircraft impossible, so Nelson rolled out a rope ladder. Most of the team reached the skid and slipped safely inside the chopper without incident, but Morales was the last man up. As he continued his climb, shots rang out—they'd been spotted. Without warning, the young pilot pulled-pitch and hauled ass while Morales clung precariously halfway up. To make matters worse, Morales hadn't had time to snap his rucksack into the bottom rung, and was trying to climb with the heavy weight still on his back. The load was about to drag him backward; all he could do was hang on for dear life. To release his grip and attempt to drop

Recon team practicing rope ladder extractions, Nha Trang. (Photo courtesy of Len Boulas)

his rucksack would have meant a tumble to the ground and a quick death. It was clear Morales didn't have the strength to hold out until the chopper reached a suitable LZ, yet he couldn't let go to snap in. He just held on and prayed for a miracle.

Nelson immediately understood Morales's plight, and told the pilot to slow down. When the pilot ignored him, Nelson slid his CAR-15 under the pilot's helmet and placed the muzzle behind his left ear. Softly, he requested the pilot to please reconsider. Taylor remarked, "Jerry was never one to mince words."[31] The pilot immediately slowed to sixty knots. Taylor continued, "Jerry slid over the open ledge and climbed toward Morales as though performing a circus trapeze act, while the ladder flapped in the wind."

Flipping to Morales's opposite side, Nelson safely snapped the two of them to the dangling rope ladder. Morales's prayers were answered.

* * * * * *

Many believe if Project Delta had made the call, their Vietnamese air assets, the 219th Special Operations Squadron (King Bees), would

---

[31] Donald Taylor, "Remembering the 281st AHC," http://www.projectdelta.net/remembering_the_281st.htm.

never have been given up. Once trained for Delta-type operations, they were as talented as the best pilots. Furthermore, the VN aircrews operated at the Delta Commander's direction; he not only paid their salaries but provided food and lodging.

Some King Bee crewmembers later transitioned to the United States and have become U.S. citizens; many attend the annual Special Operations Association Reunion (SOAR) held in Las Vegas, Nevada.

* * * * * *

Once the King Bees were pulled off to support SOG full-time, Delta initially was supported by helicopter elements from the 145th Airlift Platoon (which consolidated with the 6th Aviation Platoon, January 1966) and thereafter designated as the 2nd Platoon, 171st Aviation Company (AC). The 2/171st remained under the control of the Commander, 5th Special Forces Group, with whom Delta had to compete for support. In July 1966, and only after the 281st AHC assumed the assets of the 171st, it was attached exclusively to Project Delta for their operations.

Still, since they were handy and remained in the 5th Group compound, the attachment didn't preclude them from being pulled periodically for other 5th Group requirements. That status continued until completion of Operation Yellow Ribbon, December 1969. During that time, Delta conducted thirty-nine combat operations while using the helicopter assets of twenty-three different U.S. Army and Marine aviation units, only a few with any Project Delta experience. With outstanding results, the 281st AHC provided primary aviation support for twenty-four of these thirty-nine operations. Between the time span of Operation Yellow Ribbon and when Delta was deactivated in 1970, helicopter support was provided primarily by the units Delta supported with their Recon and Ranger assets. One thing was certain, helicopters were always in short supply—they kept getting shot down.

Captain Robert "Mo" Moberg (call-sign Bandit 21) was at the controls, with CWO Johnson as co-pilot, the day their Slick went down in A Shau Valley. The crew chief, Smith, a young door gunner, Corney, and Doc Simpson were also aboard. There were no suitable LZs, so Simpson went along as Recovery NCO; he'd operate the hoist for the jungle penetrator they would use to rescue the recon team.

Earlier, the FAC spotted the exhausted team through a small jungle clearing as they hunkered down on the side of a heavily forested hill. A Shau Valley had very few suitable LZs, and since the enemy was always aware of them, the penetrators were the primary means for extracting teams. Another chopper had already pulled out three members of the stranded team using one, having retrieved one American and two Vietnamese before ground fire drove them off. Forced to hover during the extraction, the helicopter had taken some serious fire and was hit numerous times. Fearing the helicopter might be lost, MAJ Chuck "Bruiser" Allen called off the operation before the remainder of the team could be hoisted out. Sergeant First Class Robinette (Team Leader), SSG Jay Graves (One One) and one of the Vietnamese recon men stayed behind.

Using the radio, Allen sharply chastised Robinette. "Get your shit in order and find a safe LZ!" he barked.

"I've got my shit in order," Robinette replied calmly. "Now I'm looking for that Slick you promised would get us out of here."

Basically, three types of Hughes helicopters were used for Project Delta operations. Gunships were all heavily armed, with two mini-guns and rocket pods for protecting other aircraft and troops being infiltrated or extracted from an LZ. Mini-guns, similar to Gatling guns, use multiple rotating barrels to spew their awesome firepower. The C&C ship always carried the operation's command and control element, generally the Delta Commander or one of his primary staff. During Chuck Allen's leadership, he was always on board. The Slick referred to by Robinette was without heavy armament (firepower), but had an M-60 machinegun in both side doors. These were specifically used for infiltrations and extractions either by landing, rappelling, rope ladders, McGuire Rigs or by using jungle penetrators. Generally, Slicks were always manned with a pilot, co-pilot, crew chief and either one or two door-gunners for the door-mounted 7.62 light machineguns. The Hughes (Huey) could carry a squad of combat-equipped soldiers, making it perfect for the type of operations Project Delta ran.

Mo knew Bruiser's C&C ship was nearby because he heard Allen and Robinette's verbal exchange over his headset.

The recon team, led by SFC Orville "Robbie" Robinette, had been chased for more than two days by a large NVA unit due to the scarcity of suitable LZs for pickup. In the A Shau Valley, the "Cong" owned the place. The team was near exhaustion. They already called several times the FAC spotted them. With only three of them left on the ground, Moberg worried they wouldn't be able to hold out for long. He requested the C&C pilot to direct him toward the team's location, and as he hovered, his skids skimmed the tree tops. It was a gutsy maneuver for any pilot, but Moberg knew it might be the only chance. Unable to judge distance or terrain, Moberg blindly followed the C&C's directions, expecting to feel the impact of tree limbs or rounds at any moment.

"Right three degrees...left five degrees...hold heading...."

He glanced over the nose and saw Jay Graves standing. Moberg fought to steady the helicopter as Doc Simpson operated the hoist; the agonizingly slow jungle penetrator dropped through the trees. After he'd played out more than 200 feet of cable, he yelled in frustration, "It won't reach!"

Gritting his teeth, Moberg settled his chopper down lower until cracking noises signified his rotor blades were clipping the treetops. The door gunner startled them all by opening up with his M-60; they were receiving fire from his side of the aircraft. Using his headset, Doc informed Moberg they had Jay Graves on the hoist, but Moberg couldn't move the craft for fear of dragging him through the trees. The aircraft heaved as large caliber rounds hit; the bottom wind-screen all but disappeared and the cockpit filled with blue acrid smoke. When a B40 rocket slammed into the crippled craft, the concussion knocked Moberg's right foot off the pedal. Fighting to keep his ship upright, the helicopter began drifting to the left; he struggled to correct it. Glancing quickly at CWO Johnson, his hands clutching the cyclic in a death-grip, Moberg knew he had to get his co-pilot off the controls.

"I've got it!" Moberg cried out. Startled, Johnson let go.

The aircraft kept drifting to the left, and Moberg realized he had no cyclic or pedals to control it. He made a swift decision to ditch it in the trees rather than into the valley 500 feet below.[32] Brush and tree limbs splintered and crumbled crazily around it. Bracing themselves, it took a nose dive, finally coming to a stop upside down in the tree limbs. It had

---

[32] Robert Moberg, "Shot Down with Robbie," http://www.projectdelta.net/shot_down.htm.

miraculously stopped its descent only six feet from the jungle floor. Moberg fought to get his door open, screaming, "Where the hell is my gun? Who's seen my gun?"

Doc calmly poked him in the ribs with his own M-16. "Here…take mine…and get the hell out of here before this thing blows up."

Doc and Smith had been thrown clear when they hit, both sustaining broken ribs. They quickly went back, and then scrambled toward the exit just in case the aircraft's fuel tanks lit up. Once outside the smoldering aircraft and accounted for, Doc and Moberg climbed back in again, this time to cut off the whining converters, and to retrieve the M-60 machinegun and some ammunition. Clueless as to how long they might be stranded, they knew it was going to get rough, and they'd need all the extra firepower they could muster. Doc reemerged with the M-60 and first aid/survival kit. The pilot managed to retrieve his CAR-15 and gave Doc's rifle back to him. As they stumbled up the hill toward the recon team, Jay Graves walked to Moberg and planted a big wet kiss on the top of his head.

"God damn, I knew you'd come get me, Mo," he said cheerfully.

Captain Moberg outranked Robinette, and under normal military protocol, should've taken command. But Delta Recon had its own rules. As in all operations, the One Zero might be junior in rank to other patrol members, but the one most experienced was always in charge, regardless of his rank—others followed his instructions. Robinette reminded Moberg that he was still in charge. Moberg shrugged. He was a chopper pilot—what did he know about ground combat operations? He seemed just as pleased to keep it that way, "You're doing a fine job, Robbie. Keep right on trucking. Tell me what you want me to do."

Robinette assigned positions and fields of fire along a trail above the downed helicopter for a hasty ambush. He reasoned that once the enemy realized a chopper had gone down, they'd come to investigate. Over the PRC-25, the Bruiser quickly advised them to stay put until he could identify another LZ and notify the 81st Rangers to get them out. Their water and ammo divided among them, Doc placed the M-60 in a position where he could cover the trail.

After recovering from the terrifying crash and some initial discussion, the jungle reverted to an eerie quiet; each lay silently, intently watching their assigned area. Moberg was the first to hear soft Vietnamese voices from below them on the hill. A man trotted toward the chopper, then paused about twenty yards away while staring down the hill. He came to a halt so quickly his squad began to stumble onto each other, bunching up. The small contingency of Americans had been anticipating the 81st Ranger reinforcements that Allen said were coming, and initially hoped it was them. Moberg had the best position to observe them, but the web harness and helmets seemed all wrong. These wore pith helmets—NVA headgear.

Moberg glanced at Robinette who was licking his lips and carefully taking aim with his CAR-15. As Moberg gazed over his rifle at the squad, the leader spun, his helmet star reflecting like a beacon. Eyeing the downed chopper, the leader pointed and began to scream an order when Moberg and Robinette's automatic bursts cut him down. Every American seemed to cut loose at once.

Doc's M-60 rattled off perfect three-round bursts as it plowed up the jungle. Nary a word was spoken by this seasoned bunch—the only clamor came from controlled bursts of fire, magazine changes and explosive concussions as they occasionally lobbed a grenade at an NVA position. It took only minutes to decimate the entire enemy unit. Robinette silently signaled them to pull back. Moberg helped Doc cart the heavy machinegun and extra ammo back up the hill, noting that during all the commotion, the recon guys had communicated only with hand signals, each man instinctively doing his part. They moved rapidly toward another ridgeline, just north of where the aircraft went down, and set up yet another defensive perimeter inside a clump of tall elephant grass. Remaining motionless, they detected enemy units moving up the other side, firing into the trees above them, trying to draw their fire. No one moved or responded. They knew the enemy was just trying to locate their position.

After a few more minutes, Robinette crawled to each man, whispering that the Rangers were inbound; everyone was to follow Graves as he took point and moved them farther north. As they pulled out, several Vietnamese shouted from the direction Graves had just led out. Firing erupted, and they again sought cover. Graves and the VNSF lieutenant were on point. Both fired, cutting the enemy patrol to pieces. Later, the Vietnamese lieutenant told Graves the enemy had been shouting for the Americans not to shoot, that they were out of ammunition.

Whether or not a ruse, they'd never know; the team wondered…could they have taken prisoners? Astounded by the notion, Moberg concluded, "Isn't that just like a bunch of Recon guys? Here we are, stranded, behind enemy lines, low on ammunition, and with only a slight chance of staying alive, and they're contemplating taking prisoners!"

After the ruckus finally abated, the team moved rapidly, anxious to be out of the area. They slid down the far side of the hill, away from the NVA racing up from behind. Smitty, the door gunner, carried the heavy M-60 and was having trouble keeping up; Moberg took it, then handed him his CAR-15. Jay Graves, still on point, tirelessly led as they fought through the dense undergrowth for hours without pause. Finally, he held them up and they waited. Soon, he returned—he'd made contact with the Ranger reaction force. Words were never spoken or necessary as the Rangers set up a blocking force. The exhausted patrol passed silently through their line, pausing beside a small stream at the base of the mountain where they saw orange panels laid out. Within minutes, a Marine CH-46 helicopter came in; everyone immediately climbed aboard—except for Moberg. In a daze, exhausted, spent and unable to move, Moberg stood stoically as the tailgate began to close—they were leaving him behind. The chopper ascended then settled back; the tailgate again lowered. This time Robinette's hand shot out. Grabbing Moberg by his harness, he jerked him in like a sack of potatoes.[33]

The chopper took a few rounds as it lifted off, and simultaneously everyone returned fire. Finally out of M-16 ammunition, Graves dropped it and began firing with his .45-caliber pistol. Sitting on the floor of the craft, too tired to move, Moberg stared in disbelief and shook his head. Recon guys just never knew when to quit!

After landing at Dong Ha to refuel and change aircraft, a 281st AHC Slick transported them to Hue Phu Bai. After bandaging Smith and Doc Simpson for their broken ribs, the medics spent the next two days removing thorns from their punctured bodies. Since Simpson never complained once, and no one knew his ribs were broken, they wondered how he ever endured the arduous trek through the mountains. Beyond that, they suffered no casualties other than bruised egos for losing the helicopter—and perhaps for failing to capture those prisoners.

---

[33] *Ibid.*

SIXTEEN

The Twilight Zone

THE VC RELIED HEAVILY ON BOOBY-TRAP DEVICES to slow troop progress and produce casualties; they'd dig a small hole in a trail or beside it, then fill it with sharpened bamboo stakes—often smeared with human excrement. If punctured by one of these doctored stakes, blood poisoning was imminent. Maurice "Brake" Brakeman recollects some experiences with the VC's nasty homemade booby-traps.

After an acute bout of diarrhea, he missed his regular rotation for pulling recon, but upon recovering, he was sent out with a guy he remembers only as Lieutenant Sullivan. Brake really hated going out with Sullivan; he really wasn't a bad guy, only big—and clumsy. Brakemen recalls, "He got hung up on every 'wait-a-minute' vine, and would stumble over any small rock within ten feet of the trail. He could've stood stock still and made a racket; not exactly cut out for recon...a hell-of-a-nice guy and probably would've made a fine neighbor."

It was during one of Brakeman's operations that a team member was lost due to a punji-trap. During a halt, LT Tommy Richardson stepped off the trail to defecate and committed a cardinal sin—he never looked behind him as he squatted. A feces-tipped punji punctured the back of his thigh; it became infected within minutes and eventually caused gangrene. He decided to tough it out because he didn't want to report the incident to his One Zero, but the following day, the sergeant noticed him limping in obvious pain. Insisting on examining the young officer's wound, he immediately called for extraction. The lieutenant had either been too proud, stubborn or tough to complain and admit he'd screwed up the mission. He didn't want to be the cause of cutting the recon short, just because he "had a little sticker." He was admitted to the hospital, and nearly lost his leg. The team never saw him again and that was their loss, for he'd been an old SF hand from Okinawa and potentially had the makings of a solid One Zero.

Captain Henry "Hugh" Shelton also had a run-in with one of those vicious little contraptions during a night raid with a company of Montagnards. As darkness approached, the company was fired on, the point man killed outright. All hell broke loose as more firing engulfed them from positions on the top of a nearby ridgeline. As the Americans got the Montagnard tribesmen fanned out and moving toward the top of the hill, they encountered expedient early warning devices the VC had set out, and numerous punji traps and stakes, almost impossible to see in the failing light. Feeling a burning pain in his lower leg that jolted him to an abrupt halt, Shelton reached down and discovered a punji stake had entered the front and exited through the rear of his calf. He took out his K-Bar and under extreme pain cut the stake, both in front and back, freeing himself, and then continued upward in the assault. Later that night, they removed the remainder of the embedded punji, but Shelton refused to be evacuated until the mission was completed. The following morning, a medivac ship was called in and he was flown to a field hospital. If the punji stake had been "tipped" with human waste, we might well have lost the man who would become the future Chairman of the Joint Chiefs.

* * * * * *

Herb Siugzda was born in Lithuania and survived the Nazis' brutal occupation and subsequent WWII American bombing runs. Reminiscing about one positive memory from his childhood, he was mesmerized by a tall American paratrooper with big jump boots, helmet and rifle. He wanted to be just like him; an American soldier. Immigrating to America as a young boy, he joined the Army as soon as he reached an acceptable age. The men he met there became his family. In December 1966, SSG Siugzda was assigned to a Special Forces "A" detachment in Vietnam.

Adapting quickly to combat, he soon came to the attention of others, and after being in-country for only two months, received orders for Project Delta. When he asked about it, he was told only that his new job was "classified." It seemed illogical to be so highly classified that it had to be kept a secret from a man who was going there, but he kept his mouth shut and went along. He heard persistent rumors that Project Delta was some kind of "suicide mission." He wasn't at all comfortable with becoming involved with something like that, but knowing he had very little say in the matter, he reported to Project Delta in early 1967. After years of searching, it turned out he finally found a place he wanted to call home, among men who would become closer than family.

On his first operation, Siugzda, SFC Walter "Doc" Simpson and four VNSF were among several recon teams being launched from the FOB at Hue-Phu Bai. As follow-on to Operation Pirous and Operation Samurai I, they flew out in a formation of four helicopters, each with a recon team aboard. After faking several landings to deceive the enemy of their true insertion point, they were inserted into the mountainous jungle range near A Shau Valley around dusk, 22 April 1967. Potential landing zones were scarce and the one selected had once grown corn, although since harvested. Because Siugzda was the FNG, he thought it "interesting" that the 281st AHC pilot would speed at treetop level for more than an hour and then suddenly drop from formation to hover six feet off the ground. The crew chief signaled for them to disembark.

As usual, Doc Simpson was the first to exit, followed by the four VNSF, with Siugzda bringing up the rear. Dropping into the tall vegetation six feet below, he felt a sharp pain in his left thumb; he observed a deep slice across the meaty part. Damn, he thought. Now, I've got to stay out here for five days with a sore thumb! Attempting to jog toward the tree line to join the others, he found himself anchored, unable to budge. A three-foot tall, sharp cornstalk had entered the left side of his groin and exited on the right, just below his lower abdomen.

In the rugged highlands, the VC knew there would be few LZs suitable for infiltrating recon teams. The wily VC often bobby-trapped potential sites by digging small holes filled with sharpened stakes, cam- ouflaged for concealment—punji pits. In this particular incident, where a farmer had planted corn, the VC simply used a little ingenuity to shear the cornstalks at two to three feet with an angle that produced a razor sharp point. After vegetation and elephant grass reclaimed the field, the stalks were hidden. Those jumping from an elevated helicopter became impaled on the improvised "punji stakes." Siugzda, on his first recon patrol, had fallen victim to this tactic. If the stake had been tipped with excrement, Siugzda would have died within the hour.

He saw Doc Simpson motioning impatiently for him to join the rest of the team. Recon men know insertion is the most critical time in any operation. It was apparent Doc was extremely concerned about the delay, aware that remaining for even a few minutes was dangerous. Siugzda tried to extract himself from the stake, but it held fast. He motioned to Doc that he couldn't move—signaling he had a very real problem.

Again motioning, Simpson was growing agitated and broke protocol by whispering harshly, "Bullshit! Come on, Siugz! Move your ass."

Emphatically, Siugzda signaled "no." Repeatedly pointing toward his feet, he whispered back, "I can't move, Doc."

Simpson trotted back on the LZ, amazed and speechless upon realizing the nature of Siugzda's situation. Drawing his K-bar knife, Doc knelt and hacked off the punji stake at its base. Helping his wounded comrade from the LZ, once safely inside the trees, he radioed back to the FOB, alerting them they had a seriously injured man needing immediate medical evacuation. Simpson spoke directly with Major Allen, the Delta Commander.

"We have to medivac Herb immediately. He took a punji stake through his groin."

"Tell him to cut it off and continue the mission," was Allen's short reply.

"You don't understand," Simpson said. "This isn't one of those little sticks—this thing is the size of a freaking baseball bat! He's pinned to the goddamned ground! "

By that time, darkness had fallen, and MAJ Allen informed Simpson that their LZ would be impossible to find again in the dark. Allen told them Siugzda would have to remain overnight, but that he would send a medivac chopper at first light. With the protruding three-foot stake, Siugzda's pain was growing more intense by the minute. Doc Simpson tried to remove it, but was unsuccessful—it simply wouldn't budge.

Unable to bear the pain any longer, and faced with a long night ahead, Siugzda finally whispered, "Got any morphine, Doc? I could use a little help right now."

Simpson shot him up and tried to make him comfortable as the team settled into a hasty defensive position, hoping that the VC hadn't seen them come in, just waiting until first light to attack.

The night passed without incident, and Allen was true to his word—the medivac arrived at dawn. As he climbed the rope ladder, he was extremely careful not to let the offending stake hang up. Joe Markham helped him inside the chopper, staring in amazement.

Saplings slashed downward at different angles and punji stakes, sharpened at both ends then wedged into the gash, lined trails in well defined areas. Many were tipped with human waste causing blood poisoning. (Photo courtesy of Maurice Brakeman)

"Jesus, Herb! That's not a punji stake! It's a f_ _ _ing baseball bat!"

"I'm getting really tired of hearing that, Joe."

Siugzda was evacuated to the 8th Army Field Hospital, and within twenty minutes was prepped for surgery. The doctors and nurses were all incredulous, but enthusiastically, even gleefully, snapping pictures. Siugzda fervently hoped he wouldn't end up in a medical journal or one of those "how to" books the doctors kept in their offices. The attending physician informed him the stake had narrowly missed a major artery, and the artery's proximity was directly against the stake. Attempts to remove the stake could rupture it, and Siugzda could bleed to death. After receiving a numbing injection, the doctor examined him closely, "I can't just pull this thing out. It might sever that artery."

Siugzda clinically observed the stake, trying to be helpful. "Why don't you just cut it in half at the artery, and remove it that way," he suggested helpfully.

"Oh, hey, that's not a bad idea."

"By the way, Doc. Be careful while you're cutting down there, will you?" Siugzda requested. "I don't want to wake up missing more than that corn stalk."

A surgeon arrived and informed him that his "sacks" would probably have to be removed. After Siugzda calmly explained that he was a trained killer, and that any such action would have a grave impact on the doctor's longevity, and that it would seriously lower the doctor's odds of ever seeing the States, Siugzda decided to remain awake so as to ensure his "sacks" remained firmly affixed. At his insistence, he was given a spinal block instead of general anesthesia, and the medical staff went to work. The spinal injection, combined with the anesthetic, did the job; Siugzda peacefully drifted off halfway through the operation. After he came to, a pretty recovery nurse stood over his bed.

"How many nuts do I have?" he croaked hoarsely.

"Your nuts are beautiful, soldier…now go back to sleep."

A number of Delta guys visited with him at the Army field hospital before he was transported to a hospital ship for another two months of medical care. When he was well enough to get around, and with the ship docking in the Philippines, he was finally given shore leave. According to Siugzda, "Here I was, without a uniform, my groin shaved as bald as an eagle, big, ugly stitches, and I…well, you know… wanted to see if everything still worked."

Fixated on that notion, he managed to finagle a slick-sleeve Marine private's uniform and headed downtown to get laid—for medical reasons, of course. Since all the establishments were off-limits after 2200 hours to those below the rank of SGT E-5, of course, his first encounter had to be with the shore patrol. They tried to give him a hard time, but he indignantly convinced them that he was really a Special Forces staff sergeant, despite the Marine private's uniform. After he gave them a good chewing out, he continued on his mission— that of seeking female companionship—for his medical experiment.

He admitted the first night was a total bust; on the second night, his expectations brightened. He met a beautiful young lady, and after a few drinks, they retired to her room. He flicked off the light, preparing to undress for what was to come. She flipped it back on—he turned it off—she turned it back on. Thinking "Oh, what the hell?" he undressed with the light on. When the poor girl noticed the expanse of stitches that reached from one side of his discolored purple and yellow groin to the other, she nearly fainted. Screaming and gesturing wildly, nearly incoherent, she threw his money at him, demanding he leave immediately.

"I couldn't believe it," he said reflectively. "I couldn't even make out in a whorehouse." He went on to report that eventually he learned everything would work as well as ever.

In June, Siugzda returned to Nha Trang, just as Operation Samurai II was ready to kick off. The Bruiser greeted him, personally welcoming him back.

"Don't get too comfortable. You're going back out in the morning."

This time, Siugzda roomed with SSG Fred Walz, and they soon became close friends. In 1967, Walz had recently graduated from the Special Forces Operations and Intelligence (O&I) School when his orders for Vietnam came. He ran into an old acquaintance on the flight over, SGM "Wild Bill" Fuller; he convinced Walz to join him in Project Delta.

Walz, initially assigned as a Ranger advisor, soon found himself on a three-day operation with his roommate, Herb Siugzda, SP5 Albert J. Merriman and an extraordinary young master sergeant, Edward Coffey. The force consisted of the four U.S. Special Forces and forty 81st Airborne Rangers. Reaching the LZ this time, the chopper hovered long enough for them to jump out, but Siugzda told them to land—he wasn't jumping this time! The pilot denied his request. Steadfastly refusing to jump the four to six feet to the ground, the stalemate began.

Coffey radioed MAJ Allen, who told Coffey to order him to jump. Siugzda was unimpressed. "I don't care about your orders. I just got out of the hospital for doing that crazy shit, and I'm not jumping!"

Exasperated, they circled until Coffey spotted a large bomb crater where the pilot could safely set the chopper down. They disembarked without incident. Once on the ground, the small force headed south, running into numerous fortified positions and a few huts, which the Rangers burned. Looping farther south without resistance, they drifted west, and then north toward the bomb crater for extraction. Coffey had serious misgivings about using the same site, but without any others nearby, he had little choice. A recent B-52 strike had punched a gigantic bomb crater into the soft soil at the summit of a bald hill. A steep, but heavily vegetated slope stretched to the north, and ultimately dropped off into a deep jungle valley. Another more gradual slope led south, the direction they'd traveled earlier at the start of the operation. A fairly level ridgeline stretched to the west of the crater, devoid of substantial vegetation. Coffey figured if they could set up a perimeter, they could secure the area just long enough to get the choppers back in for their extraction.

On the third day, they approached the crater and established a tight defensive perimeter. As they broke for lunch while waiting for the extraction chopper to arrive, the Rangers were suddenly sprayed with intense automatic fire from the south, instantly resulting in five casualties. Heavy firing could be heard from the opposite side of their perimeter, signifying this was a large force, confident in their ability to take on a company of seasoned Airborne Rangers. Merriman climbed to the lip of the crater and began firing down the slope, while Siugzda, inside its relative cover, attempted to establish radio communications with the FOB. He observed Coffey heading toward the heaviest conflict; he presumed the Rangers had reported casualties and Coffey was going to help.

Fred Walz cautiously made his way down the reverse face of the slope, conscious of the blanket of fire inches above his head. Crawling along a narrow path, he met one of his Ranger NCOs.

"*Bac Se* (doctor), *Bac Se*, many wounded. You come?"

Walz wasn't really a Bac Se, he was an Intelligence NCO, although he'd been cross-trained to handle most combat injuries, at least well enough to impress the indigenous troops. Walz followed him, and halfway down the hill, he discovered one of their Rangers badly wounded in the groin. Lying unconscious in a shallow indentation, he'd lost so much blood that it was filled with a muddy mess of red soup. Walz suspected he was too late to be of any help, but gave him some morphine and began to bandage his wounds. As he prepared to hoist him over his shoulder and carry him to the relative safety of the bomb crater, someone came toward them; he held up. Master Sergeant Ed Coffey, a tall, handsome NCO with a solid reputation within the Special Forces community, strolled along as if it were a Sunday morning and he was off to church, oblivious to the machinegun fire kicking up the dirt around him.

"Come on," he told Walz calmly. "Get ready to move out—we've got choppers in-bound."

Walz nodded. "Okay, but I need some cover fire. There's a little sonofabitch about a hundred yards inside the tree line that's been on my ass ever since I got here. He's probably the one that hit our Ranger."

Coffey knelt and began to fire down the slope while Walz bent over, readying himself to lift the wounded soldier. From the corner of his eye, he noticed Coffey, on one knee, slumped over his rifle, no longer firing. His heart in his throat, he immediately moved toward him; touching his shoulder, he turned him slightly to determine what was wrong. Horrified, he watched as Coffey's jaw simply fell away. A round had ripped off his lower jaw; it hung by a strand of flesh, his back teeth exposed. Fearing for his friend's life, his adrenalin kicked in, and with an amazing displey of strength, Walz hoisted Coffey over his shoulder and ran full-bore, two hundred yards up the hill to the bomb crater, ignoring the rounds kicking up dirt along his route.

Covered in Coffey's blood, he literally fell into the crater, startling Siugzda who was on the radio communicating with the incoming choppers.

Believing it was his friend Walz who'd been injured, Siugzda shouted, "Where are you hit? Where are you hit, damn it?"

Struggling to catch his breath, Walz finally gasped, "Not…me, Herb. It's…Coffey. He's hit bad."

Siugzda frantically radioed MAJ Allen who was circling over the valley. "We need an evacuation chopper, ASAP! Coffey's dying!" he shouted.

Allen's calm voice came back on, "Take a deep breath, settle down and tell me what's going on."

Siugzda took a deep breath, careful to exhale loudly while he held the key down so Allen would hear him. "We need an evacuation chopper, ASAP! Coffey's dying!" he shouted, exactly as before. Siugzda has admitted, at times, to being a wise ass.

Allen informed him another team was in trouble, too, so for the moment there were no available choppers. He said he would find one and get back to them soon. It wasn't long before a Marine CH-46 troop carrier approached, coming to land near the west side of the crater. Coffey, still conscious, pointed at his throat—he couldn't breath. Using his K-Bar knife, Siugzda slit a small hole in Coffey's trachea and inserted a plastic tube; it temporarily relieved his breathing problem.

Overcome with fear for his wounded comrade, but unable to carry both his rifle and Coffey, Siugzda let go of his rifle, hoisted Coffey to his shoulder and ran toward the helicopter, which, filled with wounded Vietnamese Rangers, was preparing to lift off. The chopper was taking fire; he could tell by the sound of the engine whining that the pilots were about to leave. Arriving, puffing heavily from the exertion of his sprint, he'd been held up at the door by a Marine crew chief.

"We're not taking any more wounded out."

"This is an American, you ass hole!"

"I don't care. The pilot said no more, and he's the boss."

Siugzda laid Coffey near two wounded Rangers, ran to the pilot's window and shouted up, "I have a badly wounded American. We have to get him out!"

The pilot just shook his head, revving up the engine. "We're taking too much fire; I need to get my crew out of here."

For a fleeting instant Siugzda fellt sorry about leaving his rifle—he could've used it. "Really?" he screamed. "You're taking fire? Well, no shit! What do you think we've been doing for the past two hours? We've had our hands full too, you know. God damn it, put this American on board, and do it now!"

The pilot looked as if he still might refuse, but then acquiesced; he indicated to get Coffey inside quickly so he could lift off. As Siugzda hurried to do his bidding, Walz came up from behind.

"I'll go with Coffey. Maybe I can help him."

Adding another man clearly didn't make the Marine pilot real happy, but he'd soon have a change of heart. Upon landing at the FOB, the pilot reported to MAJ Allen and told him why. As the pilot was preparing to lift off, a VC soldier about twenty yards away, leveled an AK-47 straight at his head. But, before he could fire, someone inside the chopper pumped half a magazine into him. It was Ed Coffey. With his head bloody with dressings and field bandages, and his M-16 across his lap, he simply sat upright and shot the VC soldier dead.[34]

Siugzda couldn't wait around to watch the chopper glide toward the west. Under heavy fire, he already returned to the crater, grateful

---

[34] Jim Morris. "Death-dealing Project Delta-Part 3: Interview with the Big 'Un." http://projectdelta.net/sof-mag3_pg1.htm

for its relative cover against the enemy's steady barrage. The radio squawked just as he reached it—a FAC had made it into their operational area and had two fast-movers standing by with 500-pound bombs. The FAC wanted precise coordinates to make a low bombing run.

"Just dump them fifty meters north of this crater," Siugzda told him.

"Say again…fifty meters? Are you crazy? Do you know what a five-hundred-pounder can do that close?" the FAC asked.

"Right now, that's the least of my worries," Siugzda replied. "There's about a million of those little bastards out there, and I want that baby unloaded right where I said to drop it."

He pulled the Rangers back from their firing positions at the lip of the crater, and they all hunkered down, waiting. A thunderous explosion ensued, but the bomb had harmlessly fallen three hundred meters to their north, deep in the valley. The enemy's firing never slacked off. Siugzda was incensed!

"FAC, get it right this time! Fifty-god-damned-do-as-I-tell-you meters! Get it right!"

"Okay, okay. It's your funeral," he replied tartly.

The next bomb landed exactly fifty meters from the lip of the crater, its concussion nearly lifted them out of the hole. As soon as the concussion echo faded, the birds began to chirp; it was quiet again, not another round was fired. Having a taste of a 500-pound bomb appeared to be sufficient; they'd withdrawn. Within minutes, another Marine chopper arrived to pick up Siugzda and his battered Rangers. Grateful to survive their ordeal, the small, depleted force was whisked back to the FOB; of the fifty fighting men inserted three days earlier, only ten would take that last chopper ride out.

Siugzda lived to fight another day; subsequently, he would receive two additional Purple Hearts for his combat wounds.

While in route, Walz, attempting to treat Coffey's wounds, removed his shirt and discovered a second, small purplish wound under his shoulder blade, and a third, crater-sized, in his chest. Despite Walz's best efforts, MSG Edward A. Coffey died before reaching the field hospital. The attending physician told MAJ Allen that a round hit Coffey in the back, exiting through his heart and creating the large chest wound. He said Coffey's mortal wound had been so severe that he never would have survived, even at the hospital. In his opinion, it

At Phu Bai, LTG Cushman, USMC (*center*) shakes SGM Harry "Crash" Whalen's (*left*) hand while MAJ Charles Allen (*right*) looks on. On the receiving line (*left to right*): Unidentified Vietnamese interpreter, MSG James Kreilick, LT Tan (VN), MSG Norman Doney. (Photo courtesy of Norman Doney)

was instant death. He was at a loss to explain how Coffey lived as long as he did, and the notion of him sitting up and firing a rifle in his condition completely defied explanation.

In an interview before his death, Chuck Allen remembered, "Just the thought of it raises the hair on the back of my neck. The doctor was right. How was Ed Coffey able to sit up and kill that VC gunning for the Marine pilot? He should've been dead."

For years, Allen would reflect on Ed Coffey's miraculous heroics, seeing them solely as instinct, from his spirit. Lieutenant General Robert Cushman once remarked to Allen after an earlier operation in support of Marines, "These men operate in the Ether Zone of military excellence." Allen later added, "He might just as well have said, 'The Twilight Zone.'"[35]

Herb Siugzda remembers Ed Coffey as one of the most pleasant and professional guys he ever met. Like most NCOs assigned to Delta, the slender black man was intelligent, level-headed and fearless.

---

[35] *Ibid.*

"When he was along, you didn't have to watch your back," said Walz, his voice cracking as he related how he'd lost Coffey on the trip back. Despite the passing years, he's been unable to diminish his anguish for not saving Coffey's life.

* * * * * *

Major Chuck Allen nominated Coffey for the Congressional Medal of Honor and many believed he should have received it. Mortally wounded, he thought only of his fellow soldiers and fought to stay alive long enough to save another. Master Sergeant Edward A. Coffey was ultimately awarded the Distinguished Service Cross for his brave actions, and, as Allen affirmed, "His memory will live on as long as one of us remains."

* * * * * *

Siugzda's next operation, Operation Sultan II, was again with Rangers SSG George Cole and LT Bill Wentz in the Plei Djereng Valley. The operation FOB was established near Pleiku. Their first two days out were unusually quiet—no contact was made nor any enemy spotted. On the third day, while exiting the dense jungle into a clearing surrounded by tall bamboo, the dry-witted Siugzda sided up to Cole, and, from the corner of his mouth, said, "They're going to hit us any minute now."

Siugzda laughed as he related it. "I was just being a wise-ass, you know…trying to be like John Wayne." He mimicked Wayne's drawl, "It's way too quiet around here, Pilgrim."

"Hell," he laughed, "I never suspected a damned thing would actually happen."

As soon as he spoke, all hell broke loose. It was a perfectly executed ambush and in a short time, the small Ranger force and four American advisors were surrounded, inundated with fire.

"They had more forces, and they could've taken us anytime, if only they had hit us in force, from one side," Siugzda said. "But they didn't. Instead, they kept banging at us all around our perimeter. I believe they hoped we'd call for extraction so they could get the choppers when they landed."

Through the years, the VC and NVA had gleaned tactics from U.S. operations, particularly regarding rescue and reinforcement practices. Often, they would hit an outpost or outlying security force, then set-up an ambush on the LZ, or on the route they knew reinforcements would use. Near the war's end, they would use the same bright orange panels the recon teams used to mark an LZ for pickup, and popped smoke to lure choppers into deadly ambushes.

Within minutes, the enemy's mortar rounds and grenades began to rain down. Siugzda was kneeling near the perimeter, firing, when blinded by a bright flash—something struck him violently in the chest. Reeling backward, his initial thoughts were that a mortar round had kicked up a rock or debris and struck him. As he felt a warm seepage through his tiger suit, he peeled back his shirt—blood spurted from a small hole in his chest. Over the deafening noise of combat, he tried to rouse the attention of others. Lieutenant Wentz saw him first, then shouted for Cole, the medic.

"Siugz is dying! He's been hit, bad!"

Instantly, Cole was beside him, concerned, frantically searching for other wounds.

"I am not dying," Siugzda told him calmly. "It's just a scratch."

"Shut up and take a deep breath," Cole directed. "I'll decide if it's a scratch or not."

Siugzda did as instructed and nearly screamed. It hurt like hell—worse than the red-hot shrapnel. "Goddamn, Doc! That hurt!"

"Yep, it should. You've got a sucking chest wound, partner. It'll hurt every time you take a breath."

"Well, no shit! I can't very well stop breathing."

"I wouldn't if I were you."

Between sporadic sniper rounds and the hum of flying shrapnel, Cole bandaged his wound. As the attacks continued, he lay helpless, unable to do anything, but it seemed the tempo was picking up. Dusk was nearly upon them. The small force knew they had to survive the night because evacuation was out of the question until morning.

Cole finished his task, propped Siugzda up, and tried to make his breathing as comfortable as possible. They all knew it would be a painfully long time before any rescue attempt. It didn't help much that the enemy continued to attack all night—not in force, but just enough to keep them awake and on edge. By daybreak, their assaults seemed to have intensified; a steady stream of automatic fire zipped by, barely a foot or two over their prone bodies. Rising only a few inches would mean certain death. Siugzda's bladder was full; he struggled painfully onto his side to relieve himself.

The FNG guy, a staff sergeant whose name has been lost, called out, "I've really got the GIs, bad. I have to take a crap."

It took about a minute of serious contemplation before Siugzda yelled back, "Well good luck. All I can tell you is just stick 'er out and cut loose. Don't get your ass shot off."

The Ranger company sustained a casualty rate of nearly thirty percent since the first round had been fired—still no choppers. Siugzda sat upright, partially leaning against a tree to help him breathe, watching as others fired to keep the enemy in check.

Suddenly, as if in slow motion, he watched as a hand grenade sailed over his head and landed a short distance from his feet. In one frozen instant, he knew he was dead. Without hesitation, the Ranger company commander, a young Vietnamese captain, fell on it, smothering the blast with his body. Practically blown apart, he was killed instantly, giving his life for those around him. Except for LT Wentz's non-lethal head wound, all others in close proximity emerged unscathed.

"Medic! Medic!" Wentz shouted, holding his bloody head. "I'm hit!"

A head wound, no matter how minor, tends to bleed profusely; often the scare is magnified by daunting images of its seriousness. Although Wentz's wound was non-threatening, it still bled copiously, soaking his uniform. Cole was at his side in a second, peering at the superficial wound.

"I'm hit!" the lieutenant cried again.

Cole was not impressed. He moved back toward his firing position. "So? Put a bandage on it, Lieutenant."

"Dammit, I'm hit in the head!"

"So, put a *large* bandage on it and keep firing."

A sudden roar drowned out his last words. Cole hit the ground, shouting, "Gunships!"

The Rangers all hugged the ground as the choppers passed overhead, their mini-guns spitting deadly tracers to within five feet of their perimeter. Siugzda felt the dirt splatter from the narrowly missing mini-gun rounds. Two Rangers were slightly wounded by the friendly fire, yet no one complained. It felt good to know they were not alone. From the air, it's hard for the pilots to determine friendly forces from enemy forces, especially when hindered by the triple-layer jungle canopy and dense bamboo, and the fact that the smoke they'd thrown to identify them had drifted. Siugzda began to wonder who'd get him first, the good guys or the bad guys.

Fred Walz was at the FOB when word came that the operation was in trouble, and that his friend and roommate, Herb Siugzda, had been "wounded again"—his third. Walz volunteered to go in with the reaction force; a company of sixty Vietnamese Rangers and four American advisors. As they approached the besieged unit, the pilot could tell it would be a tight squeeze to get all the choppers onto the small and extremely rugged LZ. Walz, seated in the open doorway, leaped out as soon as he could. Moving swiftly, he was only fifteen feet away when the chopper crashed. His American advisor, Paul Shepard, and most of the Vietnamese Rangers made it out. The crew chief was pinned under the wreckage; the pilot and co-pilot's doors both crushed too badly to open, the motor continued to run.

Walz yelled at Paul, "Hold up! We've got to get them out. It's gonna blow any minute!"

Fighting against time, they struggled with the twisted wreckage, finally retrieved the crew and moved them to a small hill nearby, then set up a hasty defensive perimeter. As soon as security was established, Walz returned to the chopper to retrieve the radio box and machinegun. He knew he had to cut the engine; the whole thing would explode when the fuel ignited. His problem: he hadn't a clue as to how to shut it down. He flipped every switch in hopes that he'd find the right one; otherwise, the damned thing would blow and take him with it.

"Fred, get your ass out of there," Paul shouted. "There's frigging Mogas all over. It's going up!"

Sensing Paul's panic, he climbed out and ran for safety to where the others huddled. Seconds later, the motor sputtered; without a whimper, it simply shut down.

"Well, I'll be a sonofa…!"

After they guided in another chopper to extract the downed crew and the Rangers left them, Walz and Paul were alone. They headed off in the same direction that they'd seen their Rangers disappear, trying to catch up. Traveling only a short distance, they came upon LT Charley Ford and CPT "Bo" Baker; both had been passengers on another chopper. One of their Vietnamese Rangers had been shot in the leg; Walz stopped to bandage it.

"Come on, Fred," Charlie Ford yelled. "We're moving out. We've got to get to "Siugz" before they get wiped out!"

Walz finished his task and ran to catch up. Siugzda would never forgive him if he wasn't among the first to reach him. As they moved, Walz detected a large group of dead Vietnamese. At first he surmised they might be Siugzda's besieged Rangers, but checking more closely, he determined they were NVA soldiers killed earlier by the encircled Ranger force.

At the sound of the helicopters, the enemy had pulled back from Siugzda's group, which allowed the entrapped Rangers to withdraw back down the hill. As more reinforcements landed, Tom Humphus led his Ranger company through the thicket, up the ridge toward the sound of firing. On the way up, he encountered LT Wentz stumbling down the path, his head covered in blood. Humphus spoke to him as they neared each other.

"Is that you, Tom?" Wentz cried. "I can't see. I'm blind. Blind!"

When he was close enough, Humphus reached out and removed Wentz's blood-coated glasses, watching quietly as relief washed over his friend's face.

"Oh," was all Wentz said. "Well shit, I ain't blind."

After pulling back from the battered Ranger force, the enemy hadn't left the area completely. That initial ambush and subsequent rescue turned into a vicious, extended encounter that lasted for two more days; for their actions, 1LT Charley Ford won a Silver Star and SSG Frederick A. Waltz was awarded the Army Commendation Medal for valor.

Walz is a sturdy, no-nonsense kind of guy. While his reflections were low-key, modest and straight forward, one sensed he might be leaving out more information about his exploits than he was willing to share. He still exudes confidence, as he did when others' lives depended on him. Herb Siugzda, a soft-spoken "Steve-McQueen-sort-of-guy" of about sixty, appears ten years younger. He is physically fit, with an impression he could still make a parachute jump, heft a heavy rucksack and trudge through dense mountainous jungle. While Siugzda tends to be more laid-back, he retains his caustic sense of humor and isn't one to get excited about much. Given a dangerous mission, one feels they would still be safe with either of these seasoned warriors and not have to worry about having their back covered.

* * * * * *

During Operation Pirous with the 3rd Marine Division, several teams were inserted into A Shau Valley from FOB-1 at Hue-Phu Bai. Deputy Commander, MAJ Charles (Bruiser) Allen, who would later take the Delta command from LTC William C. Norman, received an Army Commendation Medal for valor for his actions. Recon personnel receiving awards for bravery during Operation Pirous were: SFC Orville G. Robinette, Silver Star; SFC Joseph M. Markam, Silver Star; and SSG Herbert Siugzda, ARCM/v. Wounded yet again, Siugzda earned a Purple Heart.

SEVENTEEN

The FNG

THE FOB FOR OPERATIONS SAMURAI II AND PIROUS I was west of the small coastal town of Phu Bai, near Hue's ancient Imperial City. With an airstrip and Marine Corps dispensary nearby, B-52 set up operations south of the Marine hospital. The facilities were adjacent to a large cemetery, situated between them and the town. From Phu Bai, a decent gravel road passed by their camp to a rock quarry; there, a rifle range made it handy for Delta Recon to test fire weapons and run Immediate Action Drills. The range, while a substantial distance away, was also located high on the slope of a large hill mass, making it necessary to have a radio relay aircraft on station every day. That aircraft, an old DeHaviland Otter, was stationed at the Phu Bai airstrip. Used as everything from an airborne taxi to resupply runs for rations and beer, the Otter soon became as beloved as any other member of the team.

The Otter would land at the dirt strip on the north side of the FOB to pick up radio relay operators, and remain over night. There was usually a double-strand of concertina around the strip and the pilot was used to clearing it with his tail wheel. One day, someone decided to add

Above: Delta's trusty old Otter at Phu Bai. SSG Andy Sheppard is standing front

Right: Otter after the crash. (Both photos courtesy of Maurice Brakeman)

a third roll on top of the other two. When the pilot took off, the tail wheel caught the top wire and the additional weight was too much for the single-engine craft. It pulled the plane down, and it crashed and burned. Sergeant First Class Bartlett was Delta's relay operator that day. Everyone on board was a casualty and the Otter never flew again.

During both operations, B-52 was running recon for the Marines in and around A Shau Valley, often humorously referred to as "Happy Valley." Three antiquated French camps dotted the valley: to the north, A Luoi; Ta Bat in the center; and A Shau at the southern end. The previous year, A Shau had been occupied by a Special Forces A-Team and 200 Montagnard tribesmen until overrun by three NVA regiments.

The rough terrain east of the A Shau Valley. With its dense jungle and rivers, it had few suitable LZs—an enemy advantage, since they didn't have to spread troops too thin to watch them. The few sufficiently cleared areas were always easy "killing fields" (Photo courtesy of Steve Adams)

Only three miles from the Laotian border, the camp straddled a major trail system for supplies heading south; the NVA couldn't afford to let the camp remain—the camp fell in late 1966, the NVA losing more than 1,000 men.

At this junction, the border is a north-south range of mountainous terrain, with more high ground parallel to the long valley axis on the east. In essence, an almost perfect box, ideal for an NVA staging area, with anti-aircraft batteries dug in to afford the best field of fire. The center of the valley was under continuous surveillance; anything that moved was hit with a tactical air strike. The enemy's anti-aircraft positions not only made air strikes difficult, but as Delta Recon teams began their insertions, the focus of these big guns shifted—to the choppers.

After months of intensive defoliant spraying and air strikes, the valley center was almost devoid of vegetation; bomb craters dotted the landscape. The closer the choppers tried to advance, the more hazardous it became; it became extremely difficult to find an insertion point not already occupied by fortified enemy positions. A direct helicopter insertion on the valley floor would have been suicidal. The teams were forced to select a first, second and third choice as alternatives—often rappelling into adjacent hills and then creeping back toward their target area. This procedure was not uncommon; it was rare to find an opening large enough to land a helicopter. Utilizing alternative methods of insertion and extraction was fraught with danger, for many soldiers were often injured or killed when using improvisations, such as McGuire Rigs, rope ladders and jungle penetrators.

One such incident took place towards the end of Delta's era in War Zone D, when the Delta FOB was located at Bunard. First Lieutenant Agustin "Gus" Fabian, 1st Ranger Company Advisor, recalls his operation with a reinforced Ranger platoon on a reconnaissance in-force mission. Inserted at mid-morning, the Rangers quickly moved off the LZ into triple-canopy jungle. After completing their mission, a suitable LZ still could not be found; an FOB staff officer came up with an idea. They were dropped chainsaws and instructed to cut down trees to make a clearing for a one-ship LZ. Overhead, heavy, thick vines draped the trees making it hard to fell them.

Completing their task just before dusk, a monsoon hit only minutes before the choppers arrived. The driving force of the wind and rain not only impaired the pilots' vision, but increased the risk associated with landing in such a tight clearance. Regardless, one brave pilot attempted to descend into the small, tight space. A standard Slick with crew is designed to hold approximately a squad of combat-equipped soldiers; that is, when landing and take-off conditions are favorable. Having to descend and ascend vertically is extremely challenging and places tremendous strain on this small craft, even when lightly loaded. More Rangers loaded the ship than had been assigned, and in the extraction process as the chopper lifted off, four fell to their deaths; two onto the LZ and two others into the dense jungle. Another pilot was able to land and retrieve the Rangers on the LZ, but they died on route to the field hospital. The remaining force was extracted the following day, and then reinserted with a full company to search for and evacuate the two remaining dead Rangers. The increased activity quickly drew NVA interest, and during the second night, the enemy initiated probing attacks against the Ranger force. Before long, "Puff the Magic Dragon" arrived, which made the enemy forces pull back, finally breaking up their concentrated attack. Under continual harassing attacks, the Rangers searched the dense jungle for three days for their dead comrades; they were never found.

* * * * * *

Jay Graves vividly recollects his first time in the hole. "Doc" Simpson had sent him, along with Andre St. Laurent and five Chinese Nungs; St. Laurent briefed Graves just prior to their leaving. In his relaxed, nonchalant style, the briefing went something like this: "First we're gonna sneak around a little, maybe take a few pictures, then we're gonna shoot a bunch of folks." That was it.

They went in at last light, the helicopter hovering a few feet above an A Shau Valley river sandbar. The first two days were, for the most part, uneventful. Graves, the FNG, had the mannerisms of an owl— his eyes darted everywhere. He tried to anticipate anything out of place, a sound that might warn of enemy presence, or any nuance foreboding an ambush. By the fourth day, he settled down and relaxed a bit—then they made contact. Fifteen VC swimming in the river. St. Laurent aligned his team along the bank, called for immediate extraction and opened up, killing them all; they extracted without further incident. Graves's first enemy encounter was vicious and bloody. The memory forever seared into his mind, it set the stage for his next five years in Vietnam.

Upon returning to the FOB, St. Laurent gave Doc Simpson his report. "Jay Graves is all right—he can go in the hole with anyone."

Graves was teamed with the consummate recon man, "Moose" Monroe, a "marriage" that would last for the next five years. Graves went on to serve multiple tours and is held in high esteem as one of Delta's best and most experienced.

* * * * * *

Vietnam in July can be damned hot. Upon arrival in Cam Ranh Bay, twenty-two-year-old buck-sergeant James R. Jarrett first noticed the oppressive heat, then the smell—a reeking combination of mold and raw sewage. He would eventually get used to both. After his graduation, second in his class from Special Forces Operations and Intelligence School (O&I), he was delighted to be rid of his despised engineer and demolitions MOS for "something a bit more interesting." "Besides," he recollected, "explosives always made me nervous." At the time, he could never have imagined just how "interesting" the next few months would be.

He had heard rumors of something called Project Delta while at Fort Bragg, North Carolina; that it was the premier unit and among the most secretive of SF operations. Anxious to try out his O&I training and newly acquired Vietnamese language skills, he decided that was the place for him. His instructor felt his aptitude for excellint in language stemmed from a classical pianist background—odd skills for a man who longed to be a warrior.

After a few days at the replacement center, during which time Jarrett was issued an M-16 rifle and outfitted for combat operations, SFC Doc Simpson and SGM William Fuller came by seeking "volunteers" to fill recent B-52 recon team vacancies. The next day, Jarrett, Joe Walker and another man, referred to only as Thompson, were hand-picked and headed for the Delta compound at Nha Trang. Jarrett was assigned to bunk with Ken Edens, a tough, lean redhead, with the savvy and experience Jarrett would need to acquire to succeed in Delta Recon. They'd be "joined at the hip" for the weeks to come.

As the FNG, he spent the first two weeks in orientation and training, then was sent to help establish an FOB near An Hoa, where B-52 had been running recon teams west of Da Nang for the 5th Marines. He soon learned he'd been relegated to setting up FOB headquarters tents and latrines, and to performing menial tasks only the FNGs and support personnel were required to do. Recon guys didn't do these things— they were royalty—and that's what Jarrett wanted. Sweating in the oppressive humidity, he kept his mouth shut and labored to set up tents, wondering what the hell he was doing there.

In the Central Highlands the monsoons were about to wreak havoc and the cloudy sky seemed brooding, threatening. He wondered if helicopters could actually fly in those conditions and if he'd ever get the chance to find out. After a day and a half perspiring with the rest of the "grunts," he was summarily summoned to the "head-shed" with his M16 and field equipment. So far, the whole operation had seemed surreal and ominous. He hoped not to encounter more of the same at his first meeting.

After receiving word that Doc Simpson wanted to see him at the Tactical Operation Center (TOC), he double-timed it over, only to learn his "baptism by fire" would not be a recon operation after all, but a body recovery mission for the crew of a downed Marine chopper. Introduced to SFC Joe Singh and a nervous SP5 medic, Jarrett learned he'd be in charge of a reinforced squad of 81st Rangers who would provide security for the body recovery effort. The more highly experienced Singh would be in charge of the overall recovery detail, because Simpson said they'd likely be going into a "hot" situation.

Marine troop-carrier helicopters, dubbed "Jolly Greens," flew them to where a FAC had last seen the downed chopper, setting them down into a sea of elephant grass. The chopper lumbered off into the darkening sky, leaving him in the lonely silence of the unknown. Without a word, Singh briskly led off. Struggling to maintain Singh's pace, Jarrett quickly discovered that being in great shape wasn't all it was cracked up to be, particularly when humping a rucksack through the highlands of Vietnam. Slipping, sliding, panting and cussing, he and the new medic followed Singh and the VN Rangers, who all seemed to annoyingly glide along almost effortlessly. It would be weeks, with several more operations under his belt, before he would find his jungle legs and feel more at ease moving through the terrain.

On a charred hillside, the small group eventually broke into a large clearing. Near the bottom of a steep draw lay the incinerated hulk of a large chopper—and the bodies of the dead Marine crew. Except for trousers and boots, they'd been stripped of their gear and bore the brunt of numerous bullet wounds. Jarrett noticed none had been burned, leading him to conclude they initially escaped the crash alive, killed afterward. It was a terrible sight; it left him feeling sick and angry. To escape the gruesome sight of the mutilated Marines, more than anything else, he walked over to view the helicopter's twisted remains. Once a huge, impressive flying contraption, now nearly disintegrated, the chopper was a mass of molten metal and Plexiglas. The magnesium-clad floor and other combustible parts had fueled a fire so intense that only bits and pieces of the once proud Jolly Green remained, its rotor blades sticking upward like the ribcage of a great decaying beast.

Joe Singh jerked him back to reality.

"Jarrett! Take the Rangers, get up the slope, and set up security. Move your ass!"

Jarrett did as instructed, grateful to leave Singh and the medic while they checked the bodies, readying them for the recovery chopper. Jarrett placed the Rangers in positions that provided the best security; given the fact that he only had about a dozen men—he hoped they were enough. He felt they'd all be history if they got hit by something of any size on this scorched hillside. From his spot in the center of the Ranger's small defensive position he couldn't see Singh, and without a radio, couldn't communicate with the others. The Rangers didn't seem particularly concerned about his welfare and that worried him, too. He maneuvered until he established a direct line of sight with Singh and the medic, watching them work. Somehow, it made him feel better.

The whoop of rotor blades caught his attention; he looked up. A Marine recovery helicopter moved into position, slowly lowering a cable and sling through its open belly. He presumed either it was impossible to land the large aircraft on the steep hillside, or the pilot didn't want to stay there any longer than absolutely necessary. Jarrett could appreciate that. He wished he were someplace else, too. The rotor-wash kicked up dust and debris, obscuring the scene for a moment and making it impossible to hear. A single shot rang out, loud and clear. Jarrett saw Singh clutch his chest, double over and head for concealment in a clump of brush, the new medic close behind.

He later learned that Singh hadn't been hit squarely, but that the round had only grazed his chest, slicing through the bottom of his shirt pocket—the only casualty being the signal mirror in his pocket. Jarrett's first reaction was total confusion. It seemed clear by Singh's reaction that more firing was taking place, but the rotor-wash caused so much turbulence that he couldn't see the muzzle flashes or the bullets impacting, and he couldn't hear the shooting over the noise of the hovering helicopter. The chopper suddenly banked hard to the left, and with the recovery cable and sling still dangling, disappeared from sight. Fear gripped him as he glanced around, suddenly aware he was alone. The Rangers had all pulled back and were nowhere to be seen.

Singh, fifty meters down the slope from Jarrett, remained stationary, pinned down by the undetected sniper. He peered up the hill toward Jarrett, his expression a question mark. Jarrett shrugged, pointing simply in the direction he thought the rounds were coming. Once the chopper departed, there was total silence. The relatively inexperienced Jarrett wondered what to do next. By moving closer to the others, he risked exposing them to more sniper fire. Yet, he was equally exposed, fully expecting to be shot at any moment. He could retreat into the brush and hopefully find the Rangers, but that might place him in a position where he wouldn't be able to help his fellow Americans if they faced an all-out attack. None of the alternatives seemed acceptable.

Sporadic small arms fire erupted, and while he still couldn't tell from where, he could see the round's impact near Singh and the medic. He strained to see into the thick foliage, but still couldn't detect the enemy's position. To top it off, the weather was taking a turn for the worse and it would soon be dark. If unable to get the bodies out quickly, they'd have to remain out there overnight; he didn't want to think about that possibility. Jarrett began to fire methodically at any concealed location that might hold an enemy sniper. Just when it appeared things couldn't be worse, they got worse—Jarrett's rifle jammed. Irritated by his weapon's malfunction, his first order of business was to get it operational. He desperately needed to shoot back at someone. So in the midst of his first firefight, he simply sat and began to field-strip his rifle. As he contemplated the different components, it occurred to him that the base of the bolt was bone-dry, and he detected some carbon buildup. Retrieving his oil-based insect repellant, he sprayed it onto the bolt, oiled the rest of his weapon and began to reassemble it. He was thankful that the firing had finally abated. He never even considered the enemy might be maneuvering to get behind them; otherwise he'd really have been scared.

Before completing the task of reassembling his rifle, "things became very interesting." First, Singh was successful in contacting a FAC, who'd fired off a couple of white phosphorous rockets onto the hillside about 100 meters from Jarrett's position. Then, several gunships began to arrive, pouring mini-gun fire onto the hill around them. At last, the recovery chopper returned, the door-gunner opening fire with his M-60 machinegun. All this commotion sounded really good, but if Jarrett hoped the increased firepower might deter the enemy, he was sorely disappointed.

It seemed the enemy had been reinforced; with a vengeance, automatic small arms fire answered, but this time Jarrett made out the unmistakable resonance of a heavy machinegun added to the enemy's arsenal. He would later realize that his overwhelming impression had been the mind-numbing noise of combat. The clamor seemed to blanket him; it affected his vision, balance and even his ability to think coherently. It wouldn't have been any different if his buddies had been an arm length away instead of fifty yards; communication was impossible. Jarrett would realize that what he felt was the same as others had felt the first time under fire; with experience he would learn to control his reactions.

Singh and the medic darted through the intense fire, placing Marine bodies into the dangling sling. As soon as a body was loaded, it was winched up. It seemed agonizingly slow, one body at a time, as bullets whizzed past the chopper or kicked up dirt around them.

Jarrett scrambled to complete reassembling his weapon, irritated that he hadn't been able to shoot someone. Ready to snap his weapon closed and push the retention pin into place, the sound of the enemy heavy machinegun's changed minutely. With experience, he'd come to recognize the subtle sounds meant they were firing directly at him. Taken by surprise, he watched in dumb fascination as the heavy rounds walked a perfect line up the hill, across his position. He distinctly recalls two rounds striking dirt to the side of his left knee, another precisely between his legs, and then two more hitting just beyond his right thigh and hip. He wasn't scared, just amazed he hadn't been hit. Snapping his weapon shut, he withdrew a magazine of tracers, shoved it in, locked and loaded.

He admits he was pretty excited about finally having someone to shoot at. He never considered that he might have easily been blown to pieces by the destructive .51-caliber rounds. He yelled to Singh about spotting the shooter, but through the racket wasn't sure if Singh heard him. It just seemed very important that he tell someone. He fired several tracers to where he had spotted the heavy MG fire, and Singh, with his field experience, understood and spoke into the radio. Within minutes the gunship returned, raking that area with their mini-guns, forever silencing the .51 MG.

The other small arms fire continued and Jarrett placed his rounds wherever he believed the incoming fire originated. Suddenly, he sensed a presence and noticed the Ranger squad leader and several of his VN Rangers had crept back in; they seemed to want to press close, to touch him. Squatting, they pointed to areas where they had observed fire, grinning and jabbering in Vietnamese. Jarrett proceeded to fire tracers to where they pointed, perplexed by their behavior of crowding close and touching him. He later learned that they had watched the machinegun fire walk its path across his position, and believed that he must be charmed—protected by Buddha.

He observed that the last Marine body was slung and hoisted, and Singh was quickly approaching his location. In Vietnamese fashion, Singh squatted, seemingly undisturbed by their circumstances, or by the fact that sporadic sniper rounds continued to pop around them.

"Better travel, Jim. The FAC says the little buggers are moving in on three sides, and the gunships are running low on ammo and fuel. We can't get any fast-movers in here with this cloud cover, so we'd better haul ass in a hurry."

Without a sound, Singh started down the draw they'd slipped and slid up earlier, the Rangers in hot pursuit. If anything, their boots made the rugged draw more treacherous; Jarrett and the medic struggled to keep up. In the clouds, they could hear the comforting sound of the recovery helicopter's rotor blades beating the thick evening air. Although it was Jarrett's first combat operation, he knew they were in a tight spot and needed to get the hell out as quickly as possible. As if the enemy had decided not to let them depart, firing intensity had increased, clipping the elephant grass surrounding them. In the dim evening light he caught sight of his first green tracers streaking across the darkening sky. U.S. tracer rounds are red; the Red Chinese make green tracers—beautiful and deadly. With the gunships' racket and the noise from the recovery aircraft, identifying a threat through sound was nearly impossible. Like others before had learned, Jarrett's Vietnam experience would affect his perspective of many things; distance, noise, time, fear and feeling alone despite the presence of others.

Jarrett glanced at the young medic falling behind, struggling to keep pace; panic reflected in his eyes. He stopped and waved him past, taking up the tail-gunner position. In the blink of an eye, the time used to scan the trail behind for signs of pursuit, he turned back and found himself alone. Heart pounding wildly, he hauled ass, following the broken, bleeding trail of crushed grass that the Rangers had left, the only sign that they were ahead. Breaking through into a small saddle-shaped clearing, the chopper's rotor-wash assaulted him, slowing his progress, pushing him away from safety. When the chopper produced a high-pitched rev as if it were ready to lift off, he admits he almost had a heart attack.

Exiting the dense vegetation about ten meters from the Jolly Green's lowered tailgate, he saw Singh on the edge of it, anxiously scanning the tall grass. Jarrett leaped for the tailgate, beginning to lift, and felt Singh's hands grab his webbing as he fell forward onto the hard surface. Too exhausted to move, he gasped for breath. The VN Rangers pointed and babbled at him, their gold teeth glinting in the dim light. He thought, Buddha my ass! It had been one-hell of a first operation. The heavy chopper lurched forward, and lifted off.

At the FOB, if he had hoped to discuss the operation, he was sadly disappointed. Singh told him to get some chow—that was the end of it. They never spoke of it again. It didn't take him long to realize this was just another Project Delta workday; no-big-deal. Years later, Singh would become Jarrett's sergeant major with the 10th Special Forces Group, Fort Devens, Massachusetts. Still, the operation was never spoken of—Doc Simpson, however, did casually remark that Joe Singh had once mentioned that Jarrett had done well on his first operation.

"Could've fooled me," Jarrett said.

* * * * * *

Eventually, Jarrett transitioned from being a FNG to the number three team member following Moose Monroe, team leader, and roommate Ken Edens, assistant team leader. Moose, in Southeast Asia periodically since 1961, knew almost everything there was to know about recon and jungle survival. His competition, if any, had been Ken Edens. Jarrett decided that he'd watch these two and learn as much as he could. However, his first trip into the hole hadn't been with Moose Monroe, at all, but with Jay Graves. He soon learned there were others within Delta just as skilled in the art of combat recon.

Although he trained with high anticipation, the first time in the hole seemed foreign and surreal. Under the triple-layer canopy, the night was blanketed in an inky black; it took getting used to. Initially daunting, it soon began to feel more like an old friend. Stealth, silence and the cloak of darkness—another way to avoid detection. Around midnight, the team went on a fifty percent alert; a two-hour shift each, one American always awake. During the next five days they crept through the jungle, ghost-like, as Jarrett learned how to look and what to listen for. Eventually, he learned how to detect carefully camouflaged bunkers and obscure trail markers, and could differentiate between enemy tracks and those of indigenous farmers.

What impressed him most was that hardly anyone spoke aloud, with the exception of Graves, who, when whispering radio contacts had his face buried in his boonie hat to muffle the sound. Communication was accomplished merely by a hand or arm signal, a slight snap of the fingers or a soft whistle. He noticed how Edens and Graves shared thoughts simply with an expression; they had worked together for so long. No longer the FNG, he was still a novice; his two mentors were patient when he screwed up or made more noise than he should. Soon, he learned how to shorten his stride, balance on the steep slopes, step nimbly over rough and uneven terrain and cross a slippery stream-bed.

Jarrett was twenty-two, physically fit and could run a six-minute mile in jungle boots and fatigues. He was, as Special Forces men are known to say, "as hard as Superman's kneecap." However, he quickly learned that being in top running condition had little relationship with an ability to hump a heavy rucksack, weapon and radio gear over severe terrain while remaining silent and vigilant. By the end of his first day he was so exhausted that he couldn't eat or drink. Graves and Edens must have observed his fatigue; they didn't have him stand watch for the next two nights until he toughened into the routine.

Jarrett recollects, "They both demonstrated the quiet professionalism and leadership that is hallmark of Special Forces soldiers everywhere." They were his mentors, his heroes—he learned their lessons well.

Although their small patrol had numerous indications that the enemy was active, such as occasionally hearing their voices, no visual contact had been made for four days. They were grateful the weather remained overcast. Although an overcast sky can mute sound, the gloomy cover can be a double-edged sword. If too overcast, it's impossible to get tactical air support or a helicopter in for extraction.

Jarrett soon learned to identify natural jungle sounds; monkeys, other unidentifiable animals, birds, insects. Coming across the molted transparent skin of a monster-sized cobra, he hoped never to run into one, or one of the little bamboo krait vipers. He mastered the jungle's sounds, or lack thereof, as either the signal of human absence or presence. He was becoming seasoned.

On the fifth day out, they awoke to the sound of a distant battle being waged. A FAC flew over, advising Graves that a Marine battalion reported they were in a life and death struggle with NVA regulars, five miles away. They also were notified that they were scheduled for extraction later in the day. That news brought smiles; another team was coming in to replace them. Still, they were warned to be careful. Over-flights confirmed the area was hot, teeming with enemy activity. Their smiles quickly diminished.

Moving along a narrow valley, they headed west toward their designated extraction LZ. While small, extremely steep hills and dense vegetation blanketed the area, their map indicated cover and concealment would quickly become a problem if they continued west. Jarrett was been glad their Vietnamese counterparts seemed to be a solid lot this time out, and they had a great point man. Most likely a veteran of the French-Indochina War, in his early 40s, he was a no-nonsense, tough, experienced operative. After Jarrett's previous experiences with Vietnamese, the feeling was refreshing. He surmised they weren't much different than new American troops; they just needed training, and the opportunity to gain knowledge and experience before becoming fully competent.

The patrol moved along cautiously a few meters apart, everyone tense, alert, on guard. Jarrett had the responsibility of providing security for the left flank. He suddenly sensed tension; the hair stood on the back of his neck. On hyper-alert, weapons were carried tactically at shoulder level, muzzles depressed, swaying to the movement of the men's eyes scanning the jungle. With short steps and carefully placed boots, they visually searched shadowy corners—their feelings palpable. They weren't alone.

Entering a canyon opening, initially they were relieved to find cover. Suddenly the point man froze, bringing his rifle to combat-ready. They all took a knee. Voices! A large group was headed directly toward them. Graves urgently motioned to reverse the formation, to head back toward the last rally point, fast! Running as swiftly as possible, Jarrett wondered if he'd get hammered in the back. After 200 meters, they tumbled into a deep stream bed, hiding beneath the lip of the cut. Graves motioned for the point man and another VN to cover the left flank, and for two others, the right. Edens and Jay Graves each took the twelve o'clock position, while Jarrett covered their six. They silently observed a large enemy force advancing in the tree line they had just left, but were relieved when they turned south past the terrain the team had just raced across. They breathed a collective sigh of relief.

Graves signaled Jarrett to move closer to his and Edens's position, to get more guns into the fight, if it came to that. He crawled toward them as both flanks opened up at once. Hunkering beneath the cut of the bank, Jarrett couldn't see much, but the firing seemed to be coming from every direction. He peeked up and over the lip, detected movement in the tree line and fired off several rounds on semi-automatic. He and Edens quickly ducked, their fire instantly returned tenfold.

He noticed Edens gazing at him, bemused. "When you fire, they'll fire back," he said with a grin. Jarrett carefully peeked out again. There could easily be an NVA regiment concealed just yards away and he wouldn't be able to see them.

Graves motioned for the patrol to move—quietly—remaining in the stream bed. After a short distance, he signaled a pause. Jarrett watched as their tough, small point man slipped silently over the bank, heading back toward the tree line they'd brought under fire. Amazed by such bravery, he pondered whether he should follow. His face must have reflected this indecision because Edens shook his head; he stayed put. A few minutes passed before Graves roused the patrol to move out again. After a few minutes of brisk travel, they halted once more. Jarrett, still covering the six o'clock portion of their security perimeter, waited, straining to see anything moving. The point man disappeared into the thick jungle where enemy activity was last seen. Jarrett wondered if they would ever see him again, then a slight movement caught his eye. He raised his weapon, waiting for a target to appear.

"It's our point coming back," Edens whispered. He silently moved behind Jarrett. "Hold your fire, but cover his six until he gets inside."

The point man piled between the two of them, panting and excited. "Blood trails," he said. "One dead VC. Many more wounded."

He had retrieved the dead man's black wrist wrap and recovered two French Mat-36 rifles, both blood-stained. Viet Cong soldiers commonly used the wrist wraps to carry dried fish and rice balls. Conversely, the NVA tended to carry small packs. The recovery of the wrist wrap indicated they'd encountered VC. That was good. If these were NVA, they'd be in worse trouble.

Graves again made radio contact. Bruiser told him to move to a different LZ; they'd be extracted within a couple hours. Jarrett sighed— he'd been in the hole and might even live to make it back. And he'd be Recon—that is, if the guys gave their approval.

During the team's debriefing at the FOB, both Graves and Eden informed Simpson that Jarrett "would do"; he was fit to go as assistant team leader the next time. Subsequently, Moose requested Jarrett's assignment as his One One since Edens was due to rotate. Jarrett had made it; he was officially Recon.

Although accepted, technically he was still the FNG until given a One One slot on a future patrol. So until Ken Edens rotated and gave him his slot, for the time being, Jarrett would run his second recon mission as the third man again; this time with Monroe and Jay Graves.

During his second mission, they stopped for lunch; Graves and Monroe crouched off a short distance, eating their rice as Jarrett stood watch. Only if time permitted would the FNG also get to eat while paused, if not, he'd eat on the move. Jarrett detected movement; two armed men squatted in a nearby thicket, inching toward the Americans in a crab-walk. He moved toward Moose and Graves, softly snapping his fingers to get their attention. He whispered, "Two VC...no more than fifteen yards up the trail."

Without pause, Graves continued to eat. "So? Pop 'em...let us eat."

Jarrett crawled back a few feet, sighted and cut the two unsuspecting enemy soldiers down. They must have been the point element for a larger force; in less than a minute, the jungle opened up in a barrage of deafening gunfire. In Jarrett's words, "We were plain lucky just to make it out alive." Graves grinned when he later told Jarrett that it had been a "test," just to see if he could do it.

Jarrett learned some of his most valuable combat lessons from his life-long friend, Gary Stedman. They were involved in a nasty firefight and one of his recon men had been seriously wounded. Stedman, his personality calm compared to Jarrett's "gotta-always-be-going" temperament, first took care of the wounded man in a nearby bomb crater, and then under heavy fire, ran to another crater and hunkered down. Above the din of combat he heard Stedman intone a remark he used quite frequently when things got really hot. "This shit's just like the movies."

Upon their return to the FOB, Stedman uttered another original that continues to resonate with Jarrett. "Training gives you an edge, but luck will wield the sword."

* * * * * *

Jarrett continued to run many missions with Monroe, Graves, Stedman and Mike Norris. Moose Monroe named him "Mr. Clean" because he didn't drink, smoke or chase whores. He was determined to corrupt his new young assistant, and Jarrett admitted to being an able and willing student. After the war, Ken Edens and Moose both moved to New Mexico, within 300 miles of Jarrett's home. Jarrett said, "Moose was an awesome Special Forces soldier, and one hell of a cowboy too. He lives in Clovis, not far from me, and I think the main reason he stays in the desert is because there are no leeches."

One summer, Jarrett and Stedman worked together on a ranch, where Stedman taught him to ride a horse. The three remain close friends.

EIGHTEEN

"Break Contact...
Continue Mission!"

IN SEPTEMBER 1967, DELTA AGAIN BEGAN RUNNING operations from Vietnam's DMZ to the Central Highlands, and as the summer waned, the names of A Shau Valley, Happy Valley and An Loa would be etched forever in the memory of the men who survived them. James "Jay" Graves had been designated as team leader, the One Zero of an operation supported by the 281st; James Jarrett, his One One. Jarrett had been in the hole several times before with Graves and highly respected him as one of the best in the business—albeit a bit eccentric. Others often referred to Graves as "one crazy bastard."

One famous incident that aptly highlights this assessment of Graves' "craziness," happened after Project Delta closed in 1970 and he was assigned to the Mike Force, along with another Delta buddy, Al Schwarcbher. As the story goes, Graves seriously hit the Mike Force club—as he frequently did following an operation. It seems the Mike Force Commander had injured Graves's sensibilities, either ostensibly, or through some real or imaginary insult. His grudge, exacerbated by hard liquor, had left him in a foul mood. Wild-eyed drunk, swaying in the middle of the compound, in one hand he waved a bottle of booze, the other, an Army-issue .45-caliber automatic. He yelled loudly for either the Mike Force Commander or any of his staff to, "…come out of your holes!"

Weaving, he noticed the Commander's shiny new jeep in front of the headquarters building, staggered over and shot it—several times. In fact, he'd shoot the vehicle, take a swig, circle it for a bit and then shoot it again. After several minutes of this, the Commander's lop-sided jeep could easily have passed for metallic Swiss cheese. The scene continued as the staff and others hunkered down, their doors locked, hoping he'd soon pass out or run out of ammo. Desperate, someone thought to awaken Al Schwarcbher; maybe he could do something about the agitated Graves.

Rubbing the sleep from his eyes, Schwarcbher simply strode toward Graves, quietly looked the jeep over for several minutes and remarked, "It's dead, Jay. You killed it."

After a ten-second interval of total silence, Graves burst out laughing and laid his pistol in Schwarcbher's outstretched hand. Amazingly, the incident was never spoken of again and there were no repercussions. Graves recollected, "I should've ended up in LBJ (Long Binh Jail)." There were a lot of people who tended to agree with him.

* * * * * *

It was widely accepted that Graves was one of the best Recon men around, but he was known to do things on the spur of the moment that would break up his teammates. On one mission with James Jarrett, as they touched down, they were compromised by a force of unknown size. Quickly fading into the dense vegetation, they ran hard, trying to throw off the pursuers. Inserting before last light as standard operating procedure, it soon became too dark to travel—even for the enemy. The team selected a Remain Overnight (RON) position on the cusp of a deep ravine, quietly establishing a tight security perimeter. As soon as they were set up, they heard their pursuers about twenty meters above, on what they would discover the next morning to be a highly trafficked trail.

The enemy seemed to know they were still in the area. In the darkness, they threw rocks into the ravine to see if they could draw fire from the hidden team; some landing in their midst. They suspected these were VC and not NVA regulars. If they'd been NVA, these guys would've tossed grenades instead, or fired, hoping to hit them. Then if they heard the slightest moan, they would've been all over them. Before daylight, the team roused and silently moved out.

Graves called in with his situation report, asking to be extracted. Most of the men already knew what Bruiser would say; they had heard it so often they could easily repeat it. It was Jay Grave's turn.

"Break contact...continue mission!"

For the next three days, a thick blanket of fog and intermittent-to-heavy rain made progress extremely slow and difficult. Moving quickly wasn't an option. Despite heavy enemy concentration, they couldn't risk a broken leg or ankle, and with the wretched weather, extraction was only a remote possibility. They were on their own. Although they saw numerous indications of the enemy, they didn't make contact; but it was clear the VC knew they were nearby because they were constantly stalked. This notion did not bode well for the small patrol. The enemy knew they'd been inserted, and, if they got into serious trouble, the lousy weather would make an extraction doubtful. They hoped their adversaries were VC, not NVA. That would considerably improve their chances of getting out.

For the first three days, they played hide-and-seek with the bad guys—the majority of time by staying low, hours spent crawling on their stomachs. On the fourth day, just as they had set up a security triangle for lunch, Jarrett silently signaled that he'd spotted enemy troops; they were crawling toward them, less than thirty-five meters away. Graves nodded his understanding; both laid down a magazine of suppressing fire before retreating into the jungle. As soon as they'd moved on, the enemy returned heavy fire, churning up their old position. Jarrett noticed that when the firing commenced, the Vietnamese troops disappeared. He and Graves were alone. Down to only two rifles, they were in a serious jam.

Angered by the betrayal of their VN team members, they managed to evade the VC by taking a shortcut across several ravines, then by traversing a long ridgeline. They finally stopped to catch their breath and evaluate their situation. It didn't look good. Clearly out-gunned now that their VN guys had cut and run, their only two options were to either lay down a base of fire and run each time discovered, continuing to evade until someone could get them out, or track down their rogue VN teammates, kick their asses and restore firepower. They opted for the later; but, before they could act, someone approached from behind.

Jarrett sought cover behind a banyan tree, its extensive root system forming tendrils halfway up its trunk. The trees are valuable when used for defensive positions; the VC used them against U.S. gunship strikes. Jay, to his left, about five-to-seven meters away, held onto an M79 grenade launcher, as well as his shortened CAR-15. It was obvious the trackers were hot on their trail, advancing along the same finger of terrain they'd just left. As soon as the first enemy soldier came into view, Jay stepped from behind his tree and fired off an M-79 canister round. Eating up tree limbs and vines, it resembled a rotor-rooter churning through the vegetation. Jarrett opened up on full automatic, expending a complete magazine before pausing. Scattered screams and soft moaning followed, and then the jungle went deathly quiet.

Jay got on the radio, feeling quite lucky to make contact with the FAC on his first attempt. He hastily explained their situation. So sorry, they were told, the shitty weather precluded getting anything airborne—they were still on their own. Jarrett and Graves thought they detected stealthy movements emanating from the location where they first heard moaning, and agreed it was most likely the sounds of the enemy carrying off their dead and wounded. They agreed to move fifty meters, just in case the bad guys wanted more. Jarrett said his emotions that day were "...finely-tuned, my adrenaline was in high gear...scared, yet excited." He remembers that a ridiculous thought had crossed his mind as they were being fired on; he wished he had no shirt buttons so he could get that much closer to the ground. He continued to watch their back-trail, intent on any signs of pursuit. Then, suddenly, he smelled smoke—cigarette smoke, to be precise.

Startled, his eyes scanned the area where he'd last seen Graves crouched behind the root system of another banyan tree. He couldn't see him, but several smoke rings wafted from behind the cover. Unbelievably, he watched as Graves stepped from behind the tree. With his tongue, he removed the palate piece securing his two front teeth, stuck them toward Jarrett, wiggling them and grinning while he blew smoke circles through the gap in his teeth. The sight was so ridiculous that

Jarrett couldn't contain himself. He nearly rolled on the ground laughing. It was lucky they weren't both killed.

Once the activity settled down, they decided to continue their search for their erstwhile "allies." Aware the VC were probably still nearby, they became convinced these guys were a rather disorganized lot. That didn't mean they could get lax, however. For although their immediate foe lacked the discipline and tactical savvy of NVA regulars, he and Graves knew they could still kill. And if you made a mistake, you'd be just as dead. Jarrett took the point, heading off toward where they'd last seen their VN counterparts fade over a fifteen-foot ledge. He followed the cliff to their right, along the same long fingerling of land they'd traversed earlier, each short step precise, stealthy. Soon, he identified the place where the rest of the recon patrol had landed, near the bottom of a fifteen-foot drop. With no signs of blood to indicate differently, he ascertained the team had made it over the ledge without serious injury.

They discovered some tracks leading off and slowly followed, all the while maintaining 360 degrees of security. This was all very stressful. Then, they heard voices coming from several directions. Seems they'd stumbled into a large enemy concentration; maybe a battalion or regimental base camp. This presumption was confirmed after they crossed a highly trafficked trail, rutted with fresh vehicle tracks. Only division-sized elements had vehicles—this was not a good omen. Subtle signs indicated their VN recon guys had crossed the trail and turned toward the river—not the best of ideas, since the enemy concentrated near rivers because they were a natural travel route and provided the enemy with water and a brief respite. They had little choice—they were committed. They must go forward.

Jarrett caught a whiff of wood smoke, momentarily stopping to see if Graves had smelled it, too. Despite traveling a good distance, they were still close to some kind of large encampment; resigned to that fact that they couldn't avoid it. Activity was all around them. Stopping was not an option; they knew they had to hurry, but use extreme care. It was getting late and the tempo of enemy activity always increased after dark. Besides, they wanted to be extracted today. Jarrett picked up some familiar movements ahead and began to double-time toward them. It was their missing VN recon guys. He whistled softly, and the man in the rear turned, his expression one of simultaneous fear and relief. Jarrett grimaced, shaking his head. The man's fear was warranted, but only after they all were safely back at the FOB. This was not a time for recriminations, and leaving men behind was not an option. Recon didn't leave their men behind, regardless of how poorly they had performed.

Joined again with their VN counterparts, they headed south, where their cover would be denser. In these relatively open areas, they felt like sitting ducks. Jarrett glanced up toward the patches of blue sky as he heard a distant drone. A FAC flew over and revved his engine, a signal he wanted them to come up on the radio. Jay buried his face in his boonie hat, speaking into the handset. Bruiser wanted a situation report, the FAC would relay for him. Major Allen informed them a Slick and two gunships were inbound to pick them up, but the weather window wouldn't last long. They were to bust their hump getting to the new LZ. Bruiser reminded them that if they made it to the LZ, he'd personally be there to greet them. He didn't need to tell them, they knew he would. He always did.

Hours passed. Nearly exhausted, using only sheer guts as fuel, they finally made it to within 100 meters of the LZ before taking on sporadic small arms fire. Bruiser's C&C ship was on site, as were the gunships. He informed them jets were in-bound, only a few minutes out. He also let them know that the LZ was barely large enough to allow one Slick to make its vertical descent through triple canopy and hover just above the ground. The FAC swooped in, fired a rocket on the LZ to mark it for their recovery chopper and a loud roar shook them—the fast-movers had arrived. Graves grinned and Jarrett tried to suppress a spirited war whoop; with all the activity it was still pretty noisy. He knew the bad guys were rapidly closing in.

The recon team burst from the brush just as their Slick settled into the small hole, hovering. Jarrett dropped back to cover their six, while Graves helped the smaller VN guys climb into the wobbling chopper. These diminutive men, especially when weighted down, always had difficulty entering. One of the Delta guys was the recovery NCO; Jarrett caught site of a broad hand extending to yank one up. It might have been Gary Stedman's, but Jarrett couldn't be sure. As the team's One Zero, Graves was always the first on the ground, and the last off. While they perceived the enemy had been in hot pursuit before the air cover arrived, the prop wash and roar of the jets made it impossible to hear others approach from behind. Jarrett scoured the tall grass, fretting— the process seemed much too slow. The VN recon members bunched at the chopper's door, anxious to get inside.

Jarrett, frustrated by the bottleneck, went to the front of the chopper, intent on gaining entrance through the opposite door. Passing by the Plexiglas bubble cockpit, the startled co-pilot made eye contact, recoiling at his camouflaged, bloodied face. Within seconds, the bubble disintegrated as automatic fire struck it. Only then did he take notice of the 281st AHC pilot in the cockpit. Motionless, the pilot held the ship steady as the team struggled to get aboard. Jarrett noticed the young pilot's eyes, fixated on a vague object; his hands trying to keep the craft level and stable until every man had safely boarded. Finally, it lifted off, up and away. The chopper was banged up so badly it was forced to land at a Special Forces camp halfway to Hue.

* * * * * *

Jarrett wished he could remember the name of that young 281st AHC pilot, adamant that his brave acts were responsible for lifting them up out of the hole that day. "Without the courageous 281st pilots and crew, none of us would be home today," he said.

James Jarrett and Jay Graves remain friends. "Jay is one of the finest field soldiers I've ever been in the bush with, and I still love him like a brother," Jarrett said, then added ruefully, "The fact that he's probably clinically crazy just makes him all the more endearing."

Jarrett reinforced how Special Forces troopers are undeniably a "special" breed, and that it had been an honor and privilege to call these men brothers: "Moose" Monroe, Gary Stedman, Ken Edens, Jay Graves, Mike Norris and many others. When transitioning from SF to a different career, soldiers were often plagued by societal adjustments, and Jarrett was no exception. Initially, as a Los Angeles undercover narcotics officer, and later, as a college professor, he often felt discouraged by colleagues who didn't measure up to the high caliber of competence expected of a Special Forces soldier. It has been difficult for him to reconcile differences; he relishes his friendships with his old Delta comrades—those who know and understand.

* * * * * *

As Operation Delta Junction kicked off in the A Shau Valley, SGT Jay Graves and "Moose" Monroe had both been alerted to scrounge up some demo men. Ten camouflaged enemy trucks, presumed to be crammed full with combat goodies, were reported as setting idle in a motor pool lot. Delta would be going in "in force," hellbent on destroying every last one. D.J. Taylor, Joe Singh and SP5 Merriman, a demo expert, were assigned to head

Jay Graves with enough steaks to last the Nungs a month! (Photo courtesy of the Project Delta website)

up one team, while Monroe, Graves and a young school-trained demo man, SP4 Johnnie Link, led the other. One Ranger company would accompany them. They never knew how sorely lacking they would be in numbers as a reinforced NVA battalion waited on the LZ.

From the outset, the landing force had been trapped on the LZ. With little prospects for getting out, or for bringing more helicopters in, the only choice was to set up perimeter defensive positions and dig in. The vicious fighting would last several days; finally reinforced by another Ranger company and a Marine contingent. In all, thirteen helicopters were shot down. Merriman and Link attempted to reach a small knoll to retrieve a wounded Marine pilot. Reaching the wounded man, Link picked him up and Merriman covered for him. They were fired upon by a concealed machinegun and Merriman went down, hit in the foot. Link carried the wounded Marine to cover in a nearby crater, and then under intense fire, returned for Merriman. The machinegun continued firing as Link fell on top of Merriman to protect him from further hits, and took three rounds in the back. Captain Jim

Morris, a combat vet who previously had served with Special Forces units previously, was with them that day as a journalist for the *Green Beret Magazine*. Braving deadly fire, he dragged Link toward safety, but was hit and wounded severely himself. Staff Sergeant Anthony and SSG Stedman saw what had happened and quickly rushed to drag the wounded men into a bomb crater. Link would not survive his numerous wounds. He lasted through the night but without emergency hospital care, died the following morning; all medivac attempts were thwarted by the foul weather and deadly automatic fire. Morris's wounds were so serious they eventually forced him into early retirement from the Army.

Graves detected a pilot still seated in one of the downed infiltration helicopters. Although he appeared dead, Graves decided he could not allow him to remain any longer, sitting there under enemy fire. He had given enough. Graves and Monroe ran toward the damaged chopper to pull the dead pilot from the front seat. Graves was the first to notice SFC Thompson, Jim Morris's *Green Beret Magazine* photographer, snapping pictures near the bent tail blades.

"Better get your ass down, boy," Graves warned. "Them are real bullets you hear zinging past."

No sooner had he spoken those words, the photographer was hit, dropping instantly. Graves rushed to examine him; he'd been hit in the chest. Still breathing, pink frothy bubbles exuded from his wound; it was clear he had sustained a sucking chest wound. Under intense fire, Monroe hoisted and carried the dead pilot while Graves shouldered the wounded photographer, returning to the relative safety of a bomb crater.

* * * * * *

During the operation in the A Shau Valley, fourteen men were killed during the first two days of that battle, and thirteen aircraft destroyed, one an Air Force jet fighter. The much sought after trucks that had started the whole mess were never found.

* * * * * *

Thompson, the *Green Beret Magazine* photographer, survived. Years later, by chance, Jay Graves ran into him at Fort Bragg, N.C., and Thompson told him he was no longer with a news agency. He had become an A-team Operations NCO.

NINETEEN

Bruiser

FROM 11 AUGUST THROUGH 10 SEPTEMBER 1967, Delta Recon was back in the A Shau Valley—this time for Operation Samurai I and Samurai II, with legendary Project Delta Commander, MAJ Chuck "Bruiser" Allen leading by example. Allen was no nonsense when it came to operations; he took charge of team insertions and extractions, logged more than 500 missions in his C&C aircraft and often served on the ground with his forces. The mission came first. He expected nothing less from subordinates. Historically, Delta's recon teams were led by the most capable, experienced noncommissioned officers within Special Forces.

Higher echelons briefly experimented with having younger officers, many of whom were less experienced, accompany the teams. On a particularly dangerous mission in the An Lo Valley, LT Charlie Ford radioed Allen to inform him that he had left his weapon on the chopper during the team's insertion. The shaken officer asked for immediate extraction. Allen's reply was short and to the point: "Cut a f _ _ _ing spear. Continue mission."

Without his weapon, Ford nervously toted a grenade for the entire operation while learning a valuable lesson. He was later reassigned to the Ranger battalion, and regarded as one of the best young leaders in Project Delta. He would be awarded two Silver Stars for his actions with Delta's 81st Airborne Ranger Battalion. Bruiser Allen's lessons were hard, but constructive.

In an unfortunate training accident after returning to the States, Charlie Ford died in a helicopter crash at Fort Benning, GA.

* * * * * *

Bruiser Allen was an imposing figure; 250 pounds, all muscle. Easy-going and pleasant, he had an undeniable expression of innocence, much as a teenager might when getting away with something. A gap in his front teeth and a chipped tooth added to his "over-grown-kid" persona. Despite this affable style, the best interests of his men were always foremost, and his knowledge of Project Delta was never questioned. As far as his men were concerned, he'd written the book. Jim Tolbert recalled this about Allen: "While it's true that Special Forces NCOs were the ones on the ground and did the dirty dancing, Chuck Allen played the music, and he was never out of key."[36]

Captain Terrel "Ken" Naumann previously served with Allen on several 1st Special Forces Group assignments, so he wasn't overly surprised when he got a call while attending the Infantry Officers Advanced Course at Fort Benning, GA. He'd been attending a boring lecture when a "priority" call came in from an overseas location, pulling him from class. A gravelly voice greeted him. "Hey asshole, how you doing?"

He knew the voice instantly. It was MAJ Allen. Somehow, Allen knew Naumann was due for a Vietnam assignment; he told him not to opt for anything special—that he'd be coming to Project Delta. It never occurred to Naumann to question him. Allen wanted him, and that was good enough.

He had been around long enough to know that Allen had one of the best "spy" networks in the U.S. Army. Twelve days after his graduation, Naumann landed in Nha Trang. He reported in, and was immediately met by Allen.

---

[36] James Tolbert. "Chuck Allen and Delta." http://projectdelta.net/allen_story.htm

"Get settled. You're going to be my S3."

Working on the staff wasn't how Naumann saw himself spending the next year; he objected strenuously. He couldn't envision himself as a staff officer, even with Project Delta. He was combat arms, and he wanted to lead troops on the ground. Allen listened intently to his objections, then simply said, "Unpack, settle in, and read everything in the S3 shop so you can do the job."

That was that. Naumann would be the S3.

An I Corps operation was ongoing at that time, and Allen flew to Phu Bai the following morning. Naumann joined him two days later. He'd just arrived and dropped his bag when Allen told him to follow along. As they strode toward the flight line, Allen explained that two teams were being inserted that evening. Naumann would accompany him in the C&C chopper. He said Naumann's only mission, for the time being, was to stay within earshot, listen and learn as much as possible—and keep his mouth shut. The S2 would explain the entire mission upon their return to the FOB, and he could ask questions at that time.

"In the meantime, don't get on the chopper intercom and start talking," Allen said. "You don't know enough yet to talk." That was Naumann's first exposure to Chuck Allen's brand of combat leadership.

Approaching the launch pad, Naumann detected a distinct change in the troops' posture and demeanor; nothing particular stood out, just subtleties, like immediately picking up their gear, getting ready to go. Their mannerisms spoke volumes more than words ever could; Bruiser was there, they could go now. It was not as if anyone jumped up or saluted—just quiet, understated respect for their leader. The crews and recon teams stood silently by the helicopters, waiting as Allen passed. He asked them all the same question, "Are you ready?"

There were few smiles, just a deferent, "Yes, Sir."

It was evident the boss had arrived. No one doubted that all the men, including the helicopter crews, were indeed, ready. In turn, Allen addressed each member of every recon team. Satisfied the teams were ready to go, Allen moved to take the pre-insertion edge off with light talk, bringing a few smiles to some darkly painted faces. Naumann watched, awed by the bonding of these warriors and the ultimate trust Allen conveyed through his body language and eye contact as he shook each team member's hand and wished him luck. Their attitude conveyed he was Allen, their leader, confident that nothing had been left to chance by the Bruiser. No detail was too small that he'd overlooked it; no support required that he wouldn't supply. And if they got into trouble, he'd employ any measure at his disposal to get them out. They were ready. Allen raised his hand in a circular motion and the engines revved. He climbed aboard the C&C chopper and Naumann followed—keeping his mouth shut as they took off.

Naumann served with Allen at every FOB until after the New Year; he finally got his wish to command troops on the ground, becoming Senior Advisor to the 81st Airborne Rangers. Allen eventually told him that he'd been tagged "by name" to come to Delta, and he alone would evaluate Naumann's combat leadership performance. Allen told him, "The first time you have contact with the guys, just introduce yourself and move on. You're the FNG around here, and everyone is wondering who the hell you are because I personally picked you. Initially, you'll have no authority in the FOB, unless I lay something on you. Play it soft, let them come to you. Eventually you'll start to develop a rapport with some of them. The toughest will be Doc Simpson, the Recon Section Leader. Don't let it worry you. He's tough on everyone. No one has to like you, but you damn well have to earn their respect if they're going to listen to you."

Allen suddenly grinned, displaying his prominent gap. "Hell, what am I telling you this for? You've been around. You know what to do. I'm going to check on the teams and go to bed."

"One thing was certain," Naumann related. "Allen was a world-class combat leader. Delta accomplished its missions primarily because of his leadership—the teams knew they could depend on him."

Allen was a commanding presence unlike any others Naumann had seen. "There was little doubt that he was the boss," he said. "His leadership style didn't strike fear into anyone, but did preclude any fool-hardiness. Allen expected each Delta member to know his job and applicable SOPs, to the letter of the word, and had little trouble taking someone to task if he suspected they did not. Rarely, did he raise his voice. If someone was killed during an operation, his voice might elevate a bit, not in anger, but anguish, because a life had been lost— one he was responsible for. He was not given to verbiage, and when in a FOB, had little tolerance for it. He wanted pertinent information—clear, concise and complete, the first time around."

* * * * * *

By all accounts, Ken Naumann was a fine officer and generally liked by everyone. Of average height, his eyes, soft and baggy, made him seem more serious and much older than he was. Perhaps it was his three previous tours in Vietnam. Naumann has since passed on, but he's always mentioned with affection and great respect whenever the old Delta troopers get together.

* * * * * *

Failure simply was not in Chuck Allen's vocabulary, and under his command, the unit executed every mission in an outstanding manner. If failure was never in Allen's lexicon, neither was it in his subordinates'. He always exhibited an air of confidence, and his confidence was contagious to those around him. If he had misgivings, he kept them to himself. His close affinity with his recon personnel was apparent by his team interactions and exchanges before insertion. While it never totally eliminated the pre-insertion fear, it did reinforce the idea that if they got into trouble, he'd do whatever was necessary to get them out.

Allen understood a combat leader had to have heart, not a bleeding heart, nor one worn on the sleeve, but honest caring about the men he'd be sending into harm's way. Yet, he also understood there were times when he had to harden his heart, weigh all the factors and make an unpopular decision as to when a rescue effort should be halted; to continue might mean additional loss of personnel and equipment, in far greater numbers than the element in trouble. His teams trusted him to make the right decision on their behalf.

In the FOB, Allen was seldom given to levity. Dead serious, he understood that at any moment trouble could rear its ugly head. His mien never restricted subordinates from enjoying a bit of humor, just that he never joined in while teams where in the field. There's an old military saying, "It's lonely at the top." Although Allen could appear lonely when Delta was in the FOB, others witnessed his sense of humor after they rotated back to Nha Trang. Around headquarters, after duty hours, he could be witty, and like many others, a practical joker. As a

Left to Right: MAJ Charles "Bruiser" Allen, Project Delta Commanding Officer; CPT Ken Naumann; CPT Willis F. Larabee; Nha Trang, Vietnam, 1967. (Photo courtesy of Anita Allen)

good commander, he understood he had to alleviate combat tensions and pressures.[37] That might account for why Allen often overlooked some of the men's shenanigans when they were on stand-down.

Of the Delta men who served with him, few would deny he was the best commander in Project Delta history. Never one to avoid the fighting when he had men in combat, Bruiser Allen usually showed up, either in the air or on the ground, during every operation and as a result, he was frequently decorated for bravery. In the A Shau Valley alone, during Operation Samurai I and Samurai II, he was awarded the Silver Star and Air Medal (ARCM/v) for valor. Under his tenure as Operations Officer, and subsequently as Commander of Project Delta, the organization became one of the most decorated units in Vietnam and won acclaim for its operational capabilities. Under his leadership,

---

[37] Jerry D. Estenson. *Perceptions of Critical Leadership Attributes*, 52.

Project Delta was awarded the Presidential Unit Citation, Valorous Unit Award, Meritorious Unit Citation, Navy Unit Commendation, Vietnamese Cross of Gallantry with Palm, Civic Action Medal 1st Class and the Civic Action Honor Medal.

Author Jim Morris, a retired Special Forces major, states his most vivid memory of Allen was flying with him in his C&C ship on a mission to lift a Road Runner team out of the jungle. Allen's radio was connected simultaneously to the chopper crew; the team on the ground; his Vietnamese counterpart, MAJ Haun; to Bill Larrabee, his operations officer; and to the other Slicks and gunships in the extraction team. Allen sat in one door with an M-60 machinegun suspended from a bungee cord in front of him. Larrabee sat in the opposite door with a similar rig. Their call signs were written in gold script on the backs of their helmets. Allen's was "Bruiser," Larrabee's, "Joker."

Morris recalls the extraction of that Road Runner team as amazing to watch. Three gunships circled the team on the ground, pouring machinegun and rocket fire into the jungle while the NVA tried to kill the team. The first extraction ship eased down onto the jungle in the center of the gunships' orbit. They lifted out three of the team with McGuire Rigs; another extraction chopper got the other three. [38]

All the time, Allen was talking, directing the extraction; the chattering M-60 like a toy in his hands, never letting up once. He could have run the whole operation from the FOB like some others had done, or at an altitude of several thousand feet, but these were his guys; this is where he wanted to be.

Allen recognized his men—Rangers, Nungs, chopper pilots, crews, FACs and recon teams—were head and shoulders above others. He seemed to have a particular affinity toward his Recon guys; perhaps for who they were—had to be—to accomplish the work for which they had volunteered. He knew that without Recon, Project Delta would not exist. He knew brave men would always be available to lead an Airborne Ranger assault, more than the few uniquely qualified to run small unit recon patrols deep inside enemy territory under the enemy's nose. For those missions, his needs were for strong-minded, nerves-of-steel

---

[38] Jim Morris. *A Giant of a Man*, (short story), June 29, 2006, 4-5.

In remembrance of Major Charles Allen, Project Delta's revered coin has been inscribed with the words he made famous: "Break contact....continue mission!" (Courtesy of Project Delta website)

leaders, who possessed the rare ability to silently seek out the enemy, live in their back-yard, fight like demons when cornered—and have the guts to return, again and again. Allen understood it took a special breed of men to know they'd be dropped into areas others chose for high enemy force concentrations, and with limited intelligence on their disposition, to find and destroy them. It was difficult enough to drop them in, but then to expect them to roam about collecting information, maintain secrecy and return alive was asking a lot. That they would do it time after time was extraordinary; and this was only the basics of Delta's recon. Allen respected that.

"It's not like the Korean War," Allen said. "I mean, going on patrol overnight with thirty-five others; maybe you'd make contact and maybe you wouldn't. Recon is a whole lot different; you're completely cut off, isolated from any type of support, particularly during hours of darkness or bad weather—during those times, your support wasn't there at all.[39]

"Nobody got assigned to recon outright. The FNG was first designated for interview, then he'd stay with the recon guys for three, four or five days. At the end of that time, if those guys thought he was

---

[39] Jim Morris. "Interview with the Big 'Un,' Part 3," *Soldier of Fortune Magazine,* Sept. 1981, 47.

a good enough Joe, they'd say, 'Okay sir, we'd like to take him out.' And that's even after I, the CO, had already said, 'Hey, I want to take this guy and put him in recon.' If they didn't want him for any reason after a couple patrols, I'd back them up."

During an interview, Allen once queried author Jim Morris: "Remember Doc Simpson, my recon leader? I had a lot of faith in Doc and if he'd said, 'Everyone else thinks this guy is okay, but I really don't think he's gonna make it,' then I wouldn't accept him for recon."

Allen reinforced that if he still thought the guy was good, but just didn't seem to have the capacity for recon, he'd be reassigned to the Rangers or the Road Runners. He realized not everyone possessed the skills for recon operations. It wasn't an indictment of their abilities— just a fact. That is not to say that recon members didn't bounce back and forth between the other entities frequently.

"Was Recon then, pretty much the elite, within the elite, within the elite?" Morris asked.

"Yeah," Allen said, "it was almost the sole reason for Delta's existence."[40]

* * * * * *

Shortly before his death, Jim Tolbert, a decorated veteran who had served multiple Project Delta tours, wrote that of the seventeen commanders in Delta's brief history, he'd served with eight. These were the brightest and best officers, the most select Special Forces Commanders; they all had the innate ability to accomplish the most difficult with limited resources. By Tolbert's account, and endorsed by many of his comrades, by far, Bruiser Allen was the best—"head and shoulders" above the rest.

In 2003, at the age of 71, LTC Charles A. "Bruiser" Allen, extraordinary commander and Project Delta legend, died at Cape Fear Valley Hospital in Fayetteville, North Carolina. It was a sad day for his small, much beloved warrior brotherhood. Their loss was profound.

---

[40] *Ibid.*

TWENTY

Bad Luck B-52

NON COMMISIONED OFFICER JIM TOLBERT was one of many to tout their time with Project Delta as the best days of their lives, particularly while MAJ Chuck Allen was the Commander. Because it was "acquired" while Allen was in command, Tolbert liked to tell this tale of the bad-news jeep, which he called "Chuck Allen's jeep," even though it remained each successive commander's vehicle until Delta's demise in 1970. He claimed that it's a known fact that some people seem to be more accident prone than others. Airborne and Special Forces units soon weed them out; it's clear they would end up somewhere. But in the civilian world, it never seemed to matter. Tolbert wondered if ever a piece of equipment might also be accident prone. He thought Project Delta had just such an item—"Chuck Allen's jeep"—bumper number "Delta B-52."

When entering the compound at Nha Trang, visitors always noticed the beautifully maintained quarter-ton jeep sitting in front of the orderly room. It had classy, freshly-stenciled numbers, a like-new paint job and a spotless tarp-roof. It seems this well looked-after jeep, however, had a curse on it—that is, if one could think a piece of equipment might be cursed. Wrecked at least once during every stand-down, it spent a lot of time in the motor pool repair shop, especially at the start of every operation. In fact, it was there so frequently just before nearly every operation that superstition soon set in. Whenever the men prepared to leave on a mission, they'd check to see if the jeep was in for maintenance. If so, it would be a good trip for everyone.

Who wrecked it? No one seemed to know. Major Allen was the only one with authority to drive it. Still, the inevitable seemed to always happen; twisted out of shape, it would be sitting in the motor pool. If some of Doc Simpson's recon didn't steal it for a night downtown, then Krelick's Rangers would. And if not the Rangers, then one of Gilbert's commo crew or some of Stanfield's crazy Nungs. On every stand-down, someone would manage to slip it out, and before the night was over, wreck it. The following morning, just as mysteriously, it would show up in front of the Commander's office, skewed sideways, a fender or two missing, or its front grill caved in. Sergeant Major "Crash" Whalen, raised hell constantly about that jeep, but Allen never once mentioned it.

Since Delta's activation, the Philippine motor pool tech-rep records documented old "B-52" had been wrecked more than twenty-four times. With its extensive maintenance history, they could've easily created an additional slot to care for just this one piece of equipment; Allen could have had his own personal pit crew. Despite all its care, Allen never drove it; perhaps he too felt it was cursed. When discovered in an ill state of repair, no one ever admitted to driving it, but just like clockwork, early in the morning as stand-down ended, there it would be, parked in front of the orderly room, tore all to shit. It drove the SGM crazy, but it kept the tech-rep guys busy. Many still believe that George Pruett should've left that damned jeep in Cam Ranh Bay from where he'd originally stolen it.

Tolbert recalled the jeep's fateful last day. It was a beautiful day, the sky blue, full of cumulous cotton-ball clouds, with nary a trace of rain predicted. Walking back from downtown Nha Trang, Tolbert had just reached Dong So Ba, Number 3 Street. A loud noise startled him and he looked up; over the bay a DC-3 was spewing flames from the tail section, struggling to make that final mile to reach land. Air Vietnam, coined "Air Nouc Mam" (*nuoc mam* is a pungent fish sauce), had a bunch of the old DC-3 rejects. For the most part, they'd been fairly well maintained and air-worthy, but it was clear this one was in serious trouble. So intently had he been watching the floundering plane that Tolbert nearly failed to see Allen's bad-luck jeep as it sped by. It was heading the same direction as the plane. The pilot apparently couldn't decide whether he should land or pull up to make another pass.

A compacted dirt road led to the Delta compound; it separated Nha Trang Airbase from CIDG (Civilian Irregular Defense Group) village at the end of the main runway. The road curve, where it approached the end of the runway, had been elevated six to eight feet higher to protect the Delta compound from grazing fire, should the VC decide to attack the village. Coiled rolls of razor wire, three feet high, had been pegged down near the runway, while a cluster of cardboard and tin shacks bordered the other, forming CIDG village. From the Delta compound, school children could often be heard playing.

As Tolbert watched the aircraft's plight, his eyes gravitated toward Allen's shiny jeep as it approached the road at the end of the runway. Years later, the fact that Tolbert hadn't been offered a ride by Allen's VN driver had dogged him; he'd been grateful the offer hadn't been made. It also seemed perplexing as to why the driver hadn't noticed something as large as an airplane, all lit up like a Roman candle, traveling a hundred miles an hour straight at him. In any event, like two horses, neck and neck, "Air Nuoc Mam" and Allen's ill-fated "B-52" raced toward their destiny. The DC3 bounced twice, its engines strained, fire shooting from the passenger section. Managing to clear the raised roadway by inches, it dragged razor wire, picket fence posts and "B-52" along, then exploded in a ball of fire into the school—an instant inferno engulfed the area.

Horrified, Tolbert broke into a dead run, but by the time he reached the area, nothing could be done. The flames were so intense he couldn't get within thirty yards of the crash site. He could only watch helplessly as passengers still strapped in their seats waved frantically, crying out as they burned. For years he could recall the odor of burning flesh—and the screams.

"B-52" had made its last dispatch. Even the adaptable little tech-reps wouldn't be able to repair it this time. Never again would it be stolen from the compound, and never again used to gauge the success

Steve Adams in "B-52," MAJ Allen's ill-fated jeep. (Photo courtesy of Steve Adams)

of an upcoming operation. There would be no more joy-rides into Nha Trang, no more ass-chewing by Fuller. What remained was carted off as salvage. An unknown number of Vietnamese died the day "B-52" made its last run, including an American entangled in the razor wire as the plane dragged it across the road. Tolbert always struggled to recall the American's name, but after years of uncertainty, D.J. Taylor told him it had been Special Forces SFC Richard V. Williams, recently assigned to Project Delta. The DC-3 occupants were all killed, the CIDG School was leveled and, with only a few exceptions, all the children perished. The group got mighty drunk that evening in the Delta Club.

* * * * * *

Soldiers have a saying, "There are no atheists in a foxhole." Most Special Forces soldiers served with airborne divisions before joining SF, and many soldiers regularly attended Sunday services and offered grace before eating even a can of C-rations. Yet, Delta veterans contend they have a hard time recalling anyone saying a prayer, whether in combat or garrison, in good health or when dying. Not that these good men were atheists, but perhaps they'd just come to the conclusion that a good plan and a clean weapon would do just as well. Or maybe they were just pre-occupied with staying alive.

Typically, whenever an SF soldier was killed in combat, the 5th Special Forces Group Commander would call a mandatory formation and march the survivors to the nearest chapel. This was not the case if a Delta buddy fell; survivors were much more likely to be seen at the nearest watering hole, ordering an extra beer for the deceased and drinking it before it got warm. Any of them could be next, and that's how they wanted to be remembered. Delta men showed their respect— or disrespect—when others were alive; after they were gone, church services didn't mean all that much.

The number one rule: "Never let your buddy down!" was lived up to, or guys were shown the door in short order. Ironically, some Delta veterans, once renowned as rowdy, tough hell-raisers, embraced religion later in life.

* * * * * *

The year 1967 would close with Operation Sultan I and II—operations in the valleys of Plei Trap and Plei Djereng to support the 4th Infantry Division. Action continued until January 1968. The 81st Airborne Ranger Battalion USSF advisors were particularly bloodied during both operations. Team Sergeant Samuel S. Theriault was the first to be killed, and numerous awards for bravery were won for heroic actions. First Lieutenant Charley Ford received a second Silver Star while SSG Herbert Siugzda was awarded the BSMV and received his second and third combat wounds, which earned him two more Purple Hearts. Others awarded the BSMV were: 1LT Richard N. Ellis, 1LT William G. Wentz, (also a Purple Heart), SFC Larry L. Sites, SGT Frederick A. Walz and SGT George D. Cole. Major Willis D. Jones, 1LT Edwin Livingston and MSG James G. Kreilick were each awarded an ARCMV; SP4 Russell C. Cooper won an AMV.

TWENTY-ONE

Men of Courage and Honor

AFTER THE 281ST AHC WAS ATTACHED to Project Delta for direct support, Delta cut back on support from other organizations. Once the 281st AHC absorbed the 171st Aviation Company (including the original 145th Airlift Platoon), that unit became deeply ingrained with Delta as support camaraderie deepened; the men's bravery reflected that closeness. As for the Project Delta command group, they relished having their own U.S. helicopter assets, which enabled them to curtail relying on external aviation loans. That practice resulted in some negative operational experiences.

During Operation War Bonnet out of An Hoa, for example, the 281st extracted a recon team under intense fire. Ken Wagner recalled they had a much more positive outcome with the 281st. He was still chafed about the operation where Jerry Nelson had to resort to threats just so the pilot would slow down enough to rescue Morales from a suspended ladder.

Wagner was recovery NCO in a Slick, hoping to spot one of their recon teams standing by for extraction. They'd been on a five-day "dry hole" (having had no enemy contact) west of Thong Duc. Out for nearly a week, just as they began their ascent up the rope ladder, the enemy opened up from a ridgeline 200 meters above them. The hovering helicopter, helpless to evade the heavy ground fire, took about twenty hits, shuddering violently as each bullet ripped through it. Two accompanying gunships swarmed in quickly, suppressing the fire with an unrelenting hail of mini-gun fire. This time, there'd be no repeating what Nelson and Morales had experienced. These were members of the 281st AHC—attached to Project Delta. They knew every one of those guys on the ground. The pilot steadied the craft, seemingly impervious to the assault. Hovering smoothly while bullets tore holes in his chopper, shards of Plexiglas and metal fragments pierced his face just below his helmet visor. Although bleeding profusely, he pulled pitch only after Wagner assured him the entire team was loaded. His passengers were treated to one wild tree-top ride to the safety of the FOB, but they all got out. That remarkable 281st AHC pilot was CPT Peterson.

* * * * * *

By 1968, Alton "Moose" Monroe had more time under his belt in Vietnam than the majority of men serving. He'd first been assigned in 1963 as part of a split Special Forces A-Team, as an advisor under auspicious CIA control. From 1963 to 1969 he served several more tours with Project Delta, his stints punctuated by short trips back to the States and an assignment with SOG. Moose was highly respected in his field; a real Delta icon.

Following an operation near Hue, where Delta sustained substantial losses, Monroe was inserted as the One One for a recon mission in the Plei Trap Valley. For this operation, Delta established a FOB in Kontum. Staff Sergeant Larry P. Bartlett, a close friend of Monroe's, was designated the One Zero, while a FNG was included as the third American on the six-man recon team. Monroe remembers Bartlett as a handsome man—tall, lean, with an infectious laugh that showed a lot of teeth, each "about a foot long."

"I wouldn't say Larry was tight, exactly," Monroe recalled with affection. "He just refused to spend money. The only thing he'd ever spend a dime on was a box of them cheap cigars he always smoked. But he was one hell of a guy."

The first day out they paused beside a trail when suddenly a guy in black pajamas ambled by, saw them lurking nearby and took off running. Intuitively, Monroe didn't think he was VC, only a local rice farmer, but believed he might have information they could use. Larry Bartlett decided to catch him and let the VN recon guys question him.

"Now you've got to understand," Monroe said, "Larry was 6' 3" tall and very athletic. Bartlett took out after that little guy, and he left Larry in the dust, like he was standing still. All our indigenous guys got a real kick out of it."

No additional contact was made during the first two days. On the third, Bartlett, who'd been running point, held them up; he'd come across a small campsite with several huts stuffed with freshly harvested rice. Although the huts seemed unoccupied, the VC must have been watching it from nearby. As the team moved out, they began to receive fire. During the initial volley, Bartlett was hit in the face; the impact blew away most of his lower jaw.

A running gunfight ensued with the larger VC force in hot pursuit. As Monroe attempted to get the team and his wounded friend back to a suitable LZ for extraction, he was stymied by the rugged terrain and dense jungle. Eventually, he was forced to call a halt and asked the recovery helicopter to lower a jungle penetrator for extraction. Monroe, the first to set boots on the ground and the last to leave, managed to get them all onto the hovering helicopter.

A jungle penetrator retrieving a fully loaded six-man recon team is a slow and tenacious process. The chopper first lowers the hoist—it descends much too slowly—a man snaps in and then, as if dawdling, it is retrieved; the process is repeated until all are aboard. Maintaining a hover in a mountainous down-draft for a prolonged period is an extremely difficult task for any pilot; the task can easily deteriorate to a ride from hell with poor weather, blowing wind, too dense or too tall trees for the hoist to reach, or if the aircraft receives enemy gunfire.

Monroe watched as the last man ascended, fretful about the enemy creeping closer. As the last to hook into the hoist, he waited, intently listening as the chopper revved, struggling to lift him out. It was evident the space was too narrow, and the trees much too tall for the chopper to gain enough lift. Loaded down with the other five team members and its crew, the chopper was being pulled downward; its blades began to clip tree limbs. Monroe immediately cut himself loose, allowing the chopper to lift off. It was a selfless act by a brave man; he was alone.

Monroe knew the enemy would be converging on the site, so he moved out quickly while trying to raise another chopper on the radio. Luckily, one had been nearby. It came immediately and dropped its hoist, lifting him out. Climbing over the ledge, a grinning SSG Sewell Brown offered a helping hand.

"Man, they say that other chopper lost about three feet of its rotor blades against those trees. You were lucky, Moose!"

"How's Larry?" It was the first thing he asked.

Bartlett was so seriously wounded that he had to be medivaced to the States. A year later, during his next tour, Monroe ran into him again in the Delta Club. He was on his way "up north," to run recon for SOG. Bartlett departed for his first SOG mission soon afterward.

Larry Bartlett and SGT Richard A. Thomas are listed on the Army's roles as KIA during a classified recon SOG mission.

A recently extracted recon team. SSG Sewell Brown (*left*) and SFC Larry Bartlett (*third from left*) with three unidentified VN recon men. During his next mission, Bartlett was seriously wounded. He was evacuated to the States for medical treatment and then returned for another tour. He was KIA during an SOG classified mission. (Photo courtesy of Maurice Brakeman)

* * * * * *

Operation War Bonnet in the An Hoa river basin lasted until mid-November 1968. BS/v medals were awarded to MSG Minor B. Pylant, MSG Richard S. Sorrells, SFC Jerry L. Nelson (second award) and SGT Bobby D. Warden. It was during War Bonnet that one of the most dare-devil examples of flying ability occurred. A 281st AHC helicopter pilot, CWO Donald Torrini, would extract SFC Jerry Nelson and his team from the jaws of death. The Delta men quickly concluded that if another unit had been supporting Nelson's team that day, they doubted if any other pilot would've taken such drastic measures to extract them.[41]

Nelson had been the One Zero on a six-man "snatch" mission. With his mission to capture a POW for enemy intelligence, he jumped at his first opportunity the second day out. Quietly lying near a highly trafficked trail, he and his team members first noted groups of two and three men, periodically passing at regular intervals. He whispered to wait until the next group passed, then to "Go for it."

Settling into an improved ambush spot, he placed his team in position and waited, his team unaware the next group coming was a fifteen-man security element for a much larger NVA unit that followed. After a brief altercation, described as the customary claymore mine popping, shooting, stabbing, kicking and grenade chunking, the team had their man, eliminating the enemy's point element in the process.

Some Delta Recon vets still get quite a kick describing Nelson's POW snatch technique. "He'd try his level best to kill everyone, and then check bodies for the least wounded survivor." Nothing subtle—usually one was still alive. Despite this unorthodox technique, Nelson was normally the one selected for these missions.

Good news—the men had their POW; bad news—they'd awakened a very pissed-off company of crack NVA troops who were breathing down their necks as they dragged their wounded prisoner toward the extraction LZ. The news got worse. The team soon realized these were elite NVA troops chasing them because of the manner in which they reacted quickly, with a force to cut them off around their flank. This

---

[41] D. J. Taylor. "Remembering the 281st AHC," 3. http://www.projectdelta.net/remembering_the_281st.htm.

would block the team's only route to the designated extraction site and make it inevitable that Nelson's point man would eventually make contact with them. Once that occurred, the team knew they were in serious trouble. Blocked to the front by an encircling element, with the main force crushing behind from the rear, they had little choice as to the direction they knew they had to take. The enemy's pincher strategy was forcing them further from the LZ and toward the river; they would be trapped.

As the team reached the riverbank, Nelson discovered they were backed against a seventy-five meter-wide obstacle, too deep to ford. With each man weighed down by weapons, and a wounded prisoner on their hands, the river would be too swift to swim. Quickly surveying their situation, he concluded the tall triple-layer canopy wouldn't permit either a McGuire Rig or a rope ladder to reach. Their alternatives were rapidly dwindling. The enemy, bent on revenge and far superior in numbers, closed in for the kill. Radio communication had been virtually impossible during their hurried trek due to the dense jungle cover. From the riverbank, Nelson frantically searched for an area where he could obtain a "shiny" fix from the "Sheriff."

Chief Warrant Officer (CWO) Torrini, call sign, "Sheriff," was standing by, waiting for Nelson's call to come get them. Descending to make the recovery, it quickly became apparent there was insufficient room to maneuver through the tree cover; still, Torrini used his rotor blades to try to chop back the trees enough to shoot through. Of course, chopper blades weren't designed for this kind of treatment and the attempt failed, but he had to take some drastic measures if he hoped to get the besieged team out of this predicament.

By then, Nelson and his team were viciously fighting for their lives against an NVA force bent on their annihilation. One of the recon men cried out that he'd been hit, but Nelson didn't know who, and he was too busy to find out. Shifting his weight slightly to the right of the tree he was using for cover, he fired off a short burst from his CAR-15; two NVA soldiers crawling toward him to get within hand-grenade range were stopped in their tracks.

It was a fact—if something positive didn't happen soon, his team would be history. Most had already been wounded. With their backs against the river, extraction appeared impossible. With the enemy too close to call in tactical air support for napalm or fragmentation bombs, their situation was bleak. They resigned themselves to making the enemy's assault as costly as possible. Unbeknownst to them, above the treetops, the Sheriff had not given up.

While Torrini hovered over the team's position, trying to get low enough to extract them, he noticed some dense trees hanging over each side of the river bank that had created a tunnel of sorts. There just might be enough space beneath them for his helicopter to narrowly fit. Torrini traversed the river under intense enemy fire, searching for an opening large enough to fit his helicopter. He finally found one suitable about 500 meters down river from Nelson's team; without hesitation, he plunged toward it. The co-pilot, crew chief and door gunner all held their collective breaths as Torrini steadily lowered his chopper through the small opening. Although several rounds tore through the thin-skinned fuselage, he never once looked away from his task, intent on watching the tree branches a few feet from his rotating blades. One slight mishap, and his bird and crew would end up in the churning waters.

Coming under increasingly heavy fire, the door gunners leaped to their guns, quickly answering the enemy's fire. The door gunner's M-60s rattled non-stop, their rounds churning the mud near three enemy soldiers as they crumpled to the ground. Three more NVA soldiers scrambled to set up an automatic weapon on the riverbank, but the chattering M-60s unleashed their fury again, killing them all. Torrini remained calm as if they weren't even under attack. Protecting the craft from the enemy was his crew's job—flying was his. Without forewarning, they punched through the hole, skimming the water. Torrini's skids were in the water as he flew under the low-lying branches, the rotor blades barely clearing the overhead limbs.

Nelson, nearly resigned to their fate, couldn't believe it! A helicopter emerging from the river, hovering right behind him, its skids submerged in the swift current. It set so low that its troop deck was awash in the fast-moving flow; its M-60s devastating the enemy's frontal attack. Holding steady, as if he pulled off these feats everyday, Torrini edged his craft closer to the muddy bank, his blades literally chewing bark from the trees. The chopper's M-60s continued to lay killing fire barely a foot over their heads. The team waded, then swam the short distance to the chopper and climbed in with their POW in tow.

Once the team was aboard, Torrini had to contend with another problem; he couldn't turn the chopper around. He had to back the heavily loaded helicopter out, hovering partially submerged, to return through the opening he previously had entered. By then, the gunships had arrived and were making repeated runs, blanketing the entire area with covering fire. Determined NVA soldiers along the riverbank were met by a killing fire from these, the door-gunners and from Nelson's recon team. By the time they reached the hole in the trees where the chopper had entered, the door gunners and Nelson's team had expended all their ammo.

The helicopter was badly shot up, with the rotor blades, transmission and engine so heavily damaged, Torrini concluded he'd never make it back to Phu Bai. Finding a suitable location in a rice paddy, he carefully set his battered chopper down, transferred his crew and Nelson's recon team to another helicopter, and then watched sadly as the brave little bird was destroyed. For the team and its crew, it felt as if one of their fellow soldiers had died. Remarkably, it was the only U.S. casualty of the day.

* * * * * *

D.J. Taylor summed up the experiences of Delta Recon when he said, "Who among us will ever forget being shot out of the hole, climbing fragile rope ladders, or being extracted by McGuire Rig as an extraction helicopter labored to gain attitude...while we dangled helplessly by those thin lifelines? Or hanging 120 feet below a helicopter traveling more than sixty knots per hour, watching a 281st Charlie model gunships come at us, its mini-guns blazing and thinking, 'Oh my God! He doesn't see us down here,' then noticing the tracers whizzing past under our feet, impacting on the LZ we'd just departed. By then, he would've passed under us so close that we couldn't resist an urge to lift our feet to give him room. Those 281st gunships would continue making passes beneath us until we were at a safe altitude, well away from the hot LZ. If an enemy hoped to take a shot at us, he had to first dodge bullets from those beautiful, awesome little ships. While we were hanging helpless, unable to defend ourselves, those 281st pilots would position themselves between us and those who'd do us harm. No soldier could ask for more."

* * * * * *

Operation Alamo, in support of the 5th ARVN Division in the Song Be River area, began June 1968. On 12 September 1968, Recon Team 7, consisting of SSG Lamberto Guitron, SSG Sherman Paddock and four VNSF, located an NVA security element. The team stealthily made their way inside the enemy's perimeter, where they discovered a large weapons and ammunition cache. Withdrawing to a safer location, they called in their find, and the BDA Platoon was inserted the following day to exploit the discovery.

It soon became evident the cache was too large and too well defended for the BDA Platoon to seize, so a Ranger company was inserted on 14 September to reinforce the BDA Platoon. The security force left by NVA had no intention of letting such a large stockpile slip away without a struggle. They put up a fierce fight in an effort to save their cache, and it wasn't long before all three Ranger companies of the 81st Airborne Ranger Battalion had joined in the fray. After a short but violent battle, the Rangers pushed the enemy force back and began to move the stockpile of weapons and munitions to a nearby LZ where it was sling-loaded onto a CH-47 Chinook helicopter and flown back to Quan Loi.

As the Rangers continued to push the NVA security element farther back, they found even more stockpiled ammo; the cache was proving to be much larger than anyone had originally thought. To make matters worse, there seemed to be an increasing number of NVA and VC arriving to engage in the fight. After an estimated one-tenth of the ammunition was removed, and yet another large, booby-trapped ammo bunker discovered, the decision was made to destroy the remainder of the ammo in place. The cache was rigged to explode, and the Rangers pulled back. After the initial blasts, air strikes were called in to complete the destruction, resulting in numerous undetected ammo bunkers going up in smoke.

Up to that time, the Song Be discovery was the largest ammunition cache seizure of the war. The Project Delta S-2 believed the ammo had not come down the Ho Chi Minh Trail, but had been delivered to a port in Cambodia and trucked across the border. Why the NVA had not left it in Cambodia where it would have been relatively safe remained a mystery.

This was only one-tenth of the NVA ammo cache found by Recon Team 7 near Song Be River, 1968. (Photo courtesy D.J. Taylor)

* * * * * *

Five Purple Hearts resulted from Operation Alamo: SGT John P. Burdish, SSG Sherman A. Paddock, SGT David F. Ryder, SSG Laurence A. Young and Stephen J. Viglietta. Both SFC Jerry L. Nelson and Kenneth C. Wagner won a BSMV, while SFC Arthur F. Garcia was awarded the ACMV.

TWENTY-TWO

"You're Fired!"

WITH MORE THAN THREE YEARS IN DELTA behind him, Jim Tolbert seemed to be almost a permanent fixture around Nha Trang. A fine soldier, he'd served on a Special Forces "A" Team, been a Ranger Advisor and had even spent some time on the headquarters staff. Tolbert was a tough guy, but he'd much rather strum his guitar and sing ballads than fight the VC. He sang his country and folk music with a strong mellow voice and a cutting sense of humor.

Tolbert's Delta experience was unique; he'd been fired from Project Delta after extending for a third straight year. With an abundance of Delta and SF experience behind him, he had little trouble landing another job, eventually with SOG. This fine soldier was also a prolific songwriter, and his lyrics were at the root of the problem between him and his new commander.

Tolbert tended to refer to the newest Delta Commander, LTC Bob Moore inauspiciously as, "…a non-Special Forces lieutenant colonel; just another conventional army officer trying to get his ticket punched." His comments about Moore were in stark contrast to the high praise he'd heaped on Project Delta Commander Chuck Allen. Tolbert said the Project had been warned about Moore long before he'd arrived, and his reputation didn't begin to do him justice. It would be the only time in Delta's history that an experienced Special Forces trained officer hadn't been in command of the elite unit; how that guy had been assigned was a complete mystery, even to the 5th Group Commander and his staff.

The consensus was that he must have been a relative of one of the generals in the theater, or had some other influence pulling for him. Tolbert had strong opinions on the subject; Moore had once been a cavalry officer who General Creighton Abrams had personally assigned, intent on undermining Special Forces. He'd made no pretense of disliking them. Some said that he was probably spying on the troops, but was too stupid to do it covertly. Tolbert, in his slow southern drawl, summed it up: "Nope…he's just an asshole."

After the war, Tolbert chronicled a summation of his firing and posted it to the Project Delta website. He wasn't ashamed of being fired—he'd paid his dues. He wore his dismissal like a Purple Heart; a badge of honor. Here is his version of what transpired:

Project Delta was on stand-down from the first Trojan Horse operation near Mail Loc. Everyone was in the Delta Club letting it all hang out, as they usually did after a particularly difficult mission. What was unusual this night was that LTC Moore was with the teams, instead of at the 5th Group Officers Club hobnobbing with the group officer staff as usual. Tolbert was seated close to the bar at a round table with "Stick" Evans. With his guitar, he was entertaining himself and anyone else who'd listen. He and Stick had just returned from the cemetery, and he was trying his best to cheer up his friend and forget that god-awful place.

Billy "Stick" Evans was one of two "hill-country boys" assigned to Delta, both named Billy and considered among the best. The other was Billy Bean. While Bean had more of an Andy Capp personality—a Pall Mall cigarette perpetually hung from the corner of his mouth—he was always planning, scheming and ready for action. Evans, on the other hand, was more like a Special Ops' version of World War One's famous Sergeant York. In a firefight, while others poured on the lead with their M-16s in a "rock and roll" mode, Stick Evans was conservative about his ammunition. One shot—one kill.

Their visit to the graveyard hadn't been pleasant. It was a nasty piece of land, more garbage dump than a cemetery. Holes were evidence of rats tunneling into the graves to get at corpses; the headstones either leaned precariously or had fallen over. A foul putrid odor hung in the air; one that even the strong South China Sea breeze couldn't dissipate. A few Vietnamese squatted, burned incense, paper molds and hand-written prayers; each grieved while praying to their ancestors. They were surprised to see two Americans; after all, the Americans had put most of them there. The mourners blankly stared, silent, no smiles—unusual for Vietnamese.

Tolbert and Evans stood in silence, the scene only added to their morbid feelings of guilt. Staring down at one small concrete marker on the fresh mound of dirt, Billy Evans spoke quietly.

"I'm still here…because of him," he said softly. "I wish I could've done more for him."

Tolbert, tongue-tied, unsure of what to say, kept his mouth shut and eyes down, shifting self-consciously.

"Jim, I just can't shake the guilt of being…on this side of the dirt. That little sonofabitch died for me. He…didn't have to…do that." Evans looked up. "Ya know?"

Billy, weak from wounds received on a recent operation, had been recuperating in Nha Trang at the old CIA safe house, House 22. He'd come by to see his old friend, to ask him to visit the cemetery with him. Tolbert hadn't really wanted to go near the damned place, but…well, Stick was his friend. Friends do strange things for each other, but he really felt uncomfortable standing there. Hoping not to say anything wrong, Tolbert remained silent, listening to Stick softly cry. After he'd had a chance to think more on it, he came to the conclusion that his discomfort probably came from his own sense of guilt. It's a common feeling, the guilt that comes with still being alive when a loved one has died.

Afterward, that evening at the club, they had a few drinks and Tolbert played some silly little songs designed to make Stick smile. He remembers Moore coming to his table, standing just long enough to hear his rendition of "Burning Barrel of Shit," played to the tune of Johnnie Cash's "Burning Ring of Fire."

The detested commander listened until the song ended, turned, then walked away without a word. Tolbert said, "I guess my "Burning

Barrel of Shit" didn't impress him—or maybe he just didn't like my singing. Hell, sometimes even I don't like my singing."

But there was more to it than just a few war ballads, as Tolbert learned the following morning. Soaking in the morning sun, he was sitting on the barracks steps, feeding scraps to a small stray dog that had wandered into the compound. Like some men of this war-scarred group, the pooch had apparently found a home with Delta. Before the little cur could snatch all of Tolbert's bacon, Diaz, the unit clerk, hollered across the street.

"Tol, the Sergeant Major wants to see you. ASAP!"

He'd no sooner walked into the orderly room when Crash Whalen said curtly, "Pack your shit and hit the road."

No fanfare, not even a "kiss-my-ass-goodbye," Tolbert remembered with a small laugh. The only reason Whalen gave was that Delta had too many radio men above what they were authorized. Tolbert was well aware they had too many radio men; too many medics and too many intelligence NCOs, too. But at the moment that didn't matter.

Whalen added, "The old man said if anyone had more than one tour in the Project, I was to get rid of him."

Crash Whalen was not a big man, a few inches short of six feet, about 150 pounds soaking wet; all man, though—all soldier. Tolbert said, "I had great respect for him. It wasn't his fault, anyway. He was just doing his job. He hadn't made the decision. We both knew who had."

Years earlier, Whalen had come to Special Forces from a conventional airborne unit. His salt and pepper hair let folks know he'd been around; he was well-liked throughout the SF community and Tolbert counted him as a friend. He could tell how difficult this was for Whalen, and how uncomfortable he felt. Tolbert didn't press the issue. He'd seen others let go; this was how it was done in a Special Forces unit. "Pack your shit and hit the road"; nothing subtle about it.

As Tolbert strode from the compound, the stray dog followed along. He finally chased the mutt back; no need for both of them to be fired. No goodbyes—just pack up and move out; he never liked goodbyes anyway. He passed the spot where he and Ed Coffey had sat, paused as he remembered An Loa and Coffey's memorial service; too few words said about such a fine soldier.

As he passed through the gate, he returned the guard's salute, pausing to observe him. Since Moore took command, the Nung guards wore freshly pressed uniforms, spit-shinned boots and painted helmets; their image more in line with garrison-based Cavalry soldiers than assault troops. Maybe this was the beginning of the end after all.

"What will that asshole do next?" he thought, shaking his head.

Shouldering his duffle bag, he marched off, thinking of how hard it was to capture what once was. He enjoyed his first two tours with Delta, and it was his love for those guys that made him sign on for a third. They were on their own now—they'd just have to get along without him. He silently wished them luck.

* * * * * *

Tolbert was the second Delta man to be fired by Moore—there would be others. Collective memories recall that before LTC Robert Moore left Project Delta, he managed to dismiss a few others; some, experienced operatives and arguably the world's finest combat recon men. Because their skills were in such great demand, men who left the projects for any reason were immediately recruited; other classified SF projects and A-teams were always short experienced personnel. Others chose to remain on Special Forces A and B Detachments, while some returned to conventional units. After Tolbert left, Moore also fired Diaz, the unit clerk. Whalen stayed on to serve until Project Delta closed in 1970. Tolbert found a new home with another Special Forces project. Many with whom he served, "Bata Boot" Bennett, Doc Simpson, Stick Evans, Crash Whalen and Sweet Peter Perkins, have all now reported to the Big First Sergeant upstairs—and someone said Stanfield's Nungs ate the dog.[42]

James Tolbert passed on 10 August 2005. Retired from active duty after twenty years of service, he continued to serve his nation as a civil servant. His songs can be found on the Project Delta website and his Delta brothers still toast him at their annual reunions; perhaps the Big First Sergeant upstairs enjoys a mellow country ballad, too.

---

[42] Jim Tolbert. "The Firing," http://projectdelta.net/firing_story.htm.

TWENTY-THREE

Leave No Man Behind

THE 81ST AIRBORNE RANGER ADVISORS WERE an important part of Delta's team. In January 1968, SSG Tom Schultz was assigned to a recon team as the FNG, and on his first operation the team discovered he had a serious problem; he talked in his sleep—loudly! This certainly was not a good thing for a Recon man inside enemy controlled territory. In every other respect he was a fine addition to Recon; so, they tried everything they could think of to overcome his problem. A gag, mouth braces—nothing worked. Obviously this shortcoming detracted from his recon fitness and Schultz, too capable to simply release, was reassigned as an advisor to one of the Ranger companies.

The Rangers had several missions: search and destroy operations; engage and destroy an enemy unit after recon teams reported it; and rescue recon teams in trouble. Due to the inherent clandestine nature of the teams, the latter happened quite frequently. The teams had plenty of guts, but relatively little firepower sufficient to overcome a larger enemy force. In late spring, Schultz's company was alerted. They would be inserted into the I Corps highlands as a reaction force to assist a troubled team operating out of Hue-Phu Bai, as part of

Operation Delta Junction. Sergeant First Class Jerry L. Nelson and SSG Alfred W. Drapeau, two Delta Recon personnel Schultz knew quite well, were on the beleaguered team.

Because of other on-going missions, the 281st AHC lacked enough Huey helicopters to transport the full contingency of Rangers. To preclude multiple lifts into a potentially hot LZ, the unit's S3 Officer requested several large Marine CH-46 troop-carrier helicopters to assist them in the insertion. The 281st AHC was assigned to Project Delta and had trained with them; these guys shared the Delta brotherhood. Bravery and dedication characterized these fine pilots as they risked their lives to retrieve teams or to insert desperately needed reaction forces.

To the contrary, the Marine pilots were strangers, with no special affiliation to the men on the ground, other than the fact that they all were Americans. It wasn't as if they would intentionally place Delta elements at risk, only that they might not go "the extra mile," as the 281st AHC frequently did. Concerned they'd be using Marine helicopters on this mission, Schultz instructed the Rangers to take all M60 machineguns and place them on the relatively few available 281st Hueys. That decision would prove to be a wise one. Nelson and Drapeau's team were pinned on the western slope of a large hill mass; the plan was to insert the Rangers on the east, to preclude them from coming under the same direct enemy fire as Nelson's team.

Apparently, the Viet Cong had anticipated this strategy. As the helicopters approached the LZ they began to receive moderate fire, which dramatically increased as they drew nearer. While all the 281st helicopters continued steadily on course, hovering and discharging their cargo of Rangers under hostile fire, the Marine's CH-46 choppers broke off, turned around and left—with all their Rangers still on board! This turn of events left Schultz less than half strength to engage a large, determined enemy force. Full darkness set in and worse, instead of sixty Rangers, Schultz had less than forty. The remainder of his men sat on Marine helicopters at the Hue-Phu Bai airstrip. Nelson's recon team reported that a VC company of about 100 men were chasing them.

The depleted Ranger force under Schultz gingerly moved up the mountainside, in total darkness, constantly in radio contact with the recon team. By midnight, they knew the two units must be getting close to one another, fearful they might have an encounter with their own men. Schultz decided he'd hold up, linking up after daylight. At first light, the recon team walked out of the jungle. Drapeau walked right up to Schultz and planted a big wet kiss on his forehead.

"Man, am I glad to see you—you sweet Mother!"

Schultz reported back to the FOB; they'd made contact with their team and were ready for pick up. Since he had only forty men left, he located a three-ship LZ and gave its coordinates. Then he heard some incredible news: he'd been informed his delayed Rangers were enroute as they spoke—on Marine choppers— heading for the same LZ as the previous day. This was not good news! It went against every principle they lived—or died by. He was incensed they'd even consider using the same LZ.

"Didn't you tell those assholes we came under some serious fire yesterday when we landed?" he said angrily.

"Yep, but that's their plan. We'll see you in thirty minutes...out."

Upon reaching the designated LZ, Schultz put out a hasty defensive perimeter as security for the in-bound choppers, and his Rangers immediately came under automatic fire from the tree line, a mere hundred yards away. Schultz called for air support; a Navy A-4 instantly responded. The Navy fighter came in close, dropping a white phosphorous (WP) bomb, right on target—or as the troops phonetically coined WP, "Willy Peter," adding humor to the following account:

Having been chased constantly for three days, the recon team, nearing exhaustion, lay inside the Ranger's defensive perimeter running around the LZ, waiting for the arrival of their promised extraction chopper. During their overnight escape, the crotch seam on Jerry Nelson's tiger fatigues had split wide-open. Since underwear tends to get wet when moving through the jungle and can ball up, often resulting in skin irritation, Jerry wasn't wearing drawers. This was not unusual; some Recon men preferred not to wear skivvies, or socks, for that matter. (A mighty peculiar breed, some have admitted to dumping sand in their jungle boots when not in the field to toughen their feet.) So, here was Jerry, lying in the grass, pretty much exposed to the world, when small flecks of the "Willy Peter" breezed by and landed squarely on his bare crotch—the quiet was instantly shattered. Yelling a string of profanities, he popped up and hopped about while beating at his smoldering groin. When that technique failed, the medic poured water over the afflicted area. Even that didn't work too well, and his dance tempo increased, fueled by sage advice shouted from on-lookers. "Pack it in mud!" "Wave it in the air!"

"Fire discipline went to hell in a hand basket," Schultz said. "Those exhausted Rangers began to roll around, laughing and pointing until their tears streamed, nearly washing off their camouflage paint. They shouted out hilarious advice to Trung Se (Sergeant) Nelson, pounded each other on the back and generally enjoyed the entire spectacle. I'll tell you what—a VC squad could've walked in, gathered up all our weapons and left without a shot being fired, and we couldn't have done a damned thing to prevent it."

* * * * * *

Like the movements of a finely-tuned Rolex, Project Delta was an intricate organization of many components: the Commander, Sergeant Major and headquarters staff, which remained at either the FOB or the Delta compound in Nha Trang to resource and support the units in the field; the talented recon teams; the death-defying Slicks and gunship helicopter crews; the brave and dedicated Air Force FACs and support personnel assigned to Delta; the fearless Battle Damage Assessment unit of Nung mercenaries, both feared and admired; Montagnard Road Runners; and the tough 81st Airborne Ranger Battalion, their main reaction force.

As tough and dedicated as any Recon man, American advisors served with the 81st Rangers, frequently rotating among the Ranger Battalion, BDA Company, Road Runner and recon teams. Prior to the Tet Offensive in January 1968, other unit commanders had hardly heard of the battle-hardened 81st Airborne Rangers, yet afterwards, they were highly sought after.

Comparable to their counterparts within the American airborne divisions, the 81st Rangers had been trained as light infantry assault outfits, with emphasis on speed, daring maneuvers, intense small arms fire and violent assaults. During the Tet Offensive the Communists occupied Hue for more than a month, stubbornly battling Marine and ARVN units, while being stalked and killed in great numbers. Concurrently, the Delta Recon teams and 81st Ranger units were being launched into the A Shau Valley and deployed along the Vietnam-

Project Delta 81st Airborne Ranger Battalion advisors, FOB Phu Bai, May 1968. *Rear, L to R*: CPT Thomas Humphus, 1LT William "Bill" Wentz, 1LT Anthony Ayers, SSG Paul Hill, MSG Virgil Murphy. *Seated L to R*: SSG David Ryder, (unknown, in front of Ryder), unknown, SSG Marvin Forbes, SFC Thomas Schultz and SFC Billy Bean. (Photo courtesy of Thomas O. Humphus)

Laotian border, not only to cut off NVA reinforcements in Hue, but to hasten the retreat of enemy forces fighting there. Delta Recon teams had picked up intelligence indicating a large food and ammunition convoy from Laos was headed to re-supply VC and NVA troops in Hue, potentially readying for a second push to secure Hue from the Americans. Delta Operations Samurai I, II and III were the Allied efforts to stop the offensive in its tracks. Delta's mission for the 81st Rangers was to ambush and destroy the re-supply convoys.

As Operation Delta Junction kicked into high gear, three companies were designated to set ambushes on suspected convoy routes. During Operation Samurai IV in March 1968, Delta teams reported locating an improved road and that they had heard trucks in the area. The

Rangers' job was to see that any supplies that might be in those vehicles didn't reach the NVA offensive in Hue. Lieutenant Binh was the 5th Airborne Ranger Company Commander, LT Nguyen Hien commanded the 1st Platoon. The senior USSF advisor was LT Tom Humphus, his assistant was Australian Warrant Officer Cedric "Shorty" Turner and the NCOIC was SSG Phil Salzwedal. Specialist 5 Little Jackson was the medic attached from the Delta Medical Section.

Slicks from the 281st AHC inserted 1st and 5th Ranger Companies at 1700 hours on an LZ near a curve in the targeted road. The 281st gunships were overhead to cover the insertion. Their luck held; no enemy on the LZ and no sign of the reported NVA. Just past the curve was an under-water bridge the enemy had built that was concealed from aerial observation. After securing the LZ, the Rangers quickly assembled and 1st Company led out away from the bridge toward their preplanned ambush positions west of the LZ. The 1st Platoon's leader, LT Hien, later said he was surprised by the unit's stealth and readiness as it proceeded toward the objective. He was excited, and from his men's faces he knew their hearts were pounding just as hard as they moved into position along the Ho Chi Minh Trail.

The 3rd Ranger Company was inserted into an LZ adjacent to the road, approximately five kilometers to the west of these two companies. Their mission was to block the road to keep NVA units from reinforcing the ambushed truck convoy and destroy any NVA that escaped the ambush.

Upon reaching their objective, 1st Company moved off the road and up a ridgeline, forming a line along the ridge. They had a relatively clear view of the road across a small ravine. The 5th Company moved off the road and formed a line about thirty meters from the road, and parallel to it. Their ambush line was slightly downhill from the road, which gave any one on the road a tactical advantage over them. The two companies had effectively formed an "L" ambush, however, which would quickly overcome any such advantage.

The USSF advisors situated themselves with the company headquarters element, about ten meters behind and centered on the ambush line. The company commander shielded himself behind a large banyan tree, with LT Humphus and WO Turner on either side, using the large roots as cover. Humphus couldn't see Salzwedal and Jackson, but knew they were to the right in a shallow depression.

About an hour before dark, the 5th Company left flank signaled enemy movement on the road from the west. The movement turned out to be an NVA squad. As they approached the center of 1st Company's line, a shot rang out to Humphus's left, and all hell broke loose as the first three NVA were hit numerous times and hammered to the ground. They died instantly, but in dying, the nearest one fell forward, squeezing off a burst from his AK-47. The errant burst tore through the rotting leaves to the right of LT Humphus, hitting Jackson in the chest and Salzwedal in the left arm.

The remainder of the NVA squad went to ground against the north bank of the road, protected from 1st Company's defilade position. Their location was such that when 1st Company attempted to fire at them, their rounds struck among 5th Company's positions, and 5th Company's rounds were striking them. The NVA could not move, but they were wisely causing the Rangers plenty of grief by firing at one company and then the other, causing the Rangers to return fire into friendly ranks. Humphus finally got the Rangers to cease fire.

He contacted the 5th Company commander with a plan. "We have them pinned down and they can't move. We should send a squad left to outflank them."

There was a slight rise in the road at that point and it would provide them perfect cover to fire upon the NVA's position. The Rangers were good troops if properly led, but many times the appointed officers did not live up to their American advisor's expectations.

"No, no. VC too many, VC too many," he kept repeating.

The more Humphus encouraged him, the more he resisted, insisting that it should be 1st Company to make the move. To complicate matters, the NVA resumed firing and 1st Company opened up again, spraying the other Ranger company's position.

Frustrated, Humphus called the 281st gunships (Wolf Pack) and asked if they could see the road. They replied that they could. He asked for the "Hog," a Huey gunship with an automatic 40mm chain gun, and they came back.

"Can you paint a center line right down the middle of the road for us?"

"Can do," the Hog pilot said.

"We're 'danger close' to the road, but below it."

"No problem," the Hog replied.

Humphus told the CO to get everyone down, then told the Hog to bring it on. "Roger. We're coming in hot."

The Hog's 40mm rounds went precisely down the middle of the dirt road to the Ranger's front, shrapnel zinging through the trees all around them. The Ranger CO's face was a mask of sheer terror. As the Hog glided off, Humphus again tried to get the VN commander to send a squad down and check out the site. Again, "Too many VC," was all he got. Humphus raised the handset and pushed the 'push-to-talk' button to call for the Hog to make another run. "Wolf Pack, Wolf Pack, this is Otter, over."

The VN CO started pleading, "No, no. We go now. We go." He'd seen enough of the Hog.

The CO ordered a squad down the road and found the rest of the NVA squad—all dead. The only Ranger casualties were minor wounds from 1st Company's fire and splinters from the Hog's 40mm.

As darkness fell, the surrounding jungle turned an inky black. Humphus and Shorty Turner discussed their worries that the earlier firefight might bring a lot more NVA down on them. But as time dragged by, all remained quiet. Humphus saw someone light a cigarette near his side of the road. He could make out a shadow leaning against a tree. Shorty told him it was their Company XO, LT Lam. Suddenly, a figure in black pajamas strode along the road toward Lam. As he got closer, Lam asked who he was. The figure in black held a flashlight under his chin to illuminate his face, and told Lam his name. Then he asked Lam who he was.

"I am Lieutenant Lam, 81st Ranger Battalion," Lam said calmly. He shot the man through the head with his .45, killing him instantly. Humphus said Lam had retained the cigarette in his mouth throughout the episode.

The .45 blast sounded much like a 105 howitzer in the still of the jungle night. Shorty said, "Aw damn. We're in deep shit now." Still, nothing happened. No attack came.

Despite the effects of the jungle chill, Humphus noticed they were napping in shifts. The sound of a vehicle cut through the silence; everyone became alert. A vehicle approached, driving with its lights out. The driver stopped a short distance away and blew his horn, moved slightly forward, paused and blew it again. When it passed

These trucks were first discovered by Delta Recon teams then ambushed near "Delta Junction" by the 81st Airborne Ranger Battalion—Project Delta's reaction force, March 1968. (Photo courtesy of Thomas O. Humphus)

Humphus's position, although too dark to identify its type, he was able to tell by its impressions that it was a three-quarter-ton U.S. Army truck. The Rangers held their fire as it proceeded to the underwater bridge, turned and came back. Obviously a scout vehicle, its horn telling the trailing convoy how far it had progressed.

It was silent until daylight, when the drone of several trucks broke the morning calm. All Humphus could do now was hope the Ranger's training kicked in. The plan called for a Light Anti-Tank Weapon (LAW) to initiate the ambush by taking out the lead vehicle, thereby blocking the road and halting the others. But as plans often do once the first round is fired, this one changed immediately. The LAW misfired.

If Humphus was concerned about the Ranger's reaction, he needn't have worried. When a young Ranger private noticed the LAW was a dud, he fired his M79 grenade launcher through the windshield of the lead truck, immobilizing it and blocking the trail. The ambush initiated, everyone began firing into the valley where the convoy had stopped. After a short but intense period, Humphus called for the 281st to come get them out—their mission was complete.

Vietnamese soldiers from the 81st Airborne Ranger Battalion assigned to Project Delta as a Quick Reaction Force. (Photo courtesy of Len Boulas)

Specialist 5 Little Jackson died sometime during the night. Wrapped in his poncho and liner, they carried him to the LZ for the ride back to FOB Phu Bai. Apparently the NVA had enough of Delta's Rangers and the Wolf Pack, particularly the Hog, allowing them to leave without resistance. The NVA would welcome them back later, to the same LZ, and this time the Rangers would pay a stiff price to get in—and an even greater one to get out.

It would not be the last Project Delta blood shed during Operation Delta Junction. Intelligence reports would later confirm Humphus's bunch destroyed an NVA convoy of eight trucks laden with supplies and ammunition and caused heavy casualties to a mobile regiment of the NVA Yellow Star Division, yet escaped with a minimal number of wounded and dead. The 81st Airborne Ranger operation was considered a huge success, but this battle would be only one of many they would fight in the upcoming weeks as part of Operation Delta Junction in the enemy stronghold of A Shau Valley.

Only one week later, they returned to support Operation Delta-36, only this time the four Airborne Ranger companies encountered an even larger NVA force on the LZ. Within minutes, five helicopters were shot down, their entire load of valiant Rangers lost. One USSF was KIA and several seriously wounded.

* * * * * *

In June 1968, when the Communists initiated grandiose plans to occupy Saigon, the ARVN Command knew they were in serious trouble and called for help from all quarters. In the midst of the ruin and rubble of that war-torn city, the 81st Rangers etched their name into Vietnam's war history. The Rangers, trained exclusively to operate in jungle and mountainous terrain, chasing and fighting an elusive insurgency, were not trained to fight pitched battles on city streets. Hardly anyone surmised they'd make a difference in the nasty urban street fighting in Saigon's Gia Dinh section. Although unaccustomed to urban warfare, the Rangers aggressively assaulted seasoned NVA soldiers who had the distinctive advantage of concealed fortifications. Staff Sergeant Tom Schultz advised one of the three Ranger companies going into Gia Dinh.

Surveying the narrow streets where he was to engage the enemy, Schultz was visibly concerned about the operation's urban combat aspect. Remembering the amphibious assault they were ordered to make at Vung Ro Bay, he knew his Rangers hadn't been trained to fight in an urban warfare situation. He expressed apprehensions to the senior Special Forces advisor, MSG Murphy.

"What the hell, Murph? We're Special Forces. We fight in the jungle. What do we know about street fighting?"

Murphy laughed. "You've watched that TV show, 'Combat,' haven't you?"

"Yeah."

"Well, shit. Don't worry about it. Just do what they do."

Yeah.

Until then, the Ranger Battalion had been armed with WWII vintage M-1 rifles, carbines and a few BARs. Outgunned by the NVA and VC's highly effective AK-47 automatic rifles, the Rangers often came across as hesitant, less aggressive on the attack than American advisors would've preferred. After their first day in Saigon, it seemed to be a surprise when two duce-and-a-half truckloads of the new M-16 automatic rifles showed up. Whether the SF advisors had "borrowed" or had been issued them, was a topic often discussed among senior military officers, but never fully resolved.

Making redistribution of the new weapons more difficult was the fact that the Rangers were heavily engaged with the enemy. Schultz and other Ranger advisors quickly devised a plan. One platoon at a time, they pulled them back off the line, issued the new weapons, showed the NCOs how to lock and load them, handed out ammo magazines and sent them back into the fray; the process repeated until all had the new weapons. The Ranger's first M-16 test fire was a wet run in a built-up area against fortified enemy positions. Schultz related that once issued the new weapons, they turned into "tigers" with an astounding aggressiveness. The enemy, contemplating their options, often sought out other Vietnamese units instead of facing the ferocious Airborne Rangers with their little black rifles. While the battle for Gia Dinh raged substantially longer, the skirmish in the 81st Ranger's section lasted only three days.

"In just three days," Schultz recalled, "our Rangers wiped out a battle-seasoned, hardcore, North Vietnamese Regiment from the Order of Battle Plan. They were that good."

During the battle for Gia Dinh, often NVA soldiers held out to surrender to the Vietnamese Marines; they claimed they would've surrendered sooner had it not been for fear of the Rangers. The speed and tenacity of the Ranger's assault completely demoralized many NVA units. After a few days, some simply waited in their bunkers for someone to surrender to. Acclaim and civilian gratitude was expressed for this unit's gallant actions and lofty accomplishments. After Gia Dinh, the unit was heralded as the "81st Special Forces Battalion."

During the battle for Gia Dinh, Project Delta medic, John Burdish, earned the Bronze Star for valor when, under heavy fire, he rescued three seriously wounded Rangers from certain death. Running through a hail of bullets, he first attempted to administer first aid, but soon discovered his position too exposed to enemy fire. He hoisted one of the men and ran through the devastating fire to safety. Burdish made two more trips through the rain of bullets to carry the wounded Rangers to safety. When all the wounded were in a covered position, he provided medical assistance until they could be evacuated to the rear, winning the admiration and respect of the entire 81st Airborne Ranger Battalion. This act, along with others during operations in 1969, would cost him his right to extend with Project Delta for another year. Turning his request down, SGM "Crash" Whelan told him, "I'm sending your ass home before you get yourself killed."

The Rangers didn't stand-down as other ARVN units did, to relax and take it easy until their next mission. With procedures similar to those of the Delta Recon teams, they trained hard, continually running realistic combat exercises in the hills surrounding their Nha Trang base camp. The Ranger Battalion advisors during the action at Gia Dinh were CPT Edward M. Young, assisted by MSG Virgil Murphy, who remained throughout Saigon's urban combat, and at the company level, SSG Tom Schultz. The 81st Rangers had won tremendous praise and deep respect for their efforts in the Saigon conflict and for their combat abilities during the Tet Offensive. It was one of the few Vietnamese units where members were awarded individual U.S. decorations for valor, including the Silver Star.

* * * * * *

While running recon support for CG III Corps, Dec 1968 to March 1969 during Operation ARES in Dong Xoai, Binh Long Province, SSG John P. Burdish and SP4 William R. Pomeroy were both awarded a Purple Heart for their wounds, while SFC Charles Hiner was awarded two. Staff Sergeant Sylvester Ray and SFC Walter Simpson both received the ACMV.

TWENTY-FOUR

Back Into the Valley

IN APRIL 1969, OPERATION CASS PARK BEGAN, followed by Cass Park II, ending July 1969. Its namesake, LTC Alan H. Park, assumed command of Delta at the beginning of 1969 and remained through August 1969. Cass Park I, in support of the 101st Airborne Division's recon effort in A Shau Valley, and Cass Park II, in Happy Valley, were extremely costly and bloody operations for Project Delta. Twenty-two awards for valor and eighteen Purple Hearts came out of these operations; twenty-one VNSF were lost, three American SF recon members were listed as MIA and one USSF soldier was killed in action. Colonel Alan Park, in recalling the loss of Recon Team 3, said the scars of that operation still linger in his memory.

Recon Team-3, comprised of SSG Charles V. Newton, SGT Charles F. Prevedel, SSG Douglas E. Dahill and three VNSF personnel, infiltrated into an area about forty kilometers southeast of A Shau on the evening of 21 April 1969. The entire area around A Shau had been saturated with enemy for months, and RT-3 made contact within hours of hitting the LZ. By daylight, they'd been in a running gunfight with a far superior enemy force for hours and suffered several casualties.

Major Steven P. Solomon, Delta Operations officer, spoke with the team, reassuring them that help was on the way. Sergeant Prevedel told him they were cornered in a deep ravine between two rugged ridgelines unable to go on, had several wounded and were surrounded. Solomon advised Prevedel of LTC Park's orders for a BDA Platoon to be sent as a reaction force, arriving within the hour. Around midday, all radio contact with the team was lost. Every time Park went to ask his communication NCO about any word from the team, the silent radio seemed to scream at him to do something. He'd done all he could. Somehow, it didn't seem enough.

Park knew all the men out there, and when he learned SSG Charles Newton was on the team in jeopardy, it hit him hard. Newton was a handsome blond youth from Texas, on his second tour with Delta. In January, he was wounded while on recon and after a short stint in the Long Binh Hospital, he was sent to the States on a thirty-day convalescent leave. He arrived in his home town with a chest full of medals, including his second Bronze Star for valor, Air Medal and Purple Heart. His dress uniform trousers tucked neatly inside glossy paratrooper jump-boots, green beret cocked jauntily to the side, he was a sharp and dashing figure. In May, he married a pretty, hometown gal—two months later, he returned to Vietnam. On 22 March 1969, Charles Newton wrote home that he'd be leaving Delta's headquarters in Nha Trang for Phu Bai in a few days, he'd be out one to three months and not to worry if he didn't write for a while. The team's last radio contact said, "We're in a stream bed, surrounded and we're hit bad!" Charlie Newton wouldn't be going back to Texas.

The BDA Platoon—Delta's ferocious Nung mercenaries—with one American advisor per squad, airlifted to within 300 meters of the besieged team, but could go no further due to the overwhelming enemy force seemingly determined to have their way with the trapped team. The Nungs lost five of their thirty-man contingent in less than fifteen minutes. Receiving Solomon's report, LTC Parks ordered two of his Airborne Ranger companies to join the Nungs and try and break through from a different direction. After successfully completing an air assault and persisting against several enemy counterattacks for hours, they combed the area, but signs of RT-3 were never found; the entire team seemed to have simply vanished into the muggy jungle air.

Reports that the three missing Americans were POWs began to surface almost immediately. For years, rumors have persisted. All three Americans and the three Vietnamese are still carried on the Army's roles as Missing in Action. On 16 December 1969, five months after Charles Newton was declared MIA, the U.S. Army promoted him to sergeant first class.

* * * * * *

Meanwhile, Park had other problems. Recon Team-2 was also under heavy attack; the team's garbled messages told him young SSG Thomas K. Long, whom Park had also known personally, had been killed, more had been wounded. The operation was in deep trouble; he had to get the rest of his boys out of that damned valley. Those who served with him said Al Park was a dedicated, caring leader, usually mild and quiet, except when his men were under fire. He was well-liked and considered a good commander. After tearing into the Nungs and Rangers for failing to get one team safely out, he was determined the same thing wouldn't happen to RT-2. This time, he'd go himself.

The remainder of SSG Long's recon team was holed up in thick, triple-canopy jungle on the side of a mountain, calling for immediate extraction as the enemy moved in for the kill. They had wounded, couldn't carry them and would not leave them. A squad of 101st Airborne helicopters and Park's C&C chopper headed out to pick them up. When LTC Park arrived in the C&C ship, two of the 101st choppers were already engaging the enemy forces, while two Slicks had extracted RT-2 by McGuire Rig. It was evident that both the recovery ships and the two gun ships were taking extremely heavy fire from a well-concealed enemy. As Park watched, one of the gunships rolled onto to its side and fell to earth. As the aviation fuel ignited, it disappeared in a huge ball of fire. A 281st AHC Slick arrived on site and began to engage the enemy with its M-60 machineguns.

The pilot of the 101st recovery ship transmitted the good news. "We've got 'em all except for the two KIAs."

"Then get the hell out of there," Park said, cringing as he thought about the handsome young trooper lying dead in the jungle below him. "Sergeant Long won't mind now," he said softly into the handset. One thing was for sure: he was determined to come back and get his dead out, whatever it took.

Returning to the FOB near Hue, Park immediately dispatched the third Ranger Company to go back in for his KIA; they sustained several wounded while recovering the body of SSG Thomas Long. During the evening, Solomon would receive an unusual situation report that baffles everyone to this day. Recon Team 6 reported observing twelve VC in black pajamas and pith helmets, walking northwest, all carrying AK-47s. In the center, a Caucasian female, attired in white shirt and dark pants, her shirt tucked in, moved freely among them. Her clothing clean, neat and freshly pressed, she wore no headgear. Her hair was shoulder-length and strawberry blond; her skin smooth and fair. She probably weighed between 140 to 145 lbs, stood 5'6" tall and, according to the team, had a large bust (the FOB staff aptly noted remarks about the team's detailed description on this one point). She appeared at ease among her companions and the surroundings, under no apparent duress. This was one of the strangest intelligence reports of the war—who was this mystery woman? No one ever knew for sure, but over the next few months she was seen several more times. The troops dubbed her "Jane," alluding to another infamous Vietnam era female.

Only three days later, Park was back over the same area, circling in his C&C ship, watching while another 101st Airborne Division helicopter attempted to recover one of his teams from the elephant grass on a densely vegetated small knoll. The recovery helicopter had been flying substantially lower than the steep hills on either side, and in this situation, the enemy sharpshooters had been firing down at it. It was clear the 101st guys were taking a lot of hits. The chopper violently lurched and broke off its run, the co-pilot's hoarse voice heard over the radio.

"He's hit! My pilot's been hit in the jaw! We're breaking off—returning to the FOB for medical treatment."

"Go," Parks affirmed, as another 101st chopper dropped toward the LZ to take his place. It hovered just briefly, and then the pilot pulled pitch and shot away, gliding off in the direction of Hue Phu Bai.

"They got 'em," his C&C pilot relayed, starting to follow. The 101st pilot suddenly cut in on his radio.

"Sorry. We thought we got them all, but we're one short. I say again, we are one short. Our headcount shows someone was left on the LZ."

One of Park's senior recon men performing as recovery NCO on another, just arriving, 281st AHC Slick, quickly broke in. "Get the team out of here. We'll go back and take a look."

"It's not an American who was left, if that means anything," the 101st pilot continued. "It's one of the little people."

"That don't mean a thing," Park heard his recovery NCO say. "He's one of *our* little people, and we're going back in to get him."

"I've never been more proud of my guys than I was that day," Park said. "I can't even remember the name of that recovery NCO, but just hearing him say that…well, it didn't matter. If you were one of ours, we didn't leave you behind."

Park directed his C&C pilot to fly low so the door gunner could place covering fire on the enemy's position. In amazement, he watched as the 281st pilot flew within a few feet of the ground, using the chopper's blade-wash to separate the tall grass to spot their lost Vietnamese recon man. The young pilot, impervious to the automatic fire peppering his helicopter, made several ground level passes, the grass parting sufficiently to expose a small crumpled form, lying motionless in the grass. Delta's recovery NCO never hesitated. Leaping out, he ran through the intense automatic fire, picked up the wounded man, and carried him back, loading him inside. Safely inside, the pilot took that bird straight up as if shot from a cannon.

At the FOB, more than twenty hits had been counted in the craft, but miraculously no one else was wounded. It was the kind of bravery that often resulted in medals for those involved, but none were ever mentioned and none asked for. While the names of the 281st AHC crew, to include the courageous recovery NCO who refused to leave a Delta brother behind, have been lost to history. It's certain they'd say they were "just doing their job."

Project Delta Commanders USSF MAJ Al Park (*right*) and VNSF MAJ Haun. Operation Cass Park, 1969. (Photo courtesy of Colonel Alan Park)

SSG Rene Cardenas (*left*) and SFC
Joe Schinkelberger, Phu Bai, 1969.
The highly respected Schinkelberger
was one of the most reliable and
savvy recon men in B-52 Project
Delta. (Photo courtesy of D.J. Taylor)

* * * * * *

During the operation's twenty-
eight days, 29 March to 25 April,
1969, Project Delta suffered five
killed, thirty-three wounded and
eleven missing, including those lost
from Recon Team-6 and Road Runner Team-1. Lieutenant Colonel
Alan Park was diagnosed with hepatitis, August 1969, and medivac'ed
to the United States to recover.

TWENTY-FIVE

Conex Boogie

WHILE SOME OPERATIONS LASTED FOR A FEW DAYS, others ran in increments of up to a month. A few sort of merged as enemy concentrations were discovered in areas previously thought to be relatively clear. This had been the case for a series of operations when Project Delta, MAJ Ben Aiken, commanding, began running recon missions supporting the 3rd Marine Division, Operation Trojan Horse in the Vuong River Valley. Delta ran their missions out of Mai Loc from 8 August 1969 to 9 November 1969. Situated in the utmost northwestern corner of South Vietnam, the FOB was set up across the airstrip from the front gate of Special Forces Operational Detachment A-101, referred to as the "Window to the North."

Since the A-team's camp had been plagued by thefts, deceptions and local insurgent attacks, it wasn't long before rockets, small arms and mortars were being directed at the Delta FOB, helicopter pads and any arriving or departing aircraft. A group of Delta volunteers, led by DJ Taylor, arrived in September to run "wet" operations, training for what Steve Carpenter called, "the real thing" in either A Shau Valley or the Khe Sanh area. On one of their initial patrols, the volunteers encountered a small group engaged in stowing arms and ammo they pilfered from the A Detachment's Mai Loc base camp. A hot confrontation ensued and Tom Crosby was shot in the neck. If not for the brilliant action by Special Forces medic Dennis McVey, who managed to clamp a severed artery and control his bleeding, Crosby would have quickly bled to death.

Al Schwarcbher, who already had served a combat tour with the 101st Airborne Division and had seen action in the Dominican Republic with the 82nd Airborne, was on the team sent in to gain recon experience. Taylor, the recon team's One Zero, was given the mission to locate a VC band that had been sending sappers into the perimeter and had previously killed two U.S. Army support personnel at Mai Loc. The second day out, they heard voices. Since Schwarcbher had combat experience, Taylor sent him forward to check it out. Upon returning, he began to remove hand grenades from his pouch.

"What do you think you're doing?" Taylor asked, cocking an eyebrow.

"There's a big bunch of VC bathing in the creek just ahead, and I'm going to fire 'em up."

Taylor laughed. "Al, you're not in the 101st Airborne anymore. Quit thinking like a conventional guy. The object is to capture at least one alive for the intelligence we may get."

All the VC died anyway, including the one Taylor hoped to take as a POW. "You guys have to curb your enthusiasm a bit," was all he said.

In the fall, I Corps' weather deteriorated so badly aircraft couldn't support Delta's mission. The low cloud cover, steady rain and high winds forced Delta's commander to stand-down for a couple weeks, back to Nha Trang. This window would give him time to straighten out some conventional unit credibility problems that persisted with their support to the recon teams. The conventional unit COs didn't want to believe, or react to, the real-time information the teams had been calling in from the field. That meant the recon teams would be left out on a limb, vulnerable to enemy reaction forces. Furthermore, the FOB couldn't be left unattended and unguarded for that long, so four young recon guys volunteered to remain behind, along with an Airborne Ranger company, to keep an eye on things. Those volunteers were SSG Jim Thornton, SGT Chester Howard, SGT Bob "Archie" Inscore and SGT Steve Carpenter.

SGT Steve Carpenter (*left*) and his brother, SGT Derick Carpenter. (Photo courtesy of Steve Carpenter)

Steve Carpenter and his brother Derick were the only set of brothers to ever serve on Project Delta. While they both ran with recon teams during 1969, Doc Simpson's rules were simple: the brothers were not permitted to run recon on the same team, be in the field at the same time or together accompany Nungs or Rangers on immediate reaction missions. So, for the most part, the Carpenter brothers' missions were routine; which meant exciting, dangerous and, at times, very frightening. Steve Carpenter recalled that neither he nor his brother had ever been involved in any epic engagements that might turn the tide of the war; they just continued to volunteer for missions, and "did their jobs."

Steve remained with his three buddies to secure the FOB until their return. This was a typical FOB compound; a few tents to house recon teams, Headquarters staff and Commo Section, the briefing tent and another tent used for the Tactical Operations Center (TOC)—all within the inner-wire perimeter. The FOB's perimeter, multiple coils of concertina wire, some "noise makers" and a few Claymore mines, had been placed around the compound at strategic locations. They'd dug a mortar pit close to the Recon tent area, near metal conex containers used to store rations and equipment. The Rangers set up defensive positions around the FOB. As "stay-behinds," their routine was simple: man the TOC 24/7, conduct a few random inspections for security each day and night and spend the rest of the time drinking beer, staying dry and playing cards. Often, the day's high point might be lifting cargo pallets to determine how many venomous snakes had sought refuge from the wet weather.

One evening as Jim Thornton manned the TOC, Howard, Inscore and Carpenter were aroused by small arms fire and radio traffic from the Ranger company. They were requesting immediate fire support. As a qualified mortar man, Carpenter grabbed his weapon and web gear, ran to the mortar pit, un-wrapped it and positioned the tube for use. Howard climbed to the top of the conex container to better observe the defenses and relay the radio's fire requests. The dilemma was that Howard's position placed him directly in line between Carpenter's mortar tube and the target. When Howard called out a range, Carpenter made sight adjustments, shouted, "Fire in the hole," and dropped a round down the tube. A mortar is an indirect-fire weapon; meaning the round is designed to travel in a high, arching trajectory toward its target, passing well overhead of friendly troops in its path. After several revolutions out of the tube, the projectile loses the locking pin on the detonator and arms itself, and upon striking something solid, it explodes. Although Howard was directly in its path, there was no reason to believe he wouldn't be safe from its flight.

The first round, a white phosphorous illumination round, exited the tube with a disturbingly loud "bloop," traveling in extreme slow motion the twenty feet to where Chester Howard perched on his conex. Stunned, he watched it head toward him like a slow-pitch softball until it hit the side, just inches below his feet. Carpenter recalled how Howard's eyes grew to the size of dinner plates as he stammered through several exclamatory expressions, replete with four letter expletives. Carpenter laughed at the surreal sight of Howard's high step dance on top of the container visible amid the strobe light flashes of the ensuing firefight.

All right, so it was a bad round. Couldn't happen again, right? Carpenter charged yet another round and dropped it—with the same result. By then, the very excited Ranger at the other end of the radio began to call for high-explosive rounds. ASAP! On the surface it appeared the WP rounds must have been exposed to moisture, or the high humidity had caused them to malfunction. So Carpenter complied with the Ranger's high explosive request, dropping yet another round down the tube. This time, the round actually hit the conex higher, closer to Howard than the first two. Of course, Howard was still doing his boogie, stringing together some of the most colorful diatribes ever heard by man. This was remarkable, because some of those recon guys could really cuss! By now, Carpenter held his sides, laughing so hard he could barely prepare another round to fire. He could hear Archie Inscore's loud, distinctive laughter from somewhere behind them; both nearly hysterical with laughter. Rubbing the tears from his eyes and trying to catch his breath, Carpenter grabbed a pinch bar and opened a brand new box of mortar rounds—and began again. This time they fired like they were supposed to. After fifteen minutes of alternating illumination and high explosive rounds around the perimeter, the brief but intensive firefight was over. Eleven rounds lay at the base of the conex where Howard stood, his legs shaking, the charges rendered useless by humidity and rain. The excitement apparently over, Inscore and Carpenter still laughed so hard they rolled in the mud. Chester Howard climbed down from his perch, watched them for a minute or two and then joined in on the muddy ground. There wasn't much to laugh about in Vietnam, so when an opportunity arose it had to be done.

They gathered at the pit again the next morning to ascertain their next move. Unexploded mortar rounds can be very unstable, so they cautiously transported the unexpended mortar rounds to the bottom of a deep gully, neatly stacking them on five pounds of C-4 composite explosives. Rigging a thirty minute delayed fuse, they retreated to the recon area to wait it out. The four cracked open beers and sat on a cot, wondering aloud about just how big a bang it would make. They weren't the only ones impressed by the magnitude of the explosion, not to mention the large mushroom cloud it produced. Within minutes a jet out of Quang Tri flew over at low altitude, asking if they'd been nuked. Thornton replied sardonically, "Nope…just a couple kids having fun."

Chester Howard, a member of that trio, is a tough Texas cowboy who loves the outdoors. He grew up riding bulls and bareback broncos at rodeo events. Upon arriving in Vietnam, he first attended Recondo School and then reported in July 1969 to SGM Whalen at Project Delta. He readily admitted to having served with many icons of the Special Operations community. He ran recon missions successfully on several teams, eventually as a One Zero, leading a team of his own. He accompanied Nungs on dangerous reaction force missions, conducted "search and destroy" operations, logged hours in a FAC aircraft and had been the "belly man" on insertion and extraction missions under fire on more than one occasion. Involved in battles with both the Viet Cong and the NVA, and pursued vigorously by them, his harrowing adventures were "pretty much the norm for a Delta Recon man."

He claims never to have done anything particularly heroic—just the job for which he'd been trained. But, he admitted, "I worked on a daily basis with men I consider to be real American heroes." Still, his service record reflects several awards for acts of bravery, to include a Bronze Star for valor.

Howard served one year with Delta, but remarked he believed the sinew that held the Project together was from the men who had stayed three to five years, many staying until the war was over. Those were veterans such as SGM Harry "Crash" Whalen, once the sole survivor of a SOG recon team. Whalen, much like "Doc" Simpson, had been a seasoned Recon man who'd done it all. They'd watched over the others, fearing no rank or position when it came to protecting their guys. They never knowingly did anything to needlessly jeopardize a fellow soldier's life. Men like those two were respected, feared and revered by NCO and officer alike.

By the time Howard arrived in 1969, many men already had reputations as living legends: Alton "Moose" Monroe, Joe Alderman, Andre "Saint" St. Laurent, James "Delta Jay" Graves and Donald "DJ" Taylor. These names are still repeated often. Those who returned year after year, their time punctuated with only a short leave back home, essentially spent their youth in-country. Their family and friends were Project Delta, and that's where they wanted to be. They had the expertise to train the new volunteers to become One Ones and One Zeros in the evolving combat recon business. They were the glue that held Delta together.

"Joe Alderman was a 'soldier's soldier.' I never met a man who didn'tlike him," Howard recalled. "He got his masters degree while still in the service—a very smart fellow."

D.J. Taylor also praised Alderman. "If you looked closely on the right side of Alderman's head, even though he wore his hair a little longer to hide it, you'd notice a large scar. The story about that scar went like this:

"Joe's recon team had made contact with a large Viet Cong unit. The team sustained casualties but wouldn't leave them, so they stayed and fought to the death, eventually being overrun. Although Joe and his teammates lay either badly wounded or dead, the Viet Cong shot them all in the head one more time to be sure, stripped them of their weapons and gear and left them for dead. After several days, a platoon from the BDA Company found them. They were all being zipped up in body bags when one of the Nungs asked, 'Why is it? All the Vietnamese are bloated, stink and the maggots eat them, but one American don't stink. I don't understand.'

"Unzipping the body bag, they checked him again and discovered Joe was still alive! This story was repeated from several reliable sources, but I never asked Joe about it; figured he didn't want to talk about it anyway."

Joe Alderman completed seven years in a combat environment, more than twenty years in U.S. Army Special Forces and was a 1996 inductee into the Ranger Hall of Fame along with other famous Rangers, such as Colonel Darby. You had to have done something pretty spectacular to be an inductee.

"The strange thing," Howard recalls, "the 'old guys,' like Alderman and Doc Simpson weren't much older than the rest of us. They'd just seen more, a lot more."

Howard remembers that being in Project Delta was hard work; trips into the hole were extremely stressful, resulting in body wear-and-tear. After several years, he realized someone in the Delta leadership chain must have had their head screwed on right when they established internal policies. The "action guys" were treated as gladiators or royalty during "stand-down." In the hole, they'd sustain themselves for days with only a daily can of fruit or meat, a little rice, and water—when they could find it. Returning, they would immediately be treated to a huge steak, baked potato, fresh salad—and of course, cold beer.

JayGraves (*center*) fires the launcher as Chester Howard (*right*) handles the belt. Although this weapon tended to jam and was more fun than practical, there is no doubt concerning the psychological effect it had on the enemy. SFC Lee Coalson (*with hat*) assists. (Photo courtesy of Maurice Brakeman)

After a month in the field, they frequently received a three-day pass for any in-country destination of their choice. Traveling sans beret and in a sterile uniform, their short CAR-15 automatic weapons and lack of insignia still gave them away. Considered "spooks" by nearly everyone (a term given to CIA and intelligence operatives), they were given a wide berth. That arrangement suited most. Even if passes weren't available, they still could look forward to stand-down, which at times could be more adventurous than combat. They worked hard, played hard and almost anything went during stand-down; some guys didn't leave the Delta Club for days, running a drinking marathon straight through until called upon again. Why leave? After all, there was plenty of great food and it was the finest club in Vietnam.

* * * * * *

Before a team infiltrated, Recon members gathered, wished them luck and saw them off. It was expected. When teams made enemy contact in some god-forsaken location, a siren went off back at the FOB, the Huey's began to warm up, and medics, Nungs and Recon men all scurried to the pads, climbing aboard. No order was given; none was necessary.

* * * * * *

Chester Howard returned to the States after his tour with Delta. Graduating from Texas A&M in 1972, he resides in Houston where he continues a career as a real estate property tax consultant.

TWENTY-SIX

The Art of War: The Nung

THE NUNG, A MINORITY GROUP OF ETHNIC CHINESE ancestry, have been a subject of debate among anthropologists for years. Who are they and where did they come from? Because China once ruled for centuries what is now known as Vietnam, it is assumed that the Nung were either left over from that era or the descendents of mercenaries, who, prior to 939 A.D., settled and promulgated in Vietnam. Samples of Chinese calligraphy, religion and agricultural practices seem to support this theory best.[43]

For centuries, the Nung, famous for their bravery and ferocity in combat, have been employed by those in power as royal bodyguards, assassins and mercenaries. Special Forces, understanding early on the importance of their capabilities, sought out these weathered warriors and engaged them for their unique skills. While three companies of Nung were used by the 5th Special Forces Group Headquarters as guards, the BDA Company was seldom used for anything other than the most dangerous situations where the Delta Commander felt he needed an

---

[43] Lebar, Hickey and Musgrave. "Ethnic Groups of Mainland Southeast Asia," 236-238.

extension of power and the extra punch that only 105 seasoned, heavily-armed mercenary soldiers "with an attitude" could deliver. Those who worked with Nungs for the term of Project Delta held them in high esteem. Some of the American NCOs who led Delta's Nungs included Art Garcia, Tom Thompson, Sammy Hernandez, Jerry Nelson and Michael Stanfield.

Arthur F. Garcia served with the Nungs longer than most, and with great distinction; typical of the type of NCO who gravitated to that job. The son of Texas migrant workers, Garcia was third in a family of ten children. He quit school at the age of nine and left home seeking adventure. At the ripe age of seventeen, in 1957, a judge in Fresno, California highly recommended that he volunteer for the Army. Since the judge hadn't advised him when he could come home, the Army finally had to put him out—thirty years later. He continued to volunteer through the years, initially with paratroopers, because he heard they paid an extra $55 per month for jump pay. After several years with the 101st and 82nd Airborne Divisions, and seeking more adventure, in 1963 he volunteered to wear the Green Beret. When SOG denied his extension in Vietnam for a third year, he heard that three of his closest friends had been killed in a classified project called Project Delta. Garcia figured that was the place for him, and immediately volunteered. It was with Delta that he finally found his home—and all the adventure he could ever hope for.

Bill Fuller was Delta's SGM when Garcia arrived; SGM Whalen took his place shortly thereafter. Garcia recalls "Crash" Whalen was in a league all his own—a tough, no nonsense SOB they all loved because he took care of his guys. Doc Simpson was the Recon Section leader, while Dave Ryder ran the 81st Airborne Ranger Battalion and Gary Nichols was boss of the Road Runners. Jerry Nelson was in charge of the BDA Company when Garcia took the job, and he inherited Tommy Johnson as his assistant. He discovered that Nelson and Johnson had done a superb job of organizing and training the BDA. Garcia had only praise for all the guys he worked with in the BDA Company, saying, "There wasn't a loser in the entire bunch."

While Garcia ran the Nungs, all the recon teams had to do was call and he'd be there, regardless of the circumstances. Chester Howard reinforced that, saying, "The BDA Nungs were always managed by true professionals. Although a number of other men led the Nungs through the years, it was while SFC Arthur Garcia was in charge that he made his mark in Delta history. When a team made enemy contact, Art and his Nungs were always first to enter the AO, link-up with the besieged team and help them break contact. And they came shooting. I considered it a great honor just to be on the ground with them, and after serving on a recon team with one other American and four Vietnamese, I felt very secure with Art and his twenty-eight, armed-to-the-teeth Chinese mercenaries."

In August 1968, Delta deployed to an FOB at Quan Loi to support the 1st Infantry Division. The "Big Red One" had lost the glorious 7th North Vietnamese Army and wanted Delta to find them. On 2 September 1968, Garcia was preparing to leave for Las Vegas on thirty days R&R. The 7th NVA Division and Recon were from his thoughts. He had already packed his "Mexican Samsonite," an old C-ration box with a set of clothing and one pair of shoes, held tightly together with green "hundred-mile-an-hour" tape and twine. "Friends and movie stars" were waiting in Vegas for him, and he just couldn't wait to get there. The afternoon he was due to depart, Crash Whalen received a call from Jerry Nelson. He was somewhere in the valley—and in a jam. Nelson had been on a POW snatch and wanted Garcia to bring him a new radio. His old one had been "dinged up" during infiltration. Whalen wasn't the kind to hesitate to ask someone to give up his R&R, to go back into the hole.

Garcia never even glanced up from his packing. "Call him back, and tell him to stick it where the sun don't shine," he said. Las Vegas was waiting; he figured there were plenty of other guys around who could take the radio to Nelson.

Whalen was adamant. "Can't do that. Nelson has to snatch a prisoner, and he specifically stated he wants you there."

Garcia sighed, stared longingly out his window for about half a minute, and then handed Whalen his sorry, taped-up, tied-together-with-string, piece of luggage. "There's some money in here. If I don't come back, use it to get the guys drunk."

Within hours he was climbing down a rope ladder into a bomb crater. Two days later, after being hoisted out by McGuire Rig, the 7th North Vietnamese Army had been found.

On 8 December 1968, Garcia was lying flat on a plywood table as one of Delta's finest medics, Dennis McVey, meticulously dug pieces of shrapnel from his belly. A radio transmission had come in and the camp siren blasted its alert. A VN recon leader was missing and the team was in serious trouble. Another American ran past, pulling on his web gear and shouting that the Nungs were on the move. The BDA was getting ready to move out—but they weren't leaving without him. Garcia rolled off the table and ran to get his gear as McVey yelled after him, "Art, I didn't finish stitching that. Be careful or your guts are going to fall out!"

After they returned, having successfully rescued the beleaguered team, Rick Conway, who'd been a "straphanger" on the mission, told Garcia, "Art, I'm never going out with you again. You're crazy!"

Garcia thought he might be kidding. He headed out to see McVey and finish getting stitched up from his last trip.

Whalen disapproved Garcia's final extension with Delta. Instead of returning to the States, however, he went on to advise the Vietnamese 30th Ranger Battalion, and later ran SOG recon missions until the end of the war. He asked Whalen years afterward why his extension had been disapproved. Whalen simply said, "Why, you crazy SOB, I was just trying to keep you alive!"

* * * * * *

Sergeant First Class Garcia was awarded five Bronze Stars and the Army Commendation Medal for valor; many of the medals were received while serving as Senior NCO of Delta's BDA Company. Numerous Letters of Commendation are in his file attesting to his courage, professionalism and exemplary leadership. He went on to serve as Command Sergeant Major for 1st Special Forces Group, Airborne, Fort Lewis, Washington, from 1983 until he retired in 1986.

TWENTY-SEVEN

"Honest, Sir...I Saw Trucks!"

OF ALL THE UNEMPLOYED COMEDIANS SERVING in the Army, Roy "Squirrel" Sprouse had to be the funniest man of the lot. He'd do anything for a laugh. Born and raised in Chattanooga, Tennessee, his two half-brothers and a sister tried to keep tabs on him while he was growing up—a full-time job at best. Slight of build, with reddish hair and a toothy overbite, he was often mistaken for less than the brave and capable soldier he was. He met the world head-on with determination, skill, integrity and a self-depreciating humor that became his trademark.

To hear Sprouse tell it, his physical appearance had been the result of being born third in a set of triplets (not true) and being forced to nurse his daddy (this is probably not true either.) At the age of sixteen, he sought travel and adventure, and coerced his aunt into forging his mother's name so he could enlist in the Army. His career spanned twenty-two years; with stints in both airborne divisions and in nearly all of the U.S. Army's Special Forces Groups. He served in Project Delta from 1969-1970, on his third tour to Vietnam. As an Army instructor, his file shows that one post commander referred to him as, "The best instructor in the U.S. Army." In 1962, he married Ginny Keesee, the love of his life, and they had two children.

Sprouse, an excellent marksman and recon man, earned a reputation as a skilled scrounger. He was known to impersonate senior officers and requisition pallets of beer, soda and steaks from rear area units. He once arrived in Mai Loc riding atop a load of PSP—steel runway planks—suspended below a flying crane, with the rationale, "We need at least one chopper pad with a little less dust." Just convincing someone to give him all that PSP was remarkable, but at a time when there were only three of those awkward flying contraptions in the entire country, how he was ever able to commandeer one to deliver the PSP, was nothing less than a marvel.

One day, he marched into the Delta Club without a shirt, waving a piece of paper that proudly announced he'd just won the "Ugliest Man in the Army Contest." During the ensuing round of congratulatory drinks, he confided to the rest of the guys that soon they'd see a big "change" in his appearance. That was because he'd just completed the Charles Atlas Body Building Course and had sent off a letter to Atlas, stating that having completed the course, it was now time for Atlas to send him some muscles.

Once on a roll, Sprouse was difficult to contain. He caused many a sore rib from taking spontaneous jabs at himself. Later that same evening in the club, he climbed onto Al Schwarcbher's lap and they adlibbed a ventrilloquist routine (with Al playing Edger Bergan to Roy's Charlie McCarthy) that brought the house down. He was all business in the field, but on stand-down, he was a one-man USO show.

Al Schwarcbher remembers, "Roy had a face only a mother could love. He could make you laugh or cry, no matter what the circumstances. Many said he could've possibly been the ugliest Special Forces guy they'd ever met. Hell, Roy even said that!"

Regarding the night he and Sprouse did the ventrilloquist act, Al said this: "Everyone was slightly inebriated and the band was taking a break anyway, so Roy and I decided—what the hell—we'd liven things up a bit.

"On stage at the club, I acted the role of Edgar Bergen, and Roy would sit on my lap and be either Charlie [McCarthy] or Mortimer [Snerd]. I'd place my hand behind Roy's shirt and we'd imitate the act, with me asking him a question, and while Roy moved his mouth and head to answer, I'd move my lips slightly to appear as if it was a poor job of throwing my voice. The guys loved it so much that we had many repeat performances. My one regret is we never taped at least one of those segments. I'm sure it'd still look pretty funny. God bless Roy Sprouse."

Virtually every time Sprouse left on a mission, someone would say, "Roy, if you don't come back, can I have your Rolex wristwatch?"

As though calculating, he'd grin shyly back. "Sure. That's why I'm wearing it. So you'll have to come get me."

During Sprouse's tour with Project Delta, he became involved in one of the greatest controversies ever to befall the organization. He and Burl Cunningham were running recon for the Marines near Laos along the DMZ, in an area the Delta teams had dubbed as the "rock pile." Cunningham and their three Vietnamese stood watch as Sprouse told the Tactical Operations Center (TOC) that they had just observed 125 NVA trucks crossing the international border, headed south. The Marines obviously didn't believe him, asking question after question. In Recon, staying on the radio too long can be very detrimental to one's existence. Frustrated, the team remained overnight; early the following morning, they heard rumbling engines again in the distance. Crawling forward for a better view, they sighted the trucks again, only a couple hundred meters away. Sprouse returned to the radio and called it in once more, while Cunningham continued to observe the trucks from a few feet away. Sprouse spoke into his boonie hat, whispering so faintly his words could barely be heard.

"You know those trucks I reported going south yesterday?" he whispered. "Yeah, well they're headed back north, right now," he told the Marine officer on the other end.

Once again, he was greeted with skepticism on the part of the staff officer, but perhaps just a bit less so. "The Commander said you are to ambush them immediately," he told Sprouse.

Sprouse thought he might be joking. "You mean with my entire six-man patrol?" His appeared sarcasm lost on the Marine.

"That is affirmative."

Sprouse quickly did the math. He had a lightly armed, six-man recon patrol, stuck in the middle of territory completely controlled by the enemy, with no help within fifty miles. The weather had been so wretched they would be lucky to get a helicopter in to pick them up, let alone any gunship support. One hundred twenty-five enemy trucks equaled 125 drivers—all NVA soldiers; add 125 assistant drivers, and the sum would be 250 NVA soldiers—with guns.

Cunningham crawled up, whispering, "What did they say?"

Sprouse never blinked an eye. "They said to pull back to the LZ and wait for extraction."

After their extraction he explained to Cunningham what had really transpired. They were then told to report to the Marine Regimental Headquarters tent for a debriefing. They headed off with some trepidation; Cunningham suspected the Marines hadn't believed them and that they'd catch hell from the staff. On the other hand, Sprouse never seemed ruffled or worried, so Cunningham figured he'd let him do the talking. After all, Roy was good at talking. They were correct about the staff being miffed and skeptical about the 125 trucks the recon team had reported and never bothered to ambush.

After a long grilling by the Marine colonel, Sprouse retrieved his glasses from the briefing table, slipped them on and slowly looked up. "Honest, I'm not lying, Sir...I saw trucks!"

He had painted tiny trucks across the lens of his eyeglasses. It completely broke the staff up. For several days Roy Sprouse could be seen wearing his decorated glasses, saying "I'm not nuts...really. They just all think I'm nuts, because I keep seeing these trucks all over the place."

Martha Raye, affectionately known to her Special Forces "boys" as "Maggie," made many visits overseas to spend time with them. Besides being a qualified nurse, she was also a goodwill ambassador who always lifted spirits and raised morale. So much so, that she was given the honorary rank of lieutenant colonel and awarded the Green Beret. She and Roy Sprouse were close friends. Why not? Both were comedians.

Roy Sprouse retired from the Army in 1979, soon became restless and linked up with a civilian operation in the Rhodesia conflict. Disillusioned about the lack of air support, he returned to North Carolina and established himself as a concrete mason with home remodeling. He was disabled by a stroke in 1989 and lost some short-term memory and eyesight. Roy passed away from cancer in 2005. On the inside, Roy Sprouse was a handsome man. God bless Roy Sprouse.

Roy Sprouse and comedienne Martha "Maggie" Rae, ca. 1970. (Photo courtesy of the
family of Roy Sprouse)

* * * * * *

Delta's resources had been particularly stretched during late 1969
and early 1970, heavy enemy contact becoming almost a daily occurrence.
Captain Mayo Hadden was the S3, 1LT Gus Fabian, the Assistant S-3
(Air). Fabian recalls placing daily air strikes on reported targets, and at
times, flying as the "back-seater" in a FAC, 0-1 aircraft from the 220th
Reconnaissance Airplane Company (RAC) out of Phu Bai. The 220th
RAC were called "Cat-killers." In addition to their regular FAC pilots,
the 220th RAC provided direct support to Delta operations while at
Mai Loc.

According to Fabian, the Cat-killer pilots operated primarily north
in I Corps, and were exceptional sources of information since they
knew the area "like the back of their hand." One Cat-killer pilot, whom
Fabian holds in high esteem, was a young, experienced captain named
Jones. Fabian recalled he was flying back seat for Jones who was due to
rotate to the States after eighteen months in Vietnam. Their mission
was to fly over the extreme north-westerly section of South Vietnam,

north of the Khe Sanh plain, and into the Cam Lo Valley, to detect signs of any activity coming through the DMZ into South Vietnam.

During a low pass, CPT Jones remarked that several trees and bushes seemed out of place—a smaller tree was growing under a larger one. That was very unusual and, besides, he hadn't noticed it on a previous pass. After a failed attempt to adjust 175mm cannon fire from an USMC artillery battery located near the "rock pile" (it had been at maximum range and the dispersion pattern had been too great to be accurate), he decided to make a pass. Jones came in low, firing a WP rocket that landed near the target; he was surprised when the tree and several small bushes bolted for a ravine. Jones circled and followed the well-camouflaged NVA soldiers, then began receiving ground fire from a nearby area. Feeling his plane take hits, CPT Jones took evasive action.

Upon landing at Mai Loc, an inspection of the aircraft revealed the brake lines had been ruptured by one of the rounds; they were very lucky to have escaped unharmed.

TWENTY-EIGHT

Welcome Home, Brother

"The world has no room for cowards. We must all be ready somehow to toil, to suffer, to die. And yours is not the less noble because no drum beats before you when you go out into your daily battlefields, and no crowds shout about your coming when you return from your-daily victory or defeat."

- Robert Louis Stevenson

CONVENTIONAL OFFICERS FOUND THE MOST PERPLEXING ways to misuse Special Ops units. After the Tet Offensive, someone at the top command echelons decided Delta's recon teams should be engaged as an assault force to help clear out VC units that had taken control of the Saigon Racetrack; using it as a base to launch attacks into downtown Saigon. Major Chuck Allen had remarked more than once, "Delta is different; it's organized and trained unlike any other Army unit. Sometimes decisions about deployment are made by those who can't think past the end of their SOPs."

Delta ran into problems like this throughout the war, but the fiasco at the racetrack was one of the worst, resulting in the decimation of nearly thirty Recon personnel.

Five seasoned recon teams were immediately wasted in urban house-to-house fighting, including four Americans. Later on, others would agree that using valuable recon units for street fighting was egregious, a criminal waste of valuable talent. This situation occurred just before Allen was due to rotate; he read the Operations Reports late at night, and it brought tears to his eyes. "They lost all these guys in the first two or three days," he said. "It was a damned shame."[44]

* * * * *

Operation Delta Dagger, 10 May 1970 through 30 June 1970, began with B-52 in support of the 101st Airborne Division, Quang Tri Province. It would be Project Delta's last combat operation before deactivation. Delta's Commander, MAJ Shane N. Soldato, had recently assumed command from the highly unpopular MACV appointed officer, LTC Robert Moore. Little documentation remains about MAJ Soldato, but Jim Tolbert once met him in Nha Trang at the 5th SFGA mess hall shortly after Moore had let him go. The 5th SFGA Deputy Commander, LTC Merrick, concluded Tolbert had enough close combat for one tour, and impressed with his musical abilities, asked him to pull together some entertainment for the outlying Special Forces camps. Tolbert jumped at the chance! The entertainment was so well received that it'd been twice reported in the *Green Beret Magazine*.

Tolbert waited in the mess hall to interview a leg clerk as his new bass player when he noticed a young airborne major filling his cup at the coffee urn. It struck him that he hadn't seen that much starch in a set of fatigues since the 82nd Airborne Division at Fort Bragg, NC.[45]

In an environment of crinkled tiger stripes and sterile fatigues, the young major really stood out. His stiff uniform was pinned with qualification badges; Pathfinder and Jungle Warfare patches, a Ranger tab and Airborne tab jump wings. The major sat with Tolbert, introducing

---

[44] Jim Morris. "Interview with the Big 'Un," Part 3.

[45] Jim Tolbert. "Shane Soldato," http://projectdelta.net/soldato_story.htm.

himself as the new Project Delta Commander. Likeable and sharp, Soldato could have been a recruitment poster model. Tolbert sipped at his coffee, wondering just how this spit-and-polish young officer would fit in with the no-pretense B-52 crowd. His mannerisms left him with nostalgia for his time in the 82nd Airborne Division.

"You're from Delta?" he asked Jim, taking his seat at the table.

""Not any more," Tolbert answered. "I'm with HHC now, but I did spend some time with Delta. I got there when Allen was the commander and left after we got that puke from MACV." Jim Tolbert had never been one to mask his feelings.

"I'm taking over from him," Saldato said. "What can you tell me about the unit?"

For the next hour he unloaded a "heap of baggage" about LTC Moore, relating how that "...non-Special Forces asshole, appointed by MACV buddies to get his ticket punched, had screwed Delta so badly that he'd decimated its most experienced personnel."

He informed the new major he was just about to meet the finest bunch of combat soldiers he'd ever have the pleasure of working with. Soldato listened intently, thanked him and left. Tolbert never again saw him; Soldato would never finish his first Vietnam tour. During the young major's first month into his new assignment, his C&C ship came under heavy fire and went down in the rugged terrain of Quang Tri Province. Major Shane N. Soldato and the entire 281st AHC crew perished in the crash. Up to then, Soldato had stubbornly insisted that "Moose" Monroe, his Recon Operations NCO, go with him on every C&C flight he boarded. He wouldn't take off unless Monroe went along. Strangely, he went alone that fateful day.

Major George F. Aiken, "Gentle Ben," assumed command upon Soldato's death. It was his second tour as the Project's commander, and he would be the last Delta commander to conduct combat operations in Vietnam. Within two months, B-52 Project Delta would be deactivated.

* * * * * *

In July 1970, Project Delta finally ceased operations and the Delta men seemed to just melt away. There were few goodbyes or exchanges of reassignment information. No tears, little emotion. The last evening of the Delta Club's existence was a "members only" event, used for

Delta's going away party on the Voigt patio. Project
Delta CO, MAJ Ben "Gentle Ben" Aikens (*right, holding knife*), doing the honors. For three days, at least,
Moose Monroe (*left*) only wore shower shoes and a
towel with a snap fastener at the waist. Andre St. Laurent (center), in his blue "drinking" shirt, looks on.
(Photo courtesy of Maurice Brakeman)

sorting and packing up the plaques and awards covering the walls,
solemnly handed off to those designated for preserving them. Some
old timers occupied their favorite bar stools or stood off to themselves,
their eyes lingering sightlessly on the silent walls, reliving poignant
memories that hung heavy in the stale air. Badolati, Bott, Terry, Stark,
Pusser and all the others, they were with them again—fellow warriors
who would remain forever young in the memories of their comrades.
Glancing up from a drink, the remaining hangers-on discovered the
group dwindling as a few more silently drifted off, their numbers down
to three—then two. As if by some unspoken agreement, the last ones
ambled out. Delta Club closed for the last time.

Stalling, uncomfortable about simply walking away from a place that was ingrained into their very existence, they stretched their backs while remarking with disdain what a shit-hole it had been; then grimacing at the twilight sun, each took a final reluctant pull from their cigarettes to hide the conflicting emotions. Like holes in their psychies, their feelings were mixed and unsettled. Sadness for those absent, joy for being alive, guilt for being alive—a sense they were deserting the restless spirits of those no longer with them, those who might still linger inside the silent walls of Delta Club.

Sometimes forgetting can be harder than remembering. Sometimes leaving can be harder than staying. Sometimes living, harder than dying. But the courage that sustained them through combat did not desert them in these final moments. With some hesitation they shouldered their battered parachute bags and reluctantly trekked toward the Delta compound front gate.

Many had arrived as fuzzy-cheeked, bright-eyed young men. In leaving, although chronologically still young, their eyes looked as though they'd lived much longer. They had met the angry man, and had lived. These were the eyes of old men; they'd drained every ounce of heartbreak, knowledge and simple enjoyment from precious, sometimes precarious life. These young-old eyes had witnessed more harsh reality than others see in a lifetime—and far too much death.

Almost to a man, they believe they survived Vietnam due to their camaraderie with others in Delta. This was a lonely, dangerous line of work, with few they could depend upon, except those who experienced it with them. The hardships, danger and gamut of emotions had only served to bring them closer.

They learned about loyalty, honor, dedication, fear, hatred and love. Through the years, they've remained close. The attitudes and abilities of these brave men, in an atmosphere of unrelenting war, had set them apart. Not once did selfishness, fear or personal concern interfere with a decision to put their life on the line to assist a teammate in trouble. That unselfishness often cost limbs and the lives of good and valuable men. Those men had families and loved ones, friends and futures. They gave it all for their brothers, and would do so again.

Final review for the 5th Special Forces Group (Airborne) at their headquarters in Nha Trang, Vietnam. 1970. (Photo courtesy of Norman Doney)

It was with a strong sense of pride and commitment that most joined this elite group—but it was for the brotherhood they remained. Superbly trained, there was never any doubt they were in good hands, no matter who was selected to go with them on a mission. That training began the day they arrived at Delta's base in Nha Trang, and continued until their final day with the organization. Once trained, they trained others; undoubtedly the best-prepared soldiers in the world.

Returning home to learn their unique sacrifices had gone unnoticed or appreciated—disdained or loathed by fellow countrymen and women—their strong bond toward each other has never wavered. Instead, it's only grown stronger. Feeling unwelcome, unlike the returning veterans of the other wars America had fought, to this day they often greet each other with the familiar, "Welcome home, brother." It's the only welcome home they've ever received.

Not enough can be said of the men who served in Detachment B-52 Project Delta. Not one considered himself a hero, yet all were. Together, they formed a unique team of heroic and unselfish individuals, dedicated to accomplishing what they believed in, and did it better than anyone else—before or since. Each a triple volunteer who could have left at any time, they were proud men who wanted to be part of this remarkable group, Project Delta. Highly motivated, their skills were honed as few others in the art of warfare have ever been. Not only individual experts when in the field, but together, a superb functional team—the premier unit of its type in the United States Army—and possibly, the world. These men are brothers in the truest sense of the word. As such, they will never stand alone. Under threat of death, they stood together to the last man, and would do it again. No heroes. No rewards.

* * * * * *

Project Delta's mission was declassified in 1996. In 2001, Delta veterans began to gather annually in Las Vegas, Nevada, as part of the Special Operations Association reunion (SOAR).

"The willingness with which our young people are likely to serve in any war, no matter how justified, shall be directly proportioned to how they perceive the veterans of earlier wars were treated and appreciated by their nation."

- George Washington

Afterword

I RETURNED TO VIETNAM IN THE WINTER OF 2005, essentially to research material for this book, but perhaps also to search for the reason behind the price paid for it all. I primarily visited Hue, Marble Mountain at Da Nang and Saigon (I still refuse to call it Ho Chi Minh City). My pilgrimage took me near the Laotian border, to the old Special Forces camps at Khe Sanh and Lang Vey, which was a far more difficult journey than I presumed it would be, and ultimately led me to cancel trips to the Cu Chi Tunnels, Ba To and the A Shau Valley where I'd lost some good friends and fine people. I wisely decided that further exploration of experiences that dwelled too deeply into my psychic and emotional memory bank should be put off until some future date.

I visited the destroyed enemy tank remains in the middle of Camp Khe Sanh, and saw the various U.S. aircraft that had been downed around the camp during the Communist siege in 1968 and 1969. At the entrance to the old camp, government sponsored vendors hawk books that have rewritten history of the battle for Khe Sanh, portraying their glorious victory over the vilified Special Forces and Marine personnel defending in and around the famous site. For all their propaganda, not one word was written about the more than 100,000 Viet Cong and NVA casualties they suffered against the much smaller American forces gallantly defending it. Some glorious victory, huh?

Various combat paraphernalia left over from one of the largest battles of the Vietnam War are proudly displayed, along with carefully staged scenes showing the "conquerors" at their best. On display are selective photos of the "cowardly Americans" who, with their mere force of 6,000 troops, held off five crack divisions of North Vietnam's best for 170 days in the most savage fighting of the war. Nothing indicated how this small force decimated three of their fine divisions in the process—my words, not theirs. History, it seems, is still written by the victors—nothing new there. If we wanted to change the way their history portrays the American soldier's efforts during that conflict, our politicians should have tried harder to win. Lord knows our troops did everything expected of them.

In December 2002, retired and ailing, General Bui Tin, the North Vietnamese Army colonel who had taken the South Vietnamese's unconditional surrender in Saigon on 30 April 1975, held a short press conference in Paris, France. He said that the 1968 Tet Offensive by the North had been a disastrous mistake, an event during which the Viet Cong and the NVA were nearly wiped out as an effective fighting force. According to Bui Tin, the North's defeat had been so complete during Tet that Hanoi's government had considered pulling completely out of the South. He mentioned it had only been because of the famous photograph of Jane Fonda visiting Hanoi and condemning the American soldiers, and Nixon, declaring he would immediately begin to pull U.S. troops out the following month, that had made them hang on a little longer—thereby outlasting the Americans and winning the war.

All water under the bridge.

I have the pleasure of knowing a few fine families in Vietnam, and for the most part, they made the recent trip very enjoyable for me and my wife. Progress is evident everywhere. New buildings are going up, especially in Saigon, built mostly by the People's Republic of China and large Japanese or foreign companies. As with other global Communist endeavors, after the politicos got tired of the starving masses, their government seems to have discovered capitalism. While few American companies have taken up residency at this date, it's clear the government is rapidly moving further from traditional Communism and closer toward our capitalistic way of life. There is a hunger for American goods and foreign participation in every aspect of their fledging markets. It isn't hard to imagine Vietnam in a few short years as another Korea, Hong Kong or Japan—perhaps in the long run, we won after all.

Almost everyone in the country has a motorbike—they all seemed to be traveling on my street, and all at the same time. A smattering of modern shopping malls are wedged between tiny businesses where owners sell their wares, live and socialize on the sidewalks. Many of the new stores rival a Macy's or a Saks, complete with five-star hotels in close proximity. Although many Westerners can be seen shopping there, amazingly, the majority are Vietnamese, an indication of just how well the economy is doing—at least, for some. The local folks point with great pride to the French-constructed Notre Dame Cathedral, restored to all its glory—the only positive remark I heard about the French during my entire visit. While most didn't actually say they don't like the French, every time the subject came up, their faces grimaced as though they'd swallowed a nasty bug. I also discovered that young people can actually go to college to get a degree in tourism. Times are changing.

The red flag with its immense yellow star hangs profusely, as though it is required decor, and billboard masses depict the ultimate symbol of Communism: the obligatory hammer and sickle. Statues and portraits of their lovable Uncle Ho assault the senses at every round-a-bout and corner sidewalk and even with new construction, the People's Communist Committee buildings are among the best and most modern.

Although change is everywhere, it's said, "Some things never change." So despite all the progress, what I remember most hasn't changed much from those days when a man's life wasn't worth much—except maybe to his buddies. The poor, deformed and hopeless are still there, begging on the streets. Hungry old women sell lottery tickets eighteen hours a day for pennies, while children hawk postcards or gum to Westerners, who hurry past in an effort to escape their pitiful plight. Despite the Communist government's admonishment to not reward such deplorable activities, I would nonetheless, albeit guilt-laden, slip them a few VN Dong when the opportunity arose. Still, I never did so without wondering if the amputee scooting along on the ground had lost his limbs in the service of the South Vietnamese Government, or as a Viet Cong soldier. In the end, I guess it really doesn't matter all that much.

It was plain to see that the South Vietnamese people still love Americans. Everywhere I traveled in-country I was greeted with warm smiles and genuine hospitality. Yes, the bright smiles are still there, despite what they've endured, yet I also found a deep appreciation (from mostly the older folks) for what it cost the American soldier. They wanted to shake my hand, ask if I had been there during the war, and discovering that I had, their old eyes would suddenly grow moist. They seemed more reluctant to release my hand. While the friendliness and affection of the Vietnamese people will stay with me forever, I still harbor a myriad of mixed and confused feelings.

I only hope the good memories will be enough to overcome the raw emotion I felt when I came across the battered military ID card that'd been taken off the body of some GI during the battle for Khe Sanh; it was on display in a museum glass case for the whole world to see. I couldn't bring myself to look at the name for fear it might be someone I knew. If ever before I'd questioned what an American life had been worth to the Vietnamese people, the gut-wrenching answer came to me in the stack of GI dog tags for sale on a Saigon street vendor table—$5.00 each.

Reflections of a Delta Recon Man[46]

"I will always remember . . .

"...when we ran out of water, and nearly died from thirst, because none could be found in the area. Then a FAC flew over and dropped a six-pack of Cokes to us. All but two busted, but that kept us going until we found water outside the AO.

"...long hours and long days on dangerous missions inside the enemy's actual defenses, unable to speak for fear of being heard—always alert. Restless, our eyes darted constantly; our sweaty hands gripped plastic rifle butts. We were always at the ready, senses highly tuned, stressed to the limit until extraction time finally rolled around—then the letdown, the drinking, the silent closeness of men who'd learned to communicate without words, far better than most who use language.

"...times when the only water available was a shallow, unappetizing pool of green slime that every animal in the area used as a watering hole

329

---

[46] Gary Nichols provided the basics for "I Will Always Remember." Other Project Delta veterans modified it by adding a few personal remembrances.

and a shithouse. Choking back reluctance, we'd scraped the slime aside to fill a canteen, because it might be the last water you'd see for days. Knowing that iodine tablets were useless in this case, clenching our teeth to strain the lumps and grass out, closing our eyes—drinking.

"...taking a new man out for the first time and have him shake you all night, telling you that he's hearing sounds all around your position. Did you do that too, on your first trip into Indian country?

"...inserting at last light, doing everything right, but then hearing strange noises all around on the ground and in the trees; discovering you'd slept with a community of monkeys that hoped to join your patrol.

"...the times when no matter how hard you tried, last light of the day caught you in a place where you didn't want to be, so you slept straddling a tree-trunk to keep from rolling down a steep mountainside or into a raging river below.

"...the nights when heavy rain started right at dusk and everything you owned got soaked. Then sitting on your rucksack all night to stay out of the pooling water, while watching leeches sense warm blood, moving in on the body heat. Leech repellent was never an option; it'd leave a water-slick in the rain, or when crossing the next stream, the enemy might see it. So it wasn't used much—except maybe to dash under your arms and between your legs; it blocked the pores and helped keep you a little warmer on cold, rain-driven nights.

"...how it was when a storm hit in the middle of the night, the rain poured down your collar by the bucket-full, bolts of lightening continuously striking the ground all around like mortar fire, lifting us at least a foot off the ground, terrifying in its unrelenting power.

"...the clear cloudless nights when the ground shook and an unrealistic rumble echoed through the valley. Had someone forgotten to mention a B-52 bomb strike in your area? Would the close-in bombs fall short and take out your entire patrol?

"...the countless hours waiting for the weather to clear sufficiently for insertion. Sitting in the recon tent playing pinochle, poker or Monopoly, eating dehydrated shrimp scrounged from the Marine supply tent.

"...the parachute water jumps into Cam Ranh Bay or the South China Sea with Colonel "Splash" Kelly.

"…raising ducks to supplement the Nung's dehydrated food supply.

"…fishing in the South China Sea with C-4 and hand grenades.

"…the gigantic T-bone steaks and cold beer at the end of each mission.

"…the friendships.

"…taking an old jeep downtown and leaving it in place of the new one, having picked it up from some unsuspecting Marine. And then being chased by the MPs who never knew it was only a game, while the little Filipinos quickly painted a new B-52 Delta bumper number on it. That was fine until the 5th Group Commander decided to conduct an inventory of Delta's assets—then there was hell to pay. Still nobody got into trouble.

"…hunting water buffalo, elephant and deer. Then we'd dry the meat to make a form of jerky to brighten up the combat rations a little.

"…infiltrating on a dirt airstrip or grassy LZ with bullets tearing through the floor and the thin skin of your aircraft.

"…exfiltrating from a dirt airstrip or grassy LZ with bullets tearing through the floor and the thin skin of your aircraft.

"…the trips into the Valley of Death—the An Loa, the A Shau, Khe Sanh, Tra Bong, or a hundred other places with such names. Always announced by rocket fire and automatic weapons fire that'd cut choppers and their defenseless passengers in half.

"…the sadness of learning that a fellow soldier had been killed, was missing in action or simply shot all to hell.

"…the elation at the end of a mission, that you were still alive after a ferocious firefight and after days of running from a determined enemy. The guilt of still being alive after losing one or more of your Delta Recon team.

"…moving through the jungle during a vicious rain storm because the noise covered the sound of movement; and because no one else was crazy enough to do it—not even the enemy.

"…and, oh so many more.

Delta Recon

By Gary Nichols

I make my way, it's just twilight,
with movements slow, not to excite.
For life that dwells up in the trees,
might give away where I might be.
Each step deliberate, as if in pain,
a day of travel, so short the gain.
I take of food but once a day,
enough so strength won't slip away;

A cough, a sneeze, soft voices slurred,
this place, that noise, I shouldn't have heard.
My movement stops as muscles freeze,
I slowly hunker to my knees.
My eyes are strained, my senses keen,
listening for what can't be seen.

The hunt is on, I slowly rise,
for who sees first, the other dies.
Adrenaline rush, the taste of fear,
with life at stake, I check to rear.
A startled face, I squeeze a burst,
my ace of trump, I saw him first.

And in this place that few men know,
the smell of death on soft winds blow.
This time good luck, no need to run,
until next time my work is done.

The Wall

By D.J. Taylor

WHEN A VIETNAM VETERAN VISITS THE Vietnam War Memorial in Washington D.C., he is in for an emotional experience that he may not immediately understand. Many veterans, no matter how often they visit, are overcome with feelings of loss, hopelessness or grief that they may not have ever felt before. Some believe that this is a result of the symbolism purposely built into this memorial, and before his first visit, a Vietnam Veteran should be aware of this.

The Vietnam War Memorial was built like no other in the history of warfare. Normally, a grateful nation builds War Memorials to honor the participants, both living and dead, who participated in the conflict. These monuments have usually been designed to promote an uplifting feeling of fulfillment and accomplishment in those veterans who come to visit, but a Vietnam Veteran will find none of this at the Vietnam Memorial. Instead, he will discover that someone has simply taken his dead comrades' names, written them on a black rock and laid this rock at the bottom of a hole in the ground.

Unlike the Marine Corps War Memorial in Arlington, VA that uses as a theme a single uplifting incident of glory that all veterans can feel a part of and share in, the Vietnam War Memorial focuses on the dead and nothing else. At the Marine Corps War Memorial, one will see visiting veterans, old and young, with pride on their faces, their families in tow, and all remembering the dead as the dead would want to be remembered. When the families of the dead visit this beautiful memorial built on a hill overlooking the Nation's Capitol, they cannot help but feel proud of their fallen loved ones and of the country for which they died.

At the Vietnam War Memorial, one will see a completely different mood controlling the veterans and their families. They move slowly, speak in hushed tones and visible grief is in their faces. Unshaven and unkempt veterans loiter about. Some are clothed in parts and pieces of ragged, old, camouflaged uniforms and seem trapped in a time warp that keeps them eternally reliving unholy places and times that they should have long ago put behind themselves.

This memorial was purposefully designed and built to impart these feelings of naked grief and shame on its visitors, and it was to call attention to what the designer and promoters felt were the useless, meaningless and needless deaths of those that died in the Vietnam War.

Historians will one day put the Vietnam War into historical perspective, and they will recognize Vietnam for what it was: just one battle in the forty-year "Cold War" with the Soviet Union. It was a battle that contained the spread of Communism in South East Asia for over a decade.

This ten-year containment provided time to bolster the capabilities of Vietnam's neighbors to resist Communist aggression, and because of this, the "Domino Effect" did not take place when Vietnam finally fell. For the bankrupting philosophy of Communism to survive, it needed to expand and feed off the economies that it absorbed. For more than forty years, our country provided men and materiel to any country that needed assistance to resist Communist annexation. This "containment" policy worked, the Soviet Union collapsed, and freedom was secured for another generation of Americans.

The Americans who died in Vietnam did not die in vain, and the negative symbolism depicted in the Vietnam War Memorial will one day be recognized. There will come a day when the American people will look at that black rock in the bottom of a hole and see it for what it depicts: an open grave with a blackened corpse lying at the bottom. Then, our country will surely fill that open grave, give those patriots a proper funeral and erect on that site a memorial befitting of their sacrifice.

* * * * * *.

The Wall was written by Delta Recon man D.J. Taylor, after his first—and last—visit to the Vietnam War Memorial. More than 58,000 names are etched on the memorial. Of those, the youngest is fifteen years of age; five are sixteen; at least twelve are seventeen; the oldest, sixty-two. Eleven thousand five hundred KIA were under age twenty; eight were women.[47]

---

[47] Statistics courtesy of veterans of the 4th Battalion, 9th Infantry Regiment. http/thewall-usa.com/information.index1.htm.

Recon

By James R. Jarrett

Dedicated to my warrior brothers and teammates of Project Delta

With watchful eyes and faces grim,
Weapons black and camoed skin.

Pupils wide the tree line peer,
Heartbeats race, death so near.

Crackling radio and static hiss,
Tracers bright with near miss.

Rockets roar with sound so deep,
The blood of men begins to seep.

Darkened jungle holds the fate,
Comrades trapped beyond the gate.

Aircraft screaming fast and low,
Death pursues the team below.

Courage their shield from loss of hope,
Hope as frail as STABO rope.

Rotors whine, gunners in the door,
Swiftly go these dogs of war.

A creed unknown to most mankind,
Never leave a man behind.

When cowards to sleep have gone,
Men like these shall carry on.

For freedom's cause in lands far gone,
Remember brave men called recon.

Acknowledgments and Sources

PROJECT DELTA SURVIVORS ARE A FUNDAMENTAL element of the Special Operations Association (SOA) that meets in Las Vegas annually for their reunion. During the 2005 event, I attended and interviewed Delta veterans about their Vietnam experiences. Those interviews, or subsequent telephone conversations, are the basis for this book. The information I've portrayed has been documented with permission of participating members.

I wish to extend special thanks to Project Delta members and others who allowed me to tie up their phone for memories and for their notes of past events: Gary Nichols, Ken Edens, Alton "Moose" Monroe, Chester Howard, Jay Graves, Al Greenup, Al Park, Art Garcia, Agustin "Gus" Fabian, Andy Sheppard, Jerry Estenson, John Burdish, Andre "Saint" St. Laurent, Norm Doney, Maurice "Brake" Brakeman, Steve Carpenter, John Flanagan, James Jarrett, Bobby Pruett, William Roderick, James Dallas Chapman, Herb Siugzda, Tom Schultz and Fred Walz. Steve Sherman, as well as Neil Horn, the Project Delta website webmaster, have been extremely helpful and permitted the use of resources and data. All personal photos I've obtained through the website archives. If I've overlooked anyone, I sincerely apologize.

I choose not to circulate the manuscript to each and every member of Project Delta. On occasion the veterans have contradicted themselves on non-crucial points that didn't change the gist or accuracy of the story. I fully realize not all might accept each account as entirely accurate. To circulate it broadly would have undoubtedly resulted in bickering about dates, times, etc., or reasons why something might have or not have happened. However, I did circulate chapters to some who've participated in its development, and greatly appreciate the suggestions, constructive criticism and corrections I've heeded and incorporated. Readers should not presume these accounts are the complete or full history of this fine organization. Given the fading memories of these honorable men and the passing of key Project Delta personnel, killed either during the war or since deceased, it might be best described as a snapshot of history.

Given the resources available, I've attempted to check and crosscheck facts via face-to-face interviews, telephone conversations and documentation, and supplemented information by revisiting some of the battlefields.

It has been an honor to bring the true story of these remarkable men to the public's attention, and to be able to assist them in passing along their personal legacy to their families.

Other Sources:
Steve Sherman. *Project Delta, After Action Reports, Detachment B-52* (1964-1970).

Steve Sherman. *History of Project Delta—Part 1, Project Delta After Action Reports*, http://project-delta.net/delta_history.htm

List of those KIA, MIA, WIA and their awards, provided by Project Delta documentation: Annex A.

Colonel David Hackworth, USA (Ret). *About Face: The Odyssey of an American Warrior*. New York: Touchstone, 1990.

BDM Corporation: A Study of Strategic Lessons Learned in Vietnam, Volume 1, The Enemy (McLean, VA, November 30, 1979), 5-14.

Brigadier General Soutchay Vongsavanh, RLG [Royal Laotian Government]. "Military Operations and Activities in the Laotian

Panhandle," *Indochina Monographs* (U.S. Army Center of Military History, Washington, DC, 1981), 4.

U.S. Department of State [DOS], telegram from Sullivan to DOS, 21 June 1965, Foreign Relations of the United States [FRUS], 1964-1968, Volume 27, Laos, accessed at: www.state.gov/www/about_state/history/vol_xxviii.

5th Special Forces Group Commander's Debriefing Report on Omega, Sigma and Project Delta, June 1966–June 1967.

Kenneth Conboy. *Shadow War,* (New York: Paladin Press), 119.

"Lancers," Volume 11, Issue 2, page 9.

Don Valentine website; http://www.don-valentine.com

Jerry D. Estenson. "Autobiography," http://www.project-delta.net /bios/estenson.htm.

Project Delta After-Action Reports

U.S. Air Force. "USAF Support of Special Forces in South East Asia," HQ PACAF, Directorate, Tactical Evaluation, CHECO Division, 10, march 1969, 75.

Jerry D. Estenson, DPA, Professor College of Business Administration, California State University, Sacramento. *Leading Professionals in High-Risk Environments: Perceptions of Critical leadership Attributes Provided by Three Generations of Military Special Operations Personnel,* 66.

Tom Clancy and John Gresham. *Special Forces: A Guided Tour of U.S. Army Special Forces.* New York: Berkely Trade, 2001, 61.

Joseph L. Galloway. *A Combat Reporter Remembers the Siege at Plei Me,* http://www.projectdelta.net/plei_mei.htm [LTG Hal Moore, USA (Ret) and Galloway co-authored *We Were Soldiers Once...and Young.* This book was the basis for the screenplay and movie of the same name, which starred Mel Gibson.]

Colonel Charlie A. Beckwith, USA (Ret). *Delta Force: The Army's Elite Counterterrorist Unit* (New York: Avon, 2000).

Roger L. Albertson. "The Last Survivor: A Memorial Day Tribute," http://projectdelta.net/gray_story.htm, 2.

Brigadier General John Flanagan, U.S. Air Force Retired. *Vietnam Above the Tree Tops: A Forward Air Controller Reports.* NYC: Praeger Publishing, 1992.

Gary Nichols. "Personal Reflections," Detachment B-52 (Project Delta), 1966-1970.http://www.projectdelta.net/ nichols_story.htm

D.J. Taylor. "Remembering the 281st AHC," http://project-delta.net/remembering_the_281st.htm, 1.

Robert Moberg "Shot Down With Robbie, http://project-delta.net/shot_down.htm, 1.

Jim Morris. "Death-Dealing Project Delta; PART 3: Interview with the Big 'Un,'" http://projectdelta.net/sofmag3_pg1.htm

James Tolbert. "Chuck Allen and Delta," http://projectdelta.net /allen_story.htm

James Tolbert. "Shane Soldato," http://projectdelta.net/soldato_story.htm

Gary Nichols. "I Will Always Remember." (Modified)

"Not everyone who lost his
life in Vietnam died there...
Not everyone who came home
from Vietnam ever left there."

- *Unknown*

ANNEX A

USSF Awards and Decorations, by Operation

Early Unnamed Operations (July 1964 – Oct. 1965)

SFC Henry M. Bailey, DSCV; SSG Ronald T. Terry, DSCV and SSFV; SSG James J. Malia, SSFV; SFC Eddie J. Adams, BSFV; SFC Sterling S. Smith, ACMV; SP5 Ronald S. Gaffney*, PHFW

Operation 15-65 (July – Oct. 1965)

SFC Fred Taylor**, PHFW; SSG Henry J. Gallant**, PHFW

Plei Me (Oct 1965)

MAJ Charles Beckwith, SSFV; SFC Marion C. Hollaway, SSFV; SFC Robert J. Wren, SSFV; MAJ Charles Thompson, SSFV; CPT A.J. Baker, SSFV; SSG Larry R. Dickinson, SSFV; SGT Ronald L. Robertson, SSFV; SGT Terrence L. Morrone, BSFV; CPT Thomas W. Pusser*, PHFW; SSG Jimmie L. McBynum*, PHFW

Operations 1-66 through 13-66 (Jan. – March 1967)

SFC David W. Disharoon, SSFV; Frank N. Badolati*, SSFV and PHFW; SFC Marlin C. Cook*, SSFV and PHFW; SSG Charles F. Hiner, BSFV and PHFW; SSG Ronald T. Terry**, PHFW; SFC Jesse L. Hancock, PHFW*

Unknown Operations (June – July 1968)

SFC Paul D. Spillane*, PHFW; SGT William E. Erickson, BSMV and ACMV; SFC Frank H. Helms, PHFW; MSG Virgil Murphy, ACMV and ACMV (2nd award); CPT Roy M. Oga-sawara, BSMV; SSG David F. Ryder, ACMV; SFC Thomas F. Schultz, BSMV and ACMV; MAJ Terrel K. Naumann, PHFW; SSG Jonathan Reid, PHFW

Alamo (Sept. – Oct. 1968)

SSG John P. Burdish, BSMV and PHFW; SFC Arthur F. Garcia, ACMV; SFC Jerry Nelson, BSMV; SSG Kenneth C. Wagner, BSMV; SFC Darrel G. Elmore, ACMV; SSG Sherman A. Paddock, PHFW; SSG David F. Ryder PHFW; SSG Laurence A. Young, PHFW; SGT Stephen J. Viglietta, PHFW

War Bonnet (Oct. – Nov. 1968)

MSG Minor B. Pylant, BSMV; MSG Richard S. Sorrells, BSMV; SFC Jerry L. Nelson, BSMV (2nd award); SGT Bobby D. Warden, BSMV

Battle of Gia Dinh (Saigon Tet Offensive)

Unknown

Ares (Dec. 1968 – March 1969)

SSG John P. Burdish, PHFW (2nd award); SFC Charles Hiner, ACMV and (2) PHFW; SP4 William R. Pomeroy, PHFW; SSG Sylvester Ray, ACMV; SFC Walter Simpson, ACMV; SSG James R. Legros, ACMV; SFC Jerry Nelson, ACMV; SFC Robert A. Conaway, BSMV; SFC Arthur F. Garcia, BSMV; SGT Charles F. Prevedel, BSMV; SFC Thomas F. Schultz, PHFW; SP4 Robert H. Fegan, BSMV; SGT Joseph M. Hartman, BSMV; SSG Laurence A. Young, BSMV

Cass Park (April 1969)

SSGT John P. Burdish, BSMV (2nd award); SFC Jerry L. Nelson, ACMV; SFC Joseph A. Roy, BSMV; SSG Bobby D. Warden, BSMV; MAJ Terrel K. Naumann, AMFV; SGT Theodore D. Aslund, BSMV; SGT James D. Benoit, BSMV; SGT Michael H. Sillings, BSMV; SSG Laurence A. Young, PHFW; SSG Thomas E. Johnson, ACMV; SGT Dave L. Barta, SSFV; SSG Terry L. Bryan, BSFV and PHFW; SSG James L. Thompson, PHFW; SSG Thomas K. Long**, SSFV and PHFW; SGT Charles F. Prevedel**, PHFW; SSG Douglas E. Dahill**, PHFW; SSG Charles V. Newton*, PHFW; SSG Joseph M. Hartman, ACMV; SGT David L. Lang –ACMV and PHFW; SSG David J. Taylor, BSFV; SFC Walter L. Simpson, PHFW

Cass Park II (May – June 1969)

SSG Arvill M. Hicks, AMFV; SSG Alfred W. Drapeau, PHFW; SSG Frederick L. Foater, PHFW; SSG Theodore L. Perkins, PHFW

Trojan Horse I & II (Aug. – Oct. 1969)

CPT Howard A. Gill, ACMV, BSMV and AMFV; CPT Mayo A. Hadden, AMFV and BSMV; SGM Harry D. Whalen, BSMV; SSG Dennis C. McVey, BSMV; SSG Larry D. Henderson, PHFW; SGT Peter J. Sckipp, PHFW

Yellow Ribbon (Dec. 1969)

SSG Arno J. Voigt - ACMV

Sabre & Spurs (Feb. – March 1970)

SP4 Stephen A. Spiers* SSFV and PHFW; SSG Thomas E. Johnson, SSFV; BSMV and PHFW; SSG Joe C. Alderman, BSFV; SFC Lothar L. Williams, BSFV; SSG Warren K. Bianchi, BSMV (1) and BSMV (2), PHFW; SSG Chester Howard, BSMV; SFC Bobby G. Pruett, BSMV (1) and BSMV (2); SFC Arthur F. Garcia, BSMV (2nd award); SSG John G. Santora, BSMV; SFC Frederick A. Thaler, BSMV; CPT James L. Walden, AMFV; SFC Charles A. Flenniken, AMFV; SFC Edgar E. Foshee, ACMV; SGT Stephen A. Carpenter, ACMV; SP4 Charles E. Dirks, ACMV (1) and ACMV (2); SFC Jackie E. Upton, AMFV; SP5 Milburn R. Harris, ACMV; SFC Andre J. St Laurent, AMFV.

Cavalry Glory (March - April 1970)

SP5 Milburn R. Harris, SSFV and PHFW; SP4 Anthony M. Bradley, BSFV; SSG Curtis A. Clemonds, BSFV; SSG Samuel D. Hernandez, BSMV; SSG Thomas L. Rea, BSMV and ACMV; SFC David A. Norville, BSMV; Arthur F. Garcia, BSMV (3rd award) and ACMV (2nd award); SFC Ralph L. Hill, BSMV; SFC Howard L. Wells, BSMV; CPT Hermann Adler, AMFV

Delta Dagger (May – June 1970)

MAJ Shane N. Soldato*, SSFV and PHFW; SSG Arno Voigt*, ACMV (2nd award) and PHFW; SSG Curtis A. Clemonds, BSFV (2nd award) and PHFW; SFC Edgar E. Foshee, AMFV and PHFW; SFC Dickie D. Pirtil, BSFV; SSG Terry Dock, BSFV; CPT Cecil R. Garvin, BSFV; SFC David A. Norville, BSFV; SSG Joe C. Alderman, BSFV and AMFV; SSG William E. Dill, BSFV; SSG Alfred W. Drapeau, PHFW; CPT James L. Walden; AMFV; SSG Ulrich Bayer, ACMV; SFC Alton E. Monroe, AMFV; SSG William R. Pomeroy, BSFV; SFC Wayne E. Fleming, PHFW; SFC Charles A. Flenniken, PHFW; SSG Gary L. Reagan, AMFV; SSG John G. Santora, PHFW; MSG James L. Clow, AMFV; CPT Arthur T. Fields, PHFW; SP4 Charles E. Dirks, ACMV

*   Killed in Action

** Missing in Action

Participants in the An Loa Valley Operation, by Team

TEAM 1

Keating, Henry A. SFC (Team Leader); Whitis, Robert P. SFC; Dupuis, Norman C. SSG (WIA); Chiarello, Agostino SSG; Bell, Brooke A. SSG

TEAM 2

Webber, Frank R., Jr. SFC (Team Leader) (WIA); Cook, Marlin C. SFC (KIA); Dotson, Donald L. SSG (KIA); Hoagland, George A. SSG (KIA); Hancock, Jesse L. SFC (KIA); Hiner, Charles F. SSG (WIA)

TEAM 3

Huston, Marcus L. SFC (Team Leader); McKeith, Billy A. SSG; Gray, Wiley W. MSG; Terry, Ronald T. SSG (MIA); Hodgson, Cecil J. SFC (MIA); Badolati, Frank N. SSG (KIA)

USSF Personnel
BDA Platoon-Nung Company

SSG Burdish, John	19 Feb 68 – 19 Oct 69
SGT Robertson, Ronald L.	01 Oct 65 – 15 June 66
SP5 Wood, James M.	01 June 66 – 01 June 67
SSG Monroe, Alton E.	1968 – 1968
SSG Stanfield, Michael T.	16 Jan 68 – 01 June 68
SFC Nelson, Jerry L.	01 Sept 68 – 25 Nov 69
SFC Garcia, Arthur F.	01 Aug 69 – 15 July 70
SSG Johnson, Thomas E.	17 Sept 69 – 17 April 70

NOTE: Despite efforts to obtain a complete listing, some BDA members may not appear due to incomplete records and/or faulty memories.

USSF Personnel, Road Runners

SFC Tracy, Paul V.	01 Jan 66 – Unknown
SFC Stanley, Harold B.	25 Jan 67 – 12 Jul 67
SFC Singh, Jose J.	28 May 67 – 27 May 68
SFC Nichols, Gary	28 May 68 – 30 Sept 69
SSG Johnson, Thomas E.	30 May 68 – 06 Jul 69
SFC Upton, Jackie E.	20 Aug 69 – 25 July 70

*   Killed in Action
** Missing in Action

NOTE: Despite efforts to obtain a complete listing, some USSF Road Runner personnel may not appear due to incomplete records and/or faulty memories.

USSF Personnel Roster, Project Delta Recon Teams

Recon Officers:

1LT	Holland, Guy H. II	01 Mar 65 – 01 Jun 66
2LT	Estenson, Jerry D.	02 Jan 67 – 17 Jul 67
2LT	Richardson, Tommy L.	03 Jan 67 – 18 Aug 67
CPT	Hadden, Mayo A.	05 Jan 67 – 04 Apr 67
1LT	Coulter, Douglas E.	13 Jan 67 – 15 Aug 67
1LT	Sullivan, John M.	30 Jan 67 – 19 July 67
CPT	Shelton, Henry H.	26 Mar 67 – 12 Jul 67
2LT	Carney, Michael K.	05 Apr 67 – 27 Jun 67

Recon Team NCOICs:

MSG	Zaky, Arif R.	12 Jun 64 – 20 Jul 64
MSG	Duarte, Antonio Jr.	01 Jan 65 – 01 Sept 65

MSG Miller, John L.   01 Jan 65 – 01 Jan 66

SFC Fisher, Loyd R.   14 Sep 65 – 18 Mar 66

MSG Shoulders, James R.   01 Jan 66 – Unknown

MSG Gray, Wiley W.   01 Jun 66 – Unknown

SFC Simpson, Walter L.   08 Sep 67 – 07 Oct 68

MSG Stamper, Thomas F.   09 Sep 66 – 08 Sep 67

MSG Doney, Norman A.   01 Oct 68 – 21 Jul 68

MSG Pylant, Minor B.   14 Jul 68 – 13 Sep 68

SFC Simpson, Walter L.   01 Sep 68 – 01 Nov 69

SFC Devere, Donald   01 Nov 69 – 01 Feb 70

SFC Monroe, Alton E.   01 Feb 70 – 15 Jul 70

Recon Team Members:

SP5 Brande, Harvey G.   12 Jun 64 – Unknown

PFC Graham, Bryan G.   16 Oct 64 – 19 Apr 65

SP5 Stahl, Phillip T.   16 Oct 64 – 19 Apr 65

SFC Adams, Eddie J.   16 Oct 64 – 19 Apr 65

SFC Kipfer, Robert   16 Oct 64 – 19 Apr 65

SSG Wren, Robert J.   01 Jan 65 – Unknown

SFC Duncan, Donald W.   01 Jan 65 – Unknown

SFC Powers, James P.   01 Jan 65 – Unknown

SFC Untalan, Lucius T.   01 Mar 65 – 01 Mar 66

SFC Keating, Henry A.   01 Apr 65 – 01 Apr 66

MSG Gallant, Henry J**   21 Apr 65 – 13 Jul 65

SFC Hannah, Donald W.   01 May 65 – 01 May 66

SSG Evans, Billie R.   01 Jun 65 – 01 Jan 66

SSG Zan, Tom L.   01 Jun 65 – 28 Jan 66

SSG Badolati, Frank N. **   Unknown – 29 Jan 66

SSG Terry, Ronald T. **   01 May 65 – 29 Jan 66

SFC	Cook, Marlin C*.	01 Jun 65 – 29 Jan 66
SSG	Chiarello, Agostino	01 Aug 65 – 01 Aug 66
SSG	Dotson, Donald L.*	01 Sep 65 – 29 Jan 66
SSG	Hoagland, George A. III*	01 Sep 65 – 29 Jan 66
SSG	Bell, Brooke A.	14 Sep 65 – 18 Mar 66
SSG	Hiner, Charles F.	14 Sep 65 – 18 Mar 66
SFC	Leone, Pompeo C.	14 Sep 65 – 18 Mar 66
SSG	Raines, Rolfe J.	01 Nov 65 – 01 Dec 66
SFC	Whitis, Robert P.	01 Nov 65 – 01 Nov 66
SSG	Dupuis, Norman C.	01 Nov 65 – 01 Jul 66
SFC	Stultz, Donald E.	01 Dec 65 – 01 Dec 66
SFC	Tracy, Paul V.	01 Jan 66 – Unknown
SFC	Hollaway, Marion C. Jr.	01 Jan 66 – Unknown
SGT	McDonald, Charles A.	01 Jan 66 – 1 Dec 66
SSG	Gray, Charles H. Jr.*	01 Jan 66 – 01 Nov 66
SGT	Moreau, Eugene R.*	01 Jan 66 – 27 Aug 66
SSG	Lovejoy, Clarence	01 Jan 66 – Unknown
SSG	McKeith, Billy A.	01 Jan 66 – 01 Oct 66
SSG	Mills, Audley D.*	01 Jan 66 – Unknown
SSG	Sutter, Phillip E.	01 Jan 66 – 01 Apr 66
SFC	Bounds, Austin C.	01 Jan 66 – Unknown
SFC	Delaney, Richard A.	01 Jan 66 – Unknown
SFC	Disharoon, David W.	01 Jan 66 – Unknown
MSG	Grisham, Robert G.	01 Jan 66 – 01 Nov 66
SFC	Harper, Charles L.	01 Jan 66 – 01 Jun 66
SFC	Davis, Edward P.	01 Jan 66 – 07 Jul 66
SFC	Hancock, Jesse L.*	01 Jan 66 – 29 Jan 66
SFC	Hodgson, Cecil J. **	01 Jan 66 – 29 Jan 66
SFC	Huston, Marcus L.	01 Jan 66 – 01 Aug 66

SFC	Jones, Harry L.	01 Jan 66 – Unknown
SFC	Matteson, Marvin E. Sr.	01 Jan 66 – 01 Mar 66
SFC	Price, Robert K.	01 Jan 66 – 01 Sep 66
SFC	Telfair, Charles W. Jr.	01 Jan 66 – 01 Jul 66
SFC	Webber, Frank R. Jr.	01 Jan 66 – 01 Apr 66
SFC	Heilman, John J.	01 Jan 66 – Unknown
SFC	McShea, William J.	01 Jan 66 – Unknown
SFC	Shumate, Walter	01 Feb 66 – 01 Jan 67
SGT	Betterton, Dale C.	25 Feb 66 – 17 Mar 68
SP4	Marquis, Roland C. Jr.	01 Mar 66 – Unknown
SGT	Alderman, Joe C.	01 Mar 66 – 01 Jan 67
SSG	Landrum, Donald G.	01 Mar 66 – Unknown
SFC	Doney, Norman A.	01 Mar 66 – 01 Mar 67
SFC	Sheppard, Paul E.	01 Mar 66 – 01 Jul 66
SFC	Nichols, Gary	01 Mar 66 – 01 Sep 66
SSG	Schenkelberger, Joel R.	01 Apr 66 – 01 Oct 66
SSG	Barnes, Robert W.	01 Apr 66 – 01 Jul 66
SFC	Sommerhof, Earl T.	01 May 66 – Unknown
SFC	Kamalu, Winsley F.	01 Jun 66 – 01 Aug 66
SGT	Bott, Russell P. **	01 Jun 66 – 02 Dec 66
SFC	Stark, Willie E. **	01 Jun 66 – 01 Dec 66
SFC	Brierley, George W. Jr.	22 Aug 66 – 21 Aug 67
SFC	Brydon, Loy B.	05 Sep 66 – 01 Oct 66
SFC	Markham, Joseph M.	05 Sep 66 – 04 Sep 67
SFC	Roderick, William C.	01 Oct 66 – 11 Mar 67
SP5	Edens, Kenneth B.	06 Oct 66 – 05 Oct 67
SFC	Simpson, Walter L.	12 Nov 66 – 01 Apr 68
SSG	Gleason, William B.	20 Nov 66 – 13 Sep 67
SSG	Stedman, Gary M.	01 Dec 66 – 01 Mar 67

SSG Graves, James W.   03 Dec 66 – 01 Jul 68

SFC Archer, Allen H.*   Unknown – 22 Mar 67

SSG Budd, Gary V.   01 Jan 67 – 06 Sep 67

SFC Tucker, Oddie   01 Jan 67 – 04 Mar 67

SFC Woody, Lonnie B.   10 Jan 67 – 09 Jan 68

SFC Bartlett, Larry P.*   11 Jan 67 – 10 Jan 68

SFC Robinette, Orville G.   11 Jan 67 – 10 Jan 68

SSG Brown, Sewell T.   15 Jan 67 – 01 Jan 68

SSG Strick, Mark J.   17 Jan 67 – 12 Sep 68

SFC Seal, John A. Jr.   25 Jan 67 – 24 Jan 68

SFC Smyth, James W.   25 Jan 67 – 06 Jan 68

SSG Sheppard, Andrew D.   27 Jan 67 – 26 Jan 68

SSG Brakeman, Maurice L.   29 Jan 67 – 19 May 67

SSG Kinzer, Robert W. Jr.   02 Feb 67 – 02 Feb 68

SSG Kerley, Estille G.   01 Mar 67 – 28 Aug 67

SFC Simpson, Walter L.   01 Apr 67 – 13 Nov 67

SFC Nichols, Gary G.   01 Apr 67 – 01 Feb 68

SSG Cunningham, Burhl M.   15 Apr 66 – 01 Feb 67

SSG Monroe, Alton E.   20 May 67 – 24 Oct 68

SGT Jarrett, James R.   28 May 67 – 01 Jan 68

SP5 Johnson, Thomas E.   01 Jun 67 – 31 May 68

SGT Forbes, Marvin R.   07 July 67 – 07 Jul 68

SGT Walker, Joe J.   07 Jul 67 – 01 Jul 68

SSG Holland, James D. Jr.   26 Jul 67 – 01 May 68

PFC Santana, Anthony J.*   28 Jan 67 – 01 Jun 68

SSG Cook, Edward L.   08 Aug 67 – 06 Aug 68

SGT Norris, Michael A.   22 Aug 67 – 10 May 68

SFC Morales, Edgar   24 Aug 67 – 26 Jun 68

MSG Waltz, William D.   09 Sep 67 – 01 Jan 68

SSG Siugzda, Herbert	15 Sep 67 – 10 Apr 68
SSG Coalson, James L.	26 Sep 67 – 20 Sep 68
SSG Stedman, Gary M.	29 Sep 67 – 14 Oct 68
SFC Spilline, Paul D.*	29 Sep 67 – 25 Jul 68
SGT Guerrero, Juan J.	03 Oct 67 – Unknown
SFC Norville, David A.	09 Oct 67 – 08 Oct 68
SP5 Greenup, Alva D.	22 Oct 67 – 02 Apr 68
SSG Guitron, Lamberto Jr.	22 Oct 67 – 21 Oct 68
SSG Sanders, Robert H. *	24 Oct 67 – 01 Feb 68
SFC Smith, Robert A.	24 Oct 67 – 23 Oct 68
SFC Gifford, Douglas L.	26 Oct 67 – 25 Oct 68
SFC Bean, Billy V.	27 Nov 67 – 01 Jun 68
SP4 Chapman, Dennis E.	10 Dec 67 – 16 Feb 68
SSG Drapeau, Alfred W.	01 Jan 68 – 06 Jul 68
SSG Zumbrun, James H. *	01 Jan 68 – 01 Mar 68
SFC Nichols, Gary G.	01 Jan 68 – 20 Jul 70
SFC Tamez, Reuben G.	01 Jan 68 – 01 Feb 69
SFC Webster, Earle E.	01 Jan 68 – Unknown
MSG Sorrells, Richard S.	01 Jan 68 – Unknown
SGT Anthony, John D. Jr.	11 Jan 68 – 11 Jan 69
SSG Lefebvre, Bernard A.	13 Jan 68 – 13 Jan 69
SFC Schultz, Thomas F.	22 Jan 68 – 01 Jun 68
SSG Schmidt, Joseph F. Jr.	24 Jan 68 – 23 Jul 68
SSG Cooley, Jimmy C.	07 Feb 68 – 07 Feb 69
SFC Conaway, Richard C.	11 Feb 68 – 11 Feb 69
SSG Harris, Barron M. Jr.	12 Feb 68 – 12 Feb 69
SFC Ortiz, Alberto Jr. *	13 Feb 68 – 12 Feb 69
SFC Bruno, William H.	01 Apr 68 – 03 Oct 68
SSG Paddock, Sherman A.	05 Apr 68 – 04 Apr 69

SFC Wagner, Kenneth C.	06 May 68 – 09 May 69
SSG Young, Laurence A.	20 May 68 – 19 May 69
SP5 Merriman, Albert J.	01 Jun 68 – 11 Oct 68
SGT Peterson, Theodore R.	01 Jun 68 – 16 Jan 69
SFC Sites, Larry L.	01 Jun 68 – 23 Oct 68
SFC Roy, Joseph A.	15 Jul 68 – 02 Jul 69
SSG Graves, James W.	01 Aug 68 – 30 Jul 69
SFC Garcia, Arthur F.	10 Aug 68 – 01 Aug 69
SFC Nelson, Jerry L.	01 Sep 68 – 25 Nov 69
SGT Pervedel, Charles F.**	01 Sep 68 – 17 Apr 69
SSG Dahill, Douglas E.**	Unknown – 17 Apr 69
SGT Aslund, Theodore D.	24 Sep 68 – 23 Sep 69
SGT Sillings, Michael H.	24 Sep 68 – 23 Sep 69
SSG Warden, Bobby D.	24 Sep 68 – Unknown
SSG Perkins, Theodore L.	26 Sep 68 – 25 Sep 69
SSG Bryan, Terry L.	16 Oct 68 – 16 Apr 69
SFC Schenkelberger, Joel R.	21 Oct 68 – 16 Oct 69
SSG Huskins, David E.	30 Oct 68 – 15 Jan 69
SSG Long, Thomas K.*	30 Oct 68 – 16 Apr 69
SFC Hicks, Arville M.	01 Dec 68 – 05 May 70
SGT Lange, David L.	10 Dec 68 – 04 Jul 69
SGT Pomeroy, William R. Jr.	22 Dec 68 – 15 Dec 69
SSG Bayer, Ulrich	23 Dec 68 – 17 Jul 70
SSG Hartman, Joseph M.	23 Dec 68 – 31 May 69
SGT Klahorst, Gley R.	23 Dec 68 – 01 Jul 69
SGT Benoit, James D.	01 Jan 69 – Unknown
SSG Newton, Charles V. **	01 Jan 69 – 17 Apr 69
SFC Basil, Lewis J.	01 Jan 69 – 29 Jun 69
SFC Cook, Charles D.	01 Jan 69 – Unknown

SGT Fegan, Robert H.   02 Jan 69 – 30 Nov 69

SFC Coalson, James L.   01 Feb 69 – 10 Jun 70

SFC Thompson, Hugh C.   10 Feb 69 – 28 Jan 70

SFC Conaway, Richard A.   11 Feb 69 – 01 Nov 70

SFC Lutz, Thomas H.   03 Mar 69 – 05 Oct 69

SFC Foster, Frederick L.   09 Mar 69 – 08 Oct 70

SSG Thornton, James B.   14 Mar 69 – 01 Mar 70

SSG Drapeau, Alfred W.   25 Mar 69 – 01 Nov 69

SFC Hill, Ralph L.   03 Apr 69 – 06 Jul 70

SFC Pruett, Bobby G.   06 Apr 69 – 29 Mar 70

SGT Carpenter, Stephen A.   21 Apr 69 – 02 Apr 70

SSG Batteford, Frank P. Jr.   07 May 69 – 07 May 70

SSG Lee, Marcus D.   27 May 69 – 08 May 70

SFC Cunningham, Burhl M.   01 Jun 69 – 09 Jan 70

SSG Schwarcbher, Alex C.   03 Jun 69 – 03 Jun 70

SSG Howard, Chester B.   16 Jun 69 – 12 Jun 70

SSG Bianchi, Warren K.   06 Jul 69 – 05 Dec 69

SSG Dill, William E. Jr.   16 Aug 69 – 15 Aug 70

SSG Reagan, Gary L.   16 Aug 69 – 15 Aug 70

SFC Williams, Lothar L.   17 Aug 69 – 16 Aug 70

SSG Orem, Robert L.   19 Aug 69 – 18 Aug 70

SSG Graves, James W.   20 Aug 69 – 11 Jul 70

SSG Pearson, James S.   20 Aug 69 – 12 Aug 70

SFC Taylor, Donald J.   20 Aug 69 – 20 Jul 70

SSG Sprouse, Roy F.   25 Aug 69 – 01 Aug 70

SSG Woods, Gilbert E.   28 Aug 69 – 30 Jun 70

SFC Piersall, Oscar L.   30 Aug 69 – 20 Aug 70

SSG Humphres, William T.   20 Mar 69 – 20 Jun 69

SFC Monroe, Alton E.   07 Oct 69 – 01 Aug 70

SSG	Reeves, Jimmie P.	06 Nov 69 – 01 Sep 70
SFC	Norville, David A.	21 Nov 69 – 01 Jul 70
SSG	Pomoroy, William R. Jr.	16 Dec 69 – 15 Dec 70
SFC	Rogers, Donald D.	29 Dec 69 – 15 Jul 70
SGT	Carpenter, Derick V.	01 Jan 70 – 15 Jun 70
SGT	Inscore, Robert C. Jr.	01 Jan 70 – 25 Jul 70
SFC	Hernandez, Samuel D.	01 Oct 70 – 30 Jun 70
SFC	St Laurent, Andre J.	15 Feb 70 – 30 Jun 70
SFC	Brakeman, Maurice L.	16 Feb 70 – 30 Jun 70
SSG	Alderman, Joe C.	21 Nov 69 – 12 Jul 70

* Killed in Action

** Missing in Action

NOTE: Despite efforts to obtain a complete listing, some USSF Recon NCOIC and team member personnel may not appear due to incomplete records and/or faulty memories.

ANNEX F

B-52, Project Delta Commanders/Headquarters Staff and Attached Personnel

Commanders:

CPT	Richardson, William J. Jr.	Unknown – 12 Jun 64
MAJ	Mitchell, Howard S.	12 Jun 64 – 01 Aug 64
CPT	Richardson, William J. Jr.	01 Aug 64 – 15 Jan 65
MAJ	Strange, Arthur A.	01 Jan 65 – Unknown
MAJ	Charles A. Beckwith	17 July 65 – 01 Feb 66
CPT	Baker, "Bo" A.J.	01 Feb 66 – 01 Mar 66
MAJ	Keefe, John V.	01 Mar 66 – 01 Apr 66
LTC	Warren, John S.	01 Apr 66 – 01 Sep 66
MAJ	Luttrell, Robert E.	01 Sep 66 – 11 Oct 66
LTC	Hayes, John G.	02 Oct 66 – 02 May 67
MAJ	Asente, James	11 Nov 66 – 14 Jul 67

LTC	Norman, William C.	01 Jun 67 – 09 Jul 67
MAJ	Allen, Charles A.	15 Jul 67 – 05 Jun 68
MAJ	May, Robert M.	06 Jun 68 – 30 Jan 69
LTC	Park, Alan H.	31 Jan 69 – 19 Aug 69
LTC	Moore, Robert J.	30 Oct 69 – 10 Mar 70
MAJ	Soldato, Shane N.*	09 Jan 70 – 23 May 70
MAJ	Aiken, George F.	20 May 70 – 21 Jul 70

Deputy Commanders:

LTC	Reish, Richard D.	01 Apr 66 – 01 Aug 66
MAJ	Luttrell, Robert E.	01 Jul 66 – 01 Sep 66
MAJ	Asente, James	01 Oct 66 – 10 Nov 66
MAJ	Allen, Charles A.	02 Mar 67 – 14 Jul 67
MAJ	Jones, Willis D.	26 Aug 67 – 25 Dec 68

Executive Officers:

MAJ	Patton, Frederick C.	08 Jun 64 – 01 Aug 64
CPT	Thompson, Charles H. Jr.	01 Dec 64 – 30 Nov 65
CPT	Baker, A.J.	11 Oct 65 – 01 May 66
CPT	Bynam, Holland E.	02 Jul 66 – 04 Sep 66
MAJ	Keefe, John V.	31 Jan 66 – 01 Mar 66
CPT	Lunday, Robert G.	15 Jul 66 – 25 Feb 67
MAJ	Naumann, Terrel K.	20 Dec 68 – 18 May 69
MAJ	Jones, Willis D.	01 Nov 69 – 01 Jun 70

Detachment B-52 Sergeant Major:

SGM	Payne, Paul C.	12 Jun 64 – 14 Dec 64
SGM	McGuire, Charles T.	01 Dec 64 – 30 Nov 65
MSG	Callahan, John R.	01 Sep 65 – 01 Jan 66

SGM Brandon, Charles L.	01 Mar 66 – 01 Sep 66
SGM Johanson, John M.	01 Mar 67 – 07 Oct 67
SGM Fuller, William Jr.	06 Jul 67 – 05 Jul 68
SGM Whalen, Harry D. Jr.	10 Apr 68 – 09 Nov 69
SGM Whalen, Harry D.	10 Nov 69 – 16 Jun 70

Attached U.S. Air Force Personnel:

Air Liaison Officer/Forward Air Controllers

CPT Kerr, Kenneth L.	01 Jan 66 – Unknown
ILT Flanagan, John	01 Jan 66 – Unknown
1LT Simpson, (unknown)	01 Jan 66 – Unknown
CPT Swope, Charles F.*	01 Jan 66 – 09 Nov 66
MAJ Miller, Ralf M.	06 Jul 66 – 05 Jul 67
CPT Groth, Allan R.	06 Oct 66 – 05 Oct 67
CPT Shields, David L.	01 Jun 67 – 30 May 68
CPT Slaughter, John T. Jr.	01 Jun 67 – 31 May 68
CPT Fasick, John C. Jr.	16 Dec 67 – 15 Dec 68
MAJ Roscoe, Edward P.	19 Feb 68 – 19 Feb 69
CPT Cocke, Robert	01 Jan 68 – Unknown
1LT Locke, William J.	22 Apr 69 – 21 Apr 70
CPT Hovde, Robert J.	04 Jun 69 – 03 Jun 70
1LT Dahlen, Bernard W.	23 Jun 69 – 22 Jun 70
CPT Fulaytar, Gerald W.	12 Sep 69 – 13 Sep 70

Aircraft Chiefs

A1C Bishop, (Unk)	01 Jan 66 - Unk
A1C Jeane, Robert A.	03 Jul 66 – 02 Jul 67
SGT Cobb, Frederick L.	25 Apr 67 – 24 Apr 68

A1C Montez, Alfred   01 May 67 – 01 May 68

SGT Elrod, Daniel R.   29 Dec 67 – 28 Dec 68

A1C Trunik, Thomas   28 Oct 69 – 28 Oct 70

SSG Hudson, Johnnie L.   22 Nov 69 – 21 Nov 70

Tactical Air Control Party (TACP) Radio Operators:

SGT Poling, Harry P.   11 Jul 67 – 10 Jul 68

SGT Young, John J.   29 Oct 67 – 28 Oct 68

SGT McKenzie, James W. Jr.   26 Jun 69 – 25 Jun 70

A1C Cornwell, Monte M.   29 Sep 69 – 28 Sep 70

*   Killed in Action

** Missing in Action

NOTE: Despite efforts to obtain a complete listing, some USSF Recon NCOIC and team member personnel may not appear due to incomplete records and/or faulty memories.

ANNEX G:

USSF Roster
91st and 81st Airborne Ranger
Battalion Advisors

CPT	Smith, Paul F. Jr.	16 Oct 64 – 19 Apr 65
CPT	Pusser, Thomas W. *	28 Jan 65 – 22 Oct 65
CPT	Walker, James A.	14 Sep 65–18 Mar 66
CPT	Cone, Edward E.	01 Jan 66 – 18 Mar 66
CPT	Bynam, Holland E.	22 Jan 66 – 01 Jul 66
CPT	Leiby, James P.	02 Apr 67 – 07 Oct 67
MAJ	Baker, Everett E.	28 Jun 67 – 01 Apr 68
MAJ	Naumann, Terrel K.	15 Mar 68 – 01 Jul 68
CPT	Humphus, Thomas O.	01 Jul 68 – 06 Mar 69
CPT	Confer, Ernest J.	07 Mar 69 – 16 Aug 69
1LT	Snider, Don M.	12 Jun 64 – 14 Dec 64

1LT Hadley, Joseph A.	16 Oct 64 – 19 Apr 65
1LT Brooks, Robert L.	20 Apr 65 – 30 Nov 65
ILT White, Euell T.	14 Sep 65 – 18 Mar 66
1LT Parker, Carroll G.	01 Jan 66 – 31 Dec 66
1LT Jantovsky, Anthony J.	01 Mar 66 – 20 Sep 66
CPT Turner, Billy J.	07 Mar 66 – 01 Jul 66
CPT Hadden, Mayo A. III	05 Apr 67 – 01 Aug 67
1LT Roland, Jessie O.	16 Sep 69 – 12 Apr 70
1LT Ford, Charley J.	05 Apr 67 – 05 Jan 68
1LT Starmann, Richard G.	05 Nov 69 – 01 May 70
MSG Conrad, John W.	16 Oct 64 – 19 Apr 65
MSG Hanks, James V. Jr.	28 Jan 65 – 01 Sep 65
SFC Coehlo, Antonio J.	01 Jan 66 – Unknown
MSG Booth, Leonard N.	01 Jan 66 – 01 Sep 66
MSG Burns, Harvey L.	01 Mar 66 – 01 Mar 67
MSG Haleamau, Julian K.	15 Aug 66 – Unknown
MSG Coffey, Edward A.*	18 Jan 67 –11 Aug 67
MSG Kreilick, James G.	28 May 67 – 27 May 68
MSG West, Daniel R.	21 Mar 68 – 01 Oct 68
MSG Edgell, James W.	13 Dec 60 – 20 Mar 70
SFC Gleason, William B.	13 Sep 67 – 18 May 68
CPT Solomon, Steven P.	01 Jan 68— 30 May 68
CPT Abla, Jimmie W.	21 Jun 68 – 12 Dec 68
MSG Gambill, Richard K.	01 Jan 67 – 01 Jun 67
SFC Winder, Raymond F.	01 Jun 67 – Unknown
SSG Ryder, David F. Jr.	10 Apr 68 – 12 Feb 69
SFC Massey, Carl E.	01 Dec 68 – 01 Jan 69
SFC Bean, Billy V.	21 Mar 69 – 20 Mar 70
CPT Garvin, Cecil R.	07 Nov 69 – 23 Oct 70

MSG Murphy, Virgil	07 Apr 68 – 07 Jul 69
SSG Hill, Paul E.	13 Jul 67 – 07 Jul 68
SFC Edgell, James W.	26 Jan 68 – 13 Dec 68
SFC Schenkelberger, Joel R.	01 Feb 68 – 21 Oct 68
SSG Erickson, William E.	09 Mar 68 – 02 Dec 68
SFC Barksdale, Charles W	01 Apr 68 – 16 Feb 70
SGT Barta, Dave L. Jr.	01 Nov 68 – 22 Mar 70
SFC Voigt, Arno J.*	27 Aug 69 – 04 Jun 70
SSG Santora, John G. Jr.	20 Sep 69 – 01 Sep 70
SFC Foshee, Edgar E.	08 Oct 69 – 07 Oct 70
SFC Thaler, Frederick A.	01 Dec 69 – 01 Dec 70
SSG Terry, Dock	01 Jan 70 – 01 Jul 70
SFC Picklesimer, Billy A.	11 Mar 69 – 03 Oct 70
SFC Pirtle, Dickie D.	15 Feb 70 – 11 Jun 70
SSG Clemonds, Curtis A.	23 Mar 70 – 01 Jun 70
CPT Moore, Charles R.	01 Sep 66 – 01 Dec 66
CPT Gill, Howard A. Jr.	01 Aug 69 – 04 Sep 69
SGT Dyer, Irby III**	Unknown – 02 Dec 66
CPL Benjamin, James S.	01 Jun 66 – Unknown
SFC Nichols, Gary G.	02 Oct 66 – 01 Apr 67
SGT Viglietta, Stephen J.	01 Jan 69 – 22 Jun 69
SSG Ray, Sylvester J.	01 Sep 68 – 28 Feb 69
SFC Reid, Campbell	10 Sep 69 – 09 Jul 70
SFC Findley, Byett P.	01 Mar 66 – 30 Sept 70
1LT Hamilton, Jack L.	31 Jan 66 – 31 Jan 67
1LT Deaton, Ronald L.	01 Oct 66 – 20 Jun 67
CPT Humphus, Thomas O.	08 Feb 68 – 12 Dec 68
1LT Ayers, Anthony	17 Mar 68 – Unknown
SFC Sommerhof, Earl T.	01 Jun 66 – Unknown

SFC Elmore, Darrell G.	01 Jun 68 – 05 Dec 68
SFC Simpson, Walter L.	14 Nov 66 – 01 Apr 67
SSG Jantz, Erwin O. Jr.	01 Jun 66 – 01 Jun 67
SSG Siugzda, Herbert	16 Sep 66 – 15 Sep 67
SFC Dobbins, Richard E.	03 Feb 67 – 06 Aug 68
SFC Kirby, Stanley B.	23 Dec 67 – 05 Dec 68
SSG Sheppard, Andrew D.	26 Jan 68 – Unknown
SP4 Ward, Jimmie R.	18 Dec 66 – 17 Dec 67
SSG Stern, Michael B.	08 Jun 67 – 07 Jun 68
SGT Walz, Frederick A.	07 Jul 67 – 01 Jan 68
SGT Gardner, Michael R.	10 Jul 67 – 09 Jul 68
SFC Chapman, James D.	24 Sep 68 – 1 Sep 69
SGT Cole, George D.	18 Oct 67 – 28 Apr 68
SP5 Jackson, Little J.*	01 Mar 68 – 07 Mar 68
SGT Coates, James D.	12 Jun 64 – 14 Dec 64
SSG Hale, James A.	12 Jun 64 – 14 Dec 64
SFC Largen, Richard L.	12 Jun 64 – 14 Dec 64
SFC Vasquez, Jose E.	12 Jun 64 – 14 Dec 64
SP4 Gaffney, Ronald S.*	16 Oct 64 – 19 Feb 65
SGT Smith, Sterling S.	16 Oct 64 – 19 Apr 65
SSG Florio, William	16 Oct 64 – 19 Apr 65
SSG Malia, James J. Jr.	16 Oct 64 – 19 Apr 65
SSG Spinaio, Edward W.	16 Oct 64 – 19 Apr 65
SFC Clements, Edwin L.	01 Jun 65 – 01 Jan 66
PFC Albertson, Roger L.	14 Sep 65 – 18 Mar 66
SSG Stamm, Garry D.	14 Sep 65 – 18 Mar 66
SSG Stevenson, Vernon R.	14 Sep 65 – 18 Mar 66
SFC Boyce, Douglas E.	14 Sep 65 – 18 Mar 66
SFC Sieg, John R.	14 Sep 65 – 18 Mar 66

SSG	Reilley, John	01 Dec 65 – 01 Apr 66
SSG	Munoz, Ferdinand	01 Jan 66 – 01 Oct 66
SFC	Harper, Charles L.	01 Jun 66 – 01 Nov 66
SFC	Findley, Boyett P.	01 Oct 66 – 01 Oct 67
SFC	Pruett, George W.	29 Oct 66 – 01 Jun 67
SGT	Millam, Gary B.	01 Jan 67 – Unknown
1LT	Livingston, Edwin C. Jr.	11 Feb 67 – 06 Feb 68
SSG	Rittenhouse, Jay R.	29 Mar 67 – 26 Mar 68
SFC	Bly, Jimmy R.	30 Mar 67 – 29 Mar 68
SSG	Stanfield, Michael T.	15 Jul 67 – 16 Jan 68
1LT	Ellis, Richard N.	2 Aug 67 – 01 Aug 68
1LT	Yang Hae Chan	21 Sep 67 – 20 Sep 68
WO2	Turner, Cedric C.	21 Oct 67 – 20 Oct 68
SFC	Sites, Larry L.	24 Oct 67 – 01 Jun 68
1LT	Wentz, William G.	28 Oct 67 – 27 Oct 68
CPT	Brubaker, Paul L.	21 Nov 67 – 01 Jun 68
SFC	Arnold, Gary L.	01 Dec 67 – 04 Dec 68
SFC	Bruno, William H.	01 Jan 68 – 01 Apr 68
CPT	Ogasawara, Roy M.	01 Jan 68 – 27 May 68
SFC	Salzwedel, Phillip S.	10 Jan 68 – 25 May 70
SFC	Ku, George W.	15 Jan 68 – 13 Jan 69
1LT	Kim Tae Soon	01 Mar 68 – 01 Dec 68
SFC	Alice-Rosario, German L.	01 Apr 68 – 31 Mar 69
SSG	Sandoval, Rufus R.	17 May 68 – 16 Mar 69
CPT	Vernon, Albert E. III	28 May 68 – 12 Dec 68
SSG	Stanfield, Michael T.	01 Jun 68 – 14 Feb 69
SFC	Bean, Billy V.	01 Jun 68 – 25 Nov 68
SFC	Schultz, Thomas F.	01 Jun 68 – 21 Jan 69
1LT	Fidler, David L.	13 Jun 68 – 12 Sep 68

1LT	Mitchell, Eugene W. III	04 Oct 68 – 03 Oct 69
1LT	Jones, Allan R.	01 Dec 68 – 01 Feb 69
CPT	Abla, Jimmie W.	13 Dec 68 – 07 Mar 69
SFC	Helms, Frank H.	01 Jan 69 – 18 Jun 69
SSG	Ward, Allen T.	01 Jan 69 – Unknown
SSG	Swiatocho, Casimir S.	02 Jan 69 – 12 May 69
CPT	Wagner, Kenneth A.	04 Jan 69 – 03 Jun 69
1LT	Trevino, Visente V.	15 Feb 69 – 16 Sep 69
CPT	Thompson, Richard C.	01 Jun 69 – 07 Nov 69
1LT	Selinsky, James J.	20 Jul 69 – 19 Dec 69
1LT	Fabian, Agustin R.	09 Nov 69 – 05 Jul 70
SFC	March, Toney E.	01 Feb 70 – 01 Jul 70
SFC	Barnes, James M.	10 Feb 70 – 30 Jun 70
SFC	Tharp, Bobby J.	01 Mar 70 – 30 Jun 70
SGT	Young, David L.	06 Mar 70 – 30 Jun 70
SGT	Bryan, James E. II.	04 May 70 – 01 Jul 70
SGT	Digiovanni, Thomas D.	06 May 70 – Unknown
1LT	Markel, James P.	10 May 70 – 14 Oct 70

ANNEX H

Unit Awards

UNIT AWARDS EARNED BY THE 5TH Special Forces Group (Abn), 1st Special Forces during the Vietnam conflict:

Presidential Unit Citation

> 5th Special Forces Group (Abn), Vietnam, 1 November 1966-31 January 1968

Meritorious Unit Citation

> 5th Special Forces Group (Abn), Vietnam, 31 January 1968-31 December 1968

Vietnam Cross of Gallantry with Palm Detachment

> B-52, Project Delta, 15 May 1964-16 August 1968; Detachment A-322 (Soui Da), 18-25 August 1968; 5th Special Forces Group (Abn), 1 Oct 1964-17 May 1969

Valorous Unit Award Detachment

> B-52, Project Delta, 4 March-4 April 1968

Vietnam Civic Action Medal

> 5th Special Forces Group, (Abn), 1 January 1968-24 Sep 1970

Navy Unit Commendation Ribbon

>   Detachment B-52, Project Delta, 17 April-17 June
>   1967 and 15 July-17 August 1967

Presidential Unit Citation

>   Navy Detachment A-101 (Lang Vei), Forward Opera-
>   tions Base 3, (Khe Sanh), and Command and Control
>   (Da Nang), 20 January-1 April 1968

U.S. Army Special Forces campaign participation credits number
twelve of the Vietnam conflict and range from 15 March 1962
to 31 December 1970.

Glossary

AA	Anti Aircraft
AAR	After Action Report
AC	Aircraft Commander
ACMV	Army Commendation Medal for Valor
AHC	Army Helicopter Company
ARCMV	Air Medal for Valor
ARVN	Army Republic of Vietnam
ASAP	As Soon As Possible; usually means "immediately"
AV	Aviation
B-57	High altitude bomber aircraft
Bac Se	Vietnamese for doctor
BAR	Browning Automatic Rifle
BDA	Battle Damage Assessment
BDE	Brigade

Bn	Battalion
BSMV	Bronze Star Medal for Valor
C&C	Command & Control
CAR-15	Shortened (carbine) version of the M-16
CAV	Cavalry
CH-47	Helicopter – large troop carrier
Chinook	Large troop carrying helicopter
CIA	Central Intelligence Agency
CO	Commanding Officer
Co	Company
COL	Full Colonel
Comm	Abbreviated term for communication
CP	Command Post
CPT	Captain
CSM	Command Sergeant Major
CWO	Chief Warrant Officer
DCO	Deputy Commanding Officer
DIV	Division
DMZ	Demilitarized Zone
DSC	Distinguished Service Cross; Nation's second highest award for valor
DZ	Drop Zone
DZSO	Drop Zone Safety Officer
FAC	Forward Air Controller
FOB	Forward Operating Base
G3	Operations at the general staff level
Grunts	Regular infantry
Gunships	Helicopters armed with twin 7.62 Gatling guns, automatic 20mm grenade launchers and rockets

HCMC	Ho Chi Minh City
HE	High Explosive
HHC	Headquarters and Headquarters Company
Hq	Headquarters
Huey	Hughes helicopter
IAD	Immediate Action Drill
ICC	International Control Commission
ID	Identification
INF	Infantry
KIA	Killed in Action
L-19	Two man observation airplane
Legs	Non-Airborne soldiers
LLDB	Loc Lon Dok Biet (Vietnamese name for Special Forces)
LRRP	Long Range Reconnaissance Patrol
LSM	Small landing craft
LT	Lieutenant
LTC	Lieutenant Colonel
LZ	Landing Zone
M-16	Standard armament for Vietnam era soldiers
M-60	7.62 caliber machinegun
M-79	Handheld 40mm grenade launcher
MACV	Military Assistance Command Vietnam
MAJ	Major
Medivac	Medical evacuation (usually by air)
MG	Machine gun
MIA	Missing in Action
Montagnard	Indigenous hill tribesmen employed by Special Forces as soldiers

MP	Military Police
MSG	Master Sergeant
MSS	Mission Support Site
NCO	Noncommissioned Officer
FNG	f_ _ _ing new guy
Nung	Indigenous band of Chinese warriors
NVA	North Vietnamese Army
O&I	Operations & Intelligence
One One	Assistant recon team leader
One Zero	Recon team leader
OP	Out Post
OPCON	Operational Control
PFC	Private First Class
PH	Purple Heart; awarded for wounds received in combat
PLF	Parachute landing fall
PLT	Platoon
PM	Provost Marshal
POW	Prisoner of war
PRC-25	Standard Army radio
PSP	Metal planks used for building roads and runways
Regt	Regiment
Ret	Retired
RON	Remain overnight
RT	Recon Team
RV	Rendezvous
S2	Intelligence
S3	Operations

S4	Supply
SFC	Sergeant First Class
SFGA	Special Forces Group Airborne
SFOD	Special Forces Operational Detachment
SGM	Sergeant Major
SGT	Sergeant
Shit hook	Chinook
SITREP	Situation Report
Slick	Stripped Huey helicopter, used for transporting troops
SOA	Special Operations Association
SOG	Studies and Observation Group
SOP	Standard operating procedures
SP5	Specialist 5th Class
SS	Silver Star; awarded for valor in combat
SSG	Staff Sergeant
TAC	Tactical Air
TACP	Tactical Air Communication Personnel
TAOR	Tactical area of recon
TASS	Tactical Air Support Squadron
TDY	Temporary duty
The "World"	Term used by Vietnam era GIs to refer to the United States
The hole	Term used by recon teams for landing in a small space in the jungle
Tiger suit	Camouflage fatigues worn by Special Forces in Vietnam
TOC	Tactical Operations Center
Trung Se	Vietnamese for "sergeant"
Un-ass	Leave immediately

USAF	United States Air Force
USSF	United States Special Forces
VC	Viet Cong
VN	Vietnamese
VN Dong	Vietnamese currency
VNAF	Vietnamese Air Force
VNSF	Vietnamese Special Forces
WIA	Wounded in Action
Willy Peter	White Phosphorous
WO	Warrant Officer
WP	White phosphorous
XO	Executive Officer

About the Author

RAYMOND C. MORRIS WAS BORN IN Jefferson City, Missouri and entered the Army at the fuzzy-cheek age of seventeen. Following basic training, he was assigned to the 101st Airborne Division. With a rank of staff sergeant, in 1963-1964 he attended Officer Candidate School at Fort Benning, Georgia.

In May 1964, as a freshly minted 2LT and the OCS Honor Graduate, his new orders led him to the 6th Special Forces Group. On 2 January 1966, he was assigned as team Executive Officer for the 5th Special Forces Group Operational Detachment (SFOD) 106 at Bato, Vietnam, followed by an assignment in May 1966 with SFOD A-103, Gia Vuc, Vietnam.

In October 1966, he was selected as the Long Range Reconnaissance Platoon Leader (LRRP) for Mobile Guerilla Force A-100, with operations throughout the A Shau Valley. In 1968, an assignment transferred him to the 46th Special Forces Company in Thailand where he trained Thai Black Panther brigades in reconnaissance tactics and inserted them into Vietnam. In 1970, he'd been detailed under the auspices of CIA operations in northern Thailand, to train Laotian commandos and deploy them into Laos.

Ether Zone author 1LT Ray Morris (*second from left*) in Bato, Vietnam, 1966. Joining him (*L to R*): CPT Richard L. Gaffney, SFC Hosea Givens, SP5 Chris Coombs, SGT Brian Becker, SFC "Mac" McNulty

In 1968, Ray returned to the U.S. for Ranger School, again distinguished as the Honor Graduate, winning the Darby Award. A new assignment led him back into Southeast Asia, where for two years, from April 1971-April 1973, he was a B-detachment commander with the 1st Special Forces Group (A) in Okinawa. During this time, he was sent to Vietnam twice for temporary assignment with the classified Special Forces FANK Program.

Returning stateside, he continued his military schooling and went on to hold other key assignments, including Deputy Commander, 6th Region Criminal Investigation Division in San Francisco, CA. In 1983, he was selected to be the Deputy Commanding Officer to reactivate the 1st Special Forces Group (A) at Fort Lewis, Washington. Ray retired from active duty in 1985 after an illustrious military career spanning twenty-six years.

His love for the military has never waned. As a civilian he returned to Fort Lewis, in charge of training the Army's new Stryker Brigades prior to Iraq deployment.

His awards include: Legion of Merit, Meritorious Service Medal, Bronze Star, Vietnam Cross of Gallantry w/silver star and Cross of

Gallantry w/bronze star, Army Commendation Medal (2) and numerous service awards. He proudly earned his jump wings, U.S., Thai and Vietnamese Master Parachutist badges, Special Forces and Ranger tabs.

Ray, never one to sit on his duff too long, holds a BA in Criminal Justice from the University of Nebraska, an MBA from City University in Seattle, Washington and a Masters in Justice Administration, Wichita State University.

A lifelong history enthusiast and prolific writer, Ray has used his keen observation of the human condition as the catalyst for expansion of his interests into writing and mainstream fiction. R. C. Morris's 2004 suspense thriller, *Don't Make the Blackbirds Cry*, and psychological thriller, the 2006 *Tender Prey*, are receiving acclaim. In October 2005, commissioned by the Project Delta members to write their story, his love of Special Forces forced him to place pending fiction novels on the back burner to write *The Ether Zone*. When not writing, you will find Ray stalking giant redfish along the Florida coast. He resides near Tampa Bay and may be contacted through his website at raycmorris.com.

Other Books by R. C. Morris

Don't Make the Blackbirds Cry

Publish America
ISBN:1-4137-2506-6

Murder, Hatred, Corrupt Politics, the Klan ... A Great Thrill Ride!

An orphaned and homeless teenager has just broken in and robbed the local store. Hiding in the darkness of an alley, he witness's five young men brutally rape and murder three teenage girls, two black and one white. One perpetrator is the town's star high school quarterback while another is the sheriff's son. When one of the five turns up dead a short time later, he knows he can't come forward!

Morris's debut novel, a gritty mystery of southern culture clash and racial hatred, reminds us that the quest for justice is not always free, and often, when seeking truth or trying to right a wrong, many lives can be affected by dire or unexpected consequences.

What the critics are saying:

"Don't Make the Blackbirds Cry, with all of its unexpected twists and turns, makes this first novel by R.C. Morris a difficult book to put down!"

- Northwest Guardian

"....truly a page-turner...a fully packed adventure. This author has writing talent and showcases it well in his first debut novel. Terrifying and exciting but most certainly entertaining! ...Well crafted...a must read book."

- Military Writers Society of America

Tender Prey

*Fear Grips Seattle! A Deranged
Serial Killer is Loose.*

Have you ever known someone
who has been sexually abused? Do
you think they'd be conscious of the
effects these childhood perversions
might have on adult behavior? Do
you ever question what could possibly
motivate the bizarre acts you learn
about your friends and neighbors who
appear so normal? Then you'll want
to meet Corky!

Detective Frank Murphy and his
side-kick, John Henry Drake, get the
nod to head up the task force. Who is
committing these heinous acts?

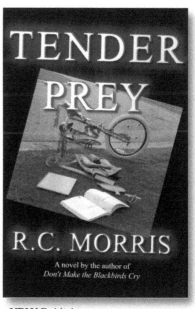

VBW Publishing
ISBN: 1-58939-812-2

What the critics are saying:

"Compelling, tantalizing and filled with complex characters and plot twists...
an intelligent treat and great entertainment! It is a terrific read for all mystery
lovers. The MWSA gives this book its highest rating of Five Stars."

- Military Writers Society of America

Both books are available at your favorite bookseller...
or visit Raycmorris.com to read excerpts

Watch for R.C. Morris's soon-to-be-released novel, "Kiss of the Viper."

Lightning Source UK Ltd.
Milton Keynes UK
UKHW022335151220
375229UK00010B/2106